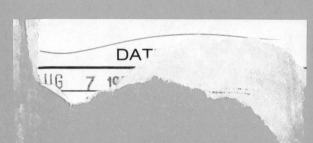

DAT

UG  7  19

*The*
*Beauty*
*Myth*

# The Beauty Myth

## How Images of Beauty Are Used Against Women

## Naomi Wolf

WILLIAM MORROW AND COMPANY, INC.

*New York*

For my parents,
Deborah and Leonard Wolf

Recognizing the importance of preserving what has been written, it is the policy of William Morrow and Company, Inc., and its imprints and affiliates to have the books it publishes printed on acid-free paper, and we exert our best efforts to that end.

Library of Congress Cataloging-in-Publication Data

Wolf, Naomi.
    The beauty myth : how images of beauty are used against
women / Naomi Wolf.
        p.   cm.
    ISBN 0-688-08510-5
    1. Feminine beauty (Aesthetics)    2. Femininity (Psychology)
3. Sex role.    I. Title.
HQ1219.W65    1991
305.42—dc20                                                          90-49983
                                                                          CIP

Printed in the United States of America

First Edition

1  2  3  4  5  6  7  8  9  10

BOOK DESIGN BY ROBIN MALKIN

# Contents

*It is far more difficult to murder a phantom than a reality.*

*—Virginia Woolf*

*I notice that it is the fashion . . . to disclaim any notion of male conspiracy in the oppression of women. . . . "For my part," I must say with William Lloyd Garrison, "I am not prepared to respect that philosophy. I believe in sin, therefore in a sinner; in theft, therefore in a thief; in slavery, therefore in a slaveholder; in wrong, therefore in a wrong-doer."*

*—Ann Jones*

*The fear of freedom is strong within us.*

*—Germaine Greer*

# The Beauty Myth

*At last*, after a long silence, women took to the streets. In the two decades of radical action that followed the rebirth of feminism in the early 1970s, Western women gained legal and reproductive rights, pursued higher education, entered the trades and the professions, and overturned ancient and revered beliefs about their social role. A generation on, do women feel free?

The affluent, educated, liberated women of the First World, who can enjoy freedoms unavailable to any women ever before, do not feel as free as they want to. And they can no longer restrict to the subconscious their sense that this lack of freedom has something to do with—with apparently frivolous issues, things that really should not matter. Many are ashamed to admit that such trivial concerns—to do with physical appearance, bodies, faces, hair, clothes—matter so much. But in spite of shame, guilt, and denial, more and more women are wondering if it isn't that they are entirely neurotic and alone but rather that something important is indeed at stake that has to do with the relationship between female liberation and female beauty.

9

The more legal and material hindrances women have broken through, the more strictly and heavily and cruelly images of female beauty have come to weigh upon us. Many women sense that women's collective progress has stalled; compared with the heady momentum of earlier days, there is a dispiriting climate of confusion, division, cynicism, and above all, exhaustion. After years of much struggle and little recognition, many older women feel burned out; after years of taking its light for granted, many younger women show little interest in touching new fire to the torch.

During the past decade, women breached the power structure; meanwhile, eating disorders rose exponentially and cosmetic surgery became the fastest-growing medical specialty. During the past five years, consumer spending doubled, pornography became the main media category, ahead of legitimate films and records combined, and thirty-three thousand American women told researchers that they would rather lose ten to fifteen pounds than achieve any other goal. More women have more money and power and scope and legal recognition than we have ever had before; but in terms of how we feel about ourselves *physically*, we may actually be worse off than our unliberated grandmothers. Recent research consistently shows that inside the majority of the West's controlled, attractive, successful working women, there is a secret "underlife" poisoning our freedom; infused with notions of beauty, it is a dark vein of self-hatred, physical obsessions, terror of aging, and dread of lost control.

It is no accident that so many potentially powerful women feel this way. We are in the midst of a violent backlash against feminism that uses images of female beauty as a political weapon against women's advancement: the beauty myth. It is the modern version of a social reflex that has been in force since the Industrial Revolution. As women released themselves from the feminine mystique of domesticity, the beauty myth took over its lost ground, expanding as it waned to carry on its work of social control.

The contemporary backlash is so violent because the ideology of beauty is the last one remaining of the old feminine ideologies that still has the power to control those women whom second wave feminism would have otherwise made relatively uncontrollable: It has grown stronger to take over the work of social coercion that myths about motherhood, domesticity, chastity, and passivity, no longer can manage. It is seeking right now to undo psychologically and covertly all the good things that feminism did for women materially and overtly.

This counterforce is operating to checkmate the inheritance of feminism on every level in the lives of Western women. Feminism gave us laws against job discrimination based on gender; immediately case law evolved in Britain and the United States that institutionalized job discrimination based on women's appearances. Patriarchal religion declined; new religious dogma, using some of the mind-altering techniques of older cults and sects, arose around age and weight to functionally supplant traditional ritual. Feminists, inspired by Friedan, broke the stranglehold on the women's popular press of advertisers for household products, who were promoting the feminine mystique; at once, the diet and skin care industries became the new cultural censors of women's intellectual space, and because of their pressure, the gaunt, youthful model supplanted the happy housewife as the arbiter of successful womanhood. The sexual revolution promoted the discovery of female sexuality; "beauty pornography"—which for the first time in women's history artificially links a commodified "beauty" directly and explicitly to sexuality—invaded the mainstream to undermine women's new and vulnerable sense of sexual self-worth. Reproductive rights gave Western women control over our own bodies; the weight of fashion models plummeted to 23 percent below that of ordinary women, eating disorders rose exponentially, and a mass neurosis was promoted that used food and weight to strip women of that sense of control. Women insisted on politicizing health; new technologies of invasive, potentially deadly "cosmetic" surgeries developed apace to re-exert old forms of medical control of women.

Every generation since about 1830 has had to fight its version of the beauty myth. "It is very little to me," said the suffragist Lucy Stone in 1855, "to have the right to vote, to own property, etcetera, if I may not keep my body, and its uses, in my absolute right." Eighty years later, after women had won the vote, and the first wave of the organized women's movement had subsided, Virginia Woolf wrote that it would still be decades before women could tell the truth about their bodies. In 1962, Betty Friedan quoted a young woman trapped in the Feminine Mystique: "Lately, I look in the mirror, and I'm so afraid I'm going to look like my mother." Eight years after that, heralding the cataclysmic second wave of feminism, Germaine Greer described "the Stereotype": "To her belongs all that is beautiful, even the very word beauty itself . . . she is a doll . . . I'm sick of the masquerade." In spite of the great revolution of the second wave, we are not exempt. Now we can look out over ruined barricades: A revolution has come upon us and changed everything in its path, enough time has passed since then for babies to have grown into women, but there still remains a final right not fully claimed.

The beauty myth tells a story: The quality called "beauty" objectively and universally exists. Women must want to embody it and men must want to possess women who embody it. This embodiment is an imperative for women and not for men, which situation is necessary and natural because it is biological, sexual, and evolutionary: Strong men battle for beautiful women, and beautiful women are more reproductively successful. Women's beauty must correlate to their fertility, and since this system is based on sexual selection, it is inevitable and changeless.

None of this is true. "Beauty" is a currency system like the gold standard. Like any economy, it is determined by politics, and in the modern age in the West it is the last, best belief system that keeps male dominance intact. In assigning value to women in a vertical hierarchy according to a culturally imposed physical standard, it is an expression of power relations in which women must unnaturally compete for resources that men have appropriated for themselves.

"Beauty" is not universal or changeless, though the West pretends that all ideals of female beauty stem from one Platonic Ideal Woman; the Maori admire a fat vulva, and the Padung, droopy breasts. Nor is "beauty" a function of evolution: Its ideals change at a pace far more rapid than that of the evolution of species, and Charles Darwin was himself unconvinced by his own explanation that "beauty" resulted from a "sexual selection" that deviated from the rule of natural selection; for women to compete with women through "beauty" is a reversal of the way in which natural selection affects all other mammals. Anthropology has overturned the notion that females must be "beautiful" to be selected to mate: Evelyn Reed, Elaine Morgan, and others have dismissed sociobiological assertions of innate male polygamy and female monogamy. Female higher primates are the sexual initiators; not only do they seek out and enjoy sex with many partners, but "every nonpregnant female takes her turn at being the most desirable of all her troop. And that cycle keeps turning as long as she lives." The inflamed pink sexual organs of primates are often cited by male sociobiologists as analogous to human arrangements relating to female "beauty," when in fact that is a universal, non-hierarchical female primate characteristic.

Nor has the beauty myth always been this way. Though the pairing of the older rich men with young, "beautiful" women is taken to be somehow inevitable, in the matriarchal Goddess religions that dominated the Mediterranean from about 25,000 B.C.E. to about 700 B.C.E., the situation was reversed: "In every culture, the Goddess has many lovers. . . . The clear pattern is of an older woman with a beautiful but expendable youth—Ishtar and Tammuz, Venus and Adonis, Cybele and Attis, Isis and Osiris . . . their only function the service of the divine 'womb.'" Nor is it something only women do and only men watch: Among the Nigerian Wodaabes, the women hold economic power and the tribe is obsessed with male beauty; Wodaabe men spend hours together in elaborate makeup sessions, and compete—provocatively painted and dressed, with swaying hips and seductive expressions—in beauty contests judged by women. There is no legitimate historical or biological justification for the beauty myth; what it is doing to women today is a result of nothing more exalted than the need of today's power structure, economy, and culture to mount a counteroffensive against women.

If the beauty myth is not based on evolution, sex, gender, aesthetics, or God, on what is it based? It claims to be about intimacy and sex and life, a celebration of women. It is actually composed of emotional distance, politics, finance, and sexual repression. The beauty myth is not about women at all. It is about men's institutions and institutional power.

The qualities that a given period calls beautiful in women are merely symbols of the female behavior that that period considers desirable: *The beauty myth is always actually prescribing behavior and not appearance.* Competition between women has been made part of the myth so that women will be divided from one another. Youth and (until recently) virginity have been "beautiful" in women since they stand for experiential and sexual ignorance. Aging in women is "unbeautiful" since women grow more powerful with time, and since the links between generations of women must always be newly broken: Older women fear young ones, young women fear old, and the beauty myth truncates for all the female life span. Most urgently, women's identity must be premised upon our "beauty" so that we will remain vulnerable to outside approval, carrying the vital sensitive organ of self-esteem exposed to the air.

Though there has, of course, been a beauty myth in some form for as long as there has been patriarchy, the beauty myth in its modern form is a fairly recent invention. The myth flourishes when material constraints on women are dangerously loosened. Before the Industrial Revolution, the average woman could not have had the same feelings about "beauty" that modern women do who experience the myth as continual comparison to a mass-disseminated physical ideal. Before the development of technologies of mass production—daguerrotypes, photographs, etc.— an ordinary woman was exposed to few such images outside the Church. Since the family was a productive unit and women's work complemented men's, the value of women who were not aristocrats or prostitutes lay in their work skills, economic shrewdness, physical strength, and fertility. Physical attraction, obviously, played its part; but "beauty" as we understand it was not, for ordinary women, a serious issue in the marriage marketplace. The beauty myth in its modern form gained ground after the upheavals of industrialization, as the work unit of the family was destroyed, and urbanization and the emerging factory system demanded what social engineers of the time termed the "separate sphere" of domesticity, which supported the new labor category of the "breadwinner" who left home for the workplace during the day. The middle class expanded, the standards of living and of literacy rose, the size of families shrank; a new class of literate, idle women developed, on whose submission to enforced domesticity the evolving system of industrial capitalism depended. Most of our assumptions about the way women have always thought about "beauty" date from no earlier than the 1830s, when the cult of domesticity was first consolidated and the beauty index invented.

For the first time new technologies could reproduce—in fashion plates, daguerreotypes, tintypes, and rotogravures—images of how women should look. In the 1840s the first nude photographs of prostitutes were taken; advertisements using images of "beautiful" women first appeared in mid-century. Copies of classical artworks, postcards of society beauties and royal mistresses, Currier and Ives prints, and porcelain figurines flooded the separate sphere to which middle-class women were confined.

Since the Industrial Revolution, middle-class Western women have been controlled by ideals and stereotypes as much as by material constraints. This situation, unique to this group, means that analyses that trace "cultural conspiracies" are uniquely plausible in relation to them. The rise of the beauty myth was just one of several emerging social fictions that masqueraded as natural components of the feminine sphere, the better to enclose those women inside it. Other such fictions arose contemporaneously: a version of childhood that required continual maternal supervision; a concept of female biology that required middle-class women to act out the roles of hysterics and hypochondriacs; a conviction that respectable women were sexually anesthetic; and a definition of women's work that occupied them with repetitive, time-consuming, and painstaking tasks such as needlepoint and lacemaking. All such Victorian inventions as these served a double function— that is, though they were encouraged as a means to expend female energy and intelligence in harmless ways, women often used them to express genuine creativity and passion.

But in spite of middle-class women's creativity with fashion and embroidery and child rearing, and, a century later, with the role of the suburban housewife that devolved from these social fictions, the fictions' main purpose was served: During a century and a half of unprecedented feminist agitation, they effectively counteracted middle-class women's dangerous new leisure, literacy, and relative freedom from material constraints.

Though these time- and mind-consuming fictions about women's natural role adapted themselves to resurface in the postwar Feminine Mystique, when the second wave of the women's movement took apart what women's magazines had portrayed as the "romance," "science," and "adventure" of homemaking and suburban family life, they temporarily failed. The cloying domestic fiction of "togetherness" lost its meaning and middle-class women walked out of their front doors in masses.

So the fictions simply transformed themselves once more: Since the women's movement had successfully taken apart most other necessary fictions of femininity, all the work of social control once spread out over the whole network of these fictions had to be reassigned to the only strand left intact, which action consequently strengthened it a hundredfold. This reimposed onto liberated women's faces and bodies all the limitations, taboos, and punishments of the repressive laws, religious injunctions and reproductive enslavement that no longer carried sufficient force. Inexhaustible but ephemeral beauty work took over from inexhaustible but ephemeral housework. As the economy, law, religion, sexual mores, education, and culture were forcibly opened up to include women more fairly, a private reality colonized female consciousness. By using ideas about "beauty," it reconstructed an alternative female world with its own laws, economy, religion, sexuality, education, and culture, each element as repressive as any that had gone before.

Since middle-class Western women can best be weakened psychologically now that we are stronger materially, the beauty myth, as it has resurfaced in the last generation, has had to draw on more technological sophistication and reactionary fervor than ever before. The modern arsenal of the myth is a dissemination of millions of images of the current ideal; although this barrage is generally seen as a collective sexual fantasy, there is in fact little that is sexual about it. It is summoned out of political fear on the part of male-dominated institutions threatened by women's freedom, and it exploits female guilt and apprehension about our own liberation—latent fears that we might be going too far. This frantic aggregation of imagery is a collective reactionary hallucination willed into being by both men and women stunned and disoriented by the rapidity with which gender relations have been transformed: a bulwark of reassurance against the flood of change. The mass depiction of the modern woman as a "beauty" is a contradiction: Where modern women are growing, moving, and expressing their individuality, as the myth has it, "beauty" is by definition inert, timeless, and generic. That this hallucination is necessary and deliberate is evident in the way "beauty" so directly contradicts women's real situation.

And the unconscious hallucination grows ever more influential and pervasive because of what is now conscious market manipulation: powerful industries—the $33-billion-a-year diet industry, the $20-billion cosmetics industry, the $300-million cosmetic surgery industry, and the $7-billion pornography industry—have arisen from the capital made out of unconscious anxieties, and are in turn able, through their influence on mass culture, to use, stimulate, and reinforce the hallucination in a rising economic spiral.

This is not a conspiracy theory; it doesn't have to be. Societies tell themselves necessary fictions in the same way that individuals and families do. Henrik Ibsen called them "vital lies," and psychologist Daniel Goleman describes them working the same way on the social level that they do within families: "The collusion is maintained by directing attention away from the fearsome fact, or by repackaging its meaning in an acceptable format." The costs of these social blind spots, he writes, are destructive communal illusions. Possibilities for women have become so open-ended that they threaten to destabilize the institutions on which a male-dominated culture has depended, and a collective panic reaction on the part of both sexes has forced a demand for counterimages.

The resulting hallucination materializes, for women, as something all too real. No longer just an idea, it becomes three-dimensional, incorporating within itself how women live and how they do not live: It becomes the Iron Maiden. The original Iron Maiden was a medieval German instrument of torture, a body-shaped casket painted with the limbs and features of a lovely, smiling young woman. The unlucky victim was slowly enclosed inside her; the lid fell shut to immobilize the victim, who died either of starvation or, less cruelly, of the metal spikes embedded in her interior. The modern hallucination in which women are trapped or trap themselves is similarly rigid, cruel, and euphemistically painted. Contemporary culture directs attention to imagery of the Iron Maiden, while censoring real women's faces and bodies.

Why does the social order feel the need to defend itself by evading the fact of real women, our faces and voices and bodies, and reducing the meaning of women to these formulaic and endlessly reproduced "beautiful" images? Though unconscious personal anxieties can be a powerful force in the creation of a vital lie, economic necessity practically guarantees it. An economy that depends on slavery needs to promote images of slaves that "justify" the institution of slavery. Western economies are absolutely dependent now on the continued underpayment of women. An ideology that makes women feel "worth less" was urgently needed to counteract the way feminism had begun to make us feel worth more. This does not require a conspiracy; merely an atmosphere. The contemporary economy depends right now on the representation of women within the beauty myth. Economist John Kenneth Galbraith offers an economic explanation for "the persistence of the view of homemaking as a 'higher calling'": the concept of women as naturally trapped within the Feminine Mystique, he feels, "has been forced on us by popular sociology, by magazines, and by fiction to disguise the fact that woman in her role of consumer has been essential to the development of our industrial society. . . . Behavior that is essential for economic reasons is transformed into a social virtue." As soon as a woman's primary social value could no longer be defined as the attainment of virtuous domesticity, the beauty myth redefined it as the attainment of virtuous beauty. It did so to substitute both a new consumer imperative and a new justification for economic unfairness in the workplace where the old ones had lost their hold over newly liberated women.

Another hallucination arose to accompany that of the Iron Maiden: The caricature of the Ugly Feminist was resurrected to dog the steps of the women's movement. The caricature is unoriginal; it was coined to ridicule the feminists of the nineteenth century. Lucy Stone herself, whom supporters saw as "a prototype of womanly grace . . . fresh and fair as the morning," was derided by detractors with "the usual report" about Victorian feminists: "a big masculine woman, wearing boots, smoking a cigar, swearing like a trooper." As Betty Friedan put it presciently in 1960, even before the savage revamping of that old caricature: "The unpleasant image of feminists today resembles less the feminists themselves than the image fostered by the interests who so bitterly opposed the vote for women in state after state." Thirty years on, her conclusion is more true than ever: That resurrected caricature, which sought to punish women for their public acts by going after their private sense of self, became the paradigm for new limits placed on aspiring women everywhere. After the success of the women's movement's second wave, the beauty myth was perfected to checkmate power at every level in individual women's lives. The modern neuroses of life in the female body spread to woman after woman at epidemic rates. The myth is undermining—slowly, imperceptibly, without our being aware of the real forces of erosion—the ground women have gained through long, hard, honorable struggle.

The beauty myth of the present is more insidious than any mystique of femininity yet: A century ago, Nora slammed the door of the doll's house; a generation ago, women turned their backs on the consumer heaven of the isolated multiapplianced home; but where women are trapped today, there is no door to slam. The contemporary ravages of the beauty backlash are destroying women physically and depleting us psychologically. If we are to free ourselves from the dead weight that has once again been made out of femaleness, it is not ballots or lobbyists or placards that women will need first; it is a new way to see.

# *Work*

$S$*ince men have* used women's "beauty" as a form of currency in circulation among men, ideas about "beauty" have evolved since the Industrial Revolution side by side with ideas about money, so that the two are virtual parallels in our consumer economy. A woman looks like a million dollars, she's a first-class beauty, her face is her fortune. In the bourgeois marriage markets of the last century, women learned to understand their own beauty as part of this economy.

By the time the women's movement had made inroads into the labor market, both women and men were accustomed to having beauty evaluated as wealth. Both were prepared for the striking development that followed: As women demanded access to power, the power structure used the beauty myth materially to undermine women's advancement.

A transformer plugs into a machine at one end, and an energy source at the other, to change an unusable current into one compatible with the machine. The beauty myth was institutionalized in the past two decades as a transformer between women and public life. It links women's energy into the machine of power while altering the machine as little as possible to accommodate them; at the same time, like the transformer, it weakens women's energy at its point of origin. It does that to ensure that the machine actually scans women's input in a code that suits the power structure.

With the decay of the Feminine Mystique, women swelled the work force. The percentage of women in the United States with jobs rose from 31.8 percent after World War II to 53.4 percent in 1984; of those aged twenty-five to fifty-four, two thirds hold jobs. In Sweden, 77 percent of women hold jobs, as do 55 percent of French women. By 1986, 63 percent of British women did paid work. As Western women entered the modern work force, the value system of the marriage market was taken over intact by the labor economy, to be used against their claims to access. The enthusiasm with which the job market assigned financial value to qualifications from the marriage market proves that the use of the beauty myth is political and not sexual: The job market refined the beauty myth as a way to legitimize employment discrimination against women.

When women breached the power structure in the 1980s, the two economies finally merged. Beauty was no longer just a symbolic form of currency; it literally *became* money. The informal currency system of the marriage market, formalized in the workplace, was enshrined in the law. Where women escaped from the sale of their sexuality in a marriage market to which they had been confined by economic dependence, their new bid for economic independence was met with a nearly identical barter system. And the higher women climbed during this period up the rungs of professional hierarchies, the harder the beauty myth has worked to undermine each step.

There has never been such a potentially destabilizing immigrant group asking for a fair chance to compete for access to power. Consider what threatens the power structure in the stereotypes of other newcomers. Jews are feared for their educational tradition and (for those from Western Europe) haut bourgeois memories. Asians in the United States and Great Britain, Algerians in France, and Turks in Germany are feared for their Third World patterns of grueling work at low pay. And the African-American underclass in the United States is feared for the explosive fusion of minority consciousness and rage. In women's easy familiarity with the dominant culture, in the bourgeois expectations of those who are middle class, in their Third World work habits, and in their potential to fuse the anger and loyalties of a galvanized underclass, the power structure correctly identifies a Frankenstein composite of its worst minority terrors. Beauty discrimination has become necessary, not from the perception that women will not be good enough, but that they will be, as they have been, twice as good.

And the old-boy network faces in this immigrant group a monster on a scale far greater than those it made out of other ethnic minorities, because women are not a minority. At 52.4 percent of the population, women are the majority.

This explains the fierce nature of the beauty backlash. This clarifies why its development has become totalitarian so fast. The pressure on the power elite can be understood by any minority ruler of an agitated majority that is beginning to appreciate its own considerable strength. In a meritocracy worth its name, the gathering gravity of events would soon and forever alter not only who the power holders are, but what power itself might look like and to what new goals it might be dedicated.

Employers did not simply develop the beauty backlash because they wanted office decoration. It evolved out of fear. That fear, from the point of view of the power structure, is firmly grounded. The beauty backlash is indeed absolutely necessary for the power structure's survival.

Women work hard—twice as hard as men.

All over the world, and for longer than records have been kept, that has been true. Historian Rosalind Miles points out that in prehistoric societies, "the labours of early women were exacting, incessant, varied and hard. If a catalogue of primitive labour were made, women would be found doing five things where men did one." In modern tribal societies, she adds, "working unceasingly during the daylight hours, women regularly produce as much as eighty per cent of the tribe's total food intake, on a daily basis . . . male members were and are doing only one-fifth of the work necessary for the group to survive, while the other four-fifths is carried out entirely by women." In seventeenth-century England the Duchess of Newcastle wrote that women "labour like beasts." Before the Industrial Revolution, "no work was too hard, no labour too strenuous, to exclude them." During nineteenth-century exploitation of the factory system, "women were universally worked harder . . . and paid less" than men, "employers everywhere agreeing that women were 'more easily induced to undergo severe bodily fatigue than men.'" Today the "primitive" five to one ratio of women's work to men's has declined to a "civilized" two to one. That ratio is fixed and international. According to the Humphrey Institute of Public Affairs: "While women represent 50 percent of the world population, they perform nearly two-thirds of all working hours, receive only one-tenth of the world income and own less than 1 percent of world property." The "Report of the World Conference for the United Nations Decade for Women" agrees: When housework is accounted for, "women around the world end up working twice as many hours as men."

Women work harder than men whether they are Eastern or Western, housewives or jobholders. A Pakistani woman spends sixty-three hours a week on domestic work alone, while a Western housewife, despite her modern appliances, works just six hours less. "Housework's modern status," writes Ann Oakley, "is non-work." A recent study shows that if housework done by married women were paid, family income would rise by 60 percent. Housework totals forty billion hours of France's labor power. Women's volunteer work in the United States amounts to $18 billion a year. The economics of industrialized countries would collapse if women didn't do the work they do for free: According to economist Marilyn Waring, throughout the West it generates between 25 and 40 percent of the gross national product.

What about the New Woman, with her responsible full-time job? Economist Nancy Barrett says that "there is no evidence of sweeping changes in the division of labor within households coincident with women's increasing labor force participation." Or: Though a woman does full-time paid work, she still does all or nearly all the unpaid work that she used to. In the United States, partners of employed women give them *less* help than do partners of housewives: Husbands of full-time homemakers help out for an hour and fifteen minutes a day, while husbands of women with full-time jobs help less than half as long—thirty-six minutes. Ninety percent of wives and 85 percent of husbands in the United States say the woman does "all or most" of the household chores. Professional women in the United States fare little better: Sociologist Arlie Hochschild found that the women in two-career couples came home to do 75 percent of household work. Married American men do only 10 percent more domestic work than they did twenty years ago. The work week of American women is twenty-one hours longer than that of men; economist Heidi Hartmann demonstrates that "men actually demand eight hours more service per week than they contribute." In Italy, 85 percent of mothers with children and full-time paid jobs are married to men who share no work in the home at all. The average European woman with a paid job has 33 percent less leisure than her husband. In Kenya, given unequal agricultural resources, women's harvests equaled men's; given equal resources, they produced bigger harvests more efficiently.

Chase Manhattan Bank estimated that American women worked each week for 99.6 hours. In the West, where paid labor centers on a forty-hour week, the unavoidable fact to confront the power structure is that women newcomers came from a group used to working more than twice as hard and long as men. And not only for less pay; for none.

Until the 1960s, the convention of referring to unpaid work at home as "not real work" helped to confound women's knowledge of their hardworking labor tradition. Such a tactic was useless once women began to do work that men recognize as male—that is, as labor worthy of its hire.

Over the past generation in the West, many of these hard workers also acquired an equal education. In the 1950s, only 20 percent of college undergraduates in the United States were women (of which only a third finished their degrees), compared with 54 percent today. By 1986, two fifths of full-time undergraduates in the United Kingdom were women. What is a nominally meritocratic system faced with, as women knock at its doors?

If interwoven in a resilient network spanning the generations, women's hard work would disproportionately multiply female excellence. The backlash was provoked because even when they were weighted with the "second shift" of domestic work, women still battered inroads into the power structure; and it was provoked because if newly raised female self-esteem were to bring this long-deferred deficit payment for the "second shift" to come due at last, its costs to employers and to the government would be staggeringly high.

In the United States between 1960 and 1990, the number of women lawyers and judges rose from 7,500 to 180,000; women doctors, from 15,672 to 108,200; women engineers, from 7,404 to 174,000. In the past fifteen years the number of women in local elected office tripled, to 18,000. Today in the United States, women fill 50 percent of entry-level management positions, 25 percent of middle management, comprise half the graduating accountants, one third of the M.B.A.s, half of graduating lawyers and a fourth of doctors, and half the officers and managers in the fifty largest commercial banks. Sixty percent of women officers in *Fortune*'s survey of top companies average $117,000 a year. Even with two shifts, at this rate, they would still challenge the status quo. *Someone had to come up with a third shift fast.*

The likelihood of backlash in some severe form was underestimated because the American mind-set celebrates winning and avoids noticing the corollary, that winners win only what losers lose. Economist Marilyn Waring concedes that "men won't easily give up a system in which half the world's population works for next to nothing" and recognizes that "precisely because that half works for so little, it may have no energy left to fight for anything else." Patricia Ireland of the National Organization for Women agrees: A real meritocracy means for men "more competition at work and more housework at home." What the aspirational message ignores is the reaction of that half of the ruling elite who hold jobs that belong by right of merit to women and who, if women were to move freely up the ladder, would inevitably lose them.

The awesome potential of this immigrant group must be thwarted, or the traditional power elite will be at a disadvantage: A white male child of the upper class is by definition someone who does not have to do two jobs or three at once, who does not feel the craving for education that comes with a heritage of illiteracy as old as written history, and who is not angry about being left out.

With what can the power structure defend itself against this onslaught? First, it can try to reinforce the Second Shift. Sixty-eight percent of women with children under eighteen are in the American work force, up from 28 percent in 1960. In the United Kingdom, 51 percent of mothers of dependent children work for pay. Forty-five percent of working women in the United States are single, divorced, widowed, or separated and are the sole economic support of their children. The failures of American and even European state-funded child care act as an effective drag on the momentum of this immigrant group. But those women who can afford to have been hiring poorer women to do their domestic work and take over their child care. So, the tactic of obstruction from lack of child care became inadequate to hold back the class of women from whom the power structure had the most to fear. What it needed was a replacement shackle, a new material burden that would drain surplus energy and lower confidence, an ideology that would produce the women workers it needs, but only in the mold in which it wants them.

Throughout the West, women's employment was stimulated by the widespread erosion of the industrial base and the shift to information and service technologies. Declining postwar birthrates and the resulting shortage of skilled labor means that women *are* welcome to the labor pool: as expendable, nonunionized, low-paid pink-collar-ghetto drudges. Economist Marvin Harris described women as a "literate and docile" labor pool, and "therefore desirable candidates for the information- and people-processing jobs thrown up by modern service industries." The qualities that best serve employers in such a labor pool's workers are: low self-esteem, a tolerance for dull repetitive tasks, lack of ambition, high conformity, more respect for men (who manage them) than women (who work beside them), and little sense of control over their lives. At a higher level, women middle managers are acceptable as long as they are male-identified and don't force too hard up against the glass ceiling; and token women at the top, in whom the female tradition has been entirely extinguished, are useful. The beauty myth is the last, best training technique to create such a work force. It does all these things to women during work hours, and then adds a Third Shift to their leisure time.

Superwoman, unaware of its full implications, had to add serious "beauty" labor to her *professional* agenda. Her new assignment grew ever more rigorous: the amounts of money, skill, and craft she must invest were to fall no lower than the amounts previously expected—before women breached the power structure—only from professional beauties in the display professions. Women took on all at once the roles of professional housewife, professional careerist, and professional beauty.

## The Professional Beauty Qualification

Before women entered the work force in large numbers, there was a clearly defined class of those explicitly paid for their "beauty": workers in the display professions—fashion mannequins, actresses, dancers, and higher-paid sex workers such as escorts. Until women's emancipation, professional beauties were usually anonymous, low in status, unrespectable. The stronger that women grow, the more prestige, fame, and money is accorded to the display professions: They are held higher and higher above the heads of rising women, for them to emulate.

What is happening today is that all the professions into which women are making strides are being rapidly reclassified—*so far as the women in them are concerned*—as display professions. "Beauty" is being categorized, in professions and trades further and further afield from the original display professions, as a version of what United States sex discrimination law calls a BFOQ (a bona fide occupational qualification) and Britain calls a GOQ (a genuine occupational qualification), such as femaleness for a wet nurse or maleness for a sperm donor.

Sex equality statutes single out the BFOQ or GOQ as an *exceptional* instance in which sex discrimination in hiring is fair because the job itself demands a specific gender; as a conscious exception to the rule of equal opportunity law, it is extremely narrowly defined. What is happening now is that a parody of the BFOQ—what I'll call more specifically the PBQ, or professional beauty qualification—is being extremely *widely* institutionalized as a condition for women's hiring and promotion. By taking over in bad faith the good-faith language of the BFOQ, those who manipulate the professional beauty qualification can defend it as being nondiscriminatory with the disclaimer that it is a necessary requirement if the job is to be properly done. Since the ever-expanding PBQ has so far been applied overwhelmingly to women in the workplace and not to men, using it to hire and promote (and harass and fire) is in fact sex discrimination and should be seen as a violation of Title VII of the 1964 Civil Rights Act in the United States and the 1975 Sex Discrimination Act in Great Britain. But three new vital lies in the ideology of "beauty" have grown during this period to camouflage the fact that the actual function of the PBQ in the workplace is to provide a risk-free, litigation-free way to discriminate against women.

Those three vital lies are: (1) "Beauty" had to be defined as a legitimate and necessary qualification for a woman's rise in power. (2) The discriminatory purpose of vital lie number one had to be masked (especially in the United States, with its responsiveness to the rhetoric of equal access) by fitting it firmly within the American dream: "Beauty" can be earned by any woman through hard work and enterprise. Those two vital lies worked in tandem to let the use of the PBQ by employers masquerade as a valid test of the woman's merit and extension of her professional duties. (3) The working woman was told she had to think about "beauty" in a way that undermined, step for step, the way she had begun to think as a result of the successes of the women's movement. This last vital lie applied to individual women's lives the central rule of the myth: For every feminist action there is an equal and opposite beauty myth reaction. In the 1980s it was evident that as women became more important, beauty too became more important. The closer women come to power, the more physical self-consciousness and sacrifice are asked of them. "Beauty" becomes the condition for a woman to take the next step. You are now too rich. Therefore, you cannot be too thin.

The fixation on "beauty" of the 1980s was a direct consequence of, and a one-to-one check and balance upon, the entry of women into powerful positions. The triumphs of "beauty" ideologies in the eighties came about as a result of real fear, on the part of the central institutions of our society, about what might

happen if free women made free progress in free bodies through a
system that calls itself a meritocracy. To return to the metaphor of
the transformer, it is the fear that the force of an unmediated
current of female energy *on a female wavelength* would break down
the delicate imbalance of the system.

The transformer's middle link is the aspirational ideology of
the women's magazines. In providing a dream language of meritocracy ("get the body you deserve"; "a gorgeous figure doesn't
come without effort"), entrepreneurial spirit ("make the most of
your natural assets"), absolute personal liability for body size and
aging ("you *can* totally reshape your body"; "your facial lines are
now within your control"), and even open admissions ("at last you
too can know the secret beautiful women have kept for years"),
they keep women consuming their advertisers' products in pursuit
of the total personal transformation in status that the consumer
society offers men in the form of money. On one hand, the aspirational promise of women's magazines that they can do it all on
their own is appealing to women who until recently were told
they could do nothing on their own. On the other, as sociologist
Ruth Sidel points out, the American Dream ultimately protects
the status quo: "It discourages those at the bottom from developing a viable political and economic analysis of the American
system [substitute: the beauty myth], instead promoting a blame-
the-victim mentality . . . a belief that if only the individual
worked harder, tried harder, he [she] would 'make it.'" But the
myth of entrepreneurial beauty, of woman against nature, hurts
women in the same way as the original model hurts men—by
leaving out the words "all else being equal."

The transfer is complete—and, coincidentally, harmful—
when through this dream, women's minds are persuaded to trim
their desires and self-esteem neatly into the discriminatory requirements of the workplace, while putting the blame for the system's failures on themselves alone.

Women accepted the professional beauty qualification more
quietly than other labor pools have reacted to unreasonable, rico-
cheting, unnegotiated employer demands. The PBQ taps reserves
of guilt that have not had time to drain: For the more fortunate
professional women, this can be guilt about wielding power, or
about "selfish" pleasure in commitment to creative work; for the

great majority who are the underpaid sole or joint supporters of children, it can be guilt about being unable to provide more, the wish to make every last effort for their families. The PBQ channels residual fears: For the middle-class woman recently valued for her willingness to conform to isolation in the home, life in the street and the office has uncharted anxieties, subjecting her as it does to public scrutiny that her mother and grandmother avoided at all costs. Working-class women have long known about brutal exploitation in the workplace that "beauty" might deflect. Women of all classes know that achievement is considered ugly and punished accordingly, and few women of any class have been used to controlling much money of their own.

Accustomed to viewing beauty as wealth, women were open to accepting a direct financial reward system that replaced the indirect reward system of the marriage market. The equation of beauty with money was not examined closely, and the power placebo of beauty was redefined to promise women the sort of power that money, in fact, gives men. Using a logic similar to that with which housewives in the 1970s added up the market value of their housework, women saw that the "meritocratic" system was too imbalanced for an isolated woman to challenge it. One part of women's psyche may have been anxious to be recognized for the work, the talent, and the money already required of them in assembling their image. And another part may have been aware that, given the dull, unglamorous nature of most women's work, the PBQ injects a dose of creativity, pleasure, and pride into the job that is usually missing from the job itself.

By the 1980s beauty had come to play in women's status-seeking the same role as money plays in that of men: a defensive proof to aggressive competitors of womanhood or manhood. Since both value systems are reductive, neither reward is ever enough, and each quickly loses any relationship to real-life values. Throughout the decade, as money's ability to buy time for comfort and leisure was abandoned in the stratospheric pursuit of wealth for wealth's sake, the competition for "beauty" saw a parallel inflation: The material pleasures once presented as its goals—sex, love, intimacy, self-expression—were lost in a desperate struggle within a sealed economy, becoming distant and quaint memories.

## The Background of the PBQ

Where did the PBQ begin? It evolved, like the beauty myth itself, alongside women's emancipation, and radiates outward to
accompany women's professional enfranchisement. It spreads,
with women's professionalization, out of American and Western
European cities into smaller towns; from the First World to the
Third World; and West to East. With the Iron Curtain drawn
back, we are due to see an acceleration of its effects in the Eastern bloc countries. Its epicenter is Manhattan, where many of the
women who have risen highest in the professional hierarchies are
concentrated.

It started in the 1960s as large numbers of educated middle-
class young women began to work in cities, living alone, between
graduation and marriage. A commercial sexualized mystique of
the airline stewardess, the model, and the executive secretary was
promoted simultaneously. (The young working woman was
blocked into a stereotype that used beauty to undermine both the
seriousness of the work that she was doing and the implications of
her new independence.) Helen Gurley Brown's 1962 best seller,
*Sex and the Single Girl*, was a survival map for negotiating this independence. But its title became a catchphrase in which the first
term canceled out the second. The working single girl had to be
seen as "sexy" so that her work, and her singleness, would not
look like what they really were: serious, dangerous, and seismic.)
If the working girl was sexy, her sexiness had to make her work
look ridiculous, because soon the girls were going to become
women.

In June 1966 the National Organization for Women was
founded in America, and that same year its members demonstrated against the firing of stewardesses at the age of thirty-two
and upon marriage. In 1967 the Equal Employment Opportunity
Commission began to hold hearings on sex discrimination. New
York women invaded the Plaza Hotel's all-male Oak Room in
February 1969. In 1970, *Time* and *Newsweek* were charged with sex
discrimination, and twelve TWA stewardesses filed a multi-
million-dollar action against the airline. Consciousness-raising

groups began to form. Women who had been politicized as students entered the job market, determined to make women's issues, rather than antiwar and free speech issues, their priority.

Away from the ferment, but well informed by it, law was quietly being made. (In 1971, a judge sentenced a woman to lose three pounds a week or go to prison.) In 1972, "beauty" was ruled to be something that could legally gain or lose women their jobs: The New York State Human Rights Appeals Board determined, in *St. Cross* v. *Playboy Club of New York*, that in one highly visible profession, a woman's "beauty" was a bona fide qualification for employment.

Margarita St. Cross was a Playboy Club waitress fired "because she had lost her Bunny Image." The club's employment standards ranked waitresses on the following scale:

1. A flawless beauty (face, figure, and grooming)
2. An exceptionally beautiful girl
3. Marginal (is aging or has developed a correctable appearance problem)
4. Has lost Bunny Image (either through aging or an uncorrectable appearance problem)

St. Cross's male counterparts who did the same work in the same place were "not subjected to appraisals of any kind."

Margarita St. Cross asked the board to decide that she was still beautiful enough to keep her job, having reached, she said, a "physiological transition from that youthful fresh, pretty look to the womanly look, mature." Hefner's spokesmen told the board that she was not. The board reached its decision through taking Hefner's word over St. Cross's—by assuming that the employer is by definition more credible about a woman's beauty than is the woman herself: that that evaluation was "well within the competence" of the Playboy Club to decide.

They did not give weight to St. Cross's expertise about what constitutes "Bunny Image." In ordinary employment disputes, the employer tries to prove that the employee deserved to be fired, while the employee tries to prove that he or she deserves to keep the job. When "beauty" is the BFOQ, though, a woman can say she's doing her job, her employer can say she isn't, and, with this ruling, the employer automatically wins.

The Appeals Board identified in its ruling a concept that it called "standards of near perfection." In a court of law, to talk about something imaginary as if it is real *makes it real*. Since 1971, the law has recognized that a standard of perfection against which a woman's body is to be judged may exist in the workplace, and that if she falls short of it, she may be fired. A "standard of perfection" for the male body has never been legally determined in the same way. While defined as materially existing, the female standard itself has never been defined. This case lay the foundations of the legal maze into which the PBQ would evolve: A woman can be fired for not looking right, but looking right remains open to interpretation.

Gloria Steinem has said, "All women are Bunnies." The St. Cross case was to resonate as an allegory of the future: Though "beauty" is arguably necessary for a Bunny to do a good job, that *concept* of female employment was adapted generally as the archetype for all women on the job. The truth of Steinem's comment deepened throughout the next two decades, wherever women tried to get and hold on to paid work.

In 1971 a prototype of *Ms.* magazine appeared. In 1972 the Equal Employment Opportunity Act was passed in the United States; Title IX outlawed sex discrimination in education. By 1972, 20 percent of management positions in America were held by women. In 1975, Catherine McDermott had to sue the Xerox Corporation because they withdrew a job offer on the grounds of her weight. The seventies saw women streaming into the professions in a way that could no longer be dismissed as intermittent or casual or secondary to their primary role as wives and mothers. In 1978 in the United States, one sixth of the master of business administration candidates and one fourth of graduating accountants were women. National Airlines fired stewardess Ingrid Fee because she was "too fat"—four pounds over the line. In 1977 Rosalynn Carter and two former first ladies spoke at the Houston convention of NOW. In 1979 the National Women's Business Enterprise Policy was created to support women's businesses; that very year a federal judge ruled that employers had the right to set appearance standards. By the new decade, United States govern-

ment policy decreed that the working woman must be taken seriously, and the law decreed that her appearance must be taken
seriously. The political function of the beauty myth is evident in
the timing of these case laws. It was not until women crowded the
public realm that laws proliferated about appearance in the workplace.

What must this creature, the serious professional woman, look
like?

Television journalism vividly proposed its answer. The avun-
cular male anchor was joined by a much younger female news-
caster with a professional prettiness level.

That double image—the older man, lined and distinguished,
seated beside a nubile, heavily made-up female junior—became
the paradigm for the relationship between men and women in the
workplace. Its allegorical force was and is pervasive: The
qualification of professional prettiness, intended at first to
sweeten the unpleasant fact of a woman assuming public authority, took on a life of its own, until professional beauties were
hired to be made over into TV journalists. By the 1980s, the
agents who headhunted anchors kept their test tapes under categories such as "Male Anchors: 40 to 50," with no corresponding
category for women, and ranked women anchors' physical appearance above their delivery skills or their experience.

The message of the news team, not hard to read, is that a
powerful man is an individual, whether that individuality is expressed in asymmetrical features, lines, gray hair, hairpieces,
baldness, bulbousness, tubbiness, facial tics, or a wattled neck;
and that his maturity is part of his power. If a single standard were
applied equally to men as to women in TV journalism, most of
the men would be unemployed. But the women beside them
need youth and beauty to enter the same soundstage. Youth and
beauty, covered in solid makeup, present the anchorwoman as
generic—an "anchorclone," in the industry's slang. What is generic is replaceable. With youth and beauty, then, the working
woman is visible, but insecure, made to feel her qualities are not
unique. But, without them, she is invisible—she falls, literally,
"out of the picture."

The situation of women in television simultaneously
symbolizes and reinforces the professional beauty qualification in

general: Seniority does not mean prestige but erasure—of TV anchors over forty, 97 percent, claims anchorwoman Christine Craft,
are male and "the other 3% are fortyish women who don't look
their age." Older anchorwomen go through "a real nightmare,"
she wrote, because soon they won't be "pretty enough to do the
news anymore." Or if an anchorwoman is "beautiful," she is
"constantly harassed as the kind of person who had gotten her job
solely because of her looks."

The message was finalized: The most emblematic working
women in the West could be visible if they were "beautiful,"
even if they were bad at their work; they could be good at their
work and "beautiful" and therefore visible, but get no credit for
merit; or they could be good and "unbeautiful" and therefore invisible, so their merit did them no good. In the last resort, they
could be as good and as beautiful as you please—for too long;
upon which, aging, they disappeared. This situation now extends
throughout the workforce.

That double standard of appearance for men and women com-
municated itself every morning and every night to the nations of
working women, whenever they tried to plug in to the events of
"their" world. Their window on historical developments was
framed by their own dilemma. To find out what is going on in the
world always involves the reminder to women that *this* is going on
in the world.

In 1983, working women received a decisive ruling on how
firmly the PBQ was established, and how far it could legally go.
The thirty-six-year-old Craft filed suit against her ex-employers,
Metromedia Inc., at Kansas City on the charge of sex discrimination. She had been dismissed on the grounds that, as Christine
Craft quotes her employer, she was "too old, too unattractive, and
not deferential to men."

Her dismissal followed months of PBQ demands made on her
time and on her purse in breach of her contract, and offensive to
her sense of self. She was subjected to fittings and makeovers by
the hour and presented with a day-by-day chart of clothing that
she would not have chosen herself and for which she was then
asked to pay. None of her male colleagues had to do those things.
Testimony from other anchorwomen showed that they had felt

forced to quit due to Metromedia's "fanatical obsession" with
their appearance.

Other women were assigned to cover the trial. Craft was hu-
miliated by her colleagues on camera. One suggested she was a
lesbian; Diane Sawyer (who, six years later, when she won a six-
figure salary, would have her appearance evaluated on *Time*'s
cover with the headline IS SHE WORTH IT?) asked Craft on a national news broadcast if she really was "'unique among women' in
[her] lack of appearance skills." Her employers had counted on
going unchallenged because of the reaction such discrimination
commonly instills in the victim of it: a shame that guarantees silence. But "Metromedia," she wrote defiantly, "was wrong if
they thought a woman would never admit to having been told she
was ugly."

Her account proves how this discrimination seeps in where
others cannot reach, poisoning the private well from which self-
esteem is drawn: "Though I may have dismissed intellectually
the statement that I was too unattractive, nonetheless in the core
of my psyche I felt that something about my face was difficult, if
not monstrous, to behold. It's hard to be even mildly flirtatious
when you're troubled by such a crippling point of view." An employer can't prove an employee incompetent simply by announc-
ing that she is. But because "beauty" lives so deep in the psyche,
where sexuality mingles with self-esteem, and since it has been
usefully defined as something that is continually bestowed from
the outside and can always be taken away, to tell a woman she is
ugly can make her feel ugly, act ugly, and, as far as her experience is concerned, *be* ugly, in the place where feeling beautiful
keeps her whole.

No woman is so beautiful—by definition—that she can be
confident of surviving a new judicial process that submits the victim to an ordeal familiar to women from other trials: looking her
up and down to see how what happened to her is her own fault.
Since there is nothing "objective" about beauty, the power elite
can, whenever necessary, form a consensus to strip "beauty"
away. To do that to a woman publicly from a witness stand is to
invite all eyes to confirm her ugliness, which then becomes the
reality that all can see. This process of legal coercion ensures that
a degrading public spectacle can be enacted at her expense

against any woman in any profession if she charges discrimination by beauty.

The moral of the Christine Craft trial was that she lost: Though two juries found for her, a male judge overturned their rulings. She seems to have been blacklisted in her profession as a result of her legal fight. Has her example affected other women in her profession? "There are thousands of Christine Crafts," one woman reporter told me. "We keep silent. Who can survive a blacklist?"

Defenders of Judge Stevens's ruling justified it on the grounds that it was not sex discrimination but market logic. If an anchorperson doesn't bring in the audiences, he or she has not done a good job. The nugget hidden here as it was applied to women— bring in audiences, sales, clients, or students *with her "beauty"*— has become the legacy of the Craft case for working women everywhere.

The outcome of the trial was one of those markers in the 1980s that a woman may have witnessed, and felt as a tightening around the neck, and knew she had to keep still about. When she read the summation, she knew that she had to distance herself from her knowledge of how much she was Christine Craft. She might have reacted by starting a new diet, or buying expensive new clothes, or scheduling an eyelift. Consciously or not, though, she probably reacted; the profession of "image consultant" grew eightfold over the decade. Women and work and "beauty" outside the sex professions fused on the day Craft lost her case, and a wider cycle of diseases was initiated. It will not, the woman might have told herself, happen to me.


## The Law Upholds the Beauty Backlash

It could and did continue to happen to working women as the law bolstered employers with a series of Byzantine rulings that ensured that the PBQ grew ever more resilient as a tool of discrimination. The law developed a tangle of inconsistencies in which women were paralyzed: While one ruling, *Miller* v. *Bank of America,* confused sexual attraction with sexual harassment and held that the law has no part to play in employment disputes that centered on it ("attractiveness," the court decided, being a "natural sex phenomenon" which "plays at least a subtle part in most personnel decisions," and, as such, the court shouldn't delve into "such matters"), the court in another case, *Barnes* v. *Costle*, concluded that if a woman's unique physical characteristics—red hair, say, or large breasts—were the reasons given by her employer for sexual harassment, then her personal appearance was the issue and not her gender, in which case she could not expect protection under Title VII of the 1964 Civil Rights Act. With these rulings a woman's beauty became at once her job and her fault.

United States law developed to protect the interests of the power structure by setting up a legal maze in which the beauty myth blocks each path so that no woman can "look right" and win. St. Cross lost her job because she was too "old" and too "ugly"; Craft lost hers because she was too "old," too "ugly," "unfeminine," and didn't dress right. This means, a woman might think, that the law will treat her fairly in employment disputes if only she does her part, looks pretty, and dresses femininely.

She would be dangerously wrong, though. Let's look at an American working woman standing in front of her wardrobe, and imagine the disembodied voice of legal counsel advising her on each choice as she takes it out on its hanger.

"Feminine, then," she asks, "in reaction to the Craft decision?"

"You'd be asking for it. In 1986, Mechelle Vinson filed a sex discrimination case in the District of Columbia against her employer, the Meritor Savings Bank, on the grounds that her boss had sexually harassed her, subjecting her to fondling, exposure, and rape. Vinson was young and 'beautiful' and carefully dressed. The district court ruled that her appearance counted against her: Testimony about her 'provocative' dress could be heard to decide whether her harassment was 'welcome.'"

"Did she dress provocatively?"

"As her counsel put it in exasperation, 'Mechelle Vinson wore *clothes*.' Her beauty in her clothes was admitted as evidence to prove that she welcomed rape from her employer."

"Well, feminine, but not too feminine, then."

"Careful: In *Hopkins* v. *Price-Waterhouse*, Ms. Hopkins was denied a partnership because she needed to learn to 'walk more femininely, talk more femininely, dress more femininely,' and 'wear makeup.'"

"Maybe she didn't deserve a partnership?"

"She brought in the most business of any employee."

"Hmm. Well, maybe a little more feminine."

"Not so fast. Policewoman Nancy Fahdl was fired because she looked 'too much like a lady.'"

"All right, less feminine. I've wiped off my blusher."

"You can lose your job if you don't wear makeup. See *Tamini* v. *Howard Johnson Company, Inc.*"

"How about this, then, sort of . . . womanly?"

"Sorry. You can lose your job if you dress like a woman. In *Andre* v. *Bendix Corporation*, it was ruled 'inappropriate for a supervisor' of women to dress like 'a woman.'"

"What am I supposed to do? Wear a sack?"

"Well, the women in *Buren* v. *City of East Chicago* had to 'dress to cover themselves from neck to toe' because the men at work were 'kind of nasty.'"

"Won't a dress code get me out of this?"

"Don't bet on it. In *Diaz* v. *Coleman*, a dress code of short skirts was set by an employer who allegedly sexually harassed his female employees because they complied with it."

It would be funny if it weren't true. And when we see that British law has evolved a legal no-win situation very close to this one, a pattern begins to emerge.

We can save the British woman the baffling guided tour through her wardrobe: It's the same situation, if not worse. The GOQ is defined as permitting "sex discrimination" when the job requires, among other things, "physical form or authenticity—for example, a model or an actor." But since 1977, *M. Schmidt* v. *Austicks Bookshops, Ltd.* has been broadly interpreted to make it legal for her to be hired or fired generally on the basis of physical appearance. Miss Schmidt lost her job and the case because she wore trousers to her work in a bookstore. The Employment Appeal Tribunal dismissed her case, which was based on the fact that the dress code was more restrictive for women than men, by ruling not only that an employer is "entitled to a large measure of discretion in controlling the image of his establishment," but also that the whole issue is insignificant: They ruled that telling a woman how to dress was no more than trivial. In *Jeremiah* v. *Ministry of Defense*, employers avoided hiring women for higher-paid work on the grounds that it was dirty and would ruin their looks. Lord Denning in his ruling mused: "A woman's hair is her crowning glory. . . . She does not like it disturbed, especially when she has just had a 'hair-do.'" The employers' counsel asserted that compelling women to ruin their hairdos at a higher rate of pay would lead to industrial unrest.

Dan Air was challenged in 1987 for hiring only pretty young women as air crews; they defended their discrimination on the basis of customer preference for pretty young women. (Two years later, the publisher of *USA Today*, in an editorial using the same logic, would call for a return to the days when stewardesses were hired pretty and young and fired upon maturing.)

In *Maureen Murphy and Eileen Davidson* v. *Stakis Leisure, Ltd.*, we can see the wave of the future. Waitresses objected to a change in "image" that put them in a "more revealing" uniform and forced them to wear makeup and nail polish. One waitress described the costumes as "straight out of *The Story of O*," consisting of a miniskirt and a plunging cleavage over an external corset or basque so tight that the women bled from it under their arms. One of the litigating women was pregnant when she was forced to wear it. Management admitted that the change was imposed on the women as a sexual draw for male customers. Waiters had no such requirements made of them. (Incidentally, the waitresses' obligation to appear in a state of undress in front of the opposite sex violates *Sisley* v. *Britannia Security Systems*, which ruled that the 1975 Sex Discrimination Act could be used to "preserve decency or privacy" from the opposite sex while "being in a state of undress.") The women's counsel got nowhere pointing out that makeup, revealing costumes, and nail polish sexualize the dress code in a way that *cannot* be parallel for men. This case too was dismissed as *de minimis*—too trivial to consider. The women lost the case but kept their jobs—for six weeks. They have both been fired; they have filed a complaint charging unfair dismissal.

So if you refuse to wear a sexually exploitive costume to work in Great Britain, you can lose your job. But in *Snowball* v. *Gardner Merchant, Ltd.*, and *Wileman* v. *Minilec Engineering, Ltd.*, a woman's perceived sexuality was ruled relevant in minimizing the harm done to her by sexual harassment. In the latter case, Miss Wileman was awarded the derisory sum of fifty pounds (seventy-five dollars) for four and a half years' harassment on the grounds that her feelings couldn't have been much injured since she wore "scanty and provocative clothing" to work: "If a girl on the shop floor goes around wearing provocative clothes and flaunting herself, it is not unlikely," the tribunal ruled, that she will get harassed. The tribunal accepted men's testimony that defined Miss Wileman's clothes as sexually inciting. Miss Wileman's plaintive echoing of Mechelle Vinson's lawyer when she protested that her clothes were definitely *not* "scanty and provocative" was ignored in the ruling.

With these rulings in place, social permission was granted for the trickle-down effect of the PBQ. It spread to receptionists and art gallery and auction house workers; women in advertising, merchandising, design, and real estate; the recording and film industries; to women in journalism and publishing.

Then to the service industries: prestige waitresses, bartenders, hostesses, catering staff. These are the beauty-intensive jobs that provide a base for the ambitions of the rural, local, and regional beauties who flow into the nation's urban centers and whose sights are set on "making it" in the display professions—ideally to become one of the 450 full-time American fashion models who constitute the elite corps deployed in a way that keeps 150 million American women in line. (The model fantasy is probably the most widespread contemporary dream shared by young women from all backgrounds.)

Then the PBQ was applied to any job that brings women in contact with the public. A woman manager I know of in one of the British John Lewis Partnership stores, who gave her job "my all," was called in by her supervisor to hear that he was very happy with her work, but that "she needed some improvement from the neck up." He wanted her to wear what she called "a mask" of makeup, and to bleach and tease her hair. "It made me feel," she said to a friend, "like all the work I did didn't matter as much as what I'd look like standing around on the floor dressed up like a bimbo. It made me feel that there was no point in my doing my job well." The men, she added, had to do nothing comparable.

Then it was applied to any job in which a woman faces one other man: A fifty-four-year-old American woman, quoted in *The Sexuality of Organization*, said her boss replaced her one day without warning. "He had told her that he 'wanted to look at a younger woman' so his 'spirits could be lifted.' She said that 'her age . . . had never bothered her before he mentioned it to her.'" Now the PBQ has spread to any job in which a woman does not work in complete isolation.

Unfortunately for them, working women do not have access to legal advice when they get dressed in the morning. But they intuit that this maze exists. Is it any surprise that, two decades into the legal evolution of the professional beauty qualification, working women are tense to the point of insanity about their appearance? Their neuroses don't arise out of the unbalanced female mind, but are sane reactions to a deliberately manipulated catch 22 in the workplace. Legally, women *don't* have a thing to wear.

Sociologists have described the effect on women of what such laws legalize. Sociologist Deborah L. Sheppard, in *The Sexuality of Organization*, describes her discovery that "the informal rules and guidelines about the appropriateness of appearance keep shifting, which helps explain the continuous appearance of books and magazines which tell women how to look and behave at work." Organizational sociologists haven't addressed the notion that they keep shifting *because they're set up to keep shifting.* "Women," Sheppard continues, "perceive themselves and other women to be confronting constantly the dualistic experience of being 'feminine' and 'businesslike' at the same time, while they do not perceive men experiencing the same contradiction." "Businesslike yet feminine" is a favorite description of clothing sold in mail-order catalogs aimed at working women, and this elusive dualism is what triggered the strong response in the United States to a series of ads for a lingerie manufacturer that showed businesswear blowing open to reveal a lace-clad nakedness. But the words "businesslike" and "feminine," as we saw, are each used to manipulate the other as well as the woman caught in the middle.

"Women," concludes Sheppard, "perceive themselves as being constantly vulnerable to unpredictable violations of the balance. . . . The area of appearance seems to be one where women feel they can most easily exert some control over how they will be responded to." But "they also perceive themselves as generally needing to take responsibility for having triggered such violations."

Women blame themselves for triggering "violations." What violations are these? A *Redbook* survey found that 88 percent of their respondents had experienced sexual harassment on the job. In the United Kingdom, 86 percent of managers and 66 percent of employees had encountered it. The British civil service found that 70 percent of its respondents had experienced it. Seventeen percent of Swedish women union members had been harassed, a figure which suggests 300,000 Swedish women harassed nationwide. Women who have been harassed, it is found, feel guilty because they fear that they "possibly provoked the comments by dressing inappropriately." Other research shows that victims of sexual harassment are rarely in a position to tell the harasser to stop.

So women dress to be businesslike yet feminine—walk the moving line, and inevitably fail: From two thirds to almost nine tenths of them experience harassment that they blame on themselves and their poor control of their appearance. Can women say, by way of their appearance at work, what they mean? No. According to *The Sexuality of Organization,* five studies have found that "a woman's . . . behaviour is noticed and labelled sexual even if it is not intended as such." Women's friendly actions are often interpreted as sexual, especially when the "nonverbal cues are ambiguous or women wear revealing clothing." As we saw, women's and men's definitions of "revealing" differ. Women's feelings of loss of control, as they try to "speak through their clothes," make sense.

The PBQ and the legal verdict that a woman's clothing invites sexual harassment both depend on women not wearing uniforms in the same workplaces where men do wear them. In 1977, when women were still new in the professions, John Molloy wrote a best-seller, *The Woman's Dress for Success Book.* Molloy had done thorough research and found that without recognizable professional wear, women had trouble eliciting respect and authority. A year after his test group adopted a "uniform," the general attitude of the women's bosses toward them had "improved dramatically," and twice as many women were recommended for promotion. In the control group there was no change. Molloy tested the "uniform" extensively, and found that a skirted suit was "the success suit"; he recommended categorically that professional women adopt it. "Without a uniform," he said, "there is no equality of image." Evidently committed to women's advances, Molloy urged women to wear the uniform in solidarity with one another; he quotes a pledge signed by corporate women that states: "I am doing this so that women may have as effective a work uniform as men and therefore be better able to compete on an equal footing."

Molloy warned what might happen if women were to adopt professional dress: "The entire fashion industry is going to be alarmed at the prospect. . . . They will see it as a threat to their domination over women. And they will be right. If women adopt the uniform, and if they ignore the absurd, profit-motivated pronouncements of the fashion industry when they select [it], they will no longer be malleable." He went on to predict the strategies to which the industry might resort to undermine the adoption of a professional uniform for women.

Eventually, *The New York Times Magazine* ran a piece declaring that Molloy's strategy was passé, and that women were so confident now that they could abandon the suit and express their "femininity" once more. Many media for which the fashion industry provided a sizable portion of their ad budget quickly followed suit. Beauty, thinness, couture, and taste had to constitute a woman's authority now that the professional uniform could not do it for her. Sadly for her, though, the evidence, according to Molloy, is that dressing for business success and dressing to be sexually appealing are practically mutually exclusive because a woman's perceived sexuality can "blot out" all other characteristics. Professional women today are expected to emulate fashion models. But in Molloy's study of one hundred male and female professionals, ninety-four chose the professionally dressed woman over the fashion model as exemplifying professional competence.

The 1980s decried Molloy's movement on the grounds that it

forced women to dress like men—though the proposed image, with its high-heeled pumps, stockings, palette of colors, makeup, and jewelry, was masculine only insofar as it established for women something recognizable as professional dress. But the fashion industry trammeled the experiment in creating businesswear for women, and they lost the instant professional status and moderate sexual camouflage that the male uniform provides. The shift in fashion ensured that the fashion industry would not suffer, while it also ensured that women would have simultaneously to work harder to be "beautiful" and work harder to be taken seriously.

Beauty provokes harassment, the law says, but it looks through men's eyes when deciding what provokes it. A woman employer may find a well-cut European herringbone twill, wantonly draped over a tautly muscled masculine flank, madly provocative, especially since it suggests male power and status, which our culture eroticizes. But the law is unlikely to see good Savile Row tailoring her way if she tells its possessor he must service her sexually or lose his job.

If, at work, women were under no more pressure to be decorative than are their well-groomed male peers in lawyer's pinstripe or banker's gabardine, the pleasure of the workplace might narrow; but so would a well-tilled field of discrimination. Since women's appearance is used to justify their sexual harassment as well as their dismissal, the statements made by women's clothing are continually, willfully misread. Since women's working clothes—high heels, stockings, makeup, jewelry, not to mention hair, breasts, legs, and hips—have already been appropriated as pornographic accessories, a judge can look at any younger woman and believe he is seeing a harassable trollop, just as he can look at any older woman and believe he is seeing a dismissable hag.

Emulating the male uniform *is* tough on women. Their urge to make traditionally masculine space less gray, sexless, and witless is an appealing wish. But their contribution did not relax the rules. Men failed to respond with whimsy, costume, or color of their own. The consequence of men wearing uniforms where women do not has simply meant that women take on the *full* penalties as well as the pleasures of physical charm in the workplace, and can legally be punished or promoted, insulted or even raped accordingly.

Women dare not yet relinquish the "advantage" this inequality in dress bestows. People put on uniforms voluntarily only when they have faith in the fair rewards of the system. They will understandably be unwilling to give up the protection of their "beauty" until they can be sure the reward system is in good working order; the professions will be unwilling to give up the controlling function of the professional beauty qualification until they are certain that women are so demoralized by it that they will pose no real threat to the way things are done. It's an uneasy truce, each side playing for time; however, when playing for time under the beauty myth, women lose.

What about the common perception that women use their "beauty" to get ahead? In fact, sociologist Barbara A. Gutek shows that there is little evidence that women even occasionally use their sexuality to get some organizational reward. It is men, she found, who use their sexuality to get ahead: "A sizeable minority of men," she found, "say they dress in a seductive manner at work," versus 1 woman in 800 who said she had used sexuality for advancement. In another study, 35 percent of men versus only 15 percent of women say that they use their appearance for rewards in the workplace.

Complicity in display does exist, of course. Does that mean the women are to blame for it? I have heard Ivy League administrators, judges discussing women attorneys, scholarship panelists, and other men employed to believe in and enforce concepts of fairness speak complacently about the uses of "feminine wiles"—a euphemism for beauty deployed to the woman's advantage. Powerful men characterize them with grudging admiration, as if "beauty's" power were an irresistible force that stunned and immobilized distinguished men, to turn them into putty in the charmer's hand. This attitude makes sure that women will have to keep using the things they sometimes use to try to get the things they seldom get.

The conventions of this gallantry are veils over the inscription in stone: It is the powerful who dictate the terms; adults, play-wrestling a child, enjoy letting the child feel it has won.

This point, where beauty forms the bridge between women

and institutions, is what women are taught to seize upon, and is then used as proof that women themselves are finally to blame. But to make herself grasp at this straw, a woman has to suppress what she knows: that the powerful ask for women to display themselves in this way. When power toys with beauty, the request for display behavior has been choreographed before the woman has had the chance to enter the room where she will be evaluated.

This request for display behavior is unspoken. It is subtle enough so that the woman cannot point to it, credibly, as an example of harassment (to be credible about being harassed, in any case, a woman must look harassable, which destroys her credibility). It usually leaves the toyed-with "beauty" no choice, short of a withdrawal so obvious as to give certain offense, but to play along. She may have to will her body to relax and not stiffen at an untoward compliment, or simply have to sit up straighter, letting her body be seen more clearly, or brush the hair from her eyes in a way that she knows flatters her face. Whatever it is she has to do, she knows it without being told, from the expression and body language of the powerful man in whose eyes her future lies.

When a brilliant critic and a beautiful woman (that's my order of priorities, not necessarily those of the men who teach her) puts on black suede spike heels and a ruby mouth before asking an influential professor to be her thesis advisor, is she a slut? Or is she doing her duty to herself, in a clear-eyed appraisal of a hostile or indifferent milieu, by taking care to nourish her real gift under the protection of her incidental one? Does her hand shape the lipstick into a cupid's bow in a gesture of free will?

*She doesn't have to do it.*

That is the response the beauty myth would like a woman to have, because then the Other Woman is the enemy. Does she in fact have to do it?

The aspiring woman does not have to do it if she has a choice. She will have a choice when a plethora of faculties in her field, headed by women and endowed by generations of female magnates and robber baronesses, open their gates to her; when multinational corporations led by women clamor for the skills of young female graduates; when there are *other* universities, with bronze busts of the heroines of half a millennium's classical learning;

when there are *other* research-funding boards maintained by the deep coffers provided by the revenues of female inventors, where half the chairs are held by women scientists. She'll have a choice when her application is evaluated blind.

Women will have the choice never to stoop, and will deserve the full censure for stooping, to consider what the demands on their "beauty" of a board of power might be, the minute they know they can count on their fair share: that 52 percent of the seats of the highest achievement are open to them. They will deserve the blame that they now get anyway only when they know that the best dream of their one life will not be forcibly compressed into an inverted pyramid, slammed up against a glass ceiling, shunted off into a stifling pink-collar ghetto, shoved back dead down a dead-end street.

## The Social Consequence of the PBQ

The professional beauty qualification works smoothly to put back into employment relations the grounds for exploitation that recent equal opportunity laws have threatened. It gives employers what they need *economically* in a female work force by affecting women *psychologically* on several levels.

*The PBQ reinforces the double standard.* Women have always been paid less than men for equal work, and the PBQ gives that double standard a new rationale where the old rationale is illegal.

Men's and women's bodies are compared in a way that symbolizes to both the comparison between men's and women's careers. Aren't men, too, expected to maintain a professional appearance? Certainly: They must conform to a standard that is well groomed, often uniformly clothed, and appropriate to their context. But to pretend that since men have appearance standards it means that the genders are treated equally is to ignore the fact that in hiring and promotion, men's and women's appearances are judged differently; and that the beauty myth reaches far beyond dress codes into a different realm. Male anchors, according to TV employer guidelines cited by law theorist Suzanne Levitt, are supposed to remember their "professional image" while female anchors are cautioned to remember "professional elegance." The double standard for appearance is a constant reminder that men are worth more and need not try as hard.

"Wherever records have survived of the pay of working people," writes Rosalind Miles, "women are shown either to receive less than men, or to get nothing at all." That is still true: In 1984 in the United States, women working year-round at full-time jobs still earned an average of only $14,780—64 percent of the $23,220 that men working full-time earned. Estimates of what they now earn range from from 54 to 66 cents to the male dollar. Taking the highest figure, it is still a difference that has narrowed only 10 cents over the past twenty years. In the United Kingdom, women earn 65.7 percent of the gross weekly earnings of men. The pay difference in the United States is maintained within the same job throughout the social structure: On the average, male lawyers aged 25–34 earn $27,563, but female lawyers the same age, $20,573; retail salesmen earn $13,002 to retail saleswomen's $7,479; male bus drivers make $15,611 and female bus drivers, $9,903; female hairdressers earn $7,603 less than male hairdressers. A barrage of imagery that makes women feel they are worth less than men, or worth only what they look like, helps keep this state of affairs going strong.

This proves again that the myth is political and not sexual: Money does the work of history more efficiently than sex. Low female self-esteem may have a sexual value to some individual men, but it has a financial value to all of society. Women's poor physical self-image today is far less a result of sexual competition than of the needs of the marketplace.

Many economists agree that women do not expect promotion and higher wages because they have been conditioned by their work experience not to expect improvements in work status: Women, writes Sidel, "are often unsure of their intrinsic worth in the marketplace." In the 1984–85 Yale University strike by the 85-percent-female clerical workers union, a basic issue, according to one organizer, was to get women to ask themselves, "What are we worth?" The biggest obstacle was "a basic lack of confidence." The beauty myth generates low self-esteem for women and high profits for corporations as a result.

Beauty ideology teaches women they have little control and

few options. Images of woman in the beauty myth are reductive and stereotyped. At any moment there are a limited number of recognizable "beautiful" faces. Through such limited perceptions of women, women come to see their options as limited: Women in the United States are clustered in 20 of 420 occupations listed by the Bureau of Labor Statistics. Seventy-five percent of American women are still employed in traditional "women's jobs," most of which are ill paid. Arlie Hochschild found that women are concentrated "in jobs that stress their physical attractiveness."

With few roles in which to see themselves and be seen, fully two thirds of American women work in service or retail jobs or in local bureaucracies, jobs with low wages and little opportunity for advancement. The few roles imagined for women are cheaply compensated: Secretaries, 99 percent of whom are female, earn an average salary of $13,000; preschool teachers, 97 percent female, $14,000; bank tellers, 94 percent female, $10,500; food service workers, 75 percent female, $8,200.

Women *do* earn more from selling their bodies than their skills. "In this context," writes legal scholar Catharine A. Mac-Kinnon, "it is instructive to ask: What is woman's best economic option?" She cites evidence that, in contrast to the salaries of the "respectable" women described above, the average streetwalker in Manhattan nets between $500 and $1,000 a week. Another of her studies shows that the one difference between the prostitutes in the sample group and other women from similar backgrounds is that the former earn twice as much; A third shows that fashion modeling and prostitution are the only professions in which women consistently earn more than men. One woman in four earns less than $10,000 a year even though working full-time; in 1989, Miss America earned $150,000, a $42,000 scholarship, and a $30,000 car.

How can a woman believe in merit in a reality like this? A job market that rewards her indirectly as if she were selling her body is simply perpetuating the traditional main employment options for women—compulsory marriage or prostitution—more politely and for half the pay. The pay-to-effort ratio at the top of the display professions, of which women are kept well-informed ("it's really gruelling under those hot lights"), is a caricature of the real relation of women's work to their pay. The gross high pay of professional beauties is a false gloss over women's actual economic situation. Hyping fantasies of discovery in the overpaid display professions, the dominant culture helps employers avoid organized resistance to the repetitiveness and low pay of real women's real work. With the aspirational link of the women's magazines in between, women learn unworthiness. The sense of professional *entitlement* a worker acquires from expecting a fair reward for a job well done thus remains conveniently distant from the expectations of working women.

Employers admit that "one way of weeding out women applicants for a job is to readvertise it at a higher salary." "When it comes to defining our worth financially," one study concludes, "we have severe doubts about ourselves." In studies of body self-perception, women regularly overestimate their body size; in a study of economic self-perception, they regularly underestimate their business expenses. The point is that the two misperceptions are causally related. By valuing women's skills at artificially low levels and tying their physical value into the workplace, the market protects its pool of cheap female labor.

The professional insecurity this situation generates cuts across the biological caste system that the PBQ sets up: It is found in "beautiful" women, since often no amount of professional success can convince them that they themselves, and not their "beauty," have earned them their positions; and it's found in "ugly" women, who learn to devalue themselves.

Pinups in the workplace are metaphors for the larger issue of how Iron Maiden imagery is used to keep women down on the job. At the Shoemaker Mine in the United States, when women coal miners joined the work force, graffiti appeared that targeted for ridicule individual women's breasts and genitals; a woman with small breasts, for instance, was called "inverted nipples." Faced with such scrutiny, reports legal scholar Rosemarie Tong, "the female miners found it increasingly difficult to maintain their self-respect, and their personal and professional lives began to deteriorate." Nevertheless, a ruling by an American court, *Rabidue* v. *Osceola Refining Co.* (1986), upheld the right of male workers to display pornography in the workplace, no matter how offensive to women workers, on the grounds that the landscape is steeped in this sort of imagery anyway.

In Great Britain, the National Council for Civil Liberties recognizes that pinups constitute sexual harassment, as they "directly undermine an individual woman's view of herself and her
ability to do her job." When unions formed discussion groups
about the subject of pinups, forty-seven of the fifty-four groups
ranked pinups as examples of sexual harassment that disturbed
women. The Society of Civil and Public Servants ranks sexually
evaluating looks, as well as pinups, as sexual harassment. Women
interviewed said that when pinups are on the walls, they feel that
"direct comparisons are being made." Pinups are used directly to
undermine women: In *Strathclyde Regional Council* v. *Porcelli*, Mrs.
Porcelli testified that her harassers often "commented on my
physical appearance in comparison with that of the nude female
depicted." But neither the American nor the British judicial system shows insight into the fact that this kind of harassment is
intended to make women in the workplace feel physically worthless, especially in comparison with the men. It is *intended* to reinstate the inequalities that women's entry into that workplace took
away. In fostering in women the feeling of ugliness—or, if their
"beauty" is the target, of exposure and foolishness—it should not
have to *lead* to another injury, as the law now defines it, in order
to be understood as discriminatory; it *is* already an injury.

*The PBQ keeps women materially and psychologically poor.* It
drains money from the very women who would pose the greatest
threat were they to learn the sense of entitlement bestowed by
economic security: Through the PBQ, even richer women are
kept away from the masculine experience of wealth. Its double
standard actually makes such women poorer than their male
peers, by cutting a greater swathe in the income of a female executive than in that of a male, and that is part of its purpose.
"Women are punished for their looks, whereas men can go far in
just a grey flannel suit," complains, ironically, a former beauty
editor of *Vogue*, who estimates that her maintenance expenses will
be about $8,000 annually. Urban professional women are devoting
up to a third of their income to "beauty maintenance," and con-
sidering it a necessary investment. Their employment contracts
are even earmarking a portion of their salary for high-fashion
clothing and costly beauty treatments. *New York Woman* describes
a typical ambitious career woman, a thirty-two-year-old who

spends "nearly a quarter of her $60,000 income . . . on self-pres-
ervation." Another "willingly spends more than $20,000 a year"
on workouts with a "cult trainer." The few women who are finally
earning as much as men are forced, through the PBQ, to pay
*themselves* significantly less than their male peers take home. It has
engineered do-it-yourself income discrimination.

When used against newly wealthy women, the PBQ helps to
enforce and rationalize discrimination at the highest levels. A
1987 U.S. Chamber of Commerce report found that corporate
women, vice presidents and above, earn 42 percent less than male
peers. Men in the twenty highest-paid professions make significantly more than women peers, says Ruth Sidel. This discrepancy
is protected by the way the PBQ leeches money and leisure *and
confidence* from this rising class, thus allowing corporations to draw
on women's expertise at the higher-paid levels, while defending
the structures of male-dominated organizations from a potential
onslaught of women who have stopped thinking poor.

*It tires women out.* As the century draws to an end, working
women are exhausted; bone-tired in a way their male colleagues
may not be able to imagine. A recent series of surveys sum-
marized in the women's press "all point to one thing: modern
women are worn out." Seventy percent of senior women executives in the United States cite tiredness as their main problem;
almost half of American eighteen- to thirty-five-year-olds feel
"tired most of the time"; 41 percent of the one thousand Danish
women questioned responded that they "felt tired at present." In
Great Britain, 95 percent of working women put "feeling unusually tired" at the head of a list of their problems. It is this
exhaustion that may call a halt to women's future collective advancement, and that is the point of it. A weariness intensified by
the rigors of the PBQ, sustained by its perpetual hunger, and renewed on its endless electronic treadmill, the PBQ may ultimately manage what direct discrimination cannot achieve.
Professional, high-achieving women have, because of it, just
enough energy, concentration, and time to do their work very
well, but too little for the kind of social activism or freewheeling
thought that would allow them to question and change the structure itself. If the rigors intensify to bring women to the physical
breaking point, they may begin to long just to go back home.

Already in the United States, there are murmurs among worn-out
career women of nostalgia for life before the mechanized stairs
that lead nowhere.

All labor systems that depend on coercing a work force into
accepting bad conditions and unfair compensation have recognized the effectiveness of keeping that work force exhausted to
keep it from making trouble.

*It inverts the male career span.* The PBQ teaches women visually
that they must yield power at the same pace at which men gain it.
Of women over sixty-five, the fastest-growing segment of the
United States population, one in five lives in poverty. A third of
people living alone in the United States are old women, of whom
half have less than $1,000 in savings. If you are a woman, writes
one economist, "you have a 60 percent shot at being poor in old
age." The average American old woman's income was 58 percent
of that of old men. In Great Britain, lone old women outnumber
lone old men by four to one; and of those, over twice as many as
old men need income support. The average West German retiring
woman gets only half the full pension. Of retiring American
women, only 20 percent have private pensions. Worldwide, just 6
percent of wage-earning women will receive a pension by the year
2000. If it is scary to be an old woman in our culture, it is not just
because you lose your complexion. Women cling to the PBQ because what it threatens is true: A young woman may indeed do
better economically by investing her sexuality while it is at an
optimum exchange rate than she does by working hard for a lifetime.

"Beauties" reach the peak of the possibilities open to them in
early youth; so do women in the economy. The PBQ reproduces
within the economy the inverted life-span of the "beauty": Despite twenty years of the second wave of the women's movement,
women's careers still are not peaking in middle and later life
alongside those of men. Though business began recruiting
women in the early 1970s, long enough ago to give them time for
significant career advancement, only 1 to 2 percent of American
upper management is female. Though half the law school graduates are women, and 30 percent of associates in private firms are
female, only 5 percent of partners are women. At the top universities in the United States and Canada, the number of women full

professors is also about 5 percent. The glass ceiling works to the advantage of the traditional elite, and its good working order is reinforced by the beauty myth.

One reaction to this is that older American women who have made advances within every profession are being forced to see the signs of age (the adjunct of male advancement) as a "need" for plastic surgery. They recognize this "need" as a professional, rather than a personal, obligation. While male peers have evidence of a generation above theirs of old, successful men who look their age, contemporary women have few such role models.

This employment demand for cosmetic surgery brings women into an alternative work reality based on ideas about the uses of human beings as workers, ideas that have not applied to men since the abolition of slavery, before which a slave owner had the right to inflict physical mutilation on his workforce. The surgical economy is no slave economy, of course; but in its increasing demand for permanent, painful, and risky alteration of the body, it constitutes—as have tattooing, branding, and scarification in other times and places—a category that falls somewhere between a slave economy and a free market. The slave owner could cut off the foot of the slave who resisted control; the employer, with this development, can, in effect, cut off parts of a woman's face. In a free market, the worker's *labor* is sold to the employer; her *body* is her own.

Cosmetic surgery and the ideology of self-improvement may have made women's hope for legal recourse to justice obsolete. We can better understand how insidious this development is if we try to imagine a racial discrimination suit brought in the face of a powerful technology that processes, with great pain, nonwhite people to look more white. A black employee can now charge, sympathetically, that he doesn't *want* to look more white, and should not have to look more white in order to keep his job. We have not yet begun the push toward civil rights for women that will entitle a woman to say that she'd rather look like herself than some "beautiful" young stranger. Though the PBQ ranks women in a similar biological caste system, female identity is not yet recognized to be remotely as legitimate as racial identity (faintly though that is recognized). It is inconceivable to the dominant culture that it should respect as a political allegiance, as deep as any ethnic or racial pride, a woman's determination to show her loyalty—in the face of a beauty myth as powerful as myths about white supremacy—to her age, her shape, her self, her life.

*It keeps women isolated.* Collective female solidarity in the workplace would force the power structure to tackle the expensive concessions that many economists now believe are necessary if women are to have truly equal opportunity: day care, flextime, job security after childbirth, and parental leave. It might also change the focus of work and the very structure of organization. The unionization of women clerical and sales workers would force Western economies into a serious recognition of what the female work force contributes: 50 percent of working women in the United Kingdom are not unionized, according to the Equal Opportunities Commission. In the United States, 86 percent are not unionized. Many economists believe that the future for unions is female—and that they are the solution to "the feminization of poverty" of the past twenty years. "The fact that unionized women workers earn, on average, 30 percent more than nonunionized women workers speaks for itself," writes one. "Collectively women workers do better." Clerical workers, a third of female wage labor, and sales and service workers, over a quarter, have been some of the hardest groups to unionize. Solidarity is hardest to find when women learn to see each other as beauties first. The myth urges women to believe that it's every woman for herself.

*It uses her body to convey her economic role.* When a woman says, "This will never be fair even if I play by their rules," she gains insight into the real workings of the myth. No amount of labor will ever be adequately compensated; she will never, hard though she may try, really "make it"; her birth is not the birth of a beauty aristocrat, that mythic species. It *isn't* fair. That's why it exists.

Women's labor for beauty, and the evaluation of women as beauties rather than as workers, issue women each day with metaphors of the real economic injustices that apply to them in the workplace: selective benefits; favoritism in promotion; no job security; a pension plan that pays out a fraction of the capital the worker has put in; a shaky shares portfolio managed by unscrupulous advisers who stand to profit from the investor's losses;

false promises and worthless contracts from management; a policy of first hired, first fired; no union, rigorous union-busting, and plenty of scab labor ready to be called in.

In a behavioral experiment Catharine MacKinnon cites, one group of chickens was fed every time they pecked; another, every second time; and the third, at random. When the food was cut off, the first group stopped trying at once, then the second group soon stopped. The third group, she writes, *"never stopped trying."*

Women, as beauty and work reward them and punish them, never come to expect consistency—but can be counted upon to keep on trying. Beauty work and the professional beauty qualification in the workplace act together to teach women that, as far as they are concerned, justice does not apply. That unfairness is presented to a woman as changeless, eternal, appropriate, and arising out of herself, as much a part of her as her height, her hair color, her gender, and the shape of her face.

# *Culture*

$S$*ince middle-class women* have been sequestered from the world, isolated from one another, and their heritage submerged with each generation, they are more dependent than men are on the cultural models on offer, and more likely to be imprinted by them. Marina Warner's *Monuments and Maidens* explains how it comes about that individual men's names and faces are enshrined in monuments, supported by identical, anonymous (and "beautiful") stone women. That situation is true of culture in general. Given few role models in the world, women seek them on the screen and the glossy page.

This pattern, which leaves out women as individuals, extends from high culture to popular mythology: "Men look at women. Women watch themselves being looked at. This determines not only the relations of men to women, but the relation of women to themselves." Critic John Berger's well-known quote has been true throughout the history of Western culture, and it is more true now than ever.

Men are exposed to male *fashion* models but do not see them as *role* models. Why do women react so strongly to nothing, really—images, scraps of paper? Is their identity so weak? Why do they feel they must treat "models"—mannequins—as if they were "models"—paradigms? Why do women react to the "ideal," whatever form she takes at that moment, as if she were a non-negotiable commandment?

## Heroines

It is not that women's identities are naturally weak. But "ideal" imagery has become obsessively important to women because it was meant to become so. Women are mere "beauties" in men's culture so that culture can be kept male. When women in culture show character, they are not desirable, as opposed to the desirable, artless ingenue. A beautiful heroine is a contradiction in terms, since heroism is about individuality, interesting and ever changing, while "beauty" is generic, boring, and inert. While culture works out moral dilemmas, "beauty" is amoral: If a woman is born resembling an art object, it is an accident of nature, a fickle consensus of mass perception, a peculiar coincidence—but it is not a moral act. From the "beauties" in male culture, women learn a bitter amoral lesson—that the moral lessons of their culture exclude them.

Since the fourteenth century, male culture has silenced women by taking them beautifully apart: The catalog of features, developed by the troubadours, first paralyzed the beloved woman into beauty's silence. The poet Edmund Spenser perfected the catalog of features in his hymn the "Epithalamion"; we inherit that catalog in forms ranging from the list-your-good-points articles in women's magazines to fantasies in mass culture that assemble the perfect women.

Culture stereotypes women to fit the myth by flattening the feminine into beauty-without-intelligence or intelligence-without-beauty; women are allowed a mind or a body but not both. A common allegory that teaches women this lesson is the pretty-plain pairing: of Leah and Rachel in the Old Testament and Mary and Martha in the New; Helena and Hermia in *A Midsummer*

*Night's Dream;* Anya and Dunyasha in Chekhov's *The Cherry Orchard;* Daisy Mae and Sadie Hawkins in Dogpatch; Glinda and the Wicked Witch of the West in Oz; Veronica and Ethel in Riverdale; Ginger and Mary Ann in *Gilligan's Island;* Janet and Chrissie in *Three's Company;* Mary and Rhoda in *The Mary Tyler Moore Show;* and so forth. Male culture seems happiest to imagine two women together when they are defined as being one winner and one loser in the beauty myth.

Women's writing, on the other hand, turns the myth on its head. Female culture's greatest writers share the search for radiance, a beauty that has meaning. The battle between the overvalued beauty and the undervalued, unglamorous but animated heroine forms the spine of the women's novel. It extends from *Jane Eyre* to today's paperback romances, in which the gorgeous nasty rival has a mane of curls and a prodigious cleavage, but the heroine only her spirited eyes. The hero's capacity to see the true beauty of the heroine is his central test.

This tradition pits beautiful, vapid Jane Fairfax ("I cannot separate Miss Fairfax from her complexion") against the subtler Emma Woodhouse in Jane Austen's *Emma;* frivolous, blond Rosamond Vincy ("What is the use of being exquisite if you are not seen by the best judges?") against "nun-like" Dorothea Casaubon in George Eliot's *Middlemarch;* manipulative, "remarkably pretty" Isabella Crawford against self-effacing Fanny Price in Austen's *Mansfield Park;* fashionable, soulless Isabella Thorpe against Catherine Morland, unsure of herself "where the beauty of her own sex is concerned," in Austen's *Northanger Abbey;* narcissistic Ginevra Fanshawe ("How do I look to-night? . . . I know I am beautiful") against the invisible Lucy Snow ("I saw myself in the glass . . . I thought little of the wan spectacle") in Charlotte Brontë's *Villette;* and, in Louisa May Alcott's *Little Women,* vain Amy March, "a graceful statue," against tomboyish Jo, who sells her "one beauty," her hair, to help her family. It descends to the present in the novels of Alison Lurie, Fay Weldon, Anita Brookner. Women's writing is full to the point of heartbreak with the injustices done by beauty—its presence as well as its absence.

But when girls read the books of masculine culture, the myth subverts what those stories seem to say. Tales taught to children as parables for proper values become meaningless for girls as the myth begins its work. Take the story of Prometheus, which appears in Sullivan Reader comic-book form for third grade American children. To a child being socialized into Western culture, it teaches that a great man risks all for intellectual daring, for progress and for the public good. But as a future woman, the little girl learns that the most beautiful woman in the world was man-made, and that *her* intellectual daring brought the first sickness and death onto men. The myth makes a reading girl skeptical of the moral coherence of her culture's stories.

As she grows up, her double vision intensifies: If she reads James Joyce's *Portrait of the Artist as a Young Man*, she is not meant to question why Stephen Dedalus is the hero of his story. But in Thomas Hardy's *Tess of the D'Urbervilles*—why did the light of description fall on her, and not on any other of the healthy, untutored Wessex farm girls dancing in circles that May morning? She was seen and found beautiful, so *things happened to her*— riches, indigence, prostitution, true love, and hanging. Her life, to say the least, became interesting, while the hard-handed threshing girls around her, her friends, not blessed or cursed with her beauty, stayed in the muddy provinces to carry on the agricultural drudgery that is not the stuff of novels. Stephen is in his story because he's an exceptional subject who must and will be known. But Tess? Without her beauty, she'd have been left out of the sweep and horror of large events. A girl learns that stories happen to "beautiful" women, whether they are interesting or not. And, interesting or not, stories do not happen to women who are not "beautiful."

Her early education in the myth makes her susceptible to the heroines of adult women's mass culture—the models in women's magazines. It is those models whom women usually mention first when they think about the myth.

## Women's Magazines

Most commentators, like this *Private Eye* satirist, ridicule women's magazines' "trivial" concerns and their editorial tone: "Women's magazine triteness . . . combines knowing chatter about blowjobs with deep reservoirs of sentimentality." Women too believe that they transmit the worst aspects of the beauty myth. Readers themselves are often ambivalent about the pleasure mixed up with anxiety that they provide. "I buy them," a young woman told me, "as a form of self-abuse. They give me a weird mixture of anticipation and dread, a sort of stirred-up euphoria. Yes! Wow! I can be better starting from right this minute! Look at her! Look at *her*! But right afterward, I feel like throwing out all my clothes and everything in my refrigerator and telling my boyfriend never to call me again and blowtorching my whole life. I'm ashamed to admit that I read them every month."

Women's magazines accompanied women's advances and the simultaneous evolution of the beauty myth. During the 1860s and 1870s, Girton and Newnham Colleges, Vassar and Radcliffe, and other institutions of higher education for women were founded, and, as historian Peter Gay writes, "women's emancipation was getting out of control." Meanwhile, the mass production of beauty images aimed at women was perfected, and *The Queen* and *Harper's Bazaar* were established; the circulation of Beeton's *English Women's Domestic Magazine* doubled to fifty thousand. The rise in women's magazines was brought about by large investments of capital combined with increased literacy and purchasing power of lower-middle- and working-class women: The democratization of beauty had begun.

Magazines first took advertisers at the turn of the century. As suffragists were chaining themselves to the gates of the White House and of Parliament, the circulation of women's magazines doubled again. By the teens, the era of the New Woman, their style had settled into what it is today: cozy, relaxed, and intimate.

The magazines, other writers have shown, reflect shifts in women's status: Victorian magazines "catered to a female sex virtually in domestic bondage," but with World War I and women's participation in it, they "quickly developed a commensurate degree of social awareness." When the male work force came back from the trenches, the magazines returned to the home. Again in the 1940s they glamorized the world of war-production paid work and war-effort volunteer work. "The press cooperated," writes John Costello in *Love, Sex and War, 1939–1945*, when "the

War Manpower Commission turned to . . . Madison Avenue to boost its national campaign to attract first-time women workers." Glamour, he claims, was a main tool in the enlistment campaign then, just as the beauty myth today serves government and the economy.

As women responded and undertook men's higher-paid work, a new sense of competence and confidence emboldened them. At the same time, writes Costello, advertisements "attempted to preserve the socially acceptable feminine image of women war workers." A Pond's cold cream ad of the time read: "We like to feel we *look* feminine even though we are doing a man-sized job . . . so we tuck flowers and ribbons in our hair and try to keep our faces looking pretty as you please." Costello quotes a cosmetics company's advertisement that admitted that while the war could not be won by lipstick, "it symbolizes one of the reasons why we are fighting . . . the precious right of women to be feminine and lovely." In the face of a great social upheaval that was giving women responsibility, autonomy, state-run child care, and good money, the advertisers needed to ensure that there would be a market left for their products. Costello notes that "it was not just the advertisements . . . magazine articles focused the ladies' attention on the need to keep their FQ (Feminine Quotient) high." The magazines needed to ensure that their readers would not liberate themselves out of their interest in women's magazines.

When the men were demobilized, Western economies faced a crisis. In the United States, the government needed "to counter fears that American soldiers would return to an employment market saturated by women." To its dismay, the Manpower Commission realized that they had been wrong in their hopes that they could exploit women's labor as a stopgap: "Behind the scenes, male-dominated bureaucracies were casting post-war plans on the assumption that most of the women would meekly return to their ageless mission as wives and mothers. But they were wrong." Very wrong: In fact, 61 to 85 percent of women, a 1944 survey found, "certainly did not want to go back to housework after the war." What the commission saw in that decided response from working women was the threat of returned veterans thrown out of work in favor of lower-paid female workers, which would lead to political unrest, even a repeat of the Depression. The year after

the war ended, the magazines swung again—more exaggeratedly
than before—back into domesticity, and three million American
and one million British women were fired or quit their jobs.

Though many writers have pointed out that women's magazines reflect historical change, fewer examine how part of their
job is to determine historical change as well. Editors do their jobs
well by reading the *Zeitgeist;* editors of women's magazines—and,
increasingly, mainstream media as well—must be alert to what
social roles are demanded of women to serve the interests of those
who sponsor their publication. Women's magazines for over a century have been one of the most powerful agents for changing
women's roles, and throughout that time—today more than
ever—they have consistently glamorized whatever the economy,
their advertisers, and, during wartime, the government, needed at
that moment from women.

By the 1950s, the traditional women's magazine's role was re-
established: "In psychological terms," writes Ann Oakley in
*Housewife,* "they enabled the harassed mother, the overburdened
housewife, to make contact with her ideal self: that self which
aspires to be a good wife, a good mother, and an efficient home-
maker. . . . Women's expected role in society [was] to strive after
perfection in all three roles." The definition of perfection, however, changes with the needs of employers, politicians, and, in
the postwar economy that depended on spiraling consumption,
advertisers.

In the 1950s, advertising revenues soared, shifting the balance
between editorial and advertising departments. Women's magazines became of interest to "the companies that, with the war
about to end, were going to have to make consumer sales take the
place of war contracts." The main advertisers in the women's
magazines responsible for the Feminine Mystique were seeking
to sell household products.

In a chapter of Betty Friedan's *The Feminine Mystique* entitled
"The Sexual Sell," she traced how American housewives' "lack
of identity" and "lack of purpose . . . [are] manipulated into dollars." She explored a marketing service and found that, of the
three categories of women, the Career Woman was "unhealthy"
from the advertisers' point of view, and "that it would be to their

advantage not to let this group get any larger . . . . they are not the ideal type of customer. *They are too critical.*"

The marketers' reports described how to manipulate housewives into becoming insecure consumers of household products: "A transfer of guilt must be achieved," they said. "Capitalize . . . on 'guilt over hidden dirt.'" Stress the "therapeutic value" of baking, they suggested: "With X mix in the home, you will be a different woman." They urged giving the housewife "a sense of achievement" to compensate her for a task that was "endless" and "time-consuming." Give her, they urged manufacturers, "specialized products for specialized tasks"; and "make housework a matter of knowledge and skill, rather than a matter of brawn and dull, unremitting effort." Identify your products with "spiritual rewards," an "almost religious feeling," "an almost religious belief." For objects with "added psychological value," the report concluded, "the price itself hardly matters." Modern advertisers are selling diet products and "specialized" cosmetics and antiaging creams rather than household goods. In 1989, "toiletries/cosmetics" ad revenue offered $650 million to the magazines, while "soaps, cleansers, and polishes" yielded only one tenth that amount. So modern women's magazines now center on beauty work rather than housework: You can easily substitute in the above quotes from the 1950s all the appropriate modern counterparts from the beauty myth.

If the ads and commercials are a "clear case of *caveat emptor,*" Friedan concluded,

the same sexual sell disguised in the editorial content is both less ridiculous and more insidious. . . . A memo need never be written, a sentence need never be spoken at an editorial conference; the men and women who make the editorial decisions often compromise their very own high standards in the interest of the advertising dollar.

That is still true.

Nothing structural has changed except the details of the dream. Betty Friedan asked:

Why is it never said that the really crucial function . . . that women serve as housewives is to *buy more things for the house*? . . . Somehow, somewhere, someone must have figured out that women will buy more things if they are kept in the underused, nameless-yearning, energy-to-get-rid-of state of being housewives. . . . It would take a pretty clever economist to figure out what would keep our affluent economy going if the housewife market began to fall off.

When the restless, isolated, bored, and insecure housewife fled the Feminine Mystique for the workplace, advertisers faced the loss of their primary consumer. How to make sure that busy, stimulated working women would keep consuming at the levels they had done when they had all day to do so and little else of interest to occupy them? A new ideology was necessary that would compel the same insecure consumerism; that ideology must be, unlike that of the Feminine Mystique, a briefcase-sized neurosis that the working woman could take with her to the office. To paraphrase Friedan, why is it never said that the really crucial function that women serve as aspiring beauties is *to buy more things for the body*? Somehow, somewhere, someone must have figured out that they will buy more things if they are kept in the self-hating, ever-failing, hungry, and sexually insecure state of being aspiring "beauties."

"Clever economists" did figure out what would keep our affluent economy going once the housewife market began to fall off after the second wave of women's advancement sparked by Friedan's book: The modern form of the beauty myth was figured out, with its $33-billion thinness industry and its $20-billion youth industry.

In the breakdown of the Feminine Mystique and the rebirth of the women's movement, the magazines and advertisers of that defunct religion were confronted with their own obsolescence. *The beauty myth, in its modern form, arose to take the place of the Feminine Mystique, to save magazines and advertisers from the economic fallout of the women's revolution.*

The beauty myth simply took over the function of Friedan's "religion" of domesticity. The terms have changed but the effect is the same. Of the women's culture of the 1950s, Friedan lamented that "there is no other way for a woman to be a heroine" than to "keep on having babies"; today, a heroine must "keep on being beautiful."

The women's movement nearly succeeded in toppling the economics of the magazines' version of femininity. During its second wave, clothing manufacturers were alarmed to find that women weren't spending much money on clothing anymore. As middle-class women abandoned their role as consuming housewives and entered the work force, their engagement with the issues of the outer world could foreseeably lead them to lose interest altogether in women's magazines' separate feminine reality. And the magazines' authority was undermined still further with the fashion upheavals that began in the late 1960s, the end of haute couture and the beginning of what fashion historians Elizabeth Wilson and Lou Taylor call "style for all." Would liberated women read women's magazines? What for? Indeed, between 1965 and 1981, British women's magazine sales fell sharply from 555.3 million to 407.4 million copies a year. The magazines' editors and publishers could foresee their traditional hold on women being loosened by the winds of social change.

High-fashion culture ended, and the women's magazines' traditional expertise was suddenly irrelevant. The Feminine Mystique evaporated; *all that was left was the body*. With the rebirth of the women's movement, *Vogue* in 1969 offered up—hopefully, perhaps desperately—the Nude Look. Women's sense of liberation from the older constraints of fashion was countered by a new and sinister relationship to their bodies, as, writes historian Roberta Pollack Seid, "*Vogue* began to focus on the body as much as on the clothes, in part because there was little they could dictate with the anarchic styles." Stripped of their old expertise, purpose, and advertising hook, the magazines invented—almost completely artificially—a new one. In a stunning move, an entire replacement culture was developed by naming a "problem" where it had scarcely existed before, centering it on women's natural state, and elevating it to *the* existential female dilemma. The number of diet-related articles rose 70 percent from 1968 to 1972. Articles on dieting in the popular press soared from 60 in the year 1979 to 66 in the *month* of January 1980 alone. By 1983–84, the *Reader's Guide to Periodical Literature* listed 103 articles; by 1984,

300 diet books were on the shelves. The lucrative "transfer of guilt" was resurrected just in time.

That "transfer of guilt" that rescued the women's magazines gained power from the caricature in the mainstream media of the heroines of the reborn women's movement, a caricature that had been done to death for over a century, always in service of the same kind of backlash; the 1848 Seneca Falls convention for a female Bill of Rights provoked editorials about "'unsexed women,'" writes Gay, which insinuated that they had become activists because "they were too repulsive to find a husband. . . . These women are entirely devoid of personal attractions." Another antifeminist publicist he quoted characterized them as a "hybrid species, half man and half woman, belonging to neither sex." When a supporter, Senator Lane of Kansas, presented a petition for the franchise on behalf of "one hundred and twenty-four beautiful, intelligent and accomplished ladies," another editorial protested that "that trick . . . will not do. We wager an apple that the ladies referred to are not 'beautiful' or accomplished. Nine out of ten of them are undoubtedly *passé*. They have hook-billed noses, crow's feet under their sunken eyes. . . ." A doctor reacting to feminist agitation characterized such "degenerate women" by "their low voices, hirsute bodies, and small breasts." According to Gay, "Feminists were denigrated as failed women, half-men, hens that crow . . . humor magazines and hostile legislators everywhere broadcast a frightening picture of appalling masculine harridans haranguing the House of Commons."

As soon as women of the 1960s spoke up, the media took on the dreamwork demanded by the vital lie of the time, and trained the beauty myth against the women's appearance. The reaction to the 1969 protest against the Miss America pageant set the stage. Coverage focused on signs reading, THERE'S ONLY ONE THING WRONG WITH MISS AMERICA—SHE'S BEAUTIFUL and JEALOUSY WILL GET YOU NOWHERE. Soon, *Esquire* was profiling Gloria Steinem as "the intellectual's pinup" and *Commentary* dismissed feminism as "a bunch . . . of ugly women screaming at each other on television." *The New York Times* quoted a traditional women's leader saying, "So many of them are just so unattractive." The 1970 march down Fifth Avenue was interpreted by the *Washington Star* as important for having

"retired the canard about women's libbers being ugly," as reporter Pete Hamill hadn't "seen so many beautiful women in
one place for years." Norman Mailer said to Germaine Greer before their famous debate at City Hall, "You're better looking
than I thought." Headlines read, WOMEN ARE REVOLTING.
Women took in the way the movement was being depicted, and
the caricatures did their work.

Though many women realized that their attention was being
focused in this way, fewer fully understood how thoroughly politically such focusing works: In drawing attention to the physical
characteristics of women leaders, *they can be dismissed as either too
pretty or too ugly.* The net effect is to prevent women's identification with the issues. If the public woman is stigmatized as too
"pretty," she's a threat, a rival—or simply not serious; if derided
as too "ugly," one risks tarring oneself with the same brush by
identifying oneself with her agenda. The political implications of
the fact that *no woman or group of women*, whether housewives,
prostitutes, astronauts, politicians or feminists, can survive un-
scathed the no-win scrutiny of the beauty myth are not yet re-
organized in their full dimensions so the divide-and-conquer
dreamwork was effective. Since "beauty" follows fashion, and the
myth determines that when something female matures it is un-
fashionable, the maturing of feminism was crudely but effectively
distorted in the lens of the myth.

The new wave of post–women's movement magazines gained
ground from the anxiety that such caricature provoked in achieving women. Nonetheless, the new wave—initiated in 1965 by the
revamped *Cosmopolitan*—is indeed revolutionary compared with
the earlier service magazines that Friedan had attacked. Their formula includes an aspirational, individualist, can-do tone that says
that you should be your best and nothing should get in your way;
a focus on personal and sexual relationships that affirms female
ambition and erotic appetite; and sexualized images of female
models that, though only slightly subtler than those aimed at
men, are meant to convey female sexual liberation. But the formula must also include an element that contradicts and then undermines the overall prowoman fare: In diet, skin care, and
surgery features, it sells women the deadliest version of the
beauty myth money can buy.

This obligatory beauty myth dosage the magazines provide elicits in their readers a raving, itching, parching product lust, and an abiding fantasy: the longing for some fairy godmother who will arrive at the reader's door and put her to sleep. When she awakens, her bathroom will be full of exactly the right skin-care products, with step-by-step instructions, and palettes of exactly the required makeup. The kindly phantom will have colored and cut the sleeper's hair to perfection, made over her face, and painlessly nipped and tucked it. In her closet she will discover a complete wardrobe arranged by season and occasion, color-coordinated and accessorized on shoe trees and in hatboxes. The refrigerator will be full of miniature vegetables, artfully displayed in prepared gourmet meals, with Perrier and Evian water virtuously ranged. She will deliver herself into a world of female consumer apotheosis, beyond appetite.

The extreme contradictions between the positive and negative elements of the magazines' message provoke extreme reactions in women (in 1970, *The Ladies' Home Journal* was the target of an angry all-woman sit-in). Why do women care so much what the magazines say and show?

They care because, though the magazines are trivialized, they represent something very important: women's mass culture. A woman's magazine is not just a magazine. The relationship between the woman reader and her magazine is so different from that between a man and his that they aren't in the same category: A man reading *Popular Mechanics* or *Newsweek* is browsing through just one perspective among countless others of general male-oriented culture, which is everywhere. A woman reading *Glamour* is holding women-oriented mass culture between her two hands.

Women are deeply affected by what their magazines tell them (or what they believe they tell them) because they are all most women have as a window on their own mass sensibility. General culture takes a male point of view on what's newsworthy, so that the Super Bowl is on the front page while a change in child care legislation is buried in a paragraph on an inside page. It also takes a male point of view about who is worth looking at: Of fifty years of *Life* magazine covers, though many showed women, only 19 of those were not actresses or models; that is, not there because of their "beauty" (indeed, true to the beauty myth, in the case of

Eleanor Roosevelt, almost every interviewer makes a reference to her famous "ugliness"). Newspapers relegate women's issues to the "women's page"; TV news programming consigns "women's stories" to the daytime. In contrast, women's magazines are the only products of popular culture that (unlike romances) change with women's reality, are mostly written by women for women about women's issues, and take women's concerns seriously.

Women react so strongly to their inconsistencies since they probably recognize that the magazines' contradictions are their own. Their economic reality is that of an individual woman writ large: They reflect the uneasy truce in which women pay for scope and power with beauty thinking. *Women's magazines themselves are subject to a textual version of the PBQ.* Like its readers, the magazine must pay for its often serious, prowoman content with beauty backlash trappings; it must do so to reassure its advertisers, who are threatened by the possible effects on women's minds of too much excellence in women's journalism. The magazines' personalities are split between the beauty myth and feminism in exactly the same way those of their readers are split.

Are the magazines trivial, degrading, and antifeminist? The beauty myth is; the editorial content by now, wherever it can escape the myth, decidedly is not. Many women who care about women's culture are drawn to tap in to this one stream of female mass consciousness, whether as editors, writers, or readers. The magazines' editorial content changed beyond recognition, for the better, after the rebirth of feminism. Twenty years ago the activists who demonstrated at the offices of *The Ladies' Home Journal* offered a utopian list of article ideas: Instead of "Zsa Zsa Gabor's Bed," they proposed "How to Get an Abortion," "How and Why Women Are Kept Apart," "How to Get a Divorce," "Developments in Day Care," and "What Our Detergents Do to the Rivers and Streams." And it happened: One recognizes each of these once-extreme suggestions as the typical fare of the new wave of women's magazines.

What is seldom acknowledged is that they have popularized feminist ideas more widely than any other medium—certainly more widely than explicitly feminist journals. It was through these glossies that issues from the women's movement swept out from the barricades and down from academic ivory towers to blow into the lives of working-class women, rural women, women without higher education. Seen in this light, they are very potent instruments of social change.

The feminist content in these magazines is of a level that could not have been imagined in Cecil Beaton's *Vogue* or in the *Redbook* targeted by Betty Friedan: Articles regularly run on abortion, rape, woman battering, sexual self-expression, and economic independence. Indeed, criticism of the beauty myth is found in them more often than anywhere else. For example, *Glamour:* "How to Make Peace with the Body You've Got"; *She:* "Fat Is Not a Sin"; *Cosmopolitan:* "What Should We Do About Pornography?" *Glamour* again: "The Appeal of Real Women," ("Make way for the smart-mouthed actresses who get the man without being gorgeous . . . whose sex appeal comes from energy, snappy banter, smartness, rather than statuesque bodies or great looks.") Even the articles that deal with emotional states and personal relationships, those most often ridiculed, are not ridiculous when one considers how communities are held together through this "emotional housework" that women are expected innately to know how to do.

When the emphasis is on the "mass" part of their appeal, the women's magazines' political importance grows clearer. Many books and journals have brought issues from the women's movement to the minority: middle-class, educated women. But the new breed of women's magazines are the first messengers in history to address the majority of women, those who are struggling financially, to tell them they have a right to define themselves first. They point out ways for them to get power: to study martial arts, to play the stock market, to take charge of their health. These magazines run women's fiction, profile female achievers, and discuss women-related legislation. If only in terms of making enough space to cover women's political and cultural experience, the most lightweight women's magazine is a more serious force for women's advancement than the most heavyweight general periodical.

They also provide a rare platform, through letters, serialization, and changing contributors, for woman-to-woman debate. Because they are the only place for women to find out what's going on in the other world—the female reality so fleetingly acknowledged by "serious" journals—women's intense love-hate reaction to them makes sense. In these respects, the magazines' role should be seen as very serious. For a mass female culture that responds to historical change, they are all that women have.

No wonder that women resent the elements of their format that follow repetitive formulas. No wonder it disturbs them when their magazines seem servile to the degrading economic bottom line of the beauty myth. Women's magazines would not provoke such strong feelings if they were merely escapist entertainment. But in the absence of mainstream journalism that treats women's issues with anything like the seriousness they deserve, women's magazines take on a burden of significance—and responsibility—that would otherwise be spread out over half the "serious" periodicals on the market.

But women's magazines do not simply mirror our own dilemma of beauty being asked as an apology for new scope and power. They intensify it. Even their editors worry that many readers have not learned how to separate out the prowoman content from the beauty myth in the magazines, whose place is primarily economic.

Unfortunately, the beauty backlash is spread and reinforced by the cycles of self-hatred provoked in women by the advertisements, photo features, and beauty copy in the glossies. These make up the beauty index, which women scan as anxiously as men scan stock reports. It promises to tell women what men truly want, what faces and bodies provoke men's fickle attentions—a seductive promise in an environment in which men and women rarely get to talk together honestly in a public setting about what each really desires. But the Iron Maiden they offer is no direct template of men's desires, any more than beefcake photos tell the whole truth about women's desires. The magazines are not oracles speaking for men. Indeed, as one study found, "our data suggest women are misinformed and exaggerate the magnitude of thinness men desire . . . they *are* misinformed, probably as a result of promotion of thinness in women through advertising in the diet industry." What editors are obliged to appear to say that *men* want from women is actually what their *advertisers* want from women.

The magazine's message *about the myth* is determined by its advertisers. But the relationship between the reader and her magazine doesn't happen in a context that encourages her to analyze how the message is affected by the advertisers' needs. It is emotional, confiding, defensive, and unequal: "the link binding readers to their magazine, the great umbilical, as some call it, the trust."

The myth isolates women by generation, and the magazines seem to offer them the wise advice, tested by experience, of an admirable older female relative. There are few other places where a modern woman can find such a role model. She is taught to dismiss her own mother's teachings about beauty, adornment, and seduction, since her mother has failed—she is aging. If she is lucky enough to have a mentor, it will be in a professional relationship, in which these intimate skills are not part of the training. The voice of the magazine gives women an invisible female authority figure to admire and obey, parallel to the mentor-protégé relationship that many men are encouraged to forge in their educations and on the job, but which women are rarely offered anywhere else but in their glossy magazines.

The voice encourages that trust. It has evolved a tone of allegiance to the reader, of being on your side with superior know-how and resources, like a woman-run social service: "Many cosmetics companies are on hand to help"; "We know how to make a difference. Let our beauty specialists guide you step by step." The magazines provide actual services, listing help lines, offering readers' polls, giving women tools for budgeting and financial information. These combine to make the magazine seem to be more than a magazine: They make it appear to be a mix of extended family, benefit agency, political party, and guild. They make it look like an interest group with the reader's best interest at heart. "A magazine," says one editor, "is like a club. Its function is to provide readers with a comfortable sense of community and pride in their identity."

Because people trust their clubs and because this voice is so attractive, it is difficult to read the magazine with a sharp eye as to how thoroughly ad revenue influences the copy. It is easy to misread the whole thing—advertisements, beauty copy, images of models—as if it were a coherent message from the editors telling women, "You should be like this." Some of the harm done by the magazines to women comes out of that misunderstanding. If we could read them in a more informed way, we could take the pleasure and leave the pain, and the magazines, with different advertisers, could do themselves the justice that they deserve in providing women with the only serious mass-market women's journalism available.

Women also respond to the beauty myth aspect of the magazines because adornment is an enormous—and often pleasing— part of female culture. And there is almost nowhere else where they can participate in women's culture in so broad a way. The myth does not only isolate women generationally, but because it encourages women's wariness of one another on the basis of their appearance, it tries to isolate them from all women they do not know and like personally. Though women have networks of intimate friends, the myth, and women's conditions until recently, have kept women from learning how to do something that makes all male social change possible: How to identify with unknown other women in a way that is not personal.

The unknown woman, the myth would like women to believe, is unapproachable; under suspicion before she opens her mouth because she's Another Woman, and beauty thinking urges women to approach one another as possible adversaries until they know they are friends. The look with which strange women sometimes appraise one another says it all: A quick up-and-down, curt and wary, it takes in the picture but leaves out the person; the shoes, the muscle tone, the makeup, are noted accurately, but the eyes glance off one another. Women can tend to resent each other if they look too "good" and dismiss one another if they look too "bad." So women too rarely benefit from the experience that makes men's clubs and organizations hold together: The solidarity of belonging to a group whose members might not be personal friends outside, but who are united in an interest, agenda, or worldview.

Ironically, the myth that drives women apart also binds them together. Commiserating about the myth is as good as a baby to bring strange women into pleasant contact, and break down the line of Other Woman wariness. A wry smile about calories, a complaint about one's hair, can evaporate the sullen examination of a rival in the fluorescent light of a ladies' room. On one hand,

women are trained to be competitors against all others for
"beauty"; on the other, when one woman—a bride, a shopper
in a boutique—needs to be adorned for a big occasion, other
women swoop and bustle around her in generous concentration
in a team formation as effortlessly choreographed as a football
play. These sweet and satisfying rituals of being all on the same
side, these all-too-infrequent celebrations of shared femaleness,
are some of the few shared female rituals left; hence their loveliness and power. But, sadly, these delightful bonds too often
dissolve when the women reenter public space and resume their
isolated, unequal, mutually threatening, jealously guarded
"beauty" status.

Women's magazines cater to that delicious sense of impersonal
female solidarity, now, compared with the high-water mark of the
second wave, so rare. They bring out of the closet women's lust
for chat across the barriers of potential jealousy and prejudgment.
What are other women really thinking, feeling, experiencing,
when they slip away from the gaze and culture of men? The magazines offer the electrifying feeling that women are too seldom
granted, though men in their groups feel it continually, of being
plugged in without hostility to a million like-minded people of
the same sex. Though the magazines' version is sadly watered
down, women are so deprived of it that it is powerful even in a
dilute concentration. Each reader, Mormon housewife in Phoe-
nix, schoolteacher in Lancashire, conceptual artist in Sydney,
welfare mother in Detroit, physics professor in Manhattan, pros-
titute in Brussels, au pair in Lyons, is dipping into the same bath
of images. All can participate in this one way in a worldwide
women's culture, which, though inadequate and ultimately
harmful, is still one of the few celebrations of female sexuality in
solidarity that women are allowed.

One sees the "perfect" face differently with this in mind. Its
power is not far-reaching because of anything innately special
about the face: Why that one? Its only power is that it has been
designated as "the face"—and that hence millions and millions of
women are looking at it together, and know it. A Christian Dior
cosmetic vision stares from a bus at a grandmother drinking a *café
con leche* on a balcony in Madrid. A cardboard blowup of the same
image gazes at the teenage Youth Training Scheme worker setting

it up in the local pharmacy in a village in Dorset. It glows over a
bazaar in Alexandria. *Cosmopolitan* appears in seventeen countries;
buying Clarins, women "join millions of women worldwide";
Weight Watchers products offer "Friends. More friends. Still
more friends."

The beauty myth, paradoxically, offers the promise of a solidarity movement, an Internationale. Where else do women get to
feel positively or even negatively connected with millions of
women worldwide? The images in women's magazines constitute
the only cultural female experience that can begin to gesture at
the breadth of solidarity possible among women, a solidarity as
wide as half the human race. It is a meager Esperanto, but in the
absence of a better language of their own they must make do with
one that is man-made and market driven, and which hurts them.

Our magazines simply reflect our own dilemma: Since much of
their message is about women's advancement, much of the
beauty myth must accompany it and temper its impact. Because
the magazines are so serious, they must also be so frivolous. Because they offer women power, they must also promote masochism. Because feminist poet Marge Piercy attacks the dieting
cult in *New Woman*, therefore the facing page must give a scare
sheet about obesity. While the editors take a step forward for
themselves and their readers, they must also take a step back into
the beauty myth for the sake of their advertisers.

Advertisers are the West's courteous censors. They blur the
line between editorial freedom and the demands of the marketplace. The magazine may project the intimate atmosphere of
clubs, guilds, or extended families, but they have to act like businesses. Because of who their advertisers are, a tacit screening
takes place. It isn't conscious policy, it doesn't circulate in
memos, it doesn't need to be thought about or spoken. It is understood that some kinds of thinking about "beauty" would alien-
ate advertisers, while others promote their products. With the
implicit need to maintain advertising revenue in order to keep
publishing, editors are not yet *able* to assign features and test
products as if the myth did not pay the bills. A women's magazine's profit does not come from its cover price, so its contents
cannot roam too far from the advertisers' wares. In a *Columbia
Journalism Review* story captioned "Magazine Crisis: Selling Out

for Ads," Michael Hoyt reports that women's magazines have always been under particular pressure from their advertisers; what's new is the intensity of the demands.

Women's magazines are not alone in this editorial obligation to the bottom line. It is on the increase outside them, too, making all media increasingly dependent on the myth. The 1980s saw a proliferation of magazines, each competing wildly for its piece of the advertising pie. The pressure is now on newspapers and news magazines: "Editors are facing a harder time maintaining their virginity," says the editor of the *Christian Science Monitor*. Lewis Lapham, editor of *Harper's,* says that New York editors speak of "the fragility of the word" and "advise discretion when approaching topics likely to alarm the buyers of large advertising space." "The American press is, and always has been, a booster press, its editorial pages characteristically advancing the same arguments as the paid advertising copy," he writes. According to *Time,* modern media management now "sees readers as a market." So publishers must seek upscale advertisers and apply pressure for upscale stories "Today, if you had Watergate, you would have to check with the marketing department," says editor Thomas Winship. The *Columbia Journalism Review* quotes the former editor of *The Boston Globe:* "'Magazines are commodities, commodities are there to sell goods, and the competition these days is ferocious.' He admits that now he too is heavily dependent on fashion ads. 'We used to have a silken curtain between advertising and editorial, but no more.' For years now, some publishers have gone out of their way to attract advertisers by creating what advertisers regard as a favorable editorial atmosphere." John R. MacArthur, editor of *Harper's,* believes, writes Hoyt, that "editing for advertisers" will destroy what makes magazines valuable: "an environment of quality and trust." Soon, if this trend continues unchecked, there will be few media left that will be free to investigate or question the beauty myth, or even offer alternatives, without worrying about the advertising repercussions.

The atmosphere is thronged with more versions of the Iron Maiden now than ever before also because of recent changes in media organization that have intensified visual competition. In 1988, the average person in the United States saw 14 percent more TV advertising than two years before, or 650 TV messages a week as part of the total of 1,000 ad messages each day. The industry calls this situation "viewer confusion": Just 1.2 of the 650 messages are remembered, down from 1.7 in 1983; the advertising business is in a growing panic.

So images of women and "beauty" become more extreme. As advertising executives told *The Boston Globe*, "You have to push a little harder . . . to jolt, shock, break through. Now that the competition is fiercer, a whole lot rougher trade takes place. [Rough trade is gay male slang for a sadistic heterosexual partner.] Today, business wants even more desperately to seduce. . . . It wants to demolish resistance." Rape is the current advertising metaphor.

In addition, film, TV, and magazines are under pressure to compete with pornography, which is now the biggest media category. Worldwide, pornography generates an estimated 7 *billion* dollars a year, more, incredibly, than the legitimate film and music industries combined. Pornographic films outnumber other films by three to one, grossing 365 million dollars a year in the United States alone, or a million dollars a day. British pornographic magazines sell twenty million copies a year at 2 to 3 pounds (about $3.20 to $4.80) a copy, grossing 500 million pounds a year. Swedish pornography earns 300–400 million kronor a year; a sex shop there offers some 500 titles, and a corner tobacconist, 20 to 30 titles. In 1981, 500,000 Swedish men bought pornographic magazines each week; by 1983, every fourth video rented in Sweden was pornographic; and by 1985, 13.6 million pornographic magazines were sold by the largest distributors in corner kiosks. Eighteen million men a month in the United States buy a total of 165 different pornographic magazines generating about half a billion dollars a year; one American man in ten reads *Playboy, Penthouse,* or *Hustler* each month; *Playboy* and *Penthouse* are the most widely read magazines in Canada. Italian men spend 600 billion lire on pornography a year, with pornographic videos representing 30–50 percent of all Italian video sales. Pornography worldwide, according to researchers, is becoming increasingly violent. (As slasher filmmaker Herschel Gordon Lewis said, "I mutilated women in our pictures because I felt it was better box office.")

To raise the level of pressure once again, this image competi-

tion is taking place during worldwide deregulation of the airwaves. In its wake, the beauty myth is exported from West to
East, and from rich to poor. United States programming is flood-
ing Europe and First World programs flood the Third World: In
Belgium, Holland, and France, 30 percent of TV is American-
made, and about 71 percent of TV programs in developing countries are imports from the rich world. In India, TV ownership
doubled in five years and advertisers have sponsored shows since
1984. Until a decade ago, most European TV was state-run; but
privatization, cable, and satellite changed all that, so that by 1995
there could be 120 channels, all but a few financed by advertising,
with revenues expected to rise from $9 billion to $25 billion by
the year 2000.

America is no exception. "The networks are running scared,"
reports *The Guardian* [London]. In ten years (1979–89), they lost
16 percent of the market to cable, independents, and video:
"The result is a glitz blitz."

With *glasnost*, the beauty myth is being imported behind the
Iron Curtain, as much to constrain a possible revival of feminism
as to simulate consumer plenty where little exists. "*Glasnost* and
*perestroika*," says Natalia Zacharova, a Soviet social critic,
". . . seem likely to bring Soviet women contradictory freedoms.
Glamour will be one of them." Her remark was prescient: *Reform*,
Hungary's revealingly named first tabloid, read by one in ten
Hungarians, has a topless or bottomless model on each page.
*Playboy* hailed Soviet Natalya Negoda as "The Soviets' first sex
star." Nationalist China entered the Miss Universe contest in
1988, the year the first Miss Moscow competition was held, following Cuba and Bulgaria. In 1990, outdated copies of *Playboy*
and women's glamour magazines began to be shipped to the Soviet bloc; we will be able to watch the beauty myth unfold there
in utero. Tatiana Mamanova, a Soviet feminist, responding to a
question about the difference between the West and Russia, replied, "The pornography . . . it's everywhere, even on billboards
. . . [it] is a different kind of assault. And it doesn't feel like
freedom to me."

## Censorship

In the free West, there is a good deal that women's magazines cannot say. In 1956 the first "arrangement" was made, when a nylon manufacturers' association booked a $12,000 space in *Woman*, and the editor agreed not to publish anything in the issue that prominently featured natural fibers. "Such silences," writes Janice Winship, "conscious or not, were to become commonplace."

Those silences we inherit, and they inhibit our freedom of speech. According to Gloria Steinem, *Ms.* lost a major cosmetics account because it featured Soviet women on its cover who were not, according to the advertiser, wearing enough makeup. Thirty-five thousand dollars worth of advertising was withdrawn from a British magazine the day after an editor, Carol Sarler, was quoted as saying that she found it hard to show women looking intelligent when they were plastered with makeup. A gray-haired editor for a leading women's magazine told a gray-haired writer, Mary Kay Blakely, that an article about the glories of gray hair cost her magazine the Clairol account for six months. An editor of *New York Woman*, a staff member told me, was informed that for financial reasons she had to put a model on the cover rather than a remarkable woman she wished to profile. Gloria Steinem remembers the difficulty of trying to fund a magazine beyond the beauty myth:

With . . . no intention of duplicating the traditional departments designed around "feminine" advertising categories— recipes to reinforce food ads, beauty features to mention beauty products, and the like—we knew it would be economically tough. (Fortunately, we didn't know *how* tough.) Attracting ads for cars, sound equipment, beer, and other things not traditionally directed to women still turns out to be easier than convincing advertisers that women look at ads for shampoo without accompanying articles on how to wash their hair, just as men look at ads for shaving products without articles on how to shave.

As she put it more wearily in a later interview in *New Woman,* "Advertisers don't believe in female opinion makers." Steinem believes that it's the advertisers who've got to change. And she believes they will, though perhaps not in her lifetime. Women need to change too, though; only when we take our own mass media seriously and resist its expectations that we will submit to still more instructions on "how to wash our hair" will advertisers concede that women's magazines must be entitled to as wide a measure of free speech as those for men.

Other censorship is more direct: Women's magazines transmit "information" about beauty products in a heavily self-censored medium. When you read about skin creams and holy oils, you are not reading free speech. Beauty editors are unable to tell the whole truth about their advertisers' products. In a *Harper's Bazaar* article, "Younger Every Day," opinions on various antiaging creams were solicited only and entirely from the presidents of ten cosmetics companies. Cosmetics and toiletry producers spend proportionately more on advertising than any other industry. The healthier the industry, the sicker are women's consumer and civil rights. Cosmetic stock is rising 15 percent yearly, and beauty copy is little more than advertising. "Beauty editors," writes Penny Chorlton in *Cover-up,* "are rarely able to write freely about cosmetics," since advertisers require an editorial promotion as a condition for placing the ad. The woman who buys a product on the recommendation of beauty copy is paying for the privilege of being lied to by two sources.

This market in turn is buoyed up by another more serious form of censorship. Dalma Heyn, editor of two women's magazines, confirms that airbrushing age from women's faces is routine. She observes that women's magazines "ignore older women or pretend they don't exist: magazines try to avoid photographs of older women, and when they feature celebrities who are over sixty, 'retouching artists' conspire to 'help' beautiful women look more beautiful; i.e., less their age."

This censorship extends beyond women's magazines to any image of an older woman: Bob Ciano, once art director of *Life* magazine, says that "no picture of a woman goes unretouched . . . even a well-known [older] woman who doesn't want to be retouched . . . we still persist in trying to make her look like she's

in her fifties." The effect of this censorship of a third of the
female life span is clear to Heyn: "By now readers have no idea
what a real woman's 60-year-old face looks like in print because
it's made to look 45. Worse, 60-year-old readers look in the mirror
and think they look too old, because they're comparing themselves to some retouched face smiling back at them from a magazine." Photographs of the bodies of models are often trimmed
with scissors. "Computer imaging"—the controversial new technology that tampers with photographic reality—has been used for
years in women's magazines' beauty advertising. Women's culture
is an adulterated, inhibited medium. How do the values of the
West, which hates censorship and believes in a free exchange of
ideas, fit in here?

This issue is not trivial. It is about the most fundamental
freedoms: the freedom to imagine one's own future and to be
proud of one's own life. Airbrushing age off women's faces has
the same political echo that would resound if all positive images
of blacks were routinely lightened. That would be making the
same value judgment about blackness that this tampering makes
about the value of the female life: that less is more. To airbrush
age off a woman's face is to erase women's identity, power, and
history.

But editors must follow the formula that works. They can't
risk providing what many readers claim they want: imagery that
includes them, features that don't talk down to them, reliable
consumer reporting. It is impossible, many editors assert, because
the readers do not yet want those things enough.

Imagine a women's magazine that positively featured round
models, short models, old models—or no models at all, but real
individual women. Let's say that it had a policy of avoiding cruelty to women, as some now have a policy of endorsing products
made free of cruelty to animals. And that it left out crash diets,
mantras to achieve self-hatred, and promotional articles for the
profession that cuts open healthy women's bodies. And let's say
that it ran articles in praise of the magnificence of visible age,
displayed loving photo essays on the bodies of women of all
shapes and proportions, examined with gentle curiosity the body's
changes after birth and breast-feeding, offered recipes without
punishment or guilt, and ran seductive portraits of men.

It would run aground, losing the bulk of its advertisers. Magazines, consciously or half-consciously, must project the attitude that looking one's age is bad because $650 million of their ad revenue comes from people who would go out of business if visible age looked good. They need, consciously or not, to promote women's hating their bodies enough to go profitably hungry, since the advertising budget for one third of the nation's food bill depends on their doing so by dieting. The advertisers who make women's mass culture possible depend on making women feel bad enough about their faces and bodies to spend more money on worthless or pain-inducing products than they would if they felt innately beautiful.

But more significantly, that magazine would run aground because women are so well schooled in the beauty myth that we often internalize it: Many of us are not yet sure ourselves that women are interesting without "beauty." Or that women's issues alone are involving enough for them to pay good money to read about if beauty thinking is not added to the mix.

Since self hatred artificially inflates the demand and the price, the overall message to women from their magazines must remain—as long as the beauty backlash is intact—negative not positive. Hence the hectoring tone that no other magazines use to address adults with money in their pockets: do's and don'ts that scold, insinuate, and condescend. The same tone in a men's magazine—*do* invest in tax-free bonds; *don't* vote Republican—is unthinkable. Since the advertisers depend on consumer behavior in women that can be brought about only through threats and compulsion, threats and compulsion weigh down the otherwise valuable editorial content of the magazines.

Women see the Face and the Body all around them now not because culture magically manifests a transparent male fantasy, but because advertisers need to sell products in a free-for-all of imagery bombardment intent on lowering women's self-esteem; and, for reasons that are political and not sexual, both men and women now pay attention to images of the Face and the Body. And it means that in the intensified competition to come, if no change of consciousness intervenes—for women's magazines cannot become more interesting until women believe that we ourselves are more interesting—the myth is bound to become many times more powerful.

And then the further the magazine guides the reader on her positive intellectual journey, the further it will drive her at the same time down the troubled route of her beauty addiction. And as the experiences along the way become ever more extreme, the stronger will grow women's maddening sense that our culture has a split personality, which it seeks to convey to us through a seductive, embarrassing, challenging, and guilt-laden quid pro quo between dazzling covers.

# *Religion*

## The Rites of Beauty

*T*he magazines transmit the beauty myth as the gospel of a new religion. Reading them, women participate in re-creating a belief system as powerful as that of any of the churches whose hold on them has so rapidly loosened.

The Church of Beauty is, like the Iron Maiden, a two-sided symbol. Women have embraced it eagerly from below as a means to fill the spiritual void that grew as their traditional relation to religious authority eroded. The social order imposes it as eagerly, to supplant religious authority as a policing force over women's lives.

The Rites of Beauty counter women's new freedom by combating women's entry into the secular public world with medieval superstition, keeping power inequalities safer than they might otherwise be. As women enter on a struggle with a world moving into a new millennium, they are increasingly weighed down with a potent belief system that keeps part of their consciousness locked in a way of thinking that the male world abandoned with the Dark Ages. If one consciousness is centered on a medieval belief system and another is thoroughly modern, the contemporary world and its power will belong to the latter. The Rites are archaic and primitive so that part of the core of female consciousness can be kept archaic and primitive.

Men too have reverent feelings about this religion of women's. The caste system based on "beauty" is defended as if it derives from an eternal truth. People assume that who don't approach the world with this kind of categorical faith in anything else. In this century, most fields of thought have been transformed by the understanding that truths are relative and perceptions subjective. But the rightness and permanence of "beauty's" caste system is taken for granted by people who study quantum physics, ethnology, civil rights law; who are atheists, who are skeptical of TV news, who don't believe that the earth was created in seven days. It is believed uncritically, as an article of faith.

The skepticism of the modern age evaporates where the subject is women's beauty. It is still—indeed, more than ever—described not as if it is determined by mortal beings, shaped by politics, history, and the marketplace, but as if there is a divine authority on high who issues deathless scripture about what it is that makes a woman good to look at.

This "truth" is seen in the way that God used to be—at the top of a chain of command, its authority linking down to His representatives on earth: beauty pageant officials, photographers, and, finally, the man in the street. Even he, the last link, has some of this divine authority over women, as Milton's Adam had over Eve: "he for God, and she for God in him." A man's right to confer judgment on any woman's beauty while remaining himself unjudged is beyond scrutiny because it is thought of as God-given. That right has become so urgently important for male culture to exercise because it is the last unexamined right remaining intact from the old list of masculine privilege: those that it was universally believed that God or nature or another absolute authority bestowed upon all men to exert over all women. As such, it is daily exercised more harshly in compensation for the other rights over women, and the other ways to control them, now lost forever.

Many writers have noticed the metaphysical similarities between beauty rituals and religious ones: Historian Joan Jacobs

Brumberg notes that even the earliest diet books' language "re-
verberated with references to religious ideas of temptation and
sin" and "echoed Calvinist struggles"; Susan Bordo speaks of
"Slenderness and the Soul"; historian Roberta Pollack Seid traces
the influence on "the weight-loss crusade" of Christian evan-
gelism in "the spectacular rise of evangelically inspired weight-
loss groups and books" (The Jesus System for Weight Control,
*God's Answer to Fat—Lose It, Pray Your Weight Away, More of Jesus
and Less of Me,* and *Help Lord—The Devil Wants Me Fat!* ). "Our
new religion," she writes of weight hysteria, ". . . offers no salvation, only a perpetually escalating cycle of sin and precarious redemption."

What has not yet been recognized is that the comparison
should be no metaphor: The rituals of the beauty backlash do not
simply echo traditional religions and cults but *functionally supplant
them.* They are *literally* reconstituting out of old faiths a new one,
*literally* drawing on traditional techniques of mystification and
thought control, to alter women's minds as sweepingly as any past
evangelical wave.

The Rites of Beauty are a heady compound of various cults
and religions. As religions go, this one is more alive and responsive than most to the changing spiritual needs of its congregants.
Bits and pieces and several belief systems are cobbled together in
it, and abandoned when they no longer serve. Like the larger
myth, the structure of its religion transforms itself with flexibility
to offset the various challenges posed to it by female autonomy.

Its imagery and its method crudely imitate medieval Catholicism. The sway it claims over women's lives is papal in its abso-
luteness. Its influence over modern women, like the medieval
Church over all of Christendom, extends far past the individual
soul to form the philosophy, politics, sexuality, and economy of
the age. The Church shaped and gave meaning not only to devo-
tional life, but to all the events of the community, brooking no
division between the secular and the religious; the Rites pervade
the days of modern women as thoroughly. Like the medieval
Church, the Rites are believed to be based on a creed as palpable
as the Rock of the Vatican: that there is such a thing as beauty,
that it is holy, and that women should seek to attain it. Both
institutions are wealthy, living off tithes; neither forgives unre-

pentant deviants and heretics. Members of both churches learn their catechism from the cradle. Both need unquestioning faith from their followers in order to sustain themselves.

Above this root of faux-medieval Catholicism, the Rites of Beauty have accumulated several newer elements: a Lutheranism in which the fashion models are the Elect, and the rest of us are the Damned; an Episcopalian adaptation to the demands of consumerism, in that women can aspire to heaven through (lucrative) good works; an Orthodox Judaism of purity compulsions, in the minute and painstaking exegesis of hundreds of laws with their commentaries on what to eat, what to wear, what to do to the body and when; and a centerpiece from the Eleusinian mysteries in the death-and-rebirth ceremony. Over all this, the maximum-indoctrination techniques of modern cult movements have been faithfully adapted. Their blunt psychological manipulations help to win converts in an age not given to spontaneous professions of faith.

The Rites of Beauty are able to isolate women so well because it is not yet publicly recognized that devotees are trapped in something more serious than a fashion and more socially pervasive than a private distortion of self-image. The Rites are not yet described in terms of what they actually represent: a new fundamentalism transforming the secular West, repressive and doctrinaire as any Eastern counterpart. As women cope with a hypermodernity to which they have only recently been admitted, a force that is in effect a mass hypnosis into a medieval worldview is pushing on them its full weight. Meanwhile, the great cathedral under whose shadow they live goes unmentioned. When other women do refer to it—self-deprecatingly, under their breath—they do so only as if to describe a hallucination that all women can see, rather than a concrete reality that no one acknowledges.

The Rites seized women's minds in the train of the women's movement because oppression abhors a vacuum; they gave back to women what women had lost when God died in the West. In the past generation, changing sexual mores loosened religious constraints on female sexual behavior; the postwar decline in Church attendance and the breakdown of the traditional family relaxed the ability of religion to dictate a morality to women. In the dangerous momentary vacuum of religious authority, a risk

was implicit that women might bestow authority on the concil-
iatory, communitarian female tradition that Carol Gilligan researched in her *In a Different Voice*. That reclamation of moral
authority could well lead women to make lasting social changes
along its lines, and have the faith to call those changes God's will.
Compassion might replace hierarchy; a traditionally feminine respect for human life might severely damage an economy based on
militarism and a job market based on the use of people as expendable resources. Women might recast human sexuality as proof of
the sacredness of the body rather than of its sinfulness, and the
old serviceable belief that equates femaleness with pollution
might become obsolete. To preempt all that, the Rites of Beauty
recently took over the job that traditional religious authority could
no longer manage with conviction. By instilling in women an in-
ternal police force, the new religion often does better than the
older ones at keeping women in order.

The new religion spread swiftly by taking advantage of
women's interim feeling of a loss of moral purpose, re-creating for
them in physical terms the earlier social roles in which "good
women" had been valued: chaste and self-denying mothers,
daughters, and wives. Older tasks of defending propriety—"fitness"—and distinguishing between decent and indecent were rit-
ually reconstructed. In the past quarter century, as society at large
slipped off the constraints of traditional religious morality, the old
moral code—diminished in scope, more constricted than ever,
but functionally unchanged—tightened on women's bodies.

For their part, many women welcomed this reassuring con-
striction on several levels. New religions spread with social chaos,
and women are making up the rules in a world that has destroyed
the old truths. This one gave them back the sense of social importance, female bonding, and the reassuring moral structure lost
with the old religion. The competitive public realm rewards amor-
ality, and women must adapt to succeed; but the Rites of Beauty
give a working woman a way to carry a harmless, private moral
order into a role in which too many old-fashioned scruples can
sabotage her career. Women as secular careerists are often isolated, but as religious followers they share a comfortable bond.

Society at large no longer places religious importance on
women's virginity or marital chastity, asks them to confess their

sins or to keep a kitchen that is scrupulously kosher. In the interim after the "good" woman's pedestal had been destroyed, but before she had acquired access to real power and authority, she was bereft of the older context in which she had been given the trappings of importance and praise. Devout women had indeed been called "good" (though they were "good" only so long as they were being devout). But in the secular age that paralleled the women's movement, though women no longer heard every Sunday that they were damned, they very rarely heard anymore that they were "saintly." Where Mary had been "blessed . . . among women," and the Jewish Woman of Valor heard that "her price is beyond rubies," all the modern woman can hope to hear is that she looks divine.

The Rites of Beauty also seduce women by meeting their current hunger for color and poetry. As they make their way into male public space that is often prosaic and emotionally dead, beauty's sacraments glow brighter than ever. As women are inundated with claims on their time, ritual products give them an alibi to take some private time for themselves. At their best, they give women back a taste of mystery and sensuality to compensate them for their days spent in the harsh light of the workplace.

Women were primed to receive the Rites by their historical relationship to the Church. Since the Industrial Revolution, the "separate sphere" to which women were relegated specifically assigned piety to femininity. That in turn justified middle-class women's separation from public life: Since women were designated as being "the pure sex," they could be obliged to stay out of the common fray, preoccupied with maintaining that purity. In the same way, women today are designated as the "beautiful" sex, which relegates them to a similarly useful preoccupation with protecting that "beauty."

The postindustrial feminization of religion did not, however, give women religious authority. "The Puritans . . . worshipped a patriarchal God, but . . . women outnumbered men in the New England Churches," writes historian Nancy Cott in *The Bonds of Womanhood*, remarking that while the female majority grew throughout the nineteenth century, the Church hierarchy remained "strictly male." The feminization of religion intensified side by side with the secularization of the male world. "Whatever expansion the Protestant religious establishment experienced in post–Civil War America, it was an expansion fueled by women rather than by men," Joan Jacobs Brumberg agrees. Women have not been admitted as ministers and rabbis until this generation. Until recently, their training has been to accept without question male clerical interpretations of what God wants women to do. Since the Industrial Revolution, their roles have involved not only religious obedience, but the humble support of Church activities, including, according to Ann Douglas in *The Feminization of American Culture*, sustaining personality cults devoted to the resident priest or minister. In short, women have a very brief tradition of participating in religious authority, and a very long one of submission to it; while seldom managing its profits, they have often given without question their widow's mite.

Victorian female piety served the same double need as the Rites: From a male-dominated society's point of view, it kept educated, leisured middle-class female energies harmlessly, even usefully, diverted from rebellion; and from those women's point of view, it gave meaning to their economically unproductive lives. The British economist Harriet Martineau observed of American middle-class women that they "pursue[d] religion as an occupation" because they were constrained from exercising their full range of moral, intellectual and physical powers in other ways." Nancy Cott writes that "the morphology of religious conversion echoed women's expected self-resignation and submissiveness while it offered enormously satisfying assurance to converts." The same seductive outlet is working the same way today.

The antiwoman bias of the Judeo-Christian tradition left fertile ground for the growth of the new religion. Its misogyny meant that women even more than men had to suspend critical thinking if they were to be believers. In rewarding women's intellectual humility, charging them with sin and sexual guilt, and offering them redemption only through submission to a male mediator, it handed over to the developing religion a legacy of female credulousness.

What exactly is this newly demanding faith into which women are being indoctrinated?

# The Structure of the New Religion

## Creation

The Judeo-Christian Creation story is the heart of the evolving religion. Because of the three verses, (Genesis 2:21–23), beginning "And the Lord God caused a deep sleep to fall upon Adam, and he slept; and he took one of his ribs. . . ," it is women who are the population of believers the Rites of Beauty manipulate. Western women absorb from those verses the sense that their bodies are second-rate, an afterthought: Though God made Adam from clay, in his own image, Eve is an expendable rib. God breathed life directly into Adam's nostrils, inspiring his body with divinity; but Eve's body is twice removed from the Maker's hand, imperfect matter born of matter.

Genesis explains why it is women who often need to offer their bodies to any male gaze that will legitimize them. "Beauty" now gives the female body the legitimacy that God withheld. Many women don't believe that they are beautiful until they win the official seal of approval that men's bodies possess in our culture simply because the Bible says they look like their Father. That seal must be bought or won from a male authority, a God the Father stand-in: surgeon, photographer, or judge. Women tend to worry about physical perfection in a way men seldom do because Genesis says that all men are created perfect, whereas Woman began as an inanimate piece of meat; malleable, unsculpted, unauthorized, raw—imperfect.

"Be ye therefore perfect, as your Father which is in Heaven is perfect," Jesus urged men. "The Past Forgiven. The Present Improved. The Future Perfect," Elizabeth Arden promises women—as model Paulina Poriskova is perfect. Women's craving for "perfection" is fired by the widespread belief that their bodies are inferior to men's—second-rate matter that ages faster. "Men age better, of course," asserts beautician Sally Wilson. "By second class," writes Oscar Wilde in his *Lecture on Art*, "I mean that which constantly decreases in value." Of course, men don't age any better physically. They age better only in terms of social status. We misperceive in this way since our eyes are trained to see time as a flaw on women's faces where it is a mark of character on men's. If men's main function were decorative and male adolescence were seen as the peak of male value, a "distinguished" middle-aged man would look shockingly flawed.

Second-rate, woman-born, the female body is always in need of completion, of man-made ways to perfect it. The Rites of Beauty offer to fire the female body in the kiln of beauty to purge its dross, to give it its "finish." The promise that Christianity makes about death, the Rites make about pain: that the believer will awaken on the other shore, in a body of light cleansed of mortal—female—stain. In the Christian heaven, one is purged of the body: "There is neither male nor female." In the Rites, women purge themselves of the stain of their gender. The new ugliness of looking female merely stands in for the old ugliness of being female. Women are often angry at impulses of self-hatred that we feel to be archaic. But in seeing how the Rites are based on the Creation story, we can forgive ourselves: The burden of a tale that for thirty-five hundred years has taught women where they came from and what they're made of is not going to be shrugged off lightly in two decades.

Men, on the other hand, since they made gods in their own image, feel that their bodies are essentially all right. Studies show that while women unrealistically distort their bodies negatively, men unrealistically distort theirs positively. The Western legacy of a religion based on the concept of men resembling God means that feeling at fault in their bodies is an article of faith for women that need not reflect reality. While only one man in ten is "strongly dissatisfied" with his body, one third of women are "strongly dissatisfied" with theirs. Though the sexes are overweight in equal proportions—about a third—95 percent of enrollees in weight-loss programs are women. Women think they have a serious problem when they are fifteen pounds above the national average; men are not concerned until they are thirty-five pounds above. Those numbers do not prove that women are an evil-looking gender, compared with the godlike race of men; if anything, more women than men resemble a cultural ideal, because they try harder. All they reflect is the Judeo-Christian tradition: Women's flesh is evidence of a God-given wrongness; whereas fat men are fat gods. The actual demographics of obesity are irrelevant because this religion is not about whose body is fat, but whose body is wrong.

The Rites designate the surgeon as Artist-Priest, a more expert Creator than the maternal body or "Mother Nature," from whom the woman had her first inadequate birth. From surgical literature, it appears that many doctors share this view of themselves: The logo for a rhinoplasty conference at the Waldorf Hotel is a female face sculpted from stone, cracked. Dr. Mohammed Fahdy, in a professional journal for plastic surgeons, describes female flesh as "clay or meat." *The New York Times* reports a symposium on beauty sponsored jointly by the New York Academy of Art and the American Academy of Cosmetic Surgery. In another *New York Times* article (aptly entitled "The Holy Grail of Good Looks"), Dr. Ronald A. Fragen admits that it is better to practice on clay faces first because "you can change your mistakes." Dr. Thomas D. Rees, in *More Than Just a Pretty Face: How Cosmetic Surgery Can Improve Your Looks and Your Life*, writes: "Even the greatest artists of all time had, occasionally, to rework a section of a painting." The cosmetic surgeon is the modern woman's divine sex symbol, claiming for himself the worship that nineteenth-century women offered the man of God.

## Original Sin

Q. I am only 21. Do I need Niôsome Système Anti-Age? . . .
A. Yes, definitely. The causes of aging have already begun, even though the signs may not yet be visible.
Q. I am over 45. Is it too late to start using Niôsome Système Anti-Age?
A. It's never too late.

The Rites of Beauty redefine original sin as being born not mortal, but female. Before the backlash, girls and old women were exempt from participation in worship—and therefore outside the ranks of potential consumers. But the Rites recast original sin in such a way that no young girl can feel it is too early to worry about the stains of female ugliness—age or fat—invisible within her from birth, waiting to be revealed. Nor can an older woman put the Rites behind her. Skin creams and diet books use the language of the parable of the prodigal son to draw their moral: Despite the sinner's wayward life, she is never forsaken and it is never too late to repent. If it's never too early or too late to forget about the Rites, there is no point in a woman's life at which she can live guilt free, to infect other women with her lapsed behavior.

An example of this theological trick is the "scientific" table of Clinique, which lists these categories under the heading "Facial Lines": Very Many, Several, Few, and Very Few. The conceptual category for None does not exist. Being undamaged is inconceivable; to exist as a woman, even as an adolescent girl, is to be damaged.

The sales effect of this condition parallels that of Christian doctrine. A worshiper who does not feel guilty cannot be counted on to support the Church; a woman who does not feel damaged cannot be relied on to spend money for her "repair." Original sin is the source of guilt. Guilt and its consequent sacrifice form the central movement of the newer religious economy as well. Ads aimed at men succeed by flattering their self-image, while ads for these ritual products work, as do ads aimed at women in general, by making women feel as guilty as possible: The sole moral responsibility for her aging or shape, she is told, rests in the woman's hands. "Even the most innocent expressions—including squinting, blinking and smiling—take a toll" (Clarins). "Since 1956, there's been no excuse for dry skin" (Revlon). "Do you laugh, cry, frown, worry, speak?" (Clarins). "Isn't it obvious what you should do for your skin now?" (Terme di Saturnia). "Stop damaging your skin" (Elizabeth Arden). "A better bust is up to you" (Clarins). "Take control of your contours" (Clarins).

## Sex into Food

Other writers have mentioned this parallel too: Kim Chernin in *The Obsession* asks: "Is it possible then that we today worry about eating and weight the way our foremothers and their doctors worried about women's sexuality?" But what has been left untraced is the exalted source of these anxieties and their true function: Modern culture represses female oral appetite as Victorian culture, through doctors, repressed female sexual appetite: *from the top of the power structure downward, for a political purpose.* When female sexual activity lost its useful penalties, the Rites replaced the fear, guilt, and shame that women had been taught must always follow pleasure.

Original sin left us sexual guilt. When the sexual revolution joined with consumerism to create the new supply of sexually available women, a physical relocation of female guilt was needed at once. The Rites of Beauty supplant virtually every Judeo-Christian prohibition against sexual appetite with a parallel taboo against oral appetite. The whole oral scenario of longing, temptation, capitulation, terror that it "will show," desperate efforts to purge the "evidence" from the body, and ultimate self-loathing can be imagined almost unchanged as the sexual reality of most unmarried young women until abortion and contraception were legal and premarital sex lost its stigma; that is, until a generation ago.

In the Church, though men were tempted by sexual lust, women were cast as its wicked embodiment. Similarly, though men have appetites and get fat, women's oral appetites are the social embodiment of shame.

"Menstruation taboos," writes Rosalind Miles, ". . . meant that for a quarter of their adult lives, one week in every four, women of earlier times were regularly stigmatized and set apart, disabled and debarred from the life of their society." Their cycle defined women as unclean, sexually repugnant during their "bad days," irrational, and unfit for public positions. Women feel similarly diminished and excluded by the "fat days" phase of their weight cycle, which serves the same purpose by characterizing women even to themselves as morally weak, tainted, and sexually unworthy. Where the menstrual taboo kept women out of public life, today women hide *themselves* away. In Orthodox Judaism, a woman in *niddah*, menstrual impurity, is forbidden to eat with her family; fat impurity does the same work.

Sexual impurity laws in general gave way to oral impurity taboos. Women were genitally chaste for God; now they are orally chaste for the God of Beauty. Sex within marriage, for procreation, was acceptable, while sex for pleasure was a sin; women make the same distinction today between eating to sustain life and eating for pleasure. The double standard that gave men and not women sexual license has become a double standard in which men have greater oral license. A sexually unchaste girl was "fallen"; women "fall off" their regimes. Women "cheated" on their husbands; now they "cheat" on their diets. A woman who eats something "forbidden" is "naughty": "It's just for tonight," she'll say. "I have lusted in my heart" becomes "All I have to do is look at one." "I'm a girl who just can't say no," announces the model promoting Jell-O gelatin, which "kind of makes you feel good about saying yes." With Wheat Thin crackers, "You don't have to hate yourself in the morning." The rosary has become a calorie counter; women say, "I have the stretch marks to show for my sins." Where once she was allowed to take communion if she made a full and sincere penance, now a woman is granted a given procedure "if she has sincerely tried diet and exercise." The state of her fat, like the state of her hymen in the past, is a community concern: "Let us pray for our sister" has become "We'll all encourage you to lose it."

## The Cycle of Purification

Beauty is heaven or a state of grace; the skin or fat cell count is the soul; ugliness is hell. "Heaven, I'm in heaven," weight-loss spa Annandale Health Hydro advertises. It "is like nowhere else on earth . . . beauty treatments to make you feel like you have wings. . . . How do you get to heaven? Just be good—and clip the coupon." Where a dessert is "temptation," seventy-calorie Alba is "salvation"; an article in *New Woman* detailing the calories in ice cream is titled "Sundae Worship."

The woman being addressed is in neither heaven nor hell— she is neither transcendent, because she is so beautiful, nor hopelessly fallen, because so ugly. She is never of the Elect, but can save herself through good works. The beauty product is her mediator: healer, angel, or spiritual guide.

She follows a calendar of excess and penance, a Mardi Gras and Lent of the body, atoning for midwinter sprees with New

Year's resolutions. At "the critical stage," as Terme di Saturnia puts it, the worshiper is evaluated by a righteous God from whom nothing can be hidden. Using the language of Yom Kippur, in which true repentance is possible for ten days, after which the Book of Life is sealed for the rest of the year, one cosmetician's ad tells New York that "what you do in the next ten days will determine what your skin looks like for the rest of the year." The "moment of truth," like the Last Judgment, weighs the penitent on a scale. "The scale," the new gospel teaches, "does not lie." "Every mouthful will show on your hips," the woman is told; "Your skin reveals what you put inside you." With those warnings she learns to "fear the Almighty from whom nothing is hidden."

What does this sense of constant surveillance do to women? In *The Female Malady: Women, Madness and English Culture, 1830–1980*, Elaine Showalter describes how surveillance is used in modern mental hospitals to keep women patients tractable. "In the asylums . . . woman are encouraged, persuaded, and taught to become surveyors, 'to watch themselves being looked at,' and to make themselves attractive objects by being surveyed." Makeup, Showalter writes, is kept in the ward box with its "stump of lipstick" and "box of blossom-pink powder." "It is not surprising," she concludes, "that in the female narrative [of schizophrenics] the hectoring spirit . . . who jeers, judges, commands and controls . . . is almost invariably male. He delivers the running critique of appearance and performance that the woman has grown up with as part of her stream of consciousness." Continual surveillance is used against political prisoners for similar reasons: An enforced lack of privacy strips dignity and breaks resistance.

This ritual use of constant surveillance is a vivid example of the real motivation behind the myth: Female thinness and youth are not in themselves next to godliness in this culture. Society really doesn't care about women's appearance per se. What genuinely matters is that women remain willing to let others tell them what they can and cannot have. Women are watched, in other words, not to make sure that they will "be good," but to make sure that they will know they are being watched.

This god is Big Brother. "Discipline is Liberation," writes exercise guru Jane Fonda, deaf to its echo: War is peace, work is freedom. And many women internalize Big Brother's eye: Weight

Watchers lets women pay for mutual surveillance; their magazines tell them to "Always wear your makeup, even if you're just walking the dog. You never know whom you might meet." Jesus said, "Watch ye therefore: for ye know not when the master of the house cometh, at even, or at midnight, or at the cockcrowing, or in the morning." "Stand naked in front of a full-length mirror and look at yourself from the front, back and sides. Take the shades from your eyes and face the truth of the situation," charges *Positively Beautiful.* "Does your flesh wobble and seem dimpled? Can you see the bulges? Are your thighs very thick? Does your stomach stick out?" This is self-scrutiny that used to be reserved for the soul.

Female nineteenth-century diarists of the soul noted every moral fluctuation, aware, in the words of one, that "the salvation of our precious souls is not to be effected independent of our exertions." The behavior modification techniques invented by psychologist Richard Stuart in 1967—the out-of-control year of the Summer of Love—had subjects record "when, where, what, and under what circumstances" they ate, thus burdening women with minute self-monitoring—just in time—for the salvation of their bodies.

The purification cycle often follows the seasons: Women who feel they have "something to hide" dread summer's approach, anxious that hot weather and full exposure will not overtake them before they have fasted and flagellated themselves into blameless readiness. Medieval Christians feared that death would overtake them while their souls were still black with sin. The magazines use the Church fathers' formula for the hidden female body, a whited sepulcher, a fair surface hiding loathsomeness: "It's easy to hide a multitude of sins under winter fashions." Only with penance can the worshiper "dare to bare all" and be like the angels of Bain de Soleil, who "have no fear of exposure." The weight-loss cycle mimics the Easter cycle: Self-scrutiny leads into self-mortification, which leads to rejoicing.

In its death-and-rebirth centerpiece, the women enter what anthropologists call the "liminal phase," a "betwixt and between" state during which, according to cult expert Willa Appel, "the novice must become nothing before [s]he can become a new something." The old identity is suspended until the new one can be assumed. A magical transition, it is surrounded with special effects that actually, not metaphorically, induce a susceptible, altered state: darkness, low music, blindfolding; the subject is often touched, bathed, and immersed in sensory stimuli such as fragrances or changes in temperature. In spas and beauty parlors, women shed their street clothes and put on identical white or colored robes. Their status is suspended when they unclasp their jewelry. They give themselves over to the touch of the masseuse or beautician. Pads are put on their eyes, scented liquids cover their faces. The waters of the Golden Door have the effect of the waters of Lourdes. The liminal moment in a make-over comes after the old makeup is removed, but before the new is applied; in surgery, when the patient, in her hospital gown, is prepared and put under. In a Lancôme ad, a woman lies on her back in a sepulchral light, seemingly dead, while a mysterious hand descends with Jesus' gesture to touch her face.

At the depth of the disorientation, the initiate into a cult often undergoes an incision or an endurance test: There is pain, hunger, or blood, real or symbolic. At that point, women are pricked with needles that emit electric shocks, or they are cut open, or burned with acid, or their hairs are plucked out by the root, or their bellies are emptied. The liminal period ends with another submersion in liquid that evokes the waters of rebirth: It is often blood, as in the Christian "blood of the lamb," or the bull's blood of the Osiris cult. This is the stage of the crucified Jesus in the tomb, the Christian under baptismal water, the patient bleeding under anesthesia, the spa devotee under wraps or steam or herbal baths.

At the end comes victory and new life: The death in the desert of the old, tainted generation is redeemed with the birth of a new one, who may enter the Promised Land. The baptized person assumes another name, a new status in the community. The newly made up or coiffed or thin woman, the woman with the surgically "new face," celebrates her fresh identity and returns to take up what she hopes will be an improved status. She is told, to prepare for reentry, to buy clothes, get a haircut, take on the accessories of an altered personality. Presented as incentive for weight loss, or camouflage for surgery, that advice is elementary magic.

The new religion improves on the others, because redemption does not last. The "supportive" rhetoric of the diet industry masks the obvious: The last thing it wants is for women to get thin once and for all. Ninety-eight percent of dieters regain the weight. "The diet industry is an entrepreneur's delight," writes Brumberg, "because the market is self-generating and intrinsically expansive. Predicated on failure . . . the interest in diet strategies, techniques and products seems unlimited." The same holds for the antiage industry, which a truly effective product (or universal female self-esteem) would destroy. Fortunately for the industry, even surgery patients continue to age at the rate of 100 percent. The "new me" is washed off with the evening's bath. The cycle must begin again from the start, since living in time and having to eat to live are both sins against the God of Beauty—and both, of course, inevitable.

When women adapt too well to the strictures of the industries, the weight or age that defines grace merely adjusts by plummeting: The models descend another ten pounds, the surgeons lower the "preventive" age for a first face-lift by another decade. From the industries' point of view, the one scenario worse than women winning at this rigged game would be for them to lose interest in playing it at all. The repeating loop of the purification cycle prevents that. A woman is scarcely given the chance to think before she must take up her burden again, the journey growing more arduous each time.

### Memento Mori

The Rites of Beauty are intended to make women archaically morbid. Five hundred years ago, men thought about their lives in relation to death as women today are asked to imagine the life span of beauty: Surrounded by sudden inexplicable deaths, medieval Christianity made the worshiper's constant awareness of mortality a lifetime obsession. The dangers of childbirth intensified the consciousness of death for women, as was exemplified by the use of Psalm 116 by women in labor: "The snares of death compassed me round, and the pains of hell gat hold on me . . . O Lord I beseech thee, deliver my soul." This once-general morbidity became primarily feminine in the nineteenth century. Scientific advances tempered men's sense of fatality, but well into the industrial age, the specter of death in the childbed forced women often to dwell upon the condition of their souls. After antisepsis lowered the maternal death rate and once women became valued as beauties rather than mothers, this preoccupation with loss was channeled into fears about the death of "beauty." So many women still feel they are surrounded by ill-understood forces that can strike at any time, destroying what has been represented to them as life itself. When a woman with her back to the TV camera describes a botched surgical job, saying, "He took away my beauty. In one blow. It's all gone," she is expressing a sense of helpless resignation that harks back to the way preindustrial societies responded to natural disaster.

To understand the primal force of this religion, we need to see that men die once and woman die twice. Women die as beauties before their bodies die.

Women today in the full bloom of beauty keep a space always in mind for its diminution and loss. Medieval death awareness that "all flesh is grass," the *memento mori*, kept men economically aligned to the Church, which could give them "new life" beyond their natural life-span. For women to be urged to think continually of beauty's fragility and transcience is a way to try to keep us subservient, by maintaining in us a fatalism that has not been part of Western men's thinking since the Renaissance. Taught that God or nature does or does not bestow "beauty" on them— randomly, beyond appeal—we live in a world in which magic, prayer, and superstition make sense.

## Light

Eve's sin meant that women are responsible for losing grace. "Grace" was redefined during the Renaissance as a secular term, and used to describe the faces and bodies of "beautiful" women.

Skin cream—the "holy oil" of the new religion—promises "radiance" in its advertising. Many religions use a light metaphor for divinity: Moses' face when he descended from Mount Sinai blazed like the sun, and medieval iconography surrounded saints with halos. The holy oil industry offers to sell back to women in tubes and bottles the light of grace, to redeem women's bodies now that the cults of virginity and of motherhood can no longer offer to surround with consecrated light the female body whose sexuality has been yielded to others.

Light is in fact the issue, central to an innate way of seeing beauty that is shared by many, if not most, women and men. This way of seeing is what the beauty myth works hard to suppress. In describing this quality of light or having it described, one becomes uneasy, quick to dismiss it as sentimentality or mysticism. The source of the denial, I think, is not that we do not see this phenomenon, but rather that we see it so very clearly; and that publicly to name it threatens some basic premises of our social organization. It is proof as nothing else is that people are not things: People "light up" and objects don't. To agree that it is real would challenge a social system that works by designating some people as more thinglike than others, and all women as more thinglike than all men.

This light doesn't photograph well, can't be measured on a scale of one to ten, won't be quantified in a lab report. But most people are aware that a radiance can emerge from faces and bodies, making them truly beautiful.

Some see that radiance as inseparable from love and intimacy, not picked up by a separate visual sense but as part of the movement or warmth of a familiar. Others might see it in a body's sexuality; still others, in vulnerability, or wit. It strikes one often from the face of someone telling a story or listening intently to someone else. Many have remarked on how the act of creation seems to illuminate people, and have noticed how it envelops most children—those who have not been told yet that they are not beautiful. We very often remember our mothers as beautiful simply because it lit them up in our eyes. If any general descriptions can be drawn, a sense of wholeness seems involved, and maybe trust. To see this light, it seems, one has to look for it. The poet May Sarton calls it "the pure light that shines from the lover." Probably everyone has a different name for it and perceives it differently; but most know that it exists for them. The point is that you have seen it—your version—and have probably been dazzled or excited or attracted; and that, according to the myth, it does not count.

Society severely limits descriptions of this light, so as to keep it from taking on the force of a social reality. Women are said to emit it, for instance, only in the act of giving their bodies to men or to children: the "radiant bride" and the "radiant mother-to-be." Straight men are almost never told that they are luminous, radiant, or dazzling. The Rites of Beauty offer to sell women back an imitation of the light that is ours already, the central grace we are forbidden to say that we see.

To do so, they ask women to negotiate a three-dimensional world by two-dimensional rules. Women "know" that fashion photographs are professionally lit to imitate this radiant quality. But since we as women are trained to see ourselves as cheap imitations of fashion photographs, rather than seeing fashion photographs as cheap imitations of women, we are urged to study ways to light up our features as if they were photographs marred by motion, acting as our own lighting designer and stylist and photographer, our faces handled like museum pieces, expertly lit with highlights, lowlights, Light Effects, Frost n' Glow, Light Powder, Iridescence, and Iridience.

Synthetic light comes with rules. Older women must not use frost effects. What light will the woman be seen in—office, daylight, candlelight? Women's mirrors have lights built in; if we're caught in an unexpected setting, we will be exposed, like a photograph that, in the wrong light, turns to nothing. That stress on special effects serves to addict women psychologically to civilized indoor lighting, traditional female space; to keep us fearful of spontaneity and digression. Beauty's self-consciousness is intended to hover at skin level in order to keep women from moving far inside to an erotic center or far afield into the big space of the public realm. It is intended to make sure we do not catch a glimpse of ourselves in a brand-new light altogether.

Other practices drive women indoors as well. Once she uses Retin-A, a woman must abandon the sun *forever*. Cosmetic surgery demands that women hide indoors away from the sun for times ranging from six weeks to six months. The discovery of "photoaging" has created a phobia of the sun entirely unrelated to the risk of skin cancer. While it is true that the ozone layer is thinning, this sun-phobia mentality is severing the bond between women and the natural world, turning nature into the fearsome enemy of the male tradition's point of view. If the female tradition were not under siege, the damaged ozone layer should be sending women out onto the environmental barricades to protect it. The beauty myth stimulates women's fears of looking older in order to drive us in the opposite direction: indoors once more, locus of the separate sphere and the Feminine Mystique; the proper place for women in every culture that most oppresses us.

Indoors or out, women must make their beauty glitter because they are *so hard for men to see.* They glitter as a bid for attention that is otherwise grudgingly given. Catching light draws the eye in a basic unsubtle reflex: Babies' undeveloped eyes follow glittering objects. It is the one way in which women are allowed to shout in order to command attention. Men who glitter, on the other hand, are either low-status or not real men: gold teeth, flashy jewelry; ice skaters, Liberace. Real men are matte. Their surfaces must not distract attention from what it is they are saying. But women of every status glint. Dale Spender, in *Man Made Language*, shows that when in conversation, men cut off women in most of the interruptions by far and that men give women's words only intermittent attention. So pyrotechnics of light and color must accompany women's speech in order to beguile an attention span that wanders when women open their mouths. What women look like is considered important because what we say is not.

## The Cult of the Fear of Age

To sell two unreal ritual product lines—ersatz light and transient thinness—the Rites of Beauty are skillfully adapting standard cult techniques to inculcate women into them. The following scene plays on television in the United States: A charismatic leader dressed in white addresses an audience, her face aglow. Women listen transfixed: Three steps are to be undertaken in total solitude. "Give this time to yourself . . . Concentrate. Really feel it," she says. "Follow the steps religiously." Women testify: "I wasn't a believer at first either. But look at me now." "I didn't want to commit to it. I'd tried everything, and I just didn't believe anything could do it for me—I've never known anything like it. It's changed my life." The camera focuses on their faces. Finally, all are wearing white and clustered around the leader, eyes shining. Cameras pan backward to the sound of a hymn. The source of the shared secret is Collagen Extract Skin Nourishment, $39.95 for a month's supply.

These video conversions only supplement the main cult action in department stores, where 50 percent of holy oil sales are made at "points of purchase." The scheme is pure religion carefully organized.

A woman enters a department store from the street, looking no doubt very mortal, her hair windblown, her own face visible. To reach the cosmetics counter, she must pass a deliberately disorienting prism of mirrors, lights, and scents that combine to submit her to the "sensory overload" used by hypnotists and cults to encourage suggestibility.

On either side of her are ranks of angels—seraphim and cherubim—the "perfect" faces of the models on display. Behind them, across a liminal counter in which is arranged the magic that will permit her to cross over, lit from below, stands the guardian angel. The saleswoman is human, she knows, but "perfected" like the angels around her, from whose ranks the woman sees her own "flawed" face, reflected back and shut out. Disoriented within the man-made heaven of the store, she can't focus on what makes both the live and pictured angels seem similarly "perfect": that they are both lacquered in heavy paint. The lacquer bears little relation to the outer world, as the out-of-place look of a fashion shoot on a city street makes clear. But the mortal world disintegrates in her memory at the shame of feeling so out of place among all the ethereal objects. Put in the wrong, the shopper longs to cross over.

Cosmetics saleswomen are trained with techniques akin to those used by professional cult converters and hypnotists. A former Children of God member says in Willa Appel's *Cults in America: Programmed for Paradise* that she sought out people in shopping malls "who looked lost and vulnerable." The woman making her way down an aisle of divinities is made to look "lost and vulnerable" in her own eyes. If she sits down and agrees to a "make-over," she's a subject for a cultic hard sell.

The saleswoman will move up close into the face of the shopper, ostensibly to apply the substances, but in fact generally much closer than she needs to be to do so. She keeps up a patter that focuses in on a blemish, wrinkles, the bags under the woman's eyes. Cult converters are trained to stand very close to their potential subjects and "stare fixedly in their eyes. . . . You'd look for the weak spots in people." The woman then hears herself convicted of the sins and errors that are putting her in jeopardy: "You use *what* on your face?" "Only twenty-three, and look at those lines." "Well, if you're happy with those pimples." "You're *destroying* the delicate skin under your eyes." "If you don't stop doing what you're doing to it, in ten years your whole face will be a mass of creases." Another cult member interviewed by Appel describes this procedure: "It was the whole thing of exuding confidence, of maintaining direct communication so forceful that you're always in complete control. . . . You have to play up the feeling that all these people have of no sense of real security, no sense of what was going to happen in the future, and the fear of just continuing to repeat old mistakes."

The shopper probably gives in, and accepts Lancôme as her personal savior. Once back in the street, though, the expensive tubes and bottles immediately lose their aura. Those who have escaped from cults feel afterward that they have emerged from something they can only dimly remember.

Advertisements in print must now approach the potential cult member with more sophistication. For two decades they have used a mysterious language the way Catholicism uses Latin, Judaism Hebrew, and Masons secret passwords: as a prestigious Logos that confers magic power on the originators of it. To the lay person, it is a gibberish of science and mock-science. For example: "Phytolyastil," "Phytophyline," "Plurisome ™"; "SEI Complex" and "biologically active tissue peptides LMP" (La Prairie); "hygrascopic elements and natural ceramides" (Chanel); "a syntropic blend of the unique Bio-Dermia ™"; "Complex #3" "Reticulin and mucopolysaccharides" (Aloegen); "Tropocollagen and hyaluronic acid" (Charles of the Ritz); "Incellate ™" (Terme di

Saturnia); "Glycosphingolipids" (GSL, Glycel); "Niosomes and Microsomes and Protectinol" (Shiseido).

"Western societies from the early centuries of the second millennium," writes Rosalind Miles, "all found their own techniques for ensuring that the 'new learning' did not penetrate the great under-class of the female sex." A long history of intellectual exclusion precedes our current intimidation by this battery of mock-authoritative language.

The ads refined this daunting nonsense language to cover the fact that skin creams do not actually do anything. The holy oil industry is a megalith that for forty years has been selling women nothing at all. According to Gerald McKnight's exposé, the industry is "little more than a massive con . . . a sweetly disguised form of commercial robbery" with profit margins of over 50 percent on a revenue of 20 *billion* dollars worldwide; in 1988 skin care grossed 3 billion in the United States alone, 337 million pounds in the United Kingdom, 8.9 trillion lire in Italy, and 69.2 million guilders in the Netherlands, up from 18.3 million in 1978.

For forty years the industry has been making false claims. Before 1987, the Food and Drug Administration just twice made minor objections. In the past two decades, holy oil makers went beyond the outrageous, claiming to retard aging (Revlon Anti-Aging Firmagel), repair the skin (Night Repair), and restructure the cell (Cellular Recovery Complex, G. M. Collin Intensive Cellular Regeneration, Elancyl Restructurant). As women encountered the computerized work force of the 1980s, the ads abandoned the filmy florals of "hope in a bottle" and adopted new imagery of bogus technology, graphs and statistics, to resonate with the authority of the microchip. Imaginary technological "breakthroughs" reinforced women's sense that the beauty index was inflating out of control, its claims reported too fast for the human brain to organize or verify.

Information overload joined new technologies in airbrushing and photo doctoring to give women the sense that scrutiny itself had become superhuman. The eye of the camera, like God's, developed a microscopic judgment that outdid the imperfect human eye, magnifying "flaws" a mortal could not detect: In the early 1980s, says Morris Herstein of Laboratoires Serobiologiques, who

characterizes himself as a "pseudo-scientist," "we were then able
to see and measure things that had been impossible before. It
came about when the technology of the space program was made
available, when we were allowed to use their sophisticated analysis techniques, the biotechnological advances which allowed us to
see things at the cellular level. Before that we had to touch and
feel." What Herstein is saying is that by measuring tissue invisible to the naked eye, beyond "touch and feel," the struggle for
beauty was transposed into a focus so minute that the struggle
itself became metaphysical. Women were asked to believe that
erasing lines so faint as to be nonexistent to the human gaze was
now a reasonable moral imperative.

The tenuous link between what the holy oils claimed to do
and what they did was finally broken, and no longer meant anything. "The numbers are meaningless until all the tests and rank-
ings are standardized," a women's magazine quotes industry
spokesman Dr. Grove, adding that "consumers should always remember that what the machine measures may not be visible to
the naked eye."

If the "enemy" is invisible, the "barrier" is invisible, the
"eroding effects" are invisible, and the holy oil's results "may not
be visible to the naked eye," we are in a dimension of pure faith,
where "graphic evidence" is provided of the "visible improvement" in the number of angels that after treatment will dance on
the head of a pin. The whole dramatic fiction of the holy oil's
fight against age began, by the mid-1980s, to unfold on an entirely make-believe stage, inventing psychic flaws to sell psychic
cures. From that point on, the features of their faces and bodies
that would make women unhappy would increasingly be those
that no one else could see. More alone than ever, women were
placed beyond the consolation of reason. Perfection had now to
hold up beyond the artist's frame, and survive the microscope.

Even many industry insiders acknowledge that the creams do
not work. According to Buddy Wedderburn, a biochemist at Uni-
lever: "The effect of rubbing collagen onto the skin is negligi-
ble. . . . I don't know of anything that gets into these areas—
certainly nothing that will stop wrinkles." Anita Roddick of The
Body Shop, the beauty care chain, says, "There is *no* application,
no topical application, that will get rid of grief or stress or heavy

lines. . . . There's nothing, but nothing, that's going to make you look younger. Nothing." Anthea Disney, editor of the women's magazine *Self*, adds, "We all know there isn't anything that will make you look younger." And as "Sam" Sugiyama, codirector of Shiseido, concludes, "If you want to avoid aging, you must live in space. There is no other way to avoid getting wrinkles, once you are out of the womb."

The professional collegial spirit that has helped keep the fraudulent nature of the industry's claims fairly quiet was belatedly broken by Professor Albert Kligman of the University of Pennsylvania—whose whistle-blowing must be put in context: He is the developer of Retin-A, the one substance that does seem to do something, including subjecting the skin to inflammation, sunlight intolerance, and continuous heavy peeling. "In the industry today," he wrote presciently to his colleagues, "fakery is replacing puffery . . . a consumer and FDA crackdown is inevitable and damaging to credibility." He goes further in interviews: "When they make a claim of anti-aging, of the stuff having deep biological effects, then they have to be stopped. It's pure bunkum . . . beyond the bounds of reason and truth." And he says that the new products "simply cannot function as their backers and makers say they do, because it is physically impossible for them to get deep enough into the skin to make any lasting difference to wrinkles. The same applies to the removal of lines or wrinkles, or the permanent prevention of the aging of cells." The hope of anything achieving such effects is, he says, "actually zero."

"Some of my colleagues," Kligman admits, "tell me, 'Women are so dumb! How can they buy all that grease and stuff? Educated women, who've been to Radcliffe and Cambridge and Oxford and the Sorbonne—what gets into them? Why do they go to Bloomingdale's and pay $250 for that hokum?'"

Women are "so dumb" because the establishment and its watchdogs share the cosmetics industry's determination that we are and must remain "so dumb." The "crackdown" came at last in the United States in 1987—but not from concern for women consumers exploited by a $20-billion-a-year fraud. The first straw was when heart specialist Dr. Christiaan Barnard brought out Glycel ("a fake, a complete fake," says Dr. Kligman). The doctor's fame and superoutrageous claims for his product ("This was the first time in history that we can recall a physician putting his name to a cosmetic line," says Stanley Kohlenberg of Sanofi Beauty Products) provoked envy in the rest of the industry. According to one of Gerald McKnight's sources: "Somebody put it to the Agency that if they did not act to pull the product off the shelves, the industry would see to it that the FDA's name was dragged through the mire." The Food and Drug Administration then went after the industry as a whole "because we were all doing it, making wild claims." The agency asked twenty-three chief cosmetics executives to account for "claims that they were flagrantly making in magazines, films and every possible area of hype . . . that they had added 'magical' anti-aging and cellular replacement ingredients to their products." The FDA asked for "immediate withdrawal of the claims or submission for testing as drugs." "We are unaware," FDA director Daniel L. Michaels wrote to them, "of any substantial scientific evidence that demonstrates the safety and effectiveness of these articles. Nor are we aware that these drugs are generally recognized as safe and effective for their intended uses." In other words, the agency said, if the creams do what you claim, they are drugs and must be tested. If they don't, you are making false claims.

Is all this proof that anyone really cares about an industry whose targets for religious fraud are women? Morris Herstein points out that "the FDA is only saying, 'Look, we're concerned about what you're *saying*, not what you're doing.' It is a dictionary problem, a lexicon problem, a question of vocabulary." The head of the agency hardly sounds adversarial. "We're not trying to punish anyone," he told Deborah Blumenthal, a reporter for *The New York Times*, in 1988. She believed that the products would stay the same, only the "surrealist nature" of some claims would disappear. Three years later, these "surrealist" claims have reemerged.

Think of the enormity: For twenty years the holy oils made "scientific" claims, using bogus charts and figures, of "proven improvement" and "visible difference" that were subject to no outside verification. Outside the United States, the same manufacturers continue to make false claims. In the United Kingdom, almost all holy oil ads ignore the British Code of Advertising warning not to "contain any claim to provide rejuvenation, that is to prevent, retard or reverse the physiological changes and degenerative conditions brought about by, or associated with, increasing age." The British Department of Trade and Industry finally followed suit in 1989 (as British dermatologist Ronald Marks said, "A lot of this stuff is cosmetic hoo-ha"), but the DTI has not yet committed the time or resources to follow through. In neither country has there been a public move to put pressure on the industry to print retractions or apologies to women; nor in the coverage of the change in regulations has the possibility been raised of financial compensation for the women consumers cheated so thoroughly for so many years.

Is it an overreaction to take such deception so seriously? Isn't women's relation to holy oils as trivial, the pathos of our faith as harmless, even endearing, as it is reflected in popular discourse? Women are poor; poorer than men. What is so important about 20 billion of our dollars a year? It would buy us, trivially enough, *each year*, roughly three times the amount of day care offered by the U.S. government: or 2,000 women's health clinics; or 75,000 women's film, music, literature, or art festivals; or 50 women's universities; or 1 million highly paid home support workers for the housebound elderly; or 1 million highly paid domestic or child care workers; or 33,000 battered-women's shelters; or 2 billion tubes of contraceptive cream; or 200,000 vans for late-night safe transport; or 400,000 full four-year university scholarships for young women who cannot afford further education; or 20 million airplane tickets around the world; or 200 million five-course dinners in four-star French restaurants; or 40 million cases of Veuve Clicquot champagne. Women are poor; poor people need luxuries. Of course women should be free to buy whatever they want, but if we are going to spend our hard-earned cash, the luxuries should deliver what they promise, not simply leech guilt money. No one takes this fraud seriously because the alternative to it is the real social threat: that women will first accept their aging, then admire it, and finally enjoy it. Wasting women's money is the calculable damage; but the damage this fraud does women through its legacy of the dread of aging is incalculable.

The Food and Drug Administration "crackdown" avoided the possibility that corrupt conditions would change to let women love the signs of their age. The language of the advertisements brilliantly and immediately shifted tone to the level of emotional coercion, each word carefully market-researched. These prose poems about women's private needs and fears are even more persuasive than the earlier scientific lies. The success of a belief system depends upon how well the religious leaders understand the emotional situation of its targets. Holy oil ads began to take the emotional pulse of their audience with state-of-the-art accuracy.

Analyzing those ads, we see that women are under terrific stress. Many, though publicly confident, are secretly feeling vulnerable, exhausted, overwhelmed, and besieged. In the new scenario, unseen dangers assault an unprotected female victim:

> "Shielded from . . . environmental irritants. . . . Buffer . . . against the elements. . . . Defense cream." (*Elizabeth Arden*) "An invisible barrier between you and environmental irritants. . . . An invisible shield." (*Estée Lauder*) "Protective . . . added defense. . . . Proteotinol, an effective complex of protective ingredients. . . . Face constant aggressions . . . today's more polluted environment . . . tiredness, stress . . . environmental aggressions and lifestyle variations." (*Clarins*) "Counteract the stresses and strains of today's lifestyle." (*Almay*) "Everyday . . . subject to damaging environmental conditions which together with stress and tiredness affect it adversely and upset its natural balance." (*RoC*) "Strengthen . . . natural defenses . . . to counteract daytime environmental stress. . . . A protective barrier against external aggressors." (*Charles of the Ritz*) "Shielded from environmental irritants. . . . Buffer . . . against the elements." (*Estée Lauder*) "Assaulted by age and ultra-violet exposure. . . . A protective barrier against the chemical and physical assaults of the environment . . . your body's natural defenses. . . . Just in time. Discover your best . . . defense." (*Clientèle*) "Cells . . . slough in clumps leaving pockets of vulnerability. . . . Exposure to your daily environment . . . fluorescent lights, overheated offices . . . causes wrinkles. . . . An invisible enemy . . . 70% of women experience invisible eroding effects." (*Orience*) "Attacked by external elements . . . external aggressions." (*Orchidea*) "Skin defender . . .

desensitizing barrier . . . neutralizes environmental irritants
. . . before it takes the abuse of another day, protect it. . . .
Alleviate years of negative influence." (*Estée Lauder*) "Under
attack every day of its life . . . an essential barrier . . . helps
it to defend itself." (*L'Oréal*)

What is this scenario to which women are so painfully recep-
tive? It is about the unspoken underside of the life of the successful, controlled working woman: about sexual violence and
street harassment and a hostile workplace. Each word strikes a
nerve of legitimate female fear that has nothing to do with aging
or with the qualities of the product. Not only are women new to
the public sphere; it *is* full of unseen dangers.

Women *are* under attack every day of our lives from "unseen
aggressors": Studies repeatedly show that at least one woman in
six has been raped, and up to 44 percent have suffered attempted
rape. We *do* have "pockets of vulnerability" subjected to assault—vaginas. The extent to which the AIDS virus has infected
women is still unknown; we *do* need "protective barriers"—con-
doms and diaphragms. In the United States, 21 percent of married women report physical abuse by their mates. One and one-
half million American women are assaulted by a partner every
year; one British woman in seven is raped by her husband.
Women respond to fantasies about protection from assault because we *are* being assaulted.

Almost all working women are clustered in twenty low-status
job categories; we *do* have an "invisible enemy"—institutional
discrimination. Verbal sexual abuse on city streets is a daily abrasive; women *are* exposed to "environmental stress." Women score
lower than men on tests to measure self-esteem; we *do* need to
overcome "years of negative influence"—internalized female self-
hatred. Almost two out of three marriages in the United States
end in divorce, at which women's standard of living declines by
73 percent while men's rises by 42 percent; women *are* "unprotected." More than 8 million American women raise at least
one child alone, of whom only 5 million are awarded child support, of which 47 percent get the full amount, 37 percent less
than half, and 28 percent nothing. Women *are* being "eroded" by
"life-style variations." American women's 1983 median income

was $6,320, while men's was over twice as much. Between two thirds and three quarters of women have been sexually harassed at work. We *do* face "environmental irritants." Overwork and low pay *does* leave us "stressed" under "fluorescent lights" in "overheated offices." Women make $.59–$.66 cents for every male dollar. We can buy a holy oil called Equalizer. Vaseline Intensive Care offers, "Finally . . . equal treatment . . . the treatment they deserve." Just 5 percent of top managers are women. Johnson and Johnson makes Purpose. The Equal Rights Amendment failed to pass in the U.S. Congress; women *do* need a buffer. Women *do* need a better defense.

Holy oils promise the protection that women no longer get from men and do not yet get from the law. They do so at the level of a dream. They offer to be a chador or chastity belt or a husband or an antiradiation suit, depending on the fear evoked, to keep the woman safe in the abrasive male world that many have entered with such flying colors.

Some of the copy appeals to the ambivalence that women feel about their stressful new roles—or rather, about entering a discriminatory system in which feminism gets the blame for subjecting women to the high stress of a sexist outer world. Many have mixed feelings about the cost of male-defined "success" and time away from children. This is the "post-feminist" school of skin care:

> "[Alleviate] stress . . . surface tension." (*Almay*) "Stressed-skin concentrate . . . triumphs in the face of adversity . . . solves the 20th Century Skin Problem." (*Elizabeth Arden*) "Stress and tension." (*Biotherm*) "Is success taking its toll on your face? . . . your lifestyle exposes you to a hectic pace and lots of stress . . . real assaults on skin (ones our mothers didn't worry about)." (*Orlane*) "Takes on the realities of your life. What's happening to you is happening to your skin . . . for the woman whose lifestyle makes incredible demands." (*Matrix*) "The busy, bustling life of modern women means that unfortunately they do not take care of their legs." (*G. M. Collin*) "When your skin is acting confused." (*Origins*)

The divorce rate in the United States nearly doubled between 1970 and 1981. Since 1960, the divorce rate has doubled in almost every country in Europe, tripled in the Netherlands, quintupled in the United Kingdom, and has risen tenfold in Barbados; in Bangladesh and Mexico, one woman in ten who has married has been divorced or separated, one in five in Colombia, one in three in Indonesia. Elizabeth Arden's Eyezone repair gel gives us the last cycle of women's history in a tube: "The vital supporting structures between the [cells] break down, leaving the skin weakened and vulnerable." Her Immunage shields one from "rays that weaken skin's support structure and devastate." Untreated skin shows "a dramatic lack of cohesion." Women's traditional support systems—the family, male financial backing, even the women's groups of feminism's second wave—have broken down. Clinique "helps support needy skin. It's a good cause." In a rescue fantasy, single or struggling women read that Estée Lauder's microsomes are "attracted like high-powered magnets [magnates?] to the surface cells that need help most, repairing, reinforcing and rebuilding." These "support systems" can now be "repaired and rebuilt" by the "dynamic action" that women can get at the pharmacist's when the nuclear family and the legislature have failed us.

The code words will change with women's subconscious anxieties. But if women want out of an expensive belief system arranged to coerce us through these messages, we will read holy oil copy knowing that it is not about the product, but is an impressively accurate portrait of the hidden demons of our time.

The ads read women's needs on a very personal level as well. Women, they know, sometimes feel a need to regress and be nurtured. With the Rites of Beauty, women are driven from the present with encouragement to recapture the past. Cults that idealize the past are called revitalization movements—Nazism being one example.

With both age and weight theology, women have memories of Eden—Timotei shampoo's "secret garden"—and its loss: As children, all women had "flawless" skin and most were lovingly fed as much as they wanted to eat. The two words whose variants are repeated so often that few ads are free of them are "revitalize" and "nourish." Almay "gives new life." RoC "revitalizes"; Au-

raseva is "revitalizing," lets one be "reborn." Clarins uses "revitalize" nine times in a one-fold leaflet. You can be "Reborn"
with Elizabeth Arden. And Guerlain gives you Revitenol. Those
two words are hypnotically repeated within single ads. "Renewal"
recurs twenty-eight times over in a one-page leaflet for a holy oil
called Millennium. The millennium heralded by the Second
Coming is when the dead will live again; and women will return
to their youth, the time when the Rites say they are most alive.

Women, advertisers know, are feeling undernourished, physically and emotionally. We repress our hunger—to acknowledge it
would be a weakness. But our nutritional deficiency shows in holy
oil copy that dwells on forbidden richness or sweetness, the honey
of the Holy Land, the mother's milk of Mary: Milk 'n Honee,
Milk Plus 6, Estée Lauder Re-Nutriv, Wheat Germ n' Honey,
Max Factor 2000 Calorie Mascara, Skin Food, Creme, Mousse,
Caviare. The woman feeds her skin the goodness she cannot take
without guilt or conflict into either mouth. In a *New York Times*
article entitled "Food for Thought," Linda Wells writes that "the
latest skin care ingredients . . . could be mistaken for the menu
at a glitzy restaurant"; she lists quail's eggs, honey, bananas, olive
oil, peanuts, caviar, sturgeon's roe, and passion fruit. The hungry
woman allows herself only on the outside what she truly desires
for the inside.

In the 1990 Virginia Slims survey of three thousand women,
fully half felt that "men were only interested in their own sexual
satisfaction." The most "intensive nourishment" is promised by
the creams for nighttime, "when your skin is able to absorb more
nourishment. This is the time to nurture it . . . [with] special
nourishments" (Almay Intensive Nourishing Complex). Nighttime is when such women will most deeply feel the lack of a
nurturer. Skin "nourishment" is scientifically impossible, since
nothing penetrates the stratum corneum. Women are feeding
their skins as a way to feed themselves the love of which many
are deprived.

Women are urged to project onto these products what they
want from their relationships with men. The first *Hite Report*
showed that women wanted more tenderness. There is a strain of
Christian mysticism, sensual and intimate, in which Christ is a
lover who offers the mystic a romantic, pure union. Jesus the

bridegroom has been a fantasy mainstay of women. The cosmetic version of God the Son is tender. He knows exactly what the supplicant needs. The oils "calm," "soothe," and "comfort"; they offer a "balm," like Gilead's, to a "sensitive" and "irritated" skin or self. Judging from the ads, women want more care and attention than they are getting from men ("They never give you any personal attention"—Clinique), as well as a slower hand, an easier touch. The oils "glide on smoothly, like silk." The genie in the bottle does what real men evidently are not doing enough: He will touch her gently, commit himself forever, empathize and care for her, do for her what women do for men. He comes in a lipstick "you can have a lasting relationship with." He offers "More Care. Pure Care," "totally taking care creams," "Special Care," "Intensive Care" (Johnson & Johnson), "Loving Care" (Clairol), "Natural Care" (Clarins). He knows her sexual pace, taking "the softly, softly approach," providing "the kind of loving" the woman has "been thirsting for." He takes the guilt from sex: She "can be restored to feelings that are purely natural." He suffereth long, and is Empathy shampoo and Kind cleanser and Caress soap and Plenitude conditioner. Magically, women's sexual needs are a source of conflict no longer: "Your skin's sensitive moments need be a problem no more. . . . You need sensitive care all over . . . it's the body's most complex organ." Others offer to "lubricate luxuriously" and to "ensure maximum penetration" and to "respond directly to your needs . . . Special Care . . . when and where you need it." ("Thou knowest," the missal prays, "what good things I stand in need of.") Female sexuality is like that, after all: "Sometimes you need a little Finesse, sometimes you need a lot."

In other moods, some women may be torn by a longing to submit again to vanished authority, to God the Father. Another sales pitch lets them kiss the rod. The woman needs "Tame," an exacting guide who will train her to contain the chaos of her natural impulses; she is offered a masculine hand to subdue her, just but merciful, gentle but firm. She needs "extra control for problem skin," as if she were a problem child: "The last thing older skin needs is to be babied." Spare the rod, she is told, spoil the complexion: "Exfoliate. Inundate. Do it as aggressively as possible" (Clinique). She can buy "corrective and preventive" action

(Estée Lauder), the idiom of juvenile detention: "Slackening skin? Be firm with your face" (Clarins).

Sacrificing ourselves for others, women respond to substances that acquire their aura from sacrifice. A substance into which death has entered must work miracles. At the Swiss spa La Prairie, freshly aborted sheep embryos are "sacrificed" each week for their "fresh and living cells." (A client speaks of it as "a spiritual experience.") Placenta is a common ingredient in face creams, as are the stomach enzymes of pigs. Mammal fetal cells have been processed into them; Orchidea offers "mammary extract." In Great Britain, France, and Canada, according to Gerald McKnight, human fetal tissue cells are sold to manufacturers of skin creams. He cites recorded cases of pregnant women in poor countries persuaded to abort their children as late as seven months, for about two hundred dollars, to a lucrative undercover trade in cosmetic fetal tissue. In seventeenth-century Romania, a countess slaughtered peasant virgins so that she could bathe in their blood and stay youthful. The vampire never ages.

Magic potency comes from financial sacrifice as well. "The actual ingredients cost 10 percent or less of what [women] pay for them," a source who has worked for Helena Rubinstein and *Vogue* told McKnight. The "hideously huge markup," she says, is to cover the cost of advertising and "research." It is understood that the unreal cost is actually part of the holy oil's attraction for women: In another Linda Wells piece in *The New York Times*, "Prices: Out of Sight," she notes that Estée Lauder raised its prices for the "prestige." "The whole industry is overpriced," says a chairman of Revlon. "The price is soaring. . . . Some companies believe that the trend is peaking out. Others, meanwhile, are pushing their prices farther into the stratosphere." High prices *make* women buy holy oils. McKnight asks: "If the cost was sharply reduced . . . would they feel as satisfied in buying the stuff? It is this aspect of the business that confuses sociologists and psychologists alike." He provides a chart that proves that the breakdown of a $7.50 product yields $0.75 worth of ingredients. Selling nothing at an extortionate price makes for low overhead.

The "confusing" appeal of high cost to women should not be so baffling. The ingredients are beside the point; even their effectiveness is beside the point. The actual sheep-grease or petroleum derivative in the pot is as irrelevant as who painted the Shroud of Turin. Unlike the high cost of face colors, which at least do what they are meant to, all that the high cost of holy oil delivers is the assuaging of guilt, of the compulsion to sacrifice. In this way, the great medieval industry of pardons and indulgences reappears as the holy oil industry of today.

The value of indulgences *is* their expense to the penitent. Their primary psychological meaning lies in how much the penitent is willing to sacrifice for the sake of forgiveness. The salesmen, too, threaten to damn the woman if she does not pay. It is not even a hell of ugliness that she fears—but a limbo of guilt. If she ages without the cream, she will be told that she has brought it on herself, from her unwillingness to make the proper financial sacrifice. If she does buy the cream—and ages, which she is bound to anyway—at least she will know how much she has paid to ward off the guilt. A hundred-dollar charge is black-and-white proof that she tried. She really tried. Fear of guilt, not fear of age, is the motivating force.

## The Cult of the Fear of Fat

Many women's alarm about age or weight—the two most developed cults in the religion—has as much to do with dismay that their minds seem so trapped in unreason as it has with "the problem" itself. The fear-of-age aspect of the Rites of Beauty uses established cult methods with a subtle hand. But the fear-of-fat aspect *actually changes the way the brain works*. Women caught in it are subjected to classic, long-established forms of thought control.

The weight mania would indeed be trivial if a woman joined the cult voluntarily, and could leave it whenever she chose. But the mentality of weight control is frightening because it draws on techniques that addict the devotee to cult thinking, and distort her sense of reality. Women who may at first choose initiation into cult thinking soon find themselves unable to stop. There are sound physical and psychological reasons for this.

The weight-control cult originated as an American phenomenon. It has spread, like other American-based cults such as Mormonism and the Unification Church, to Western Europe and the

Third World. This cult, with many others, flourished in the up-heaval and rootlessness that are the American scene.

Most cults in the United States are millenarian, revolving around a struggle between saint and sinner. Activity in the cults focuses on purifying preparations for Judgment Day. Common be-haviors are trance, paranoia, hysteria, and possession.

Cults form out of the same conditions that determined women's recent history: Active rebellion is followed by passive withdrawal. When activism is frustrated, the activists turn inward. People who follow millenarian cults are groups, writes Willa Ap-pel, "whose expectations have undergone sudden change," who feel "frustrated and confused." They are attempting "to re-create reality, to establish a personal identity in situations where the old world view has lost meaning." Millenarianism is attractive to mar-ginal people, who "have no political voice, who lack effective or-ganization, and who do not have at their disposal regular, institutionalized means of redress." The cults offer "rites of pas-sage in a society where traditional institutions seem to be failing."

That is the story of women's lives today. Though many have gained power over the past two decades, that power has not cen-tered around their female bodies, as earlier women's rites of pas-sage had done. Women still lack organizations, institutions, and a collective voice. Any urban working woman will recite a litany of "frustration and confusion" and changed expectations. Women inhabit a cult-producing reality; all that was needed was the cult. The theology of weight control fitted the need: It shares with other successful cults three building blocks.

*Cults follow an authoritarian structure.* Dieters follow "re-gimes" from which they must not deviate: "Set a watch, O Lord, before my mouth," prays the Roman Catholic Missal, "and a door round my lips." The tone of diet books and features is dogmatic and unequivocal. "Experts" direct the endeavor and always know best.

*Cults preach "renunciation of the world."* Dieters give up plea-sure in food. They avoid eating out, restrain their social lives, and withdraw from situations in which they might face temptations. Anorexics give up most earthly pleasures—movies, trinkets, jokes—as an extension of food renunciation.

*Cult members believe that they alone "are gifted with the*

*truth.*" Women with weight obsessions ignore compliments because they feel that they alone really know just how repulsive is the body hidden from view. Anorexics are sure they are embarked on a quest that no one else can understand by looking at them. Self-denial can lock women into a smug and critical condescension to other, less devout women.

According to Appel, cult members develop, from these three convictions, "an attitude of moral superiority, a contempt for secular laws, rigidity of thought, and the diminution of regard for the individual." A high premium is placed on conformity to the cult group; deviation is penalized. "Beauty" is derivative; conforming to the Iron Maiden is "beautiful." The aim of beauty thinking, about weight or age, is rigid female thought. Cult members are urged to sever all ties with the past: "I destroyed all my fat photographs"; "It's a new me!"

Mind-altering activities determine how much control a cult can exert over the minds of its members. There is a kind of beauty instruction that works along the same lines as the six practices Appel identifies that cults use for altering consciousness: prayer, meditation, chanting, group rituals, psychodrama, and confession.

This repetitive loop of trivial alertness is how women's minds are altered where food is concerned. It is common knowledge that this alertness makes women *feel* slightly mad. What has not been recognized is how it *actually* makes women slightly mad. When women find we cannot stop thinking about food, we are not neurotic—we are being quite self-aware: This form of repetition, enforced on anyone who is already under pressure, actually changes the functioning of the brain. Chanters in cults exist in a "hypnagogic state." In such a state, they are prey to aggressive or self-destructive impulses. The same trance induction takes place in the way women are instructed to think about food and fat. The same irrational feelings can terrify us. Women are led to feel that the aggression and self-destruction come from within, or are not real. But this is a genuine, formal, externally imposed implant of madness.

When a woman caught up in this kind of thinking opens her eyes in the morning, she offers up something like a prayer over the scale. Chanting is assigned in hypnotic mantras. The woman chews food thirty-two times, she drinks ten glasses of water a day, she puts her fork down between bites. "Think of holding a dime between your buttocks . . . do this whenever possible—walking, watching TV, sitting at your desk, driving in your car, standing in a bank line." She is urged to flex her vaginal muscles while waiting for an elevator, to clench her jaw while hanging up her laundry. The mantra of mantras is her constant calculation, throughout the day, of the calories taken in and expended. The calorie chant, a low hum, is so habitual to many women's minds that the Hare Krishna practice of chanting seven hours a day would be child's play to them. Like the calorie chant, a mantra is repeated on one track of the mind while the rest is busy with other activities.

The weight cult teaches meditation. There is the "one-bowl" diet, in which one sits in a quiet corner, holding a bowlful of food, and concentrates on what one wants to eat and why. Women are instructed to handle, fondle, and experience a single orange for twenty minutes. They are called to center the mind on the stomach, to make certain that "appetite" is really "hunger." Women think about food all the time because the cult skillfully insists that they do so. If a woman is fat to the detriment of her health, it is far more likely to be as a result of the cult than in spite of it.

Group rituals are many. In aerobics classes, robotic parodies of exuberant movement give women a harmless high. The same bouncing dance is practiced by the Hare Krishnas, for the same effect. There is the ritual, described by Kim Chernin, of group bingeing and purging, which is common on university campuses, and the ritual of self-abasement when women leaf through magazines together, chanting the well-known formula: "I hate her. She's so thin." "You're so thin." "Oh, come on. Me? What are you talking about?"

Psychodrama takes place when a woman is confronted by the authority. That happens when the Weight Watchers' group leader demeans the devotee publicly: "Come on now, tell us what you really ate." It can be coercion from a member of one's own family: the husband who tells the wife he is ashamed to be seen with her; the mother who buys her daughter a shirt from Bloomingdale's for every lost pound.

Confession takes place formally in diet groups, which are highly formalized and very widespread cells of ritual. Weight Watchers has enrolled 8 million American women; each week across the United States, 12,000 classes are held, spreading and reinforcing cultlike behavior. In the Netherlands, its 200 employees offer 450 courses a year for 18,000 members at seventeen guilders weekly. It has spread worldwide, with 37 million members entering twenty-four international cells over the past twenty-five years.

The six mind-altering techniques just discussed are used by the Unification Church, est, Scientology, Lifespring, and other recognized cults. They are enacted in a context of group pressure, to effect a kind of conditioning that dismantles the individual. The weight cult draws on an inexhaustible supply of group pressure. It is better positioned than other cults, because group pressure is magnified by institutional pressure and cultural pressure. The Unification Church owns just the *Washington Times*, whereas the weight cult provides revenue to most of the women's media.

Willa Appel explains that the need for order is physiological as well as intellectual. She describes pattern deprivation experiments and sense deprivation research to explain what happens to cult members during indoctrination. Unable to make sense of the battery of new, highly charged sensory input on the one hand, deprived of key stimuli on the other, they become disoriented, less able to pursue rational thought, susceptible to persuasion, and suggestible. They are able to welcome, then, a scenario in which "Good and Evil meet in ultimate battle." The barrage of beauty pornography joins with recent social upheavals to constitute an entirely new, chaotic, and disorienting environment; the food self-denial most women undergo is a form of sensory deprivation. So good and evil become thin and fat, fighting for the woman's soul.

Millenarian cults depict a dangerous, wicked outer world. The Saved, like beauties, tend to be generic, faceless. A sense of loss of control leads the faithful into purification rituals while they await the Great Day. They often need to tire themselves out: A Native American cult, the Ghost Dancers, danced themselves into collapse as they waited for the final judgment. Women's fitness rituals are exhausting them. The postmillenarian world is a

paradise that is equally vague—"When I lose this weight . . ."
"It is assumed," writes Appel of millenarian cultists, "that merely
having the power that has been so long denied will bring hap-
piness."

Like women subject to the Rites of Beauty, messianists "reject those parts of themselves that threaten their new identity."
Classic cults—and the Rites—"offer hope as well as a wonderful
new identity." People who are vulnerable to cults have a poor
sense of identity, which needs to be reinforced by "becoming another person in as many ways as possible." Few women have a
strong sense of bodily identity, and the beauty myth urges us to
see a "beautiful" mask as preferable to our own faces and bodies.
Dependency and the need for approval from others are also deter-
minants. The ideal subjects for brainwashing are people who have
"no . . . organization or occupation with which they were firmly
identified." They feel sympathy for the "underdogs of the
world," for the less fortunate or exploited. The Cultural Revolution in China taught "reeducation" leaders that the best subjects
for brainwashing were those with the most highly developed
sense of sin and guilt, and the greatest vulnerability to self-crit-
icism. It seems from these indicators that a subject most vulnerable to mind-altering messages is a late-twentieth-century working
woman, struggling to make a place for herself in a turbulent
world.

A week with the Unification Church reads like such a woman's
journal. As Appel puts it:

> The effort to try to learn the required response to gain ap-
> proval, combined with lack of sleep, inadequate nutrition,
> and constant activity that allows for no rest or reflection, be-
> gins to take a toll. The guests lose their critical faculties.
> Exhausted and emotionally overwrought, they find it easier
> to lie low, keep quiet, and not provoke the anger and disap-
> proval of the group by asking questions and expressing
> doubts about the world view they are being asked to em-
> brace.

That is a precise echo of many women's experience today.
Once inside the weight cult, one is never alone. The politeness

people extend as a matter of course to the bodies of men does not apply to those of women: Women have little physical privacy. Each change or weight fluctuation is publicly observed, judged, and discussed.

Rigid planning in cults, as in the mind of an exercise- or food-fixated woman, does away with choice: What free time the cult member has left, he or she is too exhausted to use for thinking. Nutrition patterns are altered, lowering intellectual and emotional resistance. Like the moment of sliding into size-eight jeans, "moments of 'heightened experience,'" writes Appel, "are the explicit rewards for all the hard work and self-sacrifice."

A potent cult-pressure experienced by a dieter is what the Unification church calls "love bombing": the barrage of approval from everyone around her if she "gets with the program." Love bombing carries an implicit threat: that it will be withheld. Cults reward submissiveness with love; winning love grows harder and harder, and the behavior required to do so ever more submissive.

At a certain point inside the cult of "beauty," dieting becomes anorexia or compulsive eating or bulimia. Reward and punishment are the fulcrum of cult life: According to Appel: "Now Satan lurks at every corner, awaits every careless moment . . . tempting the holy." Women with eating fixations see temptation everywhere. Since women's appetites are satanic, the cult member is in a trap from which there is no escape. "By attributing to Satan desires and thoughts that the rest of society considers natural and human," writes Appel, "cults place members in an unending emotional and intellectual bind . . . forced to reject all 'selfish' feelings within [her]self . . . they inevitably intrude." To be alive is to want to satisfy hunger, but "the constant tension of having to reject innate aspects of oneself is exhausting. The convert's own humanness places [her] membership in the group and [her] own 'salvation' in jeopardy." Says one ex-cult member, "There isn't a level of acceptance where you can just be. . . . Everything's Ultimate. My God, if you take a shit, it's Ultimate. They actually tell you to sit there and meditate while you're on the john. And you feel this tremendous guilt for not being able to be focused on the Ultimate all the time." Women learn that food and body size are Ultimate, to be meditated upon in ways, and at times, that are as degrading.

American-based cults "transformed the passivity, spiritual hunger, and desire for order" of their followers into "a profitable business form specializing in quick capital." That is true of the weight cult as well.

For deprogramming to be successful, the case must be made to the cult escapee that what she has undergone "is real and powerful," while assuring her that the craziness came from without. That approach makes sense for would-be escapees from this cult too. Women trapped cannot be deprogrammed until the case is made to them that the madness is imposed from outside the self, and that it affects their minds through time-worn, third-rate psychological sleights of hand. If those women who long to escape can believe that they have been subjected to a religious indoctrination that uses the proven techniques of brainwashing, we can feel compassion for ourselves rather than self-loathing; we can begin to see where and how our minds were changed.

## The Social Effect of the New Religion

The international consequence of indoctrinating newly enfranchised women into the Rites of Beauty is that we once more are being politically sedated. Three elements used by the Rites— hunger, fear of a chaotic future, and indebtedness—have been used throughout the world by political leaders who want to keep an aggrieved population humble and quiescent.

The Rites of Beauty maintain this sedatedness in women through their daily premise of eternal deferral.

The religion says that a woman's beauty is not her own, just as the old creed said her sexuality belonged to others. She is guilty of transgression if she desecrates that beauty with impure substances, rich foods, cheap lotions. What is beautiful about her body does not belong to her but to God. But what is ugly is hers alone, proof of her sin, worthy of any abuse. She is to touch her skin reverently, as the "beauty" of a smooth youthful face is God-given. But she may wring, beat, and electrocute her woman's thighs, the proof of her prodigal ways.

This prevents women from fully inhabiting the body, keeping

us waiting for an apotheosis that will never arrive. It is meant to keep us from being at ease in the flesh or in the present, those two erotically and politically dangerous places for a woman to be; mourning the past and fearing the future, pacified.

Deferral is the bedrock of religions that need an obedient population of worshipers: The worshiper puts up with any injustice, oppression, or abuse—any hunger—because there will be pie in the sky when you die. Deferral religions have been the province of women because they keep them occupied with a life that is not this one, and supply them with miniature versions of power that leave real power uncontested. The State has encouraged women in these activities, from the woman-dominated Eleusinian Mysteries of ancient Rome and the Mary worship of the Middle Ages to the Rites of Beauty today.

Before the beauty backlash, this state of deferral, of being always prepared, had at least some mortal orientation: One was always ready to be seen by the rescuing man. Marriage was the consummation; and, afterward, a status in the community through one's husband and children. The goal of preparedness, however repressive, was at least going to be won in this life and on this body.

The number of women is multiplying for whom that deferral means that there can be no release in this life. The new religion is in some ways even darker than the old. Earlier believers knew that death brought release and fulfillment; today's are forbidden to imagine freedom in this life or the next. Our life is a never-ending test, a morass of temptation and trial, with which they must struggle forever: "Once that weight is lost, accept the fact that watching yourself is a lifelong obligation." This life, we learn, is a vale of tears. It gives life itself a compromised meaning: The woman who dies thinnest, with the fewest wrinkles, wins.

The good bridesmaids in the New Testament hoarded their oil for the bridegroom, but the bad ones burned their fuel. Women are urged to feel we must hoard our pleasure for beauty's sake; anorexics fear losing the margin of gratification saved up in the gap below "normal" weight; and women hoard shoplifted beauty products, money, food, and rewards. We are asked to believe we will at any moment be called to account and found wanting, and cast into outer darkness: poor old age, loneliness, lovelessness.

Christopher Lasch in *The Culture of Narcissism* describes how despair of the future leads people to fixate on youth. The Rites teach women to fear our own futures, our own wants. To live in fear of one's body and one's life is not to live at all. The resulting life-fearing neuroses are everywhere. They are in the woman who will take a lover, go to Nepal, learn to skydive, swim naked, demand a raise, "when she loses this weight"—but in the eternal meantime maintains her vow of chastity or self-denial. They are in the woman who can never enjoy a meal, who never feels thin enough, or that the occasion is special enough, to drop her guard and become one with the moment. They are in the woman whose horror of wrinkles is so great that the lines around her eyes shine with sacred oil, whether at a party or while making love. Women must await forever the arrival of the angel of use, the bridegroom who will dignify the effort and redeem the cost; whose presence will allow us to inhabit and use our "protected" faces and bodies. The expense is too high to let us fire the wick, to burn our own fuel to the last drop and live by our own light in our own time.

Where the Rites of Beauty have instilled these life-fearing neuroses in modern women, they paralyze in us the implications of our new freedoms, since it profits women little if we gain the whole world only to fear ourselves.

# Sex

*Religious guilt suppresses* women's sexuality. Sex researcher Alfred Kinsey found, in the words of political analyst Debbie Taylor, that "religious beliefs had little or no effect on a man's sexual pleasure, but could slice as powerfully as the circumcision knife into a woman's enjoyment, undermining with guilt and shame any pleasure she might otherwise experience." Older patriarchal religions have sought, from Egyptian clitoridectomy and the Sudanese bamboo vaginal shaft and shield to the chastity belt of Germany, to control, as Rosalind Miles charges, "*all* women via a technique which betrays a conscious determination to deal with the 'problem' of women's sexuality by destroying it wholesale." Beauty's new religion has taken on this tradition.

Technically, the female sexual organs *are* what the older religions feared as "the insatiable cunt." Capable of multiple orgasm, continual orgasm, a sharp and breathtaking clitoral orgasm, an orgasm seemingly centered in the vagina that is emotionally overwhelming, orgasm from having the breasts stroked, and of

131

endless variations of all those responses combined, women's capacity for genital pleasure is theoretically inexhaustible.

But women's prodigious sexual capacity is not being reflected in their current sexual experience. Consistently, research figures show that the sexual revolution has left many women stranded, remote from their full ability to feel pleasure. In fact, the beauty myth hit women simultaneously with—and in backlash against— the second wave and its sexual revolution, to effect a widespread suppression of women's true sexuality. Very nearly released by the spread of contraception, legal abortion, and the demise of the sexual double standard, that sexuality was quickly restrained once again by the new social forces of beauty pornography and beauty sadomasochism, which arose to put the guilt, shame, and pain back into women's experience of sex.

The sexual urge is shaped by society. Even animals have to learn how to be sexual. It is learning rather than instinct, anthropologists now believe, which leads to successful reproductive behavior: Lab-raised monkeys are inept at sex, and human beings must also learn from external cues how to be sexual. The external cues of beauty pornography and sadomasochism reshape female sexuality into a more manageable form than it would take if truly released.

Beauty pornography looks like this: The perfected woman lies prone, pressing down her pelvis. Her back arches, her mouth is open, her eyes shut, her nipples erect; there is a fine spray of moisture over her golden skin. The position is female superior; the stage of arousal, the plateau phase just preceding orgasm. On the next page, a version of her, mouth open, eyes shut, is about to tongue the pink tip of a lipstick cylinder. On the page after, another version kneels in the sand on all fours, her buttocks in the air, her face pressed into a towel, mouth open, eyes shut. The reader is looking through an ordinary women's magazine. In an ad for Reebok shoes, the woman sees a naked female torso, eyes averted. In an ad for Lily of France lingerie, she sees a naked female torso, eyes shut; for Opium perfume, a naked woman, back and buttocks bare, falls facedown from the edge of a bed; for Triton showers, a naked woman, back arched, flings her arms upward; for Jogbra sports bras, a naked female torso is cut off at the neck. In these images, where the face is visible, it is expressionless in a rictus of ecstasy. The reader understands from them that she will have to look like that if she wants to feel like that.

Beauty sadomasochism is different: In an ad for Obsession perfume, a well-muscled man drapes the naked, lifeless body of a woman over his shoulder. In an ad for Hermès perfume, a blond woman trussed in black leather is hanging upside down, screaming, her wrists looped in chains, mouth bound. In an ad for Fuji cassettes, a female robot with a playmate's body, but made of steel, floats with her genitals exposed, her ankles bolted and her face a steel mask with slits for the eyes and mouth. In an ad for Erno Laszlo skin care products, a woman sits up and begs, her wrists clasped together with a leather leash that is also tied to her dog, who is sitting up in the same posture and begging. In an American ad for Newport cigarettes, two men tackle one woman and pull another by the hair; both women are screaming. In another Newport ad, a man forces a woman's head down to get her distended mouth around a length of spurting hose gripped in his fist; her eyes are terrified. In an ad for Saab automobiles, a shot up a fashion model's thighs is captioned, "Don't worry. It's ugly underneath." In a fashion layout in *The Observer* (London), five men in black menace a model, whose face is in shock, with scissors and hot iron rods. In *Tatler* and *Harper's and Queen*, "designer rape sequences (women beaten, bound and abducted, but immaculately turned out and artistically photographed)" appear. In Chris von Wangenheim's *Vogue* layout, Doberman pinschers attack a model. Geoffrey Beene's metallic sandals are displayed against a background of S and M accessories. The woman learns from these images that no matter how assertive she may be in the world, her private submission to control is what makes her desirable.

These images above evolved with history: Sexuality follows fashion, which follows politics. During the 1960s era of Flower Power, popular culture had love as the catchword of the hour, with sex its expression; sensuality, frivolity, and playfulness were in vogue. Men grew their hair long and adorned their bodies, highlighting a feminine side that they could explore because women were not yet thinking about their own freedom. Though they appropriated girls' pleasures, it was still a boys' party.

Until the mid-1960s, pornography was primarily a male experience; women's contact with it was confined to the covers of men's magazines on newsstands. But in the 1970s beauty pornography crossed over into the female cultural arena. As women became more free, so did pornography. *Playboy* made its debut in 1958. The Pill was marketed in the United States in 1960, and approved for prescription in Britain in 1961; the British Abortion Act became law in 1967, censorship laws in the United States were relaxed in 1969, and 1973 gave American women the right to legal abortion as a result of the U.S. Supreme Court's judgment in *Roe* v. *Wade;* most European women had access to legal abortion by 1975.

The 1970s jolted women into positions of power. As they entered the work force and were caught up in the women's movement, the nature of what women would desire became a serious issue and a serious threat. The feminine sexual style of the 1960s was abandoned in popular culture, because for women to be sexual in that way—cheerfully, sensually, playfully, without violence or shame, without dread of the consequences—would break down completely institutions that were tottering crazily enough since women had changed merely their *public* roles.

In the decade during which women became political about womanhood, popular culture recast tender, intimate sex as boring. Anonymity became the aphrodisiac of the moment: Mr. Goodbar and the zipless fuck and one-night stands. If women were going to have sexual freedom and a measure of worldly power, they'd better learn to fuck like men. The soulless blood-rush of synthesized climax over a repetitive backbeat made disco the perfect music by which to score with a stranger. Helmut Newton's leather-adorned nudes appeared in *Vogue,* and David Hamilton's photographs of naked preadolescents were sold in bookstores. The "ideal" female body was stripped down and on display all over. That gave a woman, for the first time in history, the graphic details of perfection against which to measure herself, and introduced a new female experience, the anxious and minute scrutiny of the body *as intricately connected to female sexual pleasure.* Soon, "perfection" was represented as a woman's "sexual armor," made more urgent an achievement in the 1980s when AIDS intensified an atmosphere that suggested to women that only an inhuman beauty would lead a man to risk his life for sex.

~~love?~~

## Deeper Than the Skin

In a crossover of imagery in the 1980s, the conventions of high-class pornographic photography, such as *Playboy*'s, began to be used generally to sell products to women. This made the beauty thinking that followed crucially different from all that had preceded it. Seeing a face anticipating orgasm, even if it is staged, is a powerful sell: In the absence of other sexual images, many women came to believe that they must have that face, that body, to achieve that ecstasy.

Two conventions from soft- and hard-core pornography entered women's culture: One "just" objectifies the female body, the other does violence to it. Obscenity law is based in part on the idea that you can avoid what offends you. But the terms ordinarily used in the pornography debate cannot deal adequately with this issue. Discussions of obscenity, or nakedness, or community standards do not address the harm done to women by this development: the way in which "beauty" joins pornographic conventions in advertising, fashion photography, cable TV, and even comic books to affect women and children. Men can choose to enter an adult bookstore; women and children cannot choose to avoid sexually violent or beauty-pornographic imagery that follows them home.

Sexual "explicitness" is not the issue. We could use a lot more of that, if explicit meant honest and revealing; if there were a full spectrum of erotic images of uncoerced real women and real men in contexts of sexual trust, beauty pornography could theoretically hurt no one. Defenders of pornography base their position on the idea of freedom of speech, casting pornographic imagery as language. Using their own argument, something striking emerges about the representation of women's bodies: The representation is heavily censored. Because we see many versions of the naked Iron Maiden, we are asked to believe that our culture promotes the display of female sexuality. It actually shows almost none. It censors representations of women's bodies, so that only the official versions are visible. Rather than seeing images *of* female desire or that cater *to* female desire, we see mock-ups of living mannequins, made to contort and grimace, immobilized and uncomfortable under hot lights, professional set-pieces that reveal little about female sexuality. In the United States and Great Britain, which have no tradition of public nakedness, women rarely—and almost never outside a competitive context—see what other *women* look like naked; we see only identical humanoid products based loosely on women's bodies.

Beauty pornography and sadomasochism are not explicit, but dishonest. The former claims that women's "beauty" *is* our sexuality, when the truth goes the other way around. The latter claims that women like to be forced and raped, and that sexual violence and rape are stylish, elegant, and beautiful.

Midway through the 1970s, the punk-rock scene began to glorify S and M: High school girls put safety pins through their ears, painted their lips bruise-blue, and ripped their clothing to suggest sexual battle. By the end of the decade, S and M had ascended from street fashion to high fashion in the form of studded black leather, wristcuffs, and spikes. Fashion models adopted from violent pornography the furious pouting glare of the violated woman. "Vanilla" sexual styles—loving and nonviolent—came to look passé.

In the 1980s, when many women were graduating with professional degrees, anger against women crackled the airwaves. We saw a stupendous upsurge in violent sexual imagery in which the abused was female. In 1979, Jack Sullivan in *The New York Times* identified "a popular genre of thriller that attempts to generate excitement by piling up female corpses." According to Jane Caputi, who calls the modern period the Age of Sex Crime, film portrayals based on sex abusers became common during the late 1970s and 1980s: *Dressed to Kill, Tie Me Up! Tie Me Down!, Blue Velvet, 9½ Weeks, Tightrope, Body Double,* the list goes on. That decade perfected the "first person" or "subjective camera" shot that encourages identification with the killer or rapist. In 1981, American film critics Gene Siskel and Roger Ebert denounced "women in danger" films as an antifeminist backlash; a few years later, they praised one because it lets "us" really know "how it feels to abuse women." The *Zap* underground comics of the 1970s depicted child abuse and rape at gunpoint; by 1989, *The New York Times* ran a story featuring the new sadomasochism in kids' comic books, and the British comic *Viz* began to degrade women sexually in the strip "Fat Slags." Sex just wasn't sex anymore without violence. In a world in which both sexes' guilt and angry fear surrounded the sense that women were getting out of control, the public quickly lost interest in ordinary unharmed nakedness. Presented as more compulsively engaging to the attention of men and, eventually, women, was imagery that played out anxieties from the sex war, reproducing the power inequality that recent social changes had questioned: male dominance, female submission. Female nakedness became inhuman, "perfected" beyond familiarity, freakishly like a sculpture in plastic, and often degraded or violated.

The upsurge in violent sexual imagery took its energy from male anger and female guilt at women's access to power. Where beautiful women in 1950s culture got married or seduced, in modern culture the beauty gets raped. Even if we never seek out pornography, we often see rape where sex should be. Since most women repress our awareness of that in order to survive being entertained, it can take concentration to remember. According to a Screen Actors Guild study in 1989—a year in which female leading roles made up only 14 percent of the total—a growing number of the roles for women cast them as rape victims or prostitutes. In France, TV viewers see fifteen rapes a week. That has a different effect on the audience than, for example, seeing murders: One person in four is unlikely to be murdered. But even if she avoids pornography, a woman will, by watching mainstream, middle-brow plays, films, and TV, learn the conventions of her threatened rape in detail, close up.

Rape fantasies projected into the culture are benign, we're told, even beneficial, when commentators dismiss them through what Catharine MacKinnon has satirized as "the hydraulic model" of male sexuality (it lets off steam). Men, we are given to understand, are harmlessly interested in such fantasies; *women* are harmlessly interested in them (though many women may have rape fantasies for no more subtle psychological reason than that

that image of sexuality is the primary one they witness). But what is happening now is that men and women whose private psychosexual history would not lead them to eroticize sexual violence are *learning* from such scenes to be interested in it. In other words, our culture is depicting sex as rape *so that* men and women will become interested in it.

## Beauty Pornography and Sadomasochism

The current allocation of power is sustained by a flood of hostile and violent sexual images, but threatened by imagery of mutual eroticism or female desire; the elite of the power structure seem to know this consciously enough to act on it. The imposition of beauty pornography and beauty sadomasochism from the top down shows in obscenity legislation. We saw that the language of women's naked bodies and women's faces is censored. Censorship also applies to what kind of sexual imagery and information can circulate: Sexual violence against women is not obscene whereas female sexual curiosity is. British and Canadian law interprets obscenity as the presence of an erect penis, not of vulvas and breasts; and an erection, writes Susan G. Cole in *Pornography and the Sex Crisis*, is, "according to American mores . . . not the kind of thing a distributor can put on the newsstands next to *Time*." Masters and Johnson, asked in *Playboy* to comment on the average penis size, censored their findings: They "flatly refused," worrying that it would have "a negative effect on *Playboy*'s readers," and that "everyone would walk around with a measuring stick."

This version of censorship policed the same decades that saw the pornography industry's unparalleled growth: In Sweden, where the sale of violently misogynist pornography is defended on the grounds of freedom of expression, "when a magazine appeared with a nude male for a centerspread, [the authorities] whisked [it] off the stalls in a matter of hours." Women's magazine *Spare Rib* was banned in Ireland because it showed women how to examine their breasts. The Helena Rubinstein Foundation in the United States withdrew support from a Barnard women's conference because a women's magazine on campus showed "explicit" images of women. Several art galleries banned Judy Chicago's collaborative show, *The Dinner Party,* for its depiction of the stylized genitals of heroines of women's history. The U.S. National Endowment for the Arts was attacked by Congress for sponsoring an exhibit that displayed very large penises. The Ontario Police Project P held that photos of naked women tied up, bruised, and bleeding, intended for sexual purposes, were not obscene since there were no erect penises, but a Canadian women's film was banned for a five-second shot of an erect penis being fitted with a condom. In New York subways, metropolitan policemen confiscated handmade anti-AIDS posters that showed illiterate people how to put a condom over an erect penis; they left the adjacent ads for *Penthouse,* displayed by the New York City Transit Authority, intact. Leaving aside the issue of what violent sexual imagery does, it is still apparent that there is an officially enforced double standard for men's and women's nakedness in mainstream culture that bolsters power inequities.

The practice of displaying breasts, for example, in contexts in which the display of penises would be unthinkable, is portrayed as trivial because breasts are not "as naked" as penises or vaginas; and the idea of half exposing men in a similar way is moot because men don't have body parts comparable to breasts. But if we think about how women's genitals are physically concealed, unlike men's, and how women's breasts are physically exposed, unlike men's, it can be seen differently: women's breasts, then correspond to men's penises as the vulnerable "sexual flower" on the body, so that to display the former and conceal the latter makes women's bodies vulnerable while men's are protected. Cross-culturally, unequal nakedness almost always expresses power relations: In modern jails, male prisoners are stripped in front of clothed prison guards; in the antebellum South, young black male slaves were naked while serving the clothed white masters at table. To live in a culture in which women are routinely naked where men aren't is to learn inequality in little ways all day long. So even if we agree that sexual imagery is in fact a language, it is clearly one that is already heavily edited to protect men's sexual—and hence social—confidence while undermining that of women.

## How Does It Work?

These images institutionalize heterosexual alienation by intervening in our fantasy lives. "So powerful is pornography, and so smoothly does it blend in with the advertising of products . . . that many women find their own fantasies and self-images distorted too," writes Debbie Taylor in *Women: A World Report*. Romantic fiction, she points out, is "seldom sexually explicit, tending to fade out . . . when two lovers touch lips for the first time." The same sexual evasiveness is true of nearly all dramatic presentation of mainstream culture where a love story is told. So rare is it to see sexual explicitness in the context of love and intimacy on screen that it seems our culture treats tender sexuality as if it were deviant or depraved, while embracing violent or degrading sex as right and healthy. "This leaves," Taylor says, "the sexual stage," in men's and women's minds, "vacant, and pornographic images are free to take a starring role. The two leading actors on this stage are the sadist, played by man, and the masochist, played by woman."

Until recently, the locus of sexual fantasy was peopled with images actually glimpsed or were sensations actually felt, and private imaginings taken from suggestions in the real world, a dream well where weightless images from it floated, transformed by imagination. It prepared children, with these hints and traces of other people's bodies, to become adults and enter the landscape of adult sexuality and meet the lover face to face. Lucky men and women are able to keep a pathway clear to that dream well, peopling it with scenes and images that meet them as they get older, created with their own bodies' mingling with other bodies; they choose a lover because a smell from a coat, a way of walking, the shape of a lip, belong in their imagined interior and resonate back in time and deep in the bones that recall childhood and early adolescent imagination. The locus of fantasy of a lucky man holds no robots; of a lucky woman, no predators; they reach adulthood with no violence in the garden.

Protecting one's fantasy life is becoming daily more difficult, especially for the young. The beauty barrage peoples the fantasy locus of a woman with "beautiful" naked ghosts that claim her territory, turning a dim private space into a movie set where famous strangers who have nothing to do with her display themselves. The purpose of the beauty myth of the 1980s was to people the sexual interior of men and women with violence, placing an elegantly abused iron maiden into the heart of everyone's darkness, and blasting the fertile ground of children's imaginations with visions so caustic as to render them sterile. For the time being, the myth is winning its campaign against our sexual individuality, the most movingly personal images that take their associative power from our earliest childhood, our clumsy adolescence, our first loves. It is making certain that men and women, just freed to find one another, will be sure to miss.

The usual discussions about pornography center on men and what it does to their sexual attitudes toward women. But the parallel effect of beauty pornography on women is at least as important: What does that imagery do to women's sexual attitudes toward themselves? If soft-core, nonviolent, mainstream pornography has been shown to make men less likely to believe a rape victim; if its desensitizing influence lasts a long time; if sexually violent films make men progressively trivialize the severity of the violence they see against women; and if at last only violence against women is perceived by them as erotic, is it not likely that parallel imagery aimed at women does the same to women in relation to themselves? The evidence shows that it does. Wendy Stock discovered that exposure to rape imagery increased women's sexual arousal to rape and increased their rape fantasies (though it did not convince them that women liked force in sex). Carol Krafka found that her female subjects "grew less upset with the violence [against women] the more they saw, and that they rated the material less violent" the more of it was shown to them.

In a study of women in the United States, Dr. E. Hariton found that 49 percent had submissive sexual fantasies. Legal decisions are being made out of the propagation throughout the culture of the rape fantasy: In 1989 a U.K. civil suit brought by a woman raped by her physiotherapist was denied because it was suggested that she had fantasized the rape and that such fantasies are common among women. Violent sexual imagery is also redefining the idea of sex in the law: When another young British woman brought rape charges against a police officer, the bruises

and contusions on her body, and the abrasions of his truncheon
held against her throat, were ruled to be consistent with a con-
sensual "amorous tussle."

The debate continues about whether classic pornography
makes men violent toward women. But beauty pornography is
clearly making women violent toward ourselves. The evidence
surrounds us. Here, a surgeon stretches the slit skin of the breast.
There, a surgeon presses with all his weight on a woman's chest
to break up lumps of silicone with his bare hands. There is the
walking corpse. There is the woman vomiting blood.

## Sexual Battle: Profit and Glamour

Why this flood of images now? They do not arise simply as a
market response to deep-seated, innate desires already in place.
They arise also—and primarily—to set a sexual agenda and to
*create* their versions of desire. The way to instill social values,
writes historian Susan G. Cole, is to eroticize them. Images that
turn women into objects or eroticize the degradation of women
have arisen to counterbalance women's recent self-assertion.
They are welcome and necessary because the sexes have come
too close for the comfort of the powerful; they act to keep men
and women apart, wherever the restraints of religion, law, and
economics have grown too weak to continue their work of sustaining the sex war.

Heterosexual love, before the women's movement, was undermined by women's economic dependence on men. Love
freely given between equals is the child of the women's movement, and a very recent historical possibility, and as such very
fragile. It is also the enemy of some of the most powerful interests
of this society.

If women and men in great numbers were to form bonds that
were equal, nonviolent, and sexual, honoring the female principle
no less or more than the male, the result would be more radical
than the establishment's worst nightmares of homosexual "conversions." A mass heterosexual deviation into tenderness and mutual respect would mean real trouble for the status quo since

heterosexuals are the most powerful sexual majority. The power structure would face a massive shift of allegiances: From each relationship might emerge a doubled commitment to transform society into one based publicly on what have traditionally been women's values, demonstrating all too well the appeal for both sexes of a world rescued from male dominance. The good news would get out on the street: Free women have more fun; worse, so do free men.

Male-dominated institutions—particularly corporate interests—recognize the dangers posed to them by love's escape. Women who love themselves are threatening; but men who love real women, more so. Women who have broken out of gender roles have proved manageable: Those few with power are being retrained as men. But with the apparition of numbers of men moving into passionate, sexual love of real women, serious money and authority could defect to join forces with the opposition. Such love would be a political upheaval more radical than the Russian Revolution and more destabilizing to the balance of world power than the end of the nuclear age. It would be the downfall of civilization as we know it—that is, of male dominance; and for heterosexual love, the beginning of the beginning.

Images that flatten sex into "beauty," and flatten the beauty into something inhuman, or subject her to eroticized torment, are politically and socioeconomically welcome, subverting female sexual pride and ensuring that men and women are unlikely to form common cause against the social order that feeds on their mutual antagonism, their separate versions of loneliness.

Barbara Ehrenreich, Elizabeth Hess, and Gloria Jacobs, in *Re-Making Love*, point out that the new market of sexual products demands quick-turnover sexual consumerism. That point applies beyond the sexual accessories market to the entire economy of consumption. The last thing the consumer index wants men and women to do is to figure out how to love one another: The $1.5-trillion retail-sales industry depends on sexual estrangement between men and women, and is fueled by sexual dissatisfaction. Ads do not sell sex—that would be counterproductive, if it meant that heterosexual women and men turned to one another and were gratified. What they sell is sexual discontent.

Though the survival of the planet depends on women's values

balancing men's, consumer culture depends on maintaining a broken line of communication between the sexes and promoting matching sexual insecurities. Harley-Davidsons and Cuisinarts stand in for maleness and femaleness. But sexual satisfaction eases the stranglehold of materialism, since status symbols no longer look sexual, but irrelevant. Product lust weakens where emotional and sexual lust intensifies. The price we pay for artificially buoying up this market is our heart's desire. The beauty myth keeps a gap of fantasy between men and women. That gap is made with mirrors; no law of nature supports it. It keeps us spending vast sums of money and looking distractedly around us, but its smoke and reflection interfere with our freedom to be sexually ourselves.

Consumer culture is best supported by markets made up of sexual clones, men who want objects and women who want to be objects, and the object desired ever-changing, disposable, and dictated by the market. The beautiful object of consumer pornography has a built-in obsolescence, to ensure that as few men as possible will form a bond with one woman for years or for a lifetime, and to ensure that women's dissatisfaction with themselves will grow rather than diminish over time. Emotionally unstable relationships, high divorce rates, and a large population cast out into the sexual marketplace are good for business in a consumer economy. Beauty pornography is intent on making modern sex brutal and boring and only as deep as a mirror's mercury, anti-erotic for both men and women.

But even more powerful interests than the consumer index depend on heterosexual estrangement and are threatened by heterosexual accord. The military is supported by nearly one third of the United States government's budget; militarism depends on men choosing the bond with one another over the bond with women and children. Men who loved women would shift loyalties back to the family and community from which becoming a man is one long exile. Serious lovers and fathers would be unwilling to believe the standard propaganda of militarism: that their wives and children would benefit from their heroic death. Mothers don't fear mothers; if men's love for women and for their own children led them to define themselves first as fathers and lovers, the propaganda of war would fall on deaf ears: The enemy would be a

father and partner too. This percentage of the economy is at risk
from heterosexual love. Peace and trust between men and women
who are lovers would be as bad for the consumer economy and
the power structure as peace on earth for the military-industrial
complex.

Heterosexual love threatens to lead to political change: An
erotic life based on nonviolent mutuality rather than domination
and pain teaches firsthand its appeal beyond the bedroom. A consequence of female self-love is that the woman grows convinced
of social worth. Her love for her body will be unqualified, which
is the basis of female identification. If a woman loves her own
body, she doesn't grudge what other women do with theirs; if she
loves femaleness, she champions its rights. It's true what they say
about women: Women *are* insatiable. We *are* greedy. Our appetites do need to be controlled if things are to stay in place. If
the world were ours too, if we believed we could get away with it,
we *would* ask for more love, more sex, more money, more commitment to children, more food, more care. These sexual, emotional, and physical demands *would* begin to extend to social
demands: payment for care of the elderly, parental leave, child-
care, etc. The force of female desire would be so great that society would truly have to reckon with what women want, in bed
and in the world.

The economy also depends on a male work structure that denies the family. Men police one another's sexuality, forbidding
each other to put sexual love and family at the center of their
lives; women define themselves as successful according to their
ability to sustain sexually loving relationships. If too many men
and women formed common cause, that definition of success
would make its appeal to men, liberating them from the echoing
wind-tunnel of competitive masculinity. Beauty pornography is
useful in preventing that eventuality: When aimed at men, its
effect is to keep them from finding peace in sexual love. The
fleeting chimera of the airbrushed centerfold, always receding before him, keeps the man destabilized in pursuit, unable to focus
on the beauty of the woman—known, marked, lined, familiar—
who hands him the paper every morning.

The myth freezes the sexual revolution to bring us full circle,
evading sexual love with its expensive economic price tag. The

nineteenth century constrained heterosexuality in arranged marriages; today's urban overachievers sign over their sexual fate to dating services, and their libido to work: One survey found that many yuppie couples share mutual impotence. The last century kept men and women apart in rigid gender stereotypes, as they are now estranged through rigid physical stereotypes. In the Victorian marriage market, men judged and chose; in the stakes of the beauty market, men judge and choose. It is hard to love a jailer, women knew when they had no legal rights. But it is not much easier to love a judge. Beauty pornography is a war-keeping force to stabilize the institutions of a society under threat from an outbreak of heterosexual love.

## Object Lessons

Glamorous rape scenes obviously eroticize the sex war. But what about nonviolent beauty pornography? The harm is apparent in the way such imagery represses female sexuality and lowers women's sexual self-esteem by casting sex as locked in a chastity belt to which "beauty" is the only key. Since the myth began to use female sexuality to do its political work, by pairing it with "beauty" images in a siege of repetition, it has a stronger grip on women than ever before. With sex held hostage by "beauty," the myth is no longer just skin deep, but goes to the core.

Western women's sexuality may be as endangered by the myth as the sexuality of many Eastern women is endangered through cruder practices. Kinsey's 1953 study showed that only between 70 and 77 percent of women had ever achieved orgasm, either by masturbation or intercourse. Women's sexual satisfaction has not kept pace with the ostensible progress of the "sexual revolution": Shere Hite's 1976 figures showed that only 30 percent of women have orgasms regularly from intercourse without clitoral stimulation by hand, another 19 percent with clitoral stimulation; 29 percent don't have orgasms during intercourse; 15 percent don't masturbate at all; and 11.6 percent don't have orgasms at all, ever. Helen Kaplan's 1974 research showed that 8 to 10 percent of women never have orgasms, and up to 45 percent do so during intercourse only with additional clitoral stimulation. Only 30 percent of women in Seymour Fischer's 1973 study had orgasms regularly during intercourse.

The 1980s showed surprisingly little change: By 1980, Wendy Faulkner found that only 40 percent of British women have masturbated by the age of forty, versus 90 percent of men. In a 1981 study, only 47 percent of Danish women were found ever to have masturbated to orgasm at all. In the United Kingdom, a 1989 study of 10,000 women discovered that 36 percent "rarely" or "never" experienced orgasm during intercourse and "most admitted faking it to please their husbands." Western women's sexuality may be so endangered by the myth that even Eastern circumcised women have more pleasure: Incredibly, in contrast, a major study of 4,024 circumcised Sudanese women (their clitorises removed by sunna circumcision) showed that 88 percent had experienced orgasm.

Though intercourse certainly need not be set up as the primary act around which women must adjust their pleasure, it is legitimate to ask why intercourse and masturbation, as just two sources of potential pleasure out of many, should be giving women so little satisfaction now. Western heterosexual women are not getting the pleasure from their own bodies or the bodies of men that they deserve or of which they are capable. Could there be something wrong with the way in which intercourse is culturally taught to men and women, and something wrong with the way women are asked to experience their own bodies? The beauty myth can explain much of that dissatisfaction.

The myth wants to discourage women from seeing themselves unequivocally as sexually beautiful. The damage beauty pornography does to women is less immediately obvious than the harm usually attributed to pornography: A woman who knows why she hates to see another woman hanging from a meat hook, and can state her objections, is baffled if she tries to articulate her discomfort with "soft" beauty pornography.

This fear of pornography that cannot speak its name is a quiet dismay that extends across the political spectrum. It can be found inside "free speech" feminists who oppose the antipornography movement, and inside women who don't follow feminist debate, and inside women who don't identify with the "bad" women in

hard or soft pornography, inside religious women and secular, promiscuous women and virgins, gay women and straight. The
women hurt by it do not have to be convinced of a link between
"real" pornography and sexual violence; but they cannot discuss
this harm without shame. For the woman who cannot locate in
her worldview a reasonable objection to images of naked, "beautiful" women to whom nothing bad is visibly being done, what is
it that can explain the damage she feels within?

Her silence itself comes from the myth: If women feel ugly, it
is our fault, and we have no inalienable right to feel sexually
beautiful. A woman must not admit it if she objects to beauty
pornography because it strikes to the root of her sexuality by making her feel sexually unlovely. Male or female, we all need to feel
beautiful to be open to sexual communication: "beautiful" in the
sense of welcome, desired, and treasured. Deprived of that, one
objectifies oneself or the other for self-protection.

I once talked with other young women students about the
soft-core pornography to which our college common room sub-
scribed. I had it all wrong. I mentioned politics, symbolism, male
cultural space, social exclusion, commodification. A thoughtful
young woman listened intently for a while, but without a flicker
of response in her eyes. "I'll support you," she said eventually,
"though I have no idea what you're talking about. All I know is
that they make me feel incredibly bad about myself."

The covers of soft-core magazines come close to a woman's
psyche by showing versions of the models familiar to her from her
own fantasy life, which is composed of images from film, TV, and
women's magazines. Unlike the "alien" whores of hard-core pornography, whose "beauty" is less to the point than what they can
be made to do, these models are a lesson to her: They are "her"
models undressed. "Hefner's a romantic, into the beauty of it
all," says Al Goldstein, publisher of *Screw*, "and his girls are the
girls next door. My girls are the *whores* next door, with pimples
and stretch marks and cheap black and white newsprint." If those
are the only two choices of sexual representation available to
women, no wonder they seek beauty to the point of death.

The "romantic" models give the woman a hypnotic revelation
of a perfected body to sketch in under the familiar protected face;
the rosy labia and rouged nipples can be imagined under the lace

of the Sunday supplement models, whose gleaming flanks and sinuous bellies can be imagined under the fashion layouts. To this consumer striptease she compares her own. She may feel wry humility, an antidote to desire, or she may feel a sense of narcissistic "measuring up," pornographically charged but ultimately as anti-erotic, since the woman who "fits" does not win; she is simply allowed to fill the outline of the Iron Maiden. Indeed, it is possible that "beautiful" women are more vulnerable to pornographic intervention in their fantasy lives, since they can "see" themselves in pornography where other women do not.

A woman who dislikes *Playboy* may do so because the sexual core is not easily killed. Though she may have submitted her self-image to other humiliations, in its last site of resistance, this, the sexual essence, will fight hard and long. She may resent *Playboy* because she resents feeling ugly in sex—or, if "beautiful," her body defined and diminished by pornography. It inhibits in her something she needs to live, and gives her the ultimate anaphrodisiac: the self-critical sexual gaze. Alice Walker's essay "Coming Apart" investigates the damage done: Comparing herself to her lover's pornography, her heroine "foolishly" decides that she is not beautiful.

"I fantasize," says "Betty" in Nancy Friday's collection of female sexual fantasies, *My Secret Garden,* that "I have changed into a very beautiful and glamorous woman (in real life I know I'm somewhat plain). . . . I close my eyes and seem to be watching this other beautiful woman who is me from some other place, outside myself. I can see her so vividly that I want to shout encouragement to her . . . 'Enjoy it, you deserve it.' The funny thing is that this other woman isn't me." Writes "Monica": "I was suddenly not my own self. The body . . . was not this funny fat thing of mine, it wasn't me. . . . It was my beautiful sister . . . all the time it wasn't me, it was all happening to these two beautiful people in my mind." Those voices—"it was not me"; "I was suddenly not my own self"; "it was this other beautiful woman"—are haunting. In only twenty years, the myth has slid a pane of imagery to separate women from their bodies during the act of love.

When they discuss this subject, women lean forward, their voices lower. They tell their terrible secret. It's my breasts, they say. My hips. It's my thighs. I hate my stomach. This is not aesthetic distaste, but deep sexual shame. The parts of the body vary. But what each woman who describes it shares is the conviction that *that* is what the pornography of beauty most fetishizes. Breasts, thighs, buttocks, bellies; the most sexually central parts of women, whose "ugliness" therefore becomes an obsession. Those are the parts most often battered by abusive men. The parts that sex murderers most often mutilate. The parts most often defiled by violent pornography. The parts that beauty surgeons most often cut open. The parts that bear and nurse children and feel sexual. A misogynist culture has succeeded in making women hate what misogynists hate.

"Lady, love your cunt," wrote Greer, and yet Hite's figures showed that about one woman in seven thought her vagina was "ugly"; the same number thought its smell was "bad." Lady, love your body is an even more urgent message a generation later: A third of women are "strongly dissatisfied" with their bodies, which leads them to experience "higher social anxiety, lower self-esteem, and *sexual dysfunction*" (italics added). Dr. Marcia Germaine Hutchinson estimates that 65 percent of women do not like their bodies, and that poor physical self-esteem leads women to shy away from physical intimacy. That low self-esteem and diminished sexuality are the psychic black hole that beauty pornography hollows in a woman's physical integrity.

The black hole of self-hatred can migrate: An obsession with her breasts can fade away and revulsion at the sight of her thighs can take its place. Many women read the beauty index fearfully because it often *introduces* new and unexpected points of revulsion.

How did this disastrous definition of sexuality arise? "Beauty" and sexuality are both commonly misunderstood as some transcendent inevitable fact; falsely interlocking the two makes it seem doubly true that a woman must be "beautiful" to be sexual. That of course is not true at all. The definitions of both "beautiful" and "sexual" constantly change to serve the social order, and the connection between the two is a recent invention. When society needed chastity from women, virginity and fidelity endowed women with beauty (religious fundamentalist Phyllis Schlafly recently reasserted that sex outside marriage destroyed

women's beauty), and their sexuality did not exist: Peter Gay
shows that Victorian women were assumed to be "sexually anaes-
thetic," and Wendy Faulkner quotes the conviction of Victorian
writers that middle-class women were "naturally frigid." Only recently, now that society is best served by a population of women
who are sexually available and sexually insecure, "beauty" has
been redefined as sex. Why? Because, unlike female sexuality,
innate to all women, "beauty" is hard work, few women are born
with it, and it is not free.

The disparity between "beauty" and sex in the production of
such images resonates in a memory of mine: A friend, a model, at
fifteen, showed me the prints from her first lingerie shoot, for a
big department store's Sunday supplement ads. I could hardly
recognize her: Sasha's black hair, straight and puritanical, had
been tousled and teased. Her high breasts were filmed over with a
sheen of black-and-peach silk. The woman whom Sasha had pre-
tended to become in the photo was seated on her haunches in a
stylishly unmade bed, its sheets folded back like overblown cab-
bage roses. Her bed, on which we sat looking at the prints, was
single, tucked-in, austere, covered in gray-cotton ticking. Above
us were Shakespeare's plays in dog-eared high school editions,
her biology book, and a calculator; never those ropes of pearls,
diamond cuff links, the lurid gladioli with stuck-out stamens. The
thing made from Sasha arched its back, so the undersides of her
breasts caught the glare. "Your poor back," I said, thinking of its
tense shoulder blades. Sasha had scoliosis. She had to wear a
brace made of steel and rigid foam. The brace existed in a dimension outside the cropped window, the sophisticated orange twi-
light into which we both peered. Sasha's glossed lips were parted
over her teeth as if she had plunged a hand into scalding water.
Her eyes were half closed, the Sasha in them painted out. Like
me, Sasha was a virgin.

Looking back, I can imagine how the image would come out
that weekend: exploding into a life of its own, between columns
of text. A thousand grown women, who would know secrets that
we two could not have begun to imagine, would stare at it. They
would take off their clothes and brush their teeth. They would
turn around before a mirror in the buzzing light, and the scoured
illuminated shell of Sasha's body would spin above their heads in

the dark sky. They would flick off the light and go to their wide warm lively beds, to open arms, chastened, with a heavier tread.

The link between beauty pornography and sex is not natural. It is taken for granted that the desire to have visual access to an endless number of changing centerfolds is innately male, since that form of looking is taken to be a sublimation of men's innate promiscuity. But since men are not naturally promiscuous and women are not naturally monogamous, it follows that the truism so often asserted about beauty pornography—that men need it because they are visually aroused while women aren't—is not biologically inevitable. Men are visually aroused by women's bodies and less sensitive to their arousal by women's personalities because they are trained early into that response, while women are less visually aroused and more emotionally aroused because that is their training. This asymmetry in sexual education maintains men's power in the myth: They look at women's bodies, evaluate, move on; their own bodies are not looked at, evaluated, and taken or passed over. But there is no "rock called gender" responsible for that; it can change so that real mutuality—an equal gaze, equal vulnerability, equal desire—brings heterosexual men and women together.

The asymmetry of the beauty myth tells men and women lies about each other's bodies, to keep them sexually estranged. The myth's series of physical lies negates what a heterosexual woman knows to be true about the bodies of men. Women are supposed to be the "soft-skinned" sex, but a woman knows that the aureole around a man's nipple is supremely soft, and that there are places on his body where the outer skin is softer than anywhere on a woman's: the glans, the delicate covering of the shaft. Women are the "sensitive" sex; yet there is no part of a woman's body so vulnerable as the testes. Women must keep their shirts on in every weather ostensibly because their nipples are sexual. But men's nipples are sexual too, and that doesn't keep them covered when the mercury breaks eighty. Women are "ugly" where they get stretch marks. Men get stretch marks, across their hips, of which they are often not aware. Women's breasts must be perfectly symmetrical; men's genitals sure aren't. There is a whole literature of ancient revulsion against the tastes and sights of

women's bodies; men can taste unpleasant and look perfectly alarming. Women love them anyway.

The boom in images that turn women into sexual objects accompanied the sexual revolution not to cater to men's fantasies but to defend them against their fears. When novelist Margaret Atwood asked women what they feared most from men, they replied, "We're afraid they'll kill us." When she asked men the same question about women, they replied, "We're afraid they'll laugh at us." When men control women's sexuality, they are safe from sexual evaluation. A Japanese woman of the eighth century, for instance, reports Rosalind Miles, was taught "always to say of his *membrum virile* that it is huge, wonderful, larger than any other. . . . And you will add, 'Come fill me, O my wonder!' and a few other compliments of the same kind." A sixteenth-century literate woman was less complimentary: "The old man kissed her, and it was as though a slug had dragged itself across her charming face." With women experimenting sexually, men risked hearing what women hear every day: that there are sexual standards against which they might be compared. Their fears are exaggerated: Even with sexual freedom, women maintain a strict code of etiquette. "Never," enjoins a women's magazine, "mention the size of his [penis] in public . . . and never, ever let him know that anyone else knows or you may find it shrivels up and disappears, serving you right." That quotation acknowledges that critical sexual comparison is a direct anaphrodisiac when applied to men; either we do not yet recognize that it has exactly the same effect on women, or we do not care, or *we understand on some level that right now that effect is desirable and appropriate.*

A man is unlikely to be brought within earshot of women as they judge men's appearance, height, muscle tone, sexual technique, penis size, personal grooming, or taste in clothes—all of which we do. The fact is that women are able to view men just as men view women, as subjects for sexual and aesthetic evaluation; we too are effortlessly able to choose the male "ideal" from a lineup; and if we could have male beauty as well as everything else, most of us would not say no. But so what? Given all that, women make the choice, by and large, to take men as human beings first.

Women could probably be trained quite easily to see men first as sexual things. If girls never experienced sexual violence; if a girl's only window on male sexuality were a stream of easily available, well-lit, cheap images of boys slightly older than herself, in their late teens, smiling encouragingly and revealing cuddly erect penises the color of roses or mocha, she might well look at, masturbate to, and, as an adult, "need" beauty pornography based on the bodies of men. And if those initiating penises were represented to the girl as pneumatically erectible, swerving neither left nor right, tasting of cinnamon or forest berries, innocent of random hairs, and ever ready; if they were presented alongside their measurements, length, and circumference to the quarter inch; if they seemed to be available to her with no troublesome personality attached; if her sweet pleasure seemed to be the only reason for them to exist—then a real young man would probably approach the young woman's bed with, to say the least, a failing heart.

But again, so what? Having been trained does not mean one cannot reject one's training. Men's dread of being objectified in the way they have objectified women is probably unfounded: If both genders were given the choice of seeing the other as a combination of sexual object and human being, both would recognize that fulfillment lies in excluding neither term. But it is the unfounded fears between the sexes that work best to the beauty myth's advantage.

Imagery that is focused exclusively on the female body was encouraged in an environment in which men could no longer control sex but had for the first time to win it. Women who were preoccupied with their own desirability were less likely to express and seek out what they themselves desired.

## How to Suppress Female Sexuality

Germaine Greer wrote that women will be free when they have a positive definition of female sexuality. Such a definition might well render beauty pornography completely neutral to women. A generation later, women still lack it. Female sexuality is not only negatively defined, it is negatively constructed. Women are vulnerable to absorbing the beauty myth's intervention in our sexuality because our sexual education is set up to ensure that vulnerability. Female sexuality is turned inside out from birth, so "beauty" can take its place, keeping women's eyes lowered to their own bodies, glancing up only to check their reflections in the eyes of men.

This outside-in eroticism is cultivated in women by three very unnatural pressures on female sexuality. The first is that little girls are not usually intimately cared for by fathers. The second is the strong cultural influence that positions women outside their bodies to look at women alone as sexual objects. The third is the prevalence of sexual violence that prohibits female sexuality from developing organically, and makes men's bodies appear dangerous.

1. The naked Iron Maiden affects women powerfully because most are tended in infancy by women. The female body and the female breast begin as the focus of desire for the infant girl, with the male breast and body absent. As girls grow, the myth keeps the sexual focus on the female body, but, unlike the attraction to it felt by straight men and lesbians, heterosexual women's ungratified admiration often becomes contaminated with envy, regret for lost bliss, and hostility. This situation creates in women an addiction to men's eyes, enforcing what the poet Adrienne Rich calls "compulsory heterosexuality," which forbids women from seeing other women as sources of sexual pleasure at all. Under the myth, the beauty of other women's bodies gives women pain, leading to what Kim Chernin calls our "cruel obsession with the female body." This balked relationship—which gives straight women confused, anxious pleasure when looking at another female body—leaves women in a lifelong anguish of competition that is in fact only the poisonous residue of original love.

2. The cultural inversion of female sexuality starts early, beginning with the masturbation taboo. Sexual integrity grows out of the sublime selfishness of childhood, from which sexual giving emerges as generosity rather than submissiveness. But female masturbation is also culturally censored. Early solitary desire is one of the rare memories that can remind women that we are fully sexual before "beauty" comes into the picture, and can be so

after and beyond the beauty myth; and that sexual feeling does not have to depend on being looked at.

Men take this core for granted in themselves: We see that, sanctioned by the culture, men's sexuality simply *is*. They do not have to earn it with their appearance. We see that men's desire precedes contact with women. It does not lie dormant waiting to spring into being only in response to a woman's will. Solitary male desire is represented from high culture to low, from Philip Roth, André Gide, Karl Shapiro, and James Joyce to dirty jokes told to mixed audiences. We all know about the sexual desire of adolescent boys. But scenes of young women's sexual awakening *in themselves* do not exist except in a mock-up for the male voyeur. It is hard to imagine, in a cultural vacuum, what solitary female desire looks like. Women's bodies are portrayed as attractive packaging around an empty box; our genitals are not eroticized *for women*. Men's bodies are not eroticized *for women*. Other women's bodies are not eroticized *for women*. Female masturbation is not eroticized *for women*. Each woman has to learn for herself, from nowhere, how to feel sexual (though she learns constantly how to look sexual). She is given no counterculture of female lust looking outward, no descriptions of the intricate, curious *presence* of her genital sensations or the way they continually enrich her body's knowledge. Left to herself in the dark, she has very little choice: She must absorb the dominant culture's fantasies as her own.

Ten-year-olds in the 1970s, eager for talk about sex written in a woman's voice, took turns at camp reading aloud pirated copies of *The Story of O* or *The Happy Hooker;* one is an indoctrination in masochism, the other is about soulless commercial sexual barter. Little girls for lack of anything better learn from what comes to hand. They do not lack facts; they lack a positive sexual culture: novels and poetry, film and jokes and rock and roll, written not to sell but to explore and communicate and celebrate, as the best male erotic culture is written. For girls' education, there is nothing but a woman bound to a wall, her mouth an O; or a woman with an apt business sense and a flat prose style counting her money.

Boys, though, have a sexual culture ready-made for them. They sing, playing air guitar against their groins: "Brown sugar, mm! How come you taste so good? Ahhh . . . Just like a young girl should." ("We should?" wondered the little girls. "Like brown sugar?") But of the girls' own experience, what their own senses are telling them—the prickling smell of male salt in a school corridor, the intrigue of newly darkening down on a forearm, the pitch of a voice shifting into low gear, the slouch that stretches denim over a thigh, the taste of Southern Comfort on a half-educated tongue, of filterless Lucky Strikes filched from a dresser, the corrosion of stubble, windburn—they notice it all, they see it; but they are powerless to tell it. The fact that such images elicit awkwardness in both the teller and the listener attests to how unused we are to encounter young girls in our culture as sexually awakening *subjects*. The alien beauty of the bodies of men, though girls stumble upon it in a *Phaedrus* or a *Dorian Gray*, is nowhere to be found in culture meant for them; the glamour and allure of men's bodies is not described for them in a woman's voice; and their attraction to their girlfriends is described nowhere at all.

Their sexual energy, their evaluation of adolescent boys and other girls goes thwarted, deflected back upon the girls, unspoken, and their searching hungry gaze returned to their own bodies. The questions, Whom do I desire? Why? What will I do about it? are turned around: Would I desire myself? Why? . . . Why *not*? What can I do about it?

The books and films they see survey from the young boy's point of view his first touch of a girl's thighs, his first glimpse of her breasts. The girls sit listening, absorbing, their familiar breasts estranged as if they were not part of their bodies, their thighs crossed self-consciously, learning how to leave their bodies and watch them from the outside. Since their bodies are seen from the point of view of strangeness and desire, it is no wonder that what should be familiar, felt to be whole, becomes estranged and divided into parts. What little girls learn is not the desire for the other, but the desire to be desired. Girls learn to watch their sex along with the boys; that takes up the space that should be devoted to finding out about what they are wanting, and reading and writing about it, seeking it and getting it. Sex is held hostage by beauty and its ransom terms are engraved in girls' minds early and deeply with instruments more beautiful than those which advertisers or pornographers know how to use: literature, poetry, painting, and film.

This outside-in perspective on their own sexuality leads to the confusion that is at the heart of the myth. Women come to confuse sexual looking with being looked at sexually ("Clairol . . . it's the look you want"); many confuse sexually feeling with being sexually felt ("Gillette razors . . . the way a woman wants to feel"); many confuse desiring with being desirable. "My first sexual memory," a woman tells me, "was when I first shaved my legs, and when I ran my hand down the smooth skin I felt how it would feel to someone else's hand." Women say that when they lose weight they "feel sexier"; but the nerve endings in the clitoris and nipples don't multiply with weight loss. Women tell me they're jealous of the men who get so much pleasure out of the female body; that they imagine being inside the male body that is inside their own so that they can vicariously experience desire.

Could it be then that women's famous slowness of arousal relative to men's, complex fantasy life, the lack of pleasure many experience in intercourse, is related to this cultural negation of sexual imagery that affirms the female point of view, the cultural prohibition against seeing men's bodies as instruments of pleasure? Could it relate to the taboo against representing intercourse as an opportunity for a straight woman actively to pursue, grasp, savor, and consume the male body for her satisfaction, as much as she is pursued, grasped, savored, and consumed for his?

The inversion of female sexuality keeps women from being in control of their own sexual experience. One trouble with soft-core sexual imagery aimed at young men is that the women photographed are not actually responding sexually to anything; young men grow up trained to eroticize images that teach them nothing about female desire. Nor are young *women* taught to eroticize female desire. Both men and women, then, tend to eroticize only the woman's body and the man's desire. That means that women are exaggeratedly sensitive to male desire for their own arousal, and men are exaggeratedly insensitive to female desire for theirs. The chain reaction that has women's sexual feeling depend on men's is responsible for the phenomenon described by Carol Cassell in *Swept Away: Why Women Confuse Love and Sex*. Because *notice the link?*

many women need to feel "swept away" before they can experience desire, only 48 percent of them use contraception regularly. In the United States, 48.7 percent of abortions follow from unprotected intercourse. If women's sexuality were so highly valued and attentively fostered that they could protect themselves without fear of lessened sexual feeling, half of the abortion tragedy would be a thing of the past. With the AIDS epidemic, women submitting to the "swept away" phenomenon are risking not just pregnancy but death.

3. A final explanation for women's deflected sexuality and ambivalence about intercourse relates to their lived experience of sexual force. The suggestive power of the abused Iron Maiden must be understood in a context of actual sexual violence against women.

According to the 1983 random survey conducted by Diana Russell of 930 San Francisco women, 44 percent had survived rape or attempted rape as defined by the FBI, 88 percent of those knew their attacker, and 1 woman in 7 had been raped by her husband or ex-husband. In a Dutch study of 1,054 middle-class, educated women between the ages of twenty and forty, 15.6 percent had been sexually abused by relatives, 24.4 percent had been sexually abused as children by nonrelatives, and 32.2 percent had forced sexual experiences before age sixteen. In another study of 4,700 Dutch families, 20.8 percent had experienced violence from a husband or lover, half experienced repeated acts of violence, and 1 in 25 experienced very severe violence that resulted in permanent damage. The Netherlands saw an increase of over a third in rapes reported between 1980 and 1988. In Sweden there was an increase of 70 percent of reports of violence against women between 1981 and 1988, and an increase of 50 percent of reported rapes. In Canada, 1 woman in 4 will have her first sexual experience under conditions of force, at the hands of a family member or someone close to the family. In Great Britain, 1 wife in 7 is raped by her husband. A 1981 study of 1,236 London women found that 1 in 6 had been raped and 1 in 5 had fought off attempted rape; other studies in 1985 and again in 1989 found the same proportions.

Women's experience of violence from their lovers is epidemic. In 1980, a study of 2,000 married couples in the United States found that there had been assault in 28 percent of them, with 16 percent reporting violence in the past year. One third of the violence was serious: punching, kicking, hitting with an object, assault with a knife or gun. In a 1985 follow-up survey, the percentages were the same. A Harris Poll showed violence in 21 percent of relationships, which squared with Diana Russell's 1982 random sample also showing 21 percent. In an assault, it is the woman who gets hurt in 94 to 95 percent of the cases. At least one and a half million American women are assaulted by their partners each year. One quarter of the violent crime in the United States is wife assault. Researchers in Pittsburgh tried to find a control group of nonbattered women—but 34 percent *of the control group* reported an attack from their partner. One Canadian married woman in ten is beaten by her spouse, and one in eight will be assaulted by the man she lives with. Battering accounts for one out of every four suicide attempts by women treated in the emergency rooms of metropolitan hospitals in the United States. In a National Institute of Mental Health study, 21 percent of women having emergency surgery were battered, half of all injured women using emergency services were battered, and half of all rapes of women over thirty were part of the battering syndrome. The Worldwatch Institute asserted in 1989 that violence against women was the most common crime worldwide.

Child sexual abuse, of course, links sex to force very early in a quarter to a third of the female population. Kinsey found in 1953 that nearly a quarter of the 4,000 women he surveyed had survived rape or attempted rape by adult men when they were children. Diana Russell's survey found in 1987 that 38 percent of women had been sexually abused by an adult relative, acquaintance, or stranger before age eighteen; 28 percent had been seriously abused before age fourteen, 12 percent by someone in their family. Bud Lewis, director of a *Los Angeles Times* poll conducted in 1985, found in his random survey of 2,627 men and women from all the states that 22 percent of those questioned had been sexually abused as children; of the women, 27 percent. He then asked 1,260 males if they had ever sexually abused a child; 1 man in 10 acknowledged that he had. Worldwide, research culled from countries as diverse as Australia, the United States, Egypt, Israel, and India suggests that one in four families is incestuous; in 80 to

90 percent of those cases, girls are sexually abused by a male relative, usually fathers. In Cairo, between 33 and 45 percent of families had daughters who had been sexually abused by a male relative or family friends; Kinsey found incest in 24 percent of American families, a figure that is consistent with the numbers in Australia and the United Kingdom. Two thirds of Israeli victims were younger than ten and a quarter of the victims in the United States were younger than five. Debbie Taylor, by extending the data to the rest of the world, suggests that as many as 100 *million* young girls "may be being raped by adult men—usually their fathers—often day after day, week after week, year in, year out."

The numbers are staggering; so is the thought that the beauty myth is projecting sexually violent images of women, and images of perfection that demand that women do violence to themselves, in an environment that has already linked sex to violence in some way at some time in most women's lives. Could harm done to women make them more willing to harm themselves? A *Radiance* magazine finding showed that 50 percent of anorexics in one clinic had been sexually abused. Plastic surgeon Elizabeth Morgan explored the relationship between incest and the desire for plastic surgery after many of her patients admitted they had been victims of child sexual abuse: "I came to understand that many of them wanted to erase the memory of the children they looked like when they were abused." Clinical studies of incest survivors show that they have fears that "their sexual pleasure does not come from a good place . . . most believe that they are the ones who had done something wrong, that they should be punished, and that if no one will mete out justice, they will administer it to themselves."

The most common reaction of rape survivors is a feeling of worthlessness, and then hatred of their bodies, often accompanied by eating disorders (usually compulsive eating or anorexia, to ensure that they will become "safely" very fat or thin) and sexual withdrawal. If actual sexual abuse does that to women's physical self-love, could images of sexual abuse and images that invade female sexual privacy do similar harm?

A more pervasive effect of this atmosphere, the prevalence of sexual violence and the way it is linked to women's beauty, is that women—especially, perhaps, young women who grew up with such violent imagery—are made to fear and distrust their own beauty and feel ambivalent about physically expressing, in dress, movement, or adornment, their own sexuality. Today, perhaps more than ever before, when young women dress in a sexually provocative way they are made to feel that they are engaged in something dangerous.

## The Sexuality of the Young: Changed Utterly?

It seems that exposure to chic violence and objectifying sexual imagery has already harmed the young. Theorists of eros have not come close to realizing the effect of beauty pornography on young people. Gloria Steinem and Susan Griffin separate pornography from eros—which makes sense if eros comes first in the psycho-sexual biography. Rape fantasies may be insignificant, as Barbara Ehrenreich believes, for those who grew up learning their sexuality from other human beings. But young people today did not ask for a sexuality of pleasure from distance, from danger: It was given to them. For the first time in history, children are growing up whose earliest sexual imprinting derives not from a living human being, or fantasies of their own; since the 1960s pornographic upsurge, the sexuality of children has begun to be shaped in response to cues that are no longer human. Nothing comparable has ever happened in the history of our species; it dislodges Freud. Today's children and young men and women have sexual identities that spiral around paper and celluloid phantoms: from *Playboy* to music videos to the blank female torsos in women's magazines, features obscured and eyes extinguished, they are being imprinted with a sexuality that is mass-produced, deliberately dehumanizing and inhuman.

Something ugly seems to be happening to young people's sexuality as a result: The effort to retrain sex into violence may be nearly won. Hilde Bruch calls young women born after 1960 "the anorexic generations." Since obscenity laws were relaxed in the the 1960s and children born after 1960 have grown up in an atmosphere of increasingly violent and degrading sexual imagery (from which young women are withdrawing through anorexia), we must recognize young people born after 1960 as "the pornographic generations."

Young women now are being bombarded with a kind of radiation sickness brought on by overexposure to images of beauty pornography, the only source offered them of ways to imagine female sexuality. They go out into the world sexually unprotected: stripped of the repressive assurance of their sexual value conferred by virginity or a diamond ring—one's sexuality was worth something all too concrete in the days when a man contracted to work for a lifetime to maintain access to it—and not yet armed with a sense of innate sexual pride. Before 1960, "good" and "bad," as applied to women, corresponded with "nonsexual" and "sexual." After the rise of beauty pornography and the sexual half-revolution, "good" began to mean "beautiful-(thin)-hence-sexual" and "bad" meant "ugly-(fat)-hencenonsexual."

In the past, women felt vulnerable, in the prenuptial bed, to pregnancy, illegal abortion, and abandonment. Young women today feel vulnerable to judgment; if a harsh sentence is passed (or even suspected or projected), it is not her reputation that suffers so much as the stability of her moral universe. They did not have long to explore the sexual revolution and make it their own. Before the old chains had grown cold, while young women were still rubbing the circulation back into their ankles and taking tentative steps forward, the beauty industries levied a heavy toll on further investigations, and beauty pornography offered them designer bondage.

The thirty-year education of the young in sex as stylish objectification or sadomasochism may have produced a generation that honestly believes that sex is violent and violence is sexual, so long as the violence is directed against women. If they believe that, it is not because they are psychopaths but because that representation in mainstream culture *is the norm.*

Twelve percent of British and American parents allow their children to watch violent and pornographic films. But you don't have to watch either kind of film to tune in. Susan G. Cole notes that MTV, the rock video channel in the United States, "appears to be conforming to pornographic standards" (the Playboy channel simply broadcasts its selections on "Hot Rocks"). With the evolution of rock videos, both sexes sit in a room together watching the culture's official fantasy line about what they are supposed to do together—or, more often, what she is supposed to look like while he does what he does, watching her. This material, unlike the version of it in glossy magazines, moves, complicating young women's sexual anxieties in relation to beauty in a new way, as it adds levels of instruction beyond the simple pose: Now they must take notes on how to move, strip, grimace, pout, breathe, and cry out during a "sexual" encounter. In the shift from print to videotape, their self-consciousness became three-dimensional.

So does their sense of being stylishly endangered. Sex killers are portrayed on MTV as male heroes: The Rolling Stones' "Midnight Rambler" is a paean to the Boston Strangler ("I'll stick my knife right down your throat"); Thin Lizzy sings "Killer in the House" about a rapist ("I'm looking for somebody . . . I might be looking for you"); Trevor Rubin sings "The Ripper." Motley Crue's videos have women as sexual slaves in cages. In Rick James's video he rapes his girlfriend. In Michael Jackson's "The Way You Make Me Feel," a gang stalks a lone woman. Duran Duran shows female figures in chains, and their "Girls on Film," observes Susan G. Cole, "look as if they've just stepped out of an X-rated film." In Alice Cooper's show, reports *The Guardian*, "a life-sized, woman-shaped doll lies on the floor in front of him, handcuffed, wearing ripped fishnets and a leotard. She appears to have been choked to death by a plastic hose." "I used to love her," sings Guns 'n' Roses, "but I had to kill her." Criticism of rock's extremism exposes one to the charge of being reactionary. But by resorting to these images, it is rock music that is being reactionary. Images of strangled women, women in cages, do not push any limits; they are a mainstream cliché of a mainstream social order. Rock music fails to live up to its subversive tradition when it eroticizes the same old establishment sadomasochism rather than playing with gender roles to make us look at them afresh.

Unfortunately, musical originality is not the only thing at stake: MTV sets the beauty index for young women today. If the women depicted in mass culture are "beautiful" and abused, abuse is a mark of desirability. For young men, "beauty" is defined as that which never says no, and that which is not really human: The date-rape figures show what lessons that teaches.

In 1986, UCLA researcher Neil Malamuth reported that 30
percent of college men said they would commit rape if they could
be sure of getting away with it. When the survey changed the
word "rape" into the phrase "force a woman into having sex," 58
percent said that they would do so. *Ms.* magazine commissioned a
study funded by the National Institute for Mental Health of 6,100
undergraduates, male and female, on thirty-two college campuses
across the United States. In the year prior to the *Ms.* survey,
2,971 college men had committed 187 rapes, 157 attempted
rapes, 327 acts of sexual coercion, and 854 attempts at unwanted
sexual contact. The *Ms.* study concluded that "scenes in movies
and TV that reflect violence and force in sexual relationships relate directly to acquaintance rape."

In another survey of 114 undergraduate men, these replies
emerged:

"I like to dominate a woman." 91.3%.
"I enjoy the conquest part of sex." 86.1%.
"Some women look like they're just asking to be raped."
   83.5.%
"I get excited when a woman struggles over sex." 63.5%.
"It would be exciting to use force to subdue a woman."
   61.7%.

In the *Ms.* survey, one college man in twelve, or 8 percent of
the respondents, had raped or tried to rape a woman since age
fourteen (the only consistent difference between this group and
those who had not assaulted women was that the former said they
read pornography "very frequently"). Researchers at Emory and
Auburn universities in the United States found that 30 percent of
male college students rated faces of women displaying emotional
distress—pain, fear—to be more sexually attractive than the faces
showing pleasure; of those respondents, 60 percent had committed acts of sexual aggression.

Women are faring badly. In the *Ms.* study, one in four women
respondents had had an experience that met the American legal
definition of rape or attempted rape. Among the 3,187 women
surveyed, in the preceding year, there had been 328 rapes and 534
attempted rapes; 837 women were subjected to sexual coercion, and

2,024 experienced episodes of unwanted sexual contact. Date rape shows, more than rape by a stranger, the confusion that has been generated in the young between sex and violence. Of the women raped, 84 percent knew the attacker, and 57 percent were raped on dates. Date rape, thus, is more common than left-handedness, alcoholism, and heart attacks. In 1982, an Auburn University study found that 25 percent of undergraduate women had had at least one experience of rape; 93 percent of those were by acquaintances. Of Auburn men, 61 percent had forced sexual contact on a woman against her will. A St. Cloud State University study in 1982 showed that 29 percent of the women students had been raped. Twenty percent of women students at the University of South Dakota had been date-raped; at Brown University, 16 percent had been date-raped. Eleven percent of Brown men said they had forced sex on a woman. The same year at Auburn University, 15 percent of male undergraduates said they had raped a woman on a date.

Women are four times more likely to be raped by an acquaintance than a stranger. Sexual violence is seen as normal by young women as well as young men: "Study after study has shown that women who are raped by men they know don't even identify their experiences as rape"; only 27 percent in the *Ms.* study did so. Does their inability to call what happened to them "rape" mean that they escape the aftereffects of rape? Thirty percent of raped young women, whether or not they called their experience rape, considered suicide afterward. Thirty-one percent sought psychotherapy, and 82 percent said the experience had permanently changed them. Forty-one percent of the raped women said they expected to be raped again. Posttraumatic stress syndrome was identified as a psychological disorder in 1980, and is now recognized as common among rape survivors. The women who don't call their rape by its name still suffer the same depression, self-hatred, and suicidal impulses as women who do. Their experiences are likely to imprint young women sexually: In the *Ms.* study, 41 percent of the raped young women were virgins; 38 percent were between fourteen and seventeen at the time of the attack. For both the rapists and the victims in the study, the average age at the time of the rape was eighteen and a half years old. College women are having relationships that include physical vio-

lence: Between 21 and 30 percent of young people report violence from their dating partner.

Among younger adolescents, the trend is even worse. In a
UCLA study of fourteen- to eighteen-year-olds, the researchers
wrote that "we appear to have uncovered some rather distressing
indications that a new generation is entering into the adult world
of relationships carrying along shockingly outmoded baggage."
More than 50 percent of the boys and nearly half the girls thought
it was okay for a man to rape a woman if he was sexually aroused
by her. A recent survey in Toronto reports that children are learning dominance and submission patterns at an earlier age: One in
seven boys in grade 13 reported having refused to take no for an
answer, and one in four girls of the same age reported having
been sexually forced. Eighty percent of the teenage girls reported
that they'd already been involved in violent relationships. According to Susan G. Cole, "In spite of hopes to the contrary, pornography and mass culture are working to collapse sexuality with
rape, reinforcing the patterns of male dominance and female submission so that many young people believe this is simply the way
sex is. This means that many of the rapists of the future will
believe they are behaving within socially accepted norms."

Cultural representation of glamorized degradation has created
a situation among the young in which boys rape and girls get
raped *as a normal course of events.* The boys may even be unaware
that what they are doing is wrong; violent sexual imagery may
well have raised a generation of young men who can rape women
without even knowing it. In 1987 a young New York woman, Jennifer Levin, was murdered in Central Park after sadomasochistic
sex; a classmate remarked dryly to a friend that that was the only
kind of sex that anyone he knew was having. In 1989, five New
York teenagers raped and savagely battered a young woman jog-
ger. The papers were full of stunned questions: Was it race? Was
it class? No one noticed that in the fantasy subculture fed to the
young, *it was normal.*

These figures show that much AIDS education has been utterly
naive. If a quarter of young women have at some point had control
denied them in a sexual encounter, they stand little chance of protecting themselves from the deadly disease. In a speakout on sex-

ual violence at Yale University, the most common theme was a new crime that has been largely ignored: when a woman stipulates a safe, or nonpenetrative, sexual encounter, but the man ejaculates into her against her will. AIDS education will not get very far until young men are taught how not to rape young women and how to eroticize trust and consent; and until young women are supported in the way they need to be redefining their desires. Only when that happens will sex in the age of AIDS be free of the aura of terror it now seems to carry on so many college campuses.

In recent literature and films by young people, sexual violence or alienation is the hallmark. In Steven Soderbergh's film *sex, lies, and videotape*, the hero can't make love to a real woman but masturbates to women's videotaped sexual confessions; in Bret Easton Ellis's *Less Than Zero*, bored rich kids watch snuff films—and a preadolescent girl, bound on a bed, and raped repeatedly, is a background image throughout; in Tama Janowitz's *Slaves of New York*, women are sexual slaves in exchange for housing (the Bloomingdale's ad based on the novel asks if you are "a slave to your boyfriend"); in Susan Minot's *Lust*, the heroine describes her promiscuity as making her feel "like a piece of pounded veal"; the heroine of Catherine Texier's *Love Me Tender* seeks out increasingly violent sexual humiliation ("Like the times we did it so hard," sings Sinead O'Connor, "there was blood on the wall"). Romantic, intimate sexual love in the culture of the young is mostly confined to gay relationships, as in the novels of David Leavitt, Michael Chabon, and Jeanette Winterson. It is as if, in an ambience of violent heterosexual imagery, the young have retreated into a dull, aching sexual estrangement that is beyond warfare; more like daily life in a militarized town, in which civilians and soldiers have little more to say to one another.

Evidently such imagery is bad for sex. Is it good for love?


## Beauty Against Love


Under the Feminine Mystique, men were kept ignorant of the details of women's sexuality and of childbirth. New fathers were kept in hospital waiting rooms. Apart from protecting himself from venereal diseases and shotgun weddings, a man left contraception to women. Menstruation was taboo. The dirtier aspects of housekeeping and child rearing were kept from men. These details were part of women's sphere, which separated them from men with a line they were not to cross. For a man to come in contact with the "female mysteries" of reproduction and domesticity was, it seemed, to put himself at the mercy of an emasculating magical power: It was supposed to make men pass out or become Milquetoasts or just make a terrible mess. So when the frazzled Papa handed Baby in exasperation to smug Mama, he was handing her the tribute of his ignorance, her expertise. She naturally knew best. Crossing the gender line subjected men to ridicule.

Today, many men feel free to be real fathers. Those who are glad of what their fathering has given them can look back at this scenario and see how it excluded them from something precious. Because the old-fashioned tribute left the drudgery to women, it seemed that the joke was on them. But because the tedium and hassle of "women's mysteries" are inseparable from the joy, the joke was on men too. Not long ago, the division of labor where these tasks are concerned was considered biological and changeless. It changed.

Today, the "women's mysteries" surrounding beauty in sexuality, beauty *as* sexuality, seem biological and changeless. They too are cloaked in flattery that manipulates women while they seem to give men the better sexual deal. They too burden women with obligations while keeping men, through peer pressure, far from a source of joy. A man today must face ridicule from other men if he joins his partner beyond the beauty myth. At the moment, the joke's on both of them. But that too can change.

The beauty mysteries that occupied the space vacated by the Feminine Mystique now constitute the topics that women censor in themselves. At least one major study proves that men are as exasperated with the beauty myth as women are. "Preoccupation with her appearance, concern about face and hair" ranked among the top four qualities that most annoyed men about women. These mysteries are what men do not know how to discuss with women whom they are trying to love without doing them harm. They put back what was nearly lost when women left their status as marital slaves: suspicion, hostility, incomprehension, obsequiousness, and rage.

Let's say a man really loves a woman; he sees her as his equal, his ally, his colleague; but she enters this other realm and becomes unfathomable. In the krypton spotlight, which he doesn't even see, she falls ill, out of his caste, and turns into an untouchable.

He may know her as confident; she stands on the bathroom scale and sinks into a keening of self-abuse. He knows her as mature; she comes home with a failed haircut, weeping from a vexation she is ashamed even to express. He knows her as prudent; she goes without winter boots because she spent half a week's paycheck on artfully packaged mineral oil. He knows her as sharing his love of the country; she refuses to go with him to the seaside until her springtime fast is ended. She's convivial; but she rudely refuses a slice of birthday cake, only to devour the ruins of anything at all in a frigid light at dawn.

Nothing he can say about this is right. He can't speak. Whatever he says hurts her more. If he comforts her by calling the issue trivial, he doesn't understand. It isn't trivial at all. If he agrees with her that it's serious, even worse: He can't possibly love her, he thinks she's fat and ugly. If he says he loves her just as she is, worse still: He doesn't think she's beautiful. If he lets her know that he loves her *because* she's beautiful, worst of all, though she can't talk about this to anyone. That is supposed to be what she wants most in the world, but it makes her feel bereft, unloved, and alone.

He is witnessing something he cannot possibly understand. The mysteriousness of her behavior keeps safe in his view of his lover a zone of incomprehension. It protects a no-man's-land, an uninhabitable territory between the sexes, wherever a man and a woman might dare to call a ceasefire.

Maybe he throws up his hands. Maybe he grows irritable or condescending. Unless he enjoys the power over her this gives him, he probably gets very bored. So would the woman if the man she loved were trapped inside something so pointless, where nothing she might say could reach him.

Even where a woman and a man have managed to build and inhabit that sand castle—an equal relationship—this is the unlistening tide; it ensures that there will remain a tag on the woman that marks her as the same old something else, half child, half savage. He can take his pick—here at least the old insults still apply.

Hysterical. Superstitious. Primitive. Immanent. Other.

"She's pretty, isn't she?" she says. "She's okay," he says. "Do you think I'm that pretty?" she says. "You're great," he says. "Should I cut my hair like that?" she says. "I love you the way you are," he says. "What's that supposed to mean?" she asks in a rage. The culture has set it up so that men and women must continually hurt and offend one another over this issue. Neither can win as long as beauty's power inequalities stay in place. In the dialogue, the man has said something that in a culture free of the beauty myth would be as loving as can be: He loves her, physically, because she is who she is. In our culture, though, the woman is forced to throw his gift back in his face: That is supposed to be less valuable than for him to rate her as a top-notch art object. If his loving her "the way she is" were considered more exciting than his assigning her a four-star rating, the woman could feel secure, desirable, irreplaceable—but then she wouldn't need to buy so many products. She would like herself too much. She would like other women too much. She would raise her voice.

So the beauty myth sets it up this way: A high rating as an art object is the most valuable tribute a woman can exact from her lover. If he appreciates her face and body because it is hers, that is next to worthless. It is very neat: The myth contrives to make women offend men by scrutinizing honest appreciation when they give it; it can make men offend women merely by giving them honest appreciation. It can manage to contaminate the sentence "You're beautiful," which is next to "I love you" in expressing a bond of regard between a woman and a man. A man cannot tell a woman that he loves to look at her without risking making her unhappy. If he never tells her, she is *destined* to be unhappy. And the "luckiest" woman of all, told she is loved because she's "beautiful," is often tormented because she lacks the security of being desired because she looks like who she lovably is.

This futile bickering goes far deeper than simply to show that women are insecure. It is not insecurity speaking the woman's

lines but—if she does have self-respect—hostility: Why should
her lover, just because he is male, be in a position to judge her
against other women? Why must she need to know her position
and hate needing to, and hate knowing? Why should his reply
have such exaggerated power? And it does. He does not know
that what he says will affect the way she feels when they next
make love. She is angry for a number of good reasons that may
have nothing to do with this particular man's intentions. The exchange reminds her that, in spite of a whole fabric of carefully
woven equalities, they are not equal in this way that is so crucial
that its snagged thread unravels the rest.

Just as "beauty" is not related to sex, neither is it related to
love. Even having it does not bestow love on a woman, though
the beauty myth claims that it must. It is because "beauty" is so
hostile to love that many beautiful women are so cynical about
men. "Only God, my dear," wrote Yeats blithely, "Could love
you for yourself alone/And not your yellow hair." This quote is
meant as a bit of lighthearted verse. But it is an epic tragedy in
three lines. The beautiful woman is excluded forever from the
rewards and responsibilities of particular human love, for she cannot trust that any man will love her "for herself alone." A hellish
doubt inheres in the myth that makes impersonal "beauty" a pre-
requisite for love: Where does love go when beauty vanishes?
And, if a woman cannot be loved "for herself alone," for whom is
she being loved? Auden knew that what is "bred in the bone" of
both women and men is to crave "not universal love/but to be
loved alone." The "love" the beauty myth offers is universal: this
year's full-lipped blonde, this season's disheveled tawny nymph.

But we long to be loved the way we were, if we were lucky, as
children: every toe touched, each limb exclaimed upon with delight, because it was ours alone, incomparable. As adults, we seek
that release from the scale of comparison in romantic love: In the
eyes of one's true love, even the most jaded wish to believe, each
of us will be "the most beautiful woman," because we will be
truly seen and known for ourselves. The beauty myth, though,
gives us the opposite prospect: If there is a set of features that is
lovable, those features are replaceable. Those elements that make
each woman unique—the unrepeatable irregularity of her face,
the scars of a childhood trauma, the lines and furrows of a life of

thought and laughter, grief and rage—exclude her from the ranks of mythical beauties, and from the charmed playgrounds, we are told, of love.

By having to "present" herself to her lover as "beautiful," the woman remains not fully known. She leaves his bed at dawn to paint over her face. She leaves his arms to run around a barbed-wire reservoir. She needs to flirt with strangers because his desire for her cannot fill the black hole or compensate her for what she has sacrificed. They both stay counterpoised on the mistrustful axis: her face, her body. Mary Gordon in *Final Payments* describes the way the beauty myth makes women hide from men: "I knew I could not possibly see him as I was now, with my stomach hanging over the top of my underpants, with my thighs that chafed together. . . . I would have to do so much before I could see him. For I knew, and in knowing this, I hated him for a moment, that without my beauty he would not love me." Insofar as he will never know her now, the man will never fully know her; and insofar as she cannot trust him now to love her with her "beauty" in eclipse, she can never fully trust him.

Beauty practices are being stressed so that the relationships between men and women will continue, in spite of a social movement toward equality, to feel dictatorial. Placing female pleasure, sex or food or self-esteem, into the hands of a personal judge turns the man into a legislator of the woman's pleasure, rather than her companion in it. "Beauty" today is what the female orgasm used to be: something given to women by men, if they submitted to their feminine role and were lucky.


## Men


For many men, the myth is a drug that insulates them from the dangers of self-knowledge. Contemplating an art object made out of a living woman is one way a man can fool himself that he is immortal. If the woman's eyes are his mirror, and the mirror ages, the gazing man must see that he is aging as well. A new mirror, or a fantasy mirror made of "beauty" rather than degenerating flesh and blood, saves him from this self-awareness. Contact would ruin the ideal nature of the mirror. Keats wrote in "Ode on a Grecian Urn," "She cannot fade, though thou hast not thy bliss./Forever wilt thou love and she be fair." The sentence's ambiguous grammar, which has given sleepless nights to generations of schoolgirls, reiterates the promise to women that they will get love if only they escape from time. Forever wilt thou love *because* she will be forever fair? The dark side, the girl hears, is that if she is not fair forever, he will not love her forever.

Is the beauty myth good to men? It hurts them by teaching them how to avoid loving women. It prevents men from actually seeing women. It does not, contrary to its own professed ideology, stimulate and gratify sexual longing. In suggesting a vision in place of a woman, it has a numbing effect, reducing all senses but the visual, and impairing even that.

Simone de Beauvoir said that no man is truly free to love a fat woman. If that is true, how free are men? Women can imagine the emotional aridity of men's experience of the myth if they look back on their lovers and try to imagine their women friends and colleagues criticizing them for any mate—no matter how witty, powerful, famous, sexy, rich, or kind—who did not resemble Praxiteles' Charioteer.

Women understand that there are two distinct economies: There is physical attraction, and then there is the "ideal." When a woman looks at a man, she can physically dislike the idea of his height, his coloring, his shape. But after she has liked him and loved him, she would not want him to look any other way: For many women, the body appears to grow beautiful and erotic as they grow to like the person in it. The actual body, the smell, the feel, the voice and movement, becomes charged with heat through the desirable person who animates it. Even Gertrude Stein said of Picasso, "There was nothing especially attractive about him at first sight . . . but his radiance, an inner fire one sensed in him, gave him a sort of magnetism I was unable to resist." By the same token, a woman can admire a man as a work of art but lose sexual interest if he turns out to be an idiot. The way in which women regard men's bodies sexually is proof that one *can* look at a person sexually without reducing him or her to pieces.

What becomes of the man who acquires a beautiful woman,

with her "beauty" his sole target? He sabotages himself. He has gained no friend, no ally, no mutual trust: She knows quite well why she has been chosen. He has succeeded in buying a mutually suspicious set of insecurities. He does gain something: the esteem of other men who find such an acquisition impressive.

Some men do get a sexual charge from a woman's objective "beauty," just as some women feel sexual pleasure at the thought of a man's money or power. But it is often a status high, a form of exhibitionism, that draws its power from the man imagining his buddies imagining him doing what he is doing while he does it. Some men feel a sexual thrill upon smelling the leather interior of a new Mercedes-Benz. It is not that that thrill is not real, but that it is based on the meaning assigned by other men to that leather. It is no deep psychosexual attachment to leather itself. There is certainly a reflexive—not instinctive—male response to the cold economy of the beauty myth; but that can be completely separated from sexual attraction, the warm dialogue of desire.

When men are more aroused by symbols of sexuality than by the sexuality of women themselves, they are fetishists. Fetishism treats a part as if it were the whole; men who choose a lover on the basis of her "beauty" alone are treating the woman as a fetish—that is, treating a part of her, her visual image, not even her skin, as if it were her sexual self. Freud suggests that the fetish is a talisman against the failure to perform.

The woman's value as a fetish lies in the way her "beauty" gives him status in the eyes of other men. So when a man has sex with a woman whom he has chosen for her impersonal beauty alone, there are many people in the room with him, but she is not among them. These relationships disappoint both because both must live in public to get that constant, recharging affirmation of the woman's high exchange value. But sexual relationships always go back to private space, where the beauty, as tediously human as any other woman, makes the stubborn mistake of asking to be known.

Some men by now cannot respond to anything but the Iron Maiden. A writing professor says that every year, when he assigns an essay on media imagery, young women write about their lovers' having expressed disappointment that the women don't look like those in pornography. If some men have come to "need" beauty pornography—Binet did simple experiments that proved that when sexual imagery was preceded by an image of a boot, he was able to create a sexual response to a boot—it is because the stimulus-response imprinting took place in the best of lab conditions: the ignorance that society tries to maintain in men about female sexuality.

So even those women who take men's beauty pornography to heart and try, and even succeed, in looking like it, are doomed to disappointment. Men who read it don't do so because they want *women* who look like that. The attraction of what they are holding is that it is *not* a woman, but a two-dimensional woman-shaped blank. The appeal of the material is not the fantasy that the model will come to life; it is precisely that she will not, ever. Her coming to life would ruin the vision. It is not about life.

Ideal beauty is ideal because it does not exist: The action lies in the gap between desire and gratification. Women are not perfect beauties without distance. That space, in a consumer culture, is a lucrative one. The beauty myth moves for men as a mirage; its power lies in its ever-receding nature. When the gap is closed, the lover embraces only his own disillusion.

The myth actually undermines sexual attraction. Attraction is a dialogue or dance or high-wire balancing act that depends on the unique qualities, memories, patterns of desire, of the two people involved; "beauty" is generic. Attraction is about a sexual fit: two people imagining how they will work together.

"Beauty" is only visual, more real on film or in stone than in three living dimensions. The visual is the sense monopolized by advertisers, who can manipulate it much better than can mere human beings. But with other senses, advertising is at a disadvantage: Humans can smell, taste, touch, and sound far better than the best advertisement. So humans, in order to become dependable, sexually insecure consumers, had to be trained away from these other, more sensual senses. One needs distance, even in the bedroom, to get a really good look; other senses are more intoxicating close up. "Beauty" leaves out smell, physical response, sounds, rhythm, chemistry, texture, fit, in favor of a portrait on a pillow.

The shape and weight and texture and feel of bodies is crucial to pleasure but the appealing body will not be identical. The Iron

Maiden is mass-produced. The world of attraction grows blander and colder as everyone, first women and soon men, begin to look alike. People lose one another as more masks are assumed. Cues are missed.

Sadly, the signals that allow men and women to find the partners who most please them are scrambled by the sexual insecurity initiated by beauty thinking. A woman who is self-conscious can't relax to let her sensuality come into play. If she is hungry she will be tense. If she is "done up" she will be on the alert for her reflection in his eyes. If she is ashamed of her body, its movement will be stilled. If she does not feel entitled to claim attention, she will not demand the airspace to shine in. If his field of vision has been boxed in by "beauty"—a box continually shrinking—he simply will not see her, his real love, standing right before him.

CHRISTIAN LACROIX GIVES WOMEN BACK THEIR FEMININITY, reads the fashion headline. "Femininity" is code for femaleness plus whatever a society happens to be selling. If "femininity" means female sexuality and its loveliness, women never lost it and do not need to buy it back. Wherever we feel pleasure, all women have "good" bodies. We do not have to spend money and go hungry and struggle and study to become sensual; we always were. We need not believe we must somehow *earn* good erotic care; we always deserved it.

Femaleness and its sexuality are beautiful. Women have long secretly suspected as much. In that sexuality, women are physically beautiful already; superb; breathtaking.

Many, many men see this way too. A man who wants to define himself as a real lover of women admires what shows of her past on a woman's face, before she ever saw him, and the adventures and stresses that her body has undergone, the scars of trauma, the changes of childbirth, her distinguishing characteristics, the light in her expression. The number of men who already see in this way is far greater than the arbiters of mass culture would lead us to believe, since the story they need to tell ends with the opposite moral.

The Big Lie is the notion that if a lie is big enough, people will believe it. The idea that adult women, with their fully developed array of sexual characteristics, are inadequate to stimulate and gratify heterosexual male desire, and that "beauty" is what will complete them, is the beauty myth's Big Lie. All around us, men are contradicting it. The fact is that the myth's version of sexuality is by definition just not true: Most men who are at this moment being aroused by women, flirting with them, in love with them, dreaming about them, having crushes on them, or making love to them, are doing so to women who look exactly like who they are.

The myth stereotyped sexuality into cartoons by representation: At one extreme, called "male," and reinforced by classic pornography, is anonymity, repetition, and dehumanization. At the other extreme, the "female," sexual desire is not something split off but suffusing all of life, not confined to the genitals, but flowing over the whole body; it is personal, tactile, and sensitizing.

These poles are not biological. Women raised free are doubtless more genital, healthily selfish, and aggressively curious about men's bodies than the female extreme allows; men raised free are probably more emotionally involved, vulnerable, healthily giving, and sensual over their entire bodies than the male extreme allows. Sexual beauty is an equal portion that belongs to both men and women, and the capacity to be dazzled is gender-blind. When men and women look at one another beyond the beauty myth, it will bring greater eroticism between the sexes as well as greater honesty. We are not as sexually incomprehensible to one another as we are meant right now to believe.

# Hunger

*I saw the best minds of my generation destroyed by madness, starving. . . .*

—*Allen Ginsberg,* "Howl"

*There is* a disease spreading. It taps on the shoulder America's firstborn sons, its best and brightest. At its touch, they turn away from food. Their bones swell out from receding flesh. Shadows invade their faces. They walk slowly, with the effort of old men. A white spittle forms on their lips. They can swallow only pellets of bread, and a little thin milk. First tens, then hundreds, then thousands, until, among the most affluent families, one young son in five is stricken. Many are hospitalized, many die.

The boys of the ghetto die young, and America has lived with that. But these boys are the golden ones to whom the reins of the world are to be lightly tossed: the captain of the Princeton football team, the head of the Berkeley debating club, the editor of the *Harvard Crimson*. Then a quarter of the Dartmouth rugby team falls ill; then a third of the initiates of Yale's secret societies. The heirs, the cream, the fresh delegates to the nation's forum selectively waste away.

The American disease spreads eastward. It strikes young men at the Sorbonne, in London's Inns of Court, in the administration of The Hague, in the Bourse, in the offices of *Die Zeit*, in the universities of Edinburgh and Tübingen and Salamanca. They grow thin and still more thin. They can hardly speak aloud. They lose their libido, and can no longer make the effort to joke or argue. When they run or swim, they look appalling: buttocks collapsed, tailbones protruding, knees knocked together, ribs splayed in a shelf that stretches their papery skin. There is no medical reason.

The disease mutates again. Across America, it becomes apparent that for every well-born living skeleton there are at least three other young men, also bright lights, who do something just as strange. Once they have swallowed their steaks and Rhine wine, they hide away, to thrust their fingers down their throats and spew out all the nourishment in them. They wander back into Maury's or "21," shaking and pale. Eventually they arrange their lives so they can spend hours each day hunched over like that, their highly trained minds telescoped around two shameful holes: mouth, toilet; toilet, mouth.

Meanwhile, people are waiting for them to take up their places: assistantships at *The New York Times*, seats on the stock exchange, clerkships with federal judges. Speeches need to be written and briefs researched among the clangor of gavels and the whir of fax machines. What is happening to the fine young men, in their brush cuts and khaki trousers? It hurts to look at them. At the expense-account lunches, they hide their medallions of veal under lettuce leaves. Secretly they purge. They vomit after matriculation banquets and after tailgate parties at the Game. The men's room in the Oyster Bar reeks with it. One in five, on the campuses that speak their own names proudest.

How would America react to the mass self-immolation by hunger of its favorite sons? How would Western Europe absorb the export of such a disease? One would expect an emergency response: crisis task forces convened in congressional hearing rooms, unscheduled alumni meetings, the best experts money can hire, cover stories in newsmagazines, a flurry of editorials, blame and counterblame, bulletins, warnings, symptoms, updates; an epidemic blazoned in boldface red. The sons of privilege *are* the future; the future is committing suicide.

Of course, this is actually happening right now, only with a gender difference. The institutions that shelter and promote these diseases are hibernating. The public conscience is fast asleep. Young women are dying from institutional catatonia: four hundred dollars a term from the college endowment for the women's center to teach "self-help"; fifty to buy a noontime talk from a visiting clinician. The world is not coming to an end because the cherished child in five who "chooses" to die slowly is a girl. And she is merely doing too well what she is expected to do very well in the best of times.

Up to one tenth of all young American women, up to one fifth of women students in the United States, are locked into one-woman hunger camps. When they fall, there are no memorial services, no intervention through awareness programs, no formal message from their schools and colleges that the society prefers its young women to eat and thrive rather than sicken and die. Flags are not lowered in recognition of the fact that in every black-robed ceremonial marches a fifth column of death's-heads.

Virginia Woolf in *A Room of One's Own* had a vision that someday young women would have access to the rich forbidden libraries of the men's colleges, their sunken lawns, their vellum, the claret light. She believed that would give young women a mental freedom that must have seemed all the sweeter from where she imagined it: the wrong side of the beadle's staff that had driven her away from the library because she was female. Now young women have pushed past the staff that barred Woolf's way. Striding across the grassy quadrangles that she could only write about, they are halted by an immaterial barrier she did not foresee. Their minds are proving well able; their bodies self-destruct.

When she envisaged a future for young women in the universities, Woolf's prescience faltered only from insufficient cynicism. Without it one could hardly conceive of the modern solution of the recently all-male schools and colleges to the problem of women: They admitted their minds, and let their bodies go. Young women learned that they could not live inside those gates and also inside their bodies.

The weight-loss cult recruits women from an early age, and eating diseases are the cult's bequest. Anorexia and bulimia are female maladies: From 90 to 95 percent of anorexics and bulimics are women. America, which has the greatest number of women who have made it into the male sphere, also leads the world with female anorexia. Women's magazines report that there are up to a million American anorexics, but the American Anorexia and Bulimia Association states that anorexia and bulimia strike a million American women *every year;* 30,000, it reports, also becomes emetic abusers.

Each year, according to the association, 150,000 American women die of anorexia. If so, every twelve months there are 17,024 more deaths in the United States alone than the total number of deaths from AIDS tabulated by the World Health Organization in 177 countries and territories from the beginning of the epidemic until the end of 1988; if so, more die of anorexia in the United States each year than died in ten years of civil war in Beirut. Beirut has long been front-page news. As criminally neglectful as media coverage of the AIDS epidemic has been, it still dwarfs that of anorexia; so it appears that the bedrock question—why must Western women go hungry—is one too dangerous to ask even in the face of a death toll such as this.

Joan Jacobs Brumberg in *Fasting Girls: The Emergence of Anorexia Nervosa as a Modern Disease* puts the number of anorexics at 5 to 10 percent of all American girls and women. On some college campuses, she believes, one woman student in five is anorexic. The number of women with the disease has increased dramatically throughout the Western world starting twenty years ago. Dr. Charles A. Murkovsky of Gracie Square Hospital in New York City, an eating diseases specialist, says that 20 percent of American college women binge and purge on a regular basis. Kim Chernin in *The Hungry Self* suggests that at least half the women on campuses in the United States suffer at some time from bulimia or anorexia. Roberta Pollack Seid in *Never Too Thin* agrees with the 5- to 10-percent figure for anorexia among young American women, adding that up to six times that figure on campuses are bulimic. If we take the high end of the figures, it means that of ten young American women in college, two will be anorexic and six will be bulimic; only two will be well. The norm, then, for young, middle-class American women, is to be a sufferer from some form of the eating disease.

The disease is a deadly one. Brumberg reports that 5 to 15 percent of hospitalized anorexics die in treatment, giving the disease one of the highest fatality rates for a mental illness. *The New York Times* cites the same fatality rate. Researcher L.K.G. Hsu gives a death rate of up to 19 percent. Forty to 50 percent of anorexics never recover completely, a worse rate of recovery from starvation than the 66 percent recovery rate for famine victims hospitalized in the war-torn Netherlands in 1944–45.

The medical effects of anorexia include hypothermia, edema, hypotension, bradycardia (impaired heartbeat), lanugo (growth of body hair), infertility, and death. The medical effects of bulimia include dehydration, electrolyte imbalance, epileptic seizure, abnormal heart rhythm, and death. When the two are combined, they can result in tooth erosion, hiatal hernia, abraded esophagus, kidney failure, osteoporosis, and death. Medical literature is starting to report that babies and children underfed by weight-conscious mothers are suffering from stunted growth, delayed puberty, and failure to thrive.

It is spreading to other industrialized nations: The United Kingdom now has 3.5 million anorexics or bulimics (95 percent of them female), with 6,000 new cases yearly. Another study of adolescent British girls alone shows that 1 percent are now anorexic. According to the women's press, at least 50 percent of British women suffer from disordered eating. Hilde Bruch states that in the last generation, larger patient groups have been reported in publications in Russia, Australia, Sweden, and Italy as well as Great Britain and the United States. Sweden's rate is now 1 to 2 percent of teenage girls, with the same percentage of women over sixteen being bulimic. The rate for the Netherlands is 1 to 2 percent; of Italian teenagers also, 1 percent suffer from anorexia or bulimia (95 percent of them female), a rise of 400 percent in ten years. That is just the beginning for Western Europe and Japan, since the figures resemble numbers for the United States ten years ago, and since the rate is rising, as it did in America, exponentially. The anorexic patient herself is *thinner* now than were previous generations of patients. Anorexia followed the familiar beauty myth pattern of movement: It began as a middle-class disease in the United States and has spread eastward as well as down the social ladder.

Some women's magazines report that 60 percent of American women have serious trouble eating. The majority of middle-class women in the United States, it appears, suffer a version of anorexia or bulimia; but if anorexia is defined as a compulsive fear of and fixation upon food, perhaps most Western women can be called, twenty years into the backlash, mental anorexics.

What happened? Why now? The first obvious clue is the progressive chiseling away of the Iron Maiden's body over this century of female emancipation, in reaction to it. Until seventy-five years ago in the male artistic tradition of the West, women's natural amplitude was their beauty; representations of the female nude reveled in women's lush fertility. Various distributions of sexual fat were emphasized according to fashion—big, ripe bellies from the fifteenth to the seventeenth centuries, plump faces and shoulders in the early nineteenth, progressively generous dimpled buttocks and thighs until the twentieth—but never, until women's emancipation entered law, this absolute negation of the female state that fashion historian Ann Hollander in *Seeing Through Clothes* characterizes, from the point of view of any age but our own, as "the look of sickness, the look of poverty, and the look of nervous exhaustion."

Dieting and thinness began to be female preoccupations when Western women received the vote around 1920; between 1918 and 1925, "the rapidity with which the new, linear form replaced the more curvaceous one is startling." In the regressive 1950s, women's natural fullness could be briefly enjoyed once more because their minds were occupied in domestic seclusion. But when women came en masse into male spheres, that pleasure had to be overridden by an urgent social expedient that would make women's bodies into the prisons that their homes no longer were.

A generation ago, the average model weighed 8 percent less than the average American woman, whereas today she weighs 23 percent less. Twiggy appeared in the pages of *Vogue* in 1965, simultaneous with the advent of the Pill, to cancel out its most radical implications. Like many beauty-myth symbols, she was double-edged, suggesting to women the freedom from the constraint of reproduction of earlier generations (since female fat is categorically understood by the subconscious as fertile sexuality), while reassuring men with her suggestion of female weakness, asexuality, and hunger. Her thinness, now commonplace, was shocking at the time; even *Vogue* introduced the model with anxiety: "'Twiggy' is called Twiggy because she looks as though a strong gale would snap her in two and dash her to the ground . . . Twiggy is of such a meagre constitution that other models stare at her. Her legs look as though she has not had enough milk as a baby and her face has that expression one feels Londoners wore in the blitz." The fashion writer's language is revealing: Under-nurtured, subject to being overpowered by a strong wind, her expression the daze of the besieged, what better symbol to reassure an establishment faced with women who were soon to march tens of thousands strong down Fifth Avenue?

In the twenty years after the start of the second wave of the women's movement, the weight of Miss Americas plummeted, and the average weight of Playboy Playmates dropped from 11 percent below the national average in 1970 to 17 percent below it in eight years. Model Aimee Liu in her autobiography claims that many models are anorexic; she herself continued to model as an anorexic. Of dancers, 38 percent show anorexic behavior. The average model, dancer, or actress is thinner than 95 percent of the female population. The Iron Maiden put the shape of a near skeleton and the texture of men's musculature where the shape and feel of a woman used to be, and the small elite corps of women whose bodies are used to reproduce the Iron Maiden often become diseased themselves in order to do so.

As a result, a 1985 survey says, 90 percent of respondents think they weigh too much. On any day, 25 percent of women are on diets, with 50 percent finishing, breaking, or starting one. This self-hatred was generated rapidly, coinciding with the women's movement: Between 1966 and 1969, two studies showed, the number of high school girls who thought they were too fat had risen from 50 to 80 percent. Though heiresses to the gains of the women's movement, their daughters are, in terms of this distress, no better off: In a recent study of high school girls, 53 percent were unhappy with their bodies by age thirteen; by age eighteen and over, 78 percent were dissatisfied. The hunger cult has on a major victory against women's fight for equality if the evidence of the 1984 *Glamour* survey of thirty-three thousand women is representative: 75 percent of those aged eighteen to thirty-five believed they were fat, while only 25 percent were medically overweight (the same percentage as men); 45 percent of the *underweight* women thought they were too fat. But more heartbreaking in terms of the way in which the myth is running to ground hopes for women's advancement and gratification, the

*Glamour* respondents chose losing ten to fifteen pounds above success in work or in love as their most desired goal.

Those ten to fifteen pounds, which have become a fulcrum, if these figures are indicative, of most Western women's sense of self, are the medium of what I call the One Stone Solution. One stone, the British measurement of fourteen pounds, is roughly what stands between the 50 percent of women who are not over-weight who believe they are and their ideal self. That one stone, once lost, puts these women well below the weight that is natural to them, and beautiful, if we saw with eyes unconstrained by the Iron Maiden. But the body quickly restores itself, and the cycle of gain and loss begins, with its train of torment and its risk of dis-ease, becoming a fixation of the woman's consciousness. The in-evitable cycles of failure ensured by the One Stone Solution create and continually reinforce in women our uniquely modern neurosis. This great weight-shift bestowed on women, just when we were free to begin to forget them, new versions of low self-esteem, loss of control, and sexual shame. It is a genuinely ele-gant fulfillment of a collective wish: By simply dropping the official weight one stone below most women's natural level, and redefining a woman's womanly shape as by definition "too fat," a wave of self-hatred swept over First World women, a reactionary psychology was perfected, and a major industry was born. It suavely countered the historical groundswell of female success with a mass conviction of female failure, a failure defined as im-plicit in womanhood itself.

The proof that the One Stone Solution is political lies in what women feel when they eat "too much": guilt. Why should guilt be the operative emotion, and female fat be a moral issue articula-ted with words like good and bad? If our culture's fixation on female fatness or thinness were about sex, it would be a private issue between a woman and her lover; if it were about health, between a woman and herself. Public debate would be far more hysterically focused on male fat than on female, since more men (40 percent) are medically overweight than women (32 percent) and too much fat is far more dangerous for men than for women. In fact, "there is very little evidence to support the claim that fatness causes poor health among women. . . . The results of re-cent studies have suggested that women may in fact live longer and be generally healthier if they weigh ten to fifteen percent *above* the life-insurance figures *and* they refrain from dieting," asserts *Radiance;* when poor health is correlated to fatness in women, it is due to chronic dieting and the emotional stress of self-hatred. The National Institutes of Health studies that linked obesity to heart disease and stroke were based on male subjects; when a study of females was finally published in 1990, it showed that weight made only a fraction of the difference for women that it made for men. The film *The Famine Within* cites a sixteen-country study that fails to correlate fatness to ill health. Female fat is not in itself unhealthy.

But female fat is the subject of public passion, and women feel guilty about female fat, because we implicitly recognize that under the myth, women's bodies are not our own but society's, and that thinness is not a private aesthetic, but hunger a social concession exacted by the community. A cultural fixation on female thinness is not an obsession about female beauty but an obsession about female obedience. Women's dieting has become what Yale psychologist Judith Rodin calls a "normative obsession," a never-ending passion play given international coverage out of all proportion to the health risks associated with obesity, and using emotive language that does not figure even in discussions of alcohol or tobacco abuse. The nations seize with compulsive attention on this melodrama because women and men understand that it is not about cholesterol or heart rate or the disruption of a line of tailoring, but about how much social freedom women are going to get away with or concede. The media's convulsive analysis of the endless saga of female fat and the battle to vanquish it are actually bulletins of the sex war: what women are gaining or losing in it, and how fast.

The great weight shift must be understood as one of the major historical developments of the century, a direct solution to the dangers posed by the women's movement and economic and reproductive freedom. Dieting is the most potent political sedative in women's history; a quietly mad population is a tractable one. Researchers S. C. Wooley and O. W. Wooley confirmed what most women know too well—that concern with weight leads to "a virtual collapse of self-esteem and sense of effectiveness." Researchers J. Polivy and C. P. Herman found that "prolonged and periodic caloric restriction" resulted in a distinctive personality whose traits are "passivity, anxiety and emotionality."

*It is those traits, and not thinness for its own sake, that the dominant culture wants to create in the private sense of self of recently liberated women in order to cancel out the dangers of their liberation.*

Women's advances had begun to give them the opposite traits—high self-esteem, a sense of effectiveness, activity, courage, and clarity of mind. "Prolonged and periodic caloric restriction" is a means to take the teeth out of this revolution. The great weight shift and its One Stone Solution followed the rebirth of feminism so that women just reaching for power would become weak, preoccupied, and, as it evolved, mentally ill in useful ways and in astonishing proportions. To understand how the gaunt toughness of the Iron Maiden has managed spectacularly to roll back women's advances toward equality, we have to see that what is really at stake is not fashion or beauty or sex, but a struggle over political hegemony that has become—for women, who are often unaware of the real issues behind our predicament—one of life and death.

Theories abound to explain anorexia, bulimia, and the modern thinning of the feminine. Ann Hollander proposes that the shift from portraiture to moving images made thinness suggestive of motion and speed. Susie Orbach in *Fat Is a Feminist Issue* "reads" women's fat as a statement to the mother about separation and dependence; she sees in the mother "a terrible ambivalence about feeding and nurturing" her daughter. Kim Chernin in the *The Obsession* gives a psychoanalytic reading of fear of fat as based on infantile rage against the all-powerful mother, and sees food as the primordial breast, the "lost world" of female abundance that we must recover "if we are to understand the heartland of our obsession with the female body. . . . We can understand how," Chernin writes, "in a frenzy of terror and dread, [a man] might be tempted to spin out fashionable images of [a woman] that tell her implicitly that she is unacceptable . . . when she is large." In *The Hungry Self*, Chernin interprets bulimia as a religious rite of passage. Joan Jacobs Brumberg sees food as a symbolic language, anorexia as a cry of confusion in a world of too many choices, and "the appetite as voice": "young women searching for an idiom in which to say things about themselves focused on food and styles of eating." Rudolph Bell in *Holy Anorexia* relates the disease to the religious impulses of medieval nuns, seeing starvation as purification.

Theories such as these are enlightening within a private context; but they do not go far enough. Women do not eat or starve only in a succession of private relationships, but within a public social order that has a material vested interest in their troubles with eating. Individual men don't "spin out fashionable images" (indeed, research keeps proving that they are warm to women's real shapes and unmoved by the Iron Maiden); multinational corporations do that. The many theories about women's food crises have stressed private psychology *to the neglect of* public policy, looking at women's shapes to see how they express a conflict about their society rather than looking at how their society makes use of a manufactured conflict with women's shapes. Many other theories have focused on women's reaction to the thin ideal, but have not asserted that the thin ideal is *proactive*, a preemptive strike.

We need to reexamine all the terms again, then, in the light of a public agenda. What, first, is food? Certainly, within the context of the intimate family, food is love, and memory, and language. But in the public realm, food is status and honor.

Food is the primal symbol of social worth. Whom a society values, it feeds well. The piled plate, the choicest cut, say: We think you're worth this much of the tribe's resources. Samoan women, who are held in high esteem, exaggerate how much they eat on feast days. Publicly apportioning food is about determining power relations, and sharing it is about cementing social equality: When men break bread together, or toast the queen, or slaughter for one another the fatted calf, they've become equals and then allies. The word *companion* comes from the Latin for "with" and "bread"—those who break bread together.

But under the beauty myth, now that all women's eating is a public issue, our portions testify to and reinforce our sense of social inferiority. If women cannot eat the same food as men, we cannot experience equal status in the community. As long as women are asked to bring a self-denying mentality to the communal table, it will never be round, men and women seated together; but the same traditional hierarchical dais, with a folding table for women at the foot.

In the current epidemic of rich Western women who cannot "choose" to eat, we see the continuation of an older, poorer tradition of women's relation to food. Modern Western female dieting descends from a long history. Women have always had to eat differently from men: less and worse. In Hellenistic Rome, reports classicist Sarah B. Pomeroy, boys were rationed sixteen measures of meal to twelve measures allotted to girls. In medieval France, according to historian John Boswell, women received two thirds of the grain allocated to men. Throughout history, when there is only so much to eat, women get little, or none: A common explanation among anthropologists for female infanticide is that food shortage provokes it. According to UN publications, where hunger goes, women meet it first: In Bangladesh and Botswana, female infants die more frequently than male, and girls are more often malnourished, because they are given smaller portions. In Turkey, India, Pakistan, North Africa, and the Middle East, men get the lion's share of what food there is, regardless of women's caloric needs. "It is not the caloric value of work which is represented in the patterns of food consumption" of men in relation to women in North Africa, "nor is it a question of physiological needs. . . . Rather these patterns tend to guarantee priority rights to the 'important' members of society, that is, adult men." In Morocco, if women are guests, "they will swear they have eaten already" or that they are not hungry. "Small girls soon learn to offer their share to visitors, to refuse meat and deny hunger." A North African woman described by anthropologist Vanessa Mahler assured her fellow diners that "she preferred bones to meat." Men, however, Mahler reports, "are supposed to be exempt from facing scarcity which is shared out among women and children."

"Third World countries provide examples of undernourished female and well-nourished male children, where what food there is goes to the boys of the family," a UN report testifies. Two thirds of women in Asia, half of all women in Africa, and a sixth of Latin American women are anemic—through lack of food. Fifty percent more Nepali women than men go blind from lack of food. Cross-culturally, men receive hot meals, more protein, and the first helpings of a dish, while women eat the cooling leftovers, often having to use deceit and cunning to get enough to eat. "Moreover, what food they do receive is consistently less nutritious."

This pattern is not restricted to the Third World: Most Western women alive today can recall versions of it at their mothers' or grandmothers' table: British miners' wives eating the grease-soaked bread left over after their husbands had eaten the meat; Italian and Jewish wives taking the part of the bird no one else would want.

These patterns of behavior are standard in the affluent West today, perpetuated by the culture of female caloric self-deprivation. A generation ago, the justification for this traditional apportioning shifted: Women still went without, ate leftovers, hoarded food, used deceit to get it—but blamed themselves. Our mothers still exiled themselves from the family circle that was eating cake with silver cutlery off Wedgwood china, and we would come upon them in the kitchen, furtively devouring the remains. The traditional pattern was cloaked in modern shame, but otherwise changed little. Weight control became its rationale once natural inferiority went out of fashion.

The affluent West is merely carrying on this traditional apportioning. Researchers found that parents in the United States urged boys to eat, regardless of their weight, while they did so with daughters only if they were relatively thin. In a sample of babies of both sexes, 99 percent of the boys were breast-fed, but only 66 percent of the girls, who were given 50 percent less time to feed. "Thus," writes Susie Orbach, "daughters are often fed less well, less attentively and less sensitively than they need." Women do not feel entitled to enough food because they have been taught to go with less than they need since birth, in a tradition passed down through an endless line of mothers; the public role of "honored guest" is new to us, and the culture is telling us through the ideology of caloric restriction that we are not welcome finally to occupy it.

What, then, is fat? Fat is portrayed in the literature of the myth as expendable female filth; virtually cancerous matter, an inert or treacherous infiltration into the body of nauseating bulk waste. The demonic characterizations of a simple body substance do not arise from its physical properties but from old-fashioned

misogyny, for above all fat is female; it is the medium and reg-
ulator of female sexual characteristics.

Cross-culturally, from birth, girls have 10–15 percent more fat
than boys. At puberty, male fat-to-muscle ratio decreases as the
female ratio increases. The increased fat ratio in adolescent girls is
the medium for sexual maturation and fertility. The average
healthy twenty-year-old female is made of 28.7 percent body fat.
By middle age, women cross-culturally are 38 percent body fat:
This is, contrary to the rhetoric of the myth, "not unique to the
industrialized advanced Western nations. They are norms characteristic of the female of the species." A moderately active
woman's caloric needs, again in contradiction to a central tenet of
the myth, are only 250 calories less than a moderately active
man's (2,250 to 2,500), or two ounces of cheese. Weight gain with
age is also normal cross-culturally for both sexes. The body is evidently programmed to weigh a certain amount, which weight the
body defends.

Fat is sexual in women; Victorians called it affectionately their
"silken layer." The leanness of the Iron Maiden impairs female
sexuality. One fifth of women who exercise to shape their bodies
have menstrual irregularities and diminished fertility. The body
of the model, remember, is 22 to 23 percent leaner than that of
the average woman; the average woman wants to be as lean as the
model; infertility and hormone imbalance are common among
women whose fat-to-lean ratio falls below 22 percent. Hormonal
imbalances promote ovarian and endometrial cancer and osteoporosis. Fat tissues store sex hormones, so low fat reserves are
linked with weak estrogens and low levels of all the other important sex hormones, as well as with inactive ovaries. Rose E.
Frisch in *Scientific American* refers to the fatness of Stone Age fertility figures, saying that "this historical linking of fatness and fertility actually makes biological sense" since fat regulates
reproduction. Underweight women double their risk of low-birthweight babies.

Fat is not just fertility in women, but desire. Researchers at
Michael Reese Hospital in Chicago found that plumper women
desired sex more often than thinner women. On scales of erotic
excitability and readiness, they outscored thin women by a factor
of almost two to one. To ask women to become unnaturally thin

is to ask them to relinquish their sexuality: "Studies consistently show that with dietary deprivation, sexual interests dissipate." Subjects of one experiment stopped masturbating or having sexual fantasies at 1,700 calories a day, 500 more than the Beverly Hills Diet. Starvation affects the endocrine glands; amenorrhea and delayed puberty are common features in starving women and girls; starved men lose their libido and become impotent, sometimes developing breasts. Loyola University's Sexual Dysfunction Clinic reports that weight-loss disorders have a far worse effect on female sexuality than do weight-gaining disorders; the heavier women were eager for courtship and sex, while anorexics "were so concerned with their bodies that they had fewer sexual fantasies, fewer dates, and less desire for sex." The *New England Journal of Medicine* reports that intense exercisers lose interest in sex. Joan Jacobs Brumberg agrees that "clinical materials suggest an absence of sexual activity on the part of anorexics." Pleasure in sex, Mette Bergstrom writes, "is rare for a bulimic because of a strong body hatred." "The evidence seems to suggest," writes Roberta Pollack Seid, "and common sense would confirm, that a hungry, undernourished animal is less, not more, interested in the pleasures of the flesh."

What, finally, is dieting? "Dieting," and, in Great Britain, "slimming," are trivializing words for what is in fact self-inflicted semistarvation. In India, one of the poorest countries in the world, the very poorest women eat 1,400 calories a day, or 600 more than a Western woman on the Hilton Head Diet. "Quite simply," writes Seid, dieters "are reacting the way victims of semi-starvation react . . . semi-starvation, even if caused by self-imposed diets, produces startlingly similar effects on all human beings."

The range of repulsive and pathetic behaviors exhibited by women touched by food diseases is portrayed as quintessentially feminine, proof positive of women's irrationality (replacing the conviction of menstrual irrationality that had to be abandoned when women were needed for the full-time work force). In a classic study done at the University of Minnesota, thirty-six volunteers were placed on an extended low-calorie diet and "the psychological, behavioral and physical effects were carefully documented." The subjects were young and healthy, showing "high levels of ego strength, emotional stability, and good intellectual ability." They "began a six-month period . . . in which their food intake was reduced by half—a typical weight reduction technique for women.

"After losing approximately 25% of their original body weight, pervasive effects of semistarvation were seen." The subjects "became increasingly preoccupied with food and eating, to the extent that they ruminated obsessively about meals and food, collected recipes and cookbooks, and showed abnormal food rituals, such as excessively slow eating and hoarding of food related objects." Then, the majority "suffered some form of emotional disturbance as a result of semistarvation, including depression, hypochondriasis, hysteria, angry outbursts, and, in some cases, psychotic levels of disorganization." Then, they "lost their ability to function in work and social contexts, due to apathy, reduced energy and alertness, social isolation, and decreased sexual interest." Finally, "within weeks of reducing their food intake," they "reported relentless hunger, as well as powerful urges to break dietary rules. Some succumbed to eating binges, followed by vomiting and feelings of self-reproach. Ravenous hunger persisted, even following large meals during refeeding." Some of the subjects "found themselves eating continuously, while others engaged in uncontrollable cycles of gorging and vomiting." The volunteers "became terrified of going outside the experiment environment where they would be tempted by the foods they had agreed not to eat . . . when they did succumb, they made hysterical, half-crazed confessions." They became irritable, tense, fatigued, and full of vague complaints. "Like fugitives, [they] could not shed the feeling they were being shadowed by a sinister force." For some, doctors eventually had to prescribe tranquilizers.

The subjects were a group of completely normal healthy college men.

During the great famine that began in May 1940 during the German occupation of the Netherlands, the Dutch authorities maintained rations at between 600 and 1,600 calories a day, or what they characterized as the level of semistarvation. The worst sufferers were defined as starving when they had lost 25 percent of their body weight, and were given precious supplements. Photos taken of clothed starving Dutch women are striking for how preternaturally modern they look.

At 600–1,600 calories daily, the Dutch suffered semistarvation; the Diet Centers' diet is fixed at 1,600 calories. When they had lost 25 percent of their body weight, the Dutch were given crisis food supplementation. The average healthy woman has to lose almost exactly as much to fit the Iron Maiden. In the Lodz Ghetto in 1941, besieged Jews were allotted starvation rations of 500–1200 calories a day. At Treblinka, 900 calories was scientifically determined to be the minimum necessary to sustain human functioning. At "the nation's top weight-loss clinics," where "patients" are treated for up to a year, the rations are the same.

The psychological effects of self-inflicted semistarvation are identical to those of involuntary semistarvation. By 1980 more and more researchers were acknowledging the considerable emotional and physical consequences of chronic dieting, including "symptoms such as irritability, poor concentration, anxiety, depression, apathy, lability of mood, fatigue and social isolation." Magnus Pyke, describing the Dutch famine, writes that "starvation is known to affect people's minds and these people in Holland became mentally listless, apathetic and constantly obsessed with thoughts of food." Bruch notes that with involuntary progressive semistarvation, "there is a coarsening of emotions, sensitivity and other human traits." Robert Jay Lifton found that World War II victims of starvation "experienced feelings of guilt over having done something bad for which they are now being punished, and dreams and fantasies of food of every kind in limitless amounts." Starving destroys individuality; "anorexic patients," like others who starve, asserts Hilde Bruch, "exhibited remarkably uniform behavior and emotional patterns until they gained some weight." "Food deprivation," Roberta Pollack Seid sums it up, "triggers food obsessions for both physical and psychological reasons. . . . undernourishment produces lassitude, depression and irritability. Body metabolism slows down. . . . And hunger drives the hungry person to obsess about food." The psychological terror of hunger is cross-cultural: Orphans adopted from poor countries cannot control their compulsion to smuggle and hide food, sometimes even after living for years in a secure environment.

Authoritative evidence is mounting that eating diseases are

caused mainly by dieting. Ilana Attie and J. Brooks-Gunn quote investigators who found "chronic, restrained eating" to "constitute a cumulative stress of such magnitude that dieting itself may be 'a sufficient condition for the development of anorexia nervosa or bulimia.'" Roberta Pollack Seid reaches the same conclusion. "Ironically, dieting . . . itself may provoke obsessive behaviour and binge-eating. It may indeed *cause* both eating disorders and obesity itself." Sustained caloric deprivation appears to be a severe shock to the body that it remembers with destructive consequences. Seid writes that "women's problems with food seem to stem . . . from their effort to get an ultra-lean body. . . . The only way 95% can get it is by putting themselves on deprivatory diets." Attie and Brooks-Gunn concur: "Much of the behavior thought to cause anorexia nervosa and bulimia may actually be a consequence of starvation. . . . The normal weight dieter who diets to look and feel thin also is vulnerable to disturbed emotional, cognitive and behavioral patterns by virtue of the constant stress of trying to stay below the body's 'natural' or biologically regulated weight." Dieting and fashionable thinness make women seriously unwell.

Now, if female fat is sexuality and reproductive power; if food is honor; if dieting is semistarvation; if women have to lose 23 percent of their body weight to fit the Iron Maiden and chronic psychological disruption sets in at a body weight loss of 25 percent; if semistarvation is physically and psychologically debilitating, and female strength, sexuality, and self-respect pose the threats explored earlier against the vested interests of society; if women's journalism is sponsored by a $33-billion industry whose capital is made out of the political fear of women; then we can understand why the Iron Maiden is so thin. The thin "ideal" is not beautiful aesthetically; she is beautiful as a political solution.

The compulsion to imitate her is not something trivial that women choose freely to do to ourselves. It is something serious being done to us to safeguard political power. Seen in this light, it is inconceivable that women would not have to be compelled to grow thin at this point in our history.

The ideology of semistarvation undoes feminism; what happens to women's bodies happens to our minds. If women's bodies are and have always been wrong whereas men's are right, then women are wrong and men are right. Where feminism taught women to put a higher value on ourselves, hunger teaches us how to erode our self-esteem. If a woman can be made to say, "I hate my fat thighs," it is a way she has been made to hate femaleness. The more financially independent, in control of events, educated and sexually autonomous women become in the world, the more impoverished, out of control, foolish, and sexually insecure we are asked to feel in our bodies.

Hunger makes women feel poor and think poor. A wealthy woman on a diet feels physically at the mercy of a scarcity economy; the rare woman who makes $100,000 a year has a bodily income of 1,000 calories a day. Hunger makes successful women feel like failures: An architect learns that her work crumbles; a politician who oversees a long-range vision is returned to the details, to add up every bite; a woman who can afford to travel can't "afford" rich foreign foods. It undermines each experience of control, economic security, and leadership that women have had only a generation to learn to enjoy. Those who were so recently freed to think beyond the basics are driven, with this psychology, back to the feminine mental yoke of economic dependence: fixation on getting sustenance and safety. Virginia Woolf believed that "one cannot think well, sleep well, love well if one has not dined well." "The lamp in the spine does not light on beef and prunes," she wrote, contrasting the dispiriting food of poverty, of the hard-pressed women's colleges with that of the rich men's colleges, the "soles sunk in a deep dish, over which the college cook has spread a counterpane of the whitest cream." Now that some women at last have achieved the equivalent of £500 a year and a room of their own, it is back once more to four ounces of boiled beef and three unsweetened prunes, and the unlit lamp.

The anorexic may begin her journey defiant, but from the point of view of a male-dominated society, she ends up as the perfect woman. She is weak, sexless, and voiceless, and can only with difficulty focus on a world beyond her plate. The woman has been killed off in her. She is almost not there. Seeing her like this, unwomaned, it makes crystalline sense that a half-conscious but virulent mass movement of the imagination created the vital lie of skeletal female beauty. A future in which industrialized nations are peopled with anorexia-driven women is one of few conceivable that would save the current distribution of wealth and power from the claims made on it by women's struggle for equality.

For theorists of anorexia to focus on the individual woman, even within her family, misses the tactical heart of this struggle. Economic and political retaliation against female appetite is far stronger at this point than family dynamics.

This can no longer be explained as a private issue. If suddenly 60 to 80 percent of college women can't eat, it's hard to believe that suddenly 60 to 80 percent of their families are dysfunctional in this particular way. There is a disease in the air; its cause was generated with intent; and young women are catching it.

Just as the thin Iron Maiden is not actually beautiful, anorexia, bulimia, even compulsive eating, symbolically understood, are not actually diseases. They *begin*, as Susie Orbach notes, as sane and mentally healthy responses to an insane social reality: that most women can feel good about themselves only in a state of permanent semistarvation. The anorexic refuses to let the official cycle master her: By starving, she masters it. A bulimic may recognize the madness of the hunger cult, its built-in defeat, its denial of pleasure. A mentally healthy person will resist having to choose between food and sexuality—sexuality being bought, today, by maintenance of the official body. By vomiting, she gets around the masochistic choice. Eating diseases are often interpreted as symptomatic of a neurotic need for control. But surely it is a sign of mental health to try to control something that is trying to control you, especially if you are a lone young woman and it is a massive industry fueled by the needs of an entire determined world order. Self-defense is the right plea when it comes to eating disasters; not insanity. Self-defense bears no stigma, whereas madness is a shame.

Victorian female hysteria, mysterious at the time, makes sense now that we see it in the light of the social pressures of sexual self-denial and incarceration in the home. Anorexia should be as simple to understand. What hysteria was to the nineteenth-century fetish of the asexual woman locked in the home, anorexia is to the late-twentieth-century fetish of the hungry woman.

Anorexia is spreading because it works. Not only does it solve the dilemma of the young woman faced with the hunger cult, it also protects her from street harassment and sexual coercion; construction workers leave walking skeletons alone. Having no fat means having no breasts, thighs, hips, or ass, which for once means not having asked for it. Women's magazines tell women they *can* control their bodies; but women's experiences of sexual harassment make them feel they *cannot* control what their bodies are said to provoke. Our culture gives a young woman only two dreams in which to imagine her body, like a coin with two faces: one pornographic, the other anorexic; the first for nighttime, the second for day—the one, supposedly, for men and the other for other women. She does not have the choice to refuse to toss it— nor, yet, to demand a better dream. The anorexic body is sexually safer to inhabit than the pornographic.

At the same time, it works for male-dominated institutions by processing women smoothly, unwomaned, into positions closer to power. It is "trickling down" to women of all social classes from elitist schools and universities because that is where women are getting too close to authority. There, it is emblematic of how hunger checkmates power in any woman's life: Hundreds of thousands of well-educated young women, living and studying at the fulcrum of cultural influence, are causing no trouble. The anorexic woman student, like the anti-Semitic Jew and the self-hating black, fits in. She is politically castrate, with exactly enough energy to do her schoolwork, neatly and completely, and to run around the indoor track in eternal circles. She has no energy to get angry or get organized, to chase sex, to yell through a bullhorn, asking for money for night buses or for women's studies programs or to know where all the women professors are. Administering a coed class half full of mentally anorexic women is an experience distinct from that of administering a class half full of healthy, confident young women. The woman in these women canceled out, it is closer to the administration of young men only, which was how things were comfortably managed before.

For women to stay at the official extreme of the weight spectrum requires 95 percent of us to infantilize or rigidify to some degree our mental lives. The beauty of thinness lies not in what it does to the body but to the mind, since *it is not female thinness that is prized, but female hunger, with thinness merely symptomatic*. Hunger attractively narrows the focus of a mind that has "let itself go."

Babies cannot feed themselves; invalids and the orthodox require special diets. Dieting makes women think of ourselves as sick, religious babies. Only this new mystique could prove strong and deep-reaching enough to take on the work given up by domestic isolation and enforced chastity. "Natural" is a word that is rightly challenged. But if there is a most natural urge, it is to satisfy hunger. If there is a natural female shape, it is the one in which women are sexual and fertile and *not always thinking about it*. To maintain hunger where food is available, as Western women are doing, is to submit to a life state as unnatural as anything with which the species has come up yet. It is more bizarre than cannibalism.

Dieting is the essence of contemporary femininity. Denying oneself food is seen as good in a woman, bad in a man. For women, the Austin (Texas) Stress Clinic found, "dieting concern" was strongly related to "positive feminine traits"; for men, food restraint was related to "socially undesirable femininity." Where the feminine woman of the Feminine Mystique denied herself gratification in the world, the current successful and "mature" model of femininity submits to a life of self-denial in her body.

But this hallmark of enviable adjustment has as little innate validity as the earlier one. It too is based upon a vital lie. Where "immature" women in the 1950s wanted clitoral orgasms while "mature" ones passively yielded, today oral desire is interpreted in a similar sexual code. It is considered immature for women to eat heartily, since they're told they risk their sexuality; they are seen as mature if they starve, promised to win sexuality that way. In the 1970s, when clitoral pleasure was reclaimed, many women must have wondered how they had lived in an atmosphere that denied it. In the 1980s women were forced to deny their tongues and mouths and lips and bellies. In the 1990s, if women can reclaim the pleasure of appetite, we may wonder what possessed us during the long, mean, pointless years of hunger. Women's self-denial where food is concerned is represented today as good for her mate and even better for herself. Beyond the beauty myth, feminine hunger will look as obviously destructive to the well-being of women and their loved ones as their earlier enforced suffocation in the home looks to us from here.

Sex, food, and flesh; it is only political ideology—not health, not men's desires, not any law of loveliness—that keeps women from believing we can have all three. Young women believe what they have no memory to question, that they may not have sex, food, and flesh in any abundance; that those three terms cancel each other out.

## Dead Easy

It is dead easy to become an anorexic. When I was twelve I went to visit an older, voluptuous cousin. "I try," she said, to explain the deep-breathing exercises she did before bedtime, "to visualize my belly as something I can love and accept and live with." Still compact in a one-piece kid's body, I was alarmed to think that womanhood involved breaking apart into pieces that floated around, since my cousin seemed to be trying to hold herself together by a feat of concentration. It was not a comforting thought. The buds of my breasts hurt already. As she did her exercises, I leafed through a copy of *Cosmopolitan*, which had an article demonstrating to women how to undress and pose and move in bed with their partners so as to disguise their fatness.

My cousin looked me over. "Do you know how much you weigh?" No, I told her. "Why don't you just hop on the scale?" I could feel how much my cousin wished to inhabit a simple, slight twelve-year-old body. That could only mean, I thought, that when I was a woman, I would want to get out of my own body into some little kid's.

A year later, while bent over the drinking fountain in the hall of my junior high school, Bobby Werner, whom I hardly knew, gave me a hard poke in the soft part of my stomach, just below the navel. It would be a decade before I would remember that he was the class fat boy.

That evening I let the juice of the lamb chop congeal on my plate. I could see viscous nodules of fat, a charred outer edge of yellow matter, cooling from liquid to solid, marked USDA CHOICE in edible blue dye. The center bone, serrated, had been cloven with a powerful rotary blade. I felt a new feeling, a nausea wicked with the pleasure of loathing. Rising hungry from the table, a jet of self-righteousness lit up under my esophagus, intoxicating me. All night long I inhaled it.

The next day I passed the small notepad kept by the dishwasher. I knew what it said, though it was my mother's and private: "½ grpfruit. Blk. coff. 4 Wheat Thins. 1 Popsicle." A black scrawl: "*binge.*" I wanted to tear it up. Some memoir.

I had no more patience for the trivial confessions of women. I could taste from my mouth that my body had entered ketosis, imbalanced electrolytes—good. The girl stood on the burning deck. I put the dishes in the sink with a crash of declaration.

At thirteen, I was taking in the caloric equivalent of the food energy available to the famine victims of the siege of Paris. I did my schoolwork diligently and kept quiet in the classroom. I was a wind-up obedience toy. Not a teacher or principal or guidance counselor confronted me with an objection to my evident deportation in stages from the land of the living.

There were many starving girls in my junior high school, and every one was a teacher's paragon. We were allowed to come and go, racking up gold stars, as our hair fell out in fistfuls and the pads flattened behind the sockets of our eyes. When our eyeballs moved, we felt the resistance. They allowed us to haul our bones around the swinging rope in gym class, where nothing but the force of an exhausted will stood between the ceiling, to which we clung with hands so wasted the jute seemed to abrade the cartilage itself, and the polished wooden floor thirty-five feet below.

An alien voice took mine over. I have never been so soft-spoken. It lost expression and timbre and sank to a monotone, a dull murmur the opposite of strident. My teachers approved of me. They saw nothing wrong with what I was doing, and I could swear they looked straight at me. My school had stopped dissecting alleycats, since it was considered inhumane. There was no interference in my self-directed science experiment: to find out just how little food could keep a human body alive.

The dreams I could muster were none of the adolescent visions that boys have, or free and healthy girls; no fantasies of sex or escape, rebellion or future success. All the space I had for dreaming was taken up by food. When I lay on my bed, in that posture of adolescent reverie, I could find no comfort. My bones pressed sharply into the mattress. My ribs were hooks and my spine a dull blade and my hunger a heavy shield, all I had to stave off the trivialities that would attach themselves like parasites to my body the minute it made a misstep into the world of women. My doctor put his hand on my stomach and said he could feel my spine. I turned an eye cold with loathing on women who evidently lacked the mettle to suffer as I was suffering.

I made a drawing: myself, small, small, curled in a sort of burrow, surrounded by nesting materials, with a store of nuts and raisins, protected. This smallness and hiddenness was what I craved at the time of life when Stephen Dedalus longed to burst like a meteor on the world. What did that drawing mean? It was not a longing to return to the womb, but to return to my body. I was not longing to be safe from the choices of the world, but from the obligation to enter into a combat in which I could only believe if I forgot all about myself, and submitted to starting again dumber, like someone hit hard on the back of the head.

I'd have to forget they were my friends and believe they were really my enemies: the other playground gamblers of jacks, my fellow thieves of Pepsi-flavored lip gloss: Gemma and Stacey and Kim, who used to stand beside me in a row in the dark master bedroom, staring into the mirror. Our chins lit up from below by a candle, we chanted, scared rigid, *We're not afraid of Bloody Mary*. I knew that if I let myself fall forward into time, I would never be able to stand like that again: shoulder to shoulder before the one mirror, with the ghoul on the far side of the glass; nothing in ourselves, nothing in each other.

Adolescent starvation was, for me, a prolonged reluctance to be born into woman if that meant assuming a station of beauty. Children resist being baffled with convention, and often see social madness in full dimensions. In seventh grade, we knew what was coming, and we all went berserk with cogent fear; not a normal craziness of adolescence, but panic at what unnaturally loomed. Like a life-sized game of Mother May I, we knew that beauty was going to say, "Freeze," and wherever we were, that would be it.

"We learned the truth at seventeen," mourned a song that was popular that year, "that love was meant for beauty queens." We traded new bathing suits, and ruined them, and swore we wouldn't forgive the borrower. When Gemma and Kim mooned at

Stacey's Polaroid, Kim said, "Oh, don't worry about the picture, you were closer to the camera." Gemma twisted her neck in front of the mirror, looking for the horrible truth, while Kim wondered how her mother's words came out of her own brain.

Confiding Julie, the first to get breasts, was cynical by Thanksgiving. Since no one else looked like the class slut, she was given the position, and she soon capitulated. She bleached her hair with Sun In, and started to mess around with boys who played in garage rock bands. Marianne, because she had long legs and a stem neck, rushed from school to her pliés at the barre, her hair in a bun, her head held high, to arch and sweep and bow toward the mirror until night fell. Cara delivered her audition piece flat, but since she had a wheat-colored rope of braid that brushed her waist, she would be Titania in the school play. Emily, blunt-nosed and loud, could outact Cara in her sleep; when she saw the cast list she turned silently to her best friend, who handed her a box of milk chocolate creams. Tall, strong, bony Evvy watched Elise try out her maddening dimple. She cornered her outside class to ask her if she thought she was cute. Elise said yes, and Evvy threw a pipette of acid, stolen from the biology lab, in her face. Dodie hated her tight black hair that wouldn't grow. She crept up behind blond Karen in home ec class and hacked out a fistful with pinking shears. Even Karen understood that it wasn't personal.

The things we saw women doing for beauty looked crazy. I wanted to travel, but I saw that beauty led women in circles. My mother, a beautiful woman, got too little of the pleasures that I could understand. I saw that her beauty hurt her: teeth-gritting abstinence at celebration dinners, fury on the scale, angry rub-downs, self-accusing photographs posted over the refrigerator. She'd won—why wasn't that enough? It would be nice to be beautiful like her, I figured, sure; but nothing about it seemed nice enough to make up for that endless degradation.

Anorexia was the only way I could see to keep the dignity in my body that I had had as a kid, and that I would lose as a woman. It was the only choice that really looked like one: By refusing to put on a woman's body and receive a rating, I chose not to have all my future choices confined to little things, and not to have the choices made for me, on the basis of something meaningless to me, in the larger things. But as time went on, my choices grew smaller and smaller. Beef bouillion or hot water with lemon? The bouillion had twenty calories—I'd take the water. The lemon had four; I could live without it. Just.

Now, when I can bring myself to think of that time at all—another blackout, by beauty, of the cities of memory—my sadness can't shake off the rage that follows it close behind. To whom do I petition for that lost year? How many inches in height did I lose from having calcium withheld from my bones, their osteoblasts struggling without nourishment to multiply? How many years sooner will a brittle spine bend my neck down? In the Kafkaesque departments of this bureau of hunger, which charged me guilty for a crime no more specific than inhabiting a female body, what door do I knock upon? Who is obliged to make reparations to me for the thought abandoned, the energy never found, the explorations never considered? Who owes me for the year-long occupation of a mind at the time of its most urgent growth?

In our interpretation of the damages done by the beauty myth, it is not yet possible to lay blame anywhere but on oneself. I can say finally, for myself at least: at thirteen, to starve half to death? Not guilty. Not that child. There is certainly a charge of guilt to be made, long overdue. But it doesn't belong to me. It belongs somewhere, and to something, else.

The youngest victims, from earliest childhood, learn to starve and vomit from the overwhelmingly powerful message of our culture, which I found no amount of parental love and support strong enough to override. I knew my parents wanted me not to starve because they loved me; but their love contradicted the message of the larger world, which wanted me to starve in order to love me. It is the larger world's messages, young women know, to which they will have to listen if they are to leave their parents' protection. I kept a wetted finger up to the winds of that larger world: Too thin yet? I was asking it. What about now? No? Now?

The larger world never gives girls the message that their bodies are valuable simply because they are inside them. Until our culture tells young girls that they are welcome in any shape—that women are valuable to it with or without the excuse of "beauty"—girls will continue to starve. And institutional messages then reward young women's education in hunger. But when the lesson has been taken too dangerously to heart, they ignore the consequences, reinforcing the disease. Anorexics want to be saved; but they cannot trust individual counselors, family members, or friends; that is too uncertain. They are walking question marks challenging—pleading—with schools, universities, and the other mouthpieces that transmit what is culturally acceptable in women, to tell them unequivocally: This is intolerable. This is unacceptable. We don't starve women here. We value women. By turning an indifferent eye to the ravages of the backlash among their young women, schools and universities are killing off America's daughters; and Europe is learning to do the same to its own. You don't need to die to count as a casualty. An anorexic cannot properly be called alive. To be anorexic is to keep a close daily tally of a slow death; to be a member of the walking undead.

Since institutions are treating this epidemic as one of those embarrassing feminine things imported into the cloister like tampon dispensers or commoner's gowns worn over skirts, there is no formal mourning. Women students are kept from openly recognizing what they privately know is going on around them. They are not permitted to claim this epidemic as real, and deadly, and taking place beside and inside them. So they have to repress horrifying knowledge, or trivialize it, or blame the sufferer. Another one sickens. Another disappears. Another one bites the dust.

In college, we never had a chance to mourn for Sally. Dressed like a tatty rag doll, in faded ginghams and eyelet lace, she wore a peacock feather in an old hat. She kept her round kwashiorkor belly politely hidden and her vicious intelligence sheathed, but she was able to shred an argument into so much cotton wool and negligently hold up a conclusion sharp as quartz. Her small voice would come to a flat halt and her lips press whitely together. At parties she'd lean back her flossy head, so much too big for her body, to get the leverage to bang it again and again into the nearest wall; her brain loosened for comfort, she would dance like a Halloween creepie, waving her disjointed limbs. It was a campus set piece: "Play something good for Sally to dance to."

She left suddenly. Her roommates had to pack her things up after her: the postage scales for weighing the day's half bread roll;

the fifteen-pound hand weights; the essay of devastating clarity left on her desk half-finished.

When I was told her strength had run out, I remembered one bright blue afternoon in autumn, when a group of students came out of a classroom, arguing, high on words. She dropped her books with a crash. Flinging back her shoulders, from which her sweater hung letting in great pockets of icy air, she turned in a slow pirouette, and leaped right up into the knot of the group. A boy caught her before she fell, and offered her to me, wriggling like a troublesome baby.

I held her between my forearms without strain. She'd made it. She had escaped gravity. Her limbs were as light as hollow birch branches, the scrolls of their bark whole, but the marrow crumbled, the sap gone brittle. I folded her up easily, because there was nothing to her.

Bundles of twigs, bones in worn-soled Nikes, slapping forward into a relentless weather; the young women cast shadows of Javanese stick-puppets, huge-headed, disappearing in a sideways light. Dry-mouthed like the old, unsteady, they head home on swollen knees while it is still morning.

Nothing justifies comparison with the Holocaust; but when confronted with a vast number of emaciated bodies starved not by nature but by men, one must notice a certain resemblance. The starving body cannot know it is middle-class. The imprisoned body cannot tell that it is considered free. The experience of living in a severely anorexic body, even if that body is housed in an affluent suburb, is the experience of a body living in Bergen-Belsen—if we imagine for the Belsen inmate a 40-percent chance of imprisonment forever and a 15-percent chance of death. These experiences are closer to one another than either is to that of a middle-class body that is not in prison in the affluent First World. Though I am trying to avoid the imagery of death camps, it returns. These young women weigh no more than the bodies documented in the archives of what is legitimately called Hell. They have, at their sickest, no more to eat; and they have no choice. For an unknown reason that must be physiological, at a certain point in their starvation they lose the ability to stop starving, the choice to eat. Finally—as is seldom acknowledged—they are

hungry; I was hungry every conscious moment; I was hungry in
my sleep.

Women must claim anorexia as political damage done to us by
a social order that considers our destruction insignificant because
of what we are—less. We should identify it as Jews identify the
death camps, as homosexuals identify AIDS: as a disgrace that is
not our own, but that of an inhumane social order.

Anorexia is a prison camp. One fifth of well-educated American young women are inmates. Susie Orbach compared anorexia
to the hunger strikes of political prisoners, particularly the suffragists. But the time for metaphors is behind us. To be anorexic
or bulimic *is* to be a political prisoner.

## The Third Wave: Frozen in Motion

If we look at most young women's inert relationship to feminism,
we can see that with anorexia and bulimia, the beauty myth is
winning its offensive. Where are the women activists of the new
generation, the fresh blood to infuse energy into second-wave
burnout and exhaustion? Why are so many so quiet? On campuses, up to a fifth of them are so quiet because they are starving
to death. Starving people are notorious for a lack of organizational
enthusiasm. Roughly another 50 percent are overcome with a
time-devouring and shameful addiction to puking their guts out in
the latrines of the major centers of higher learning. The same
young women who would seem to be its heiresses are not taking
up the banner of the women's movement for perhaps no more
profound reason than that many of them are too physically ill to
do much more than cope with immediate personal demands. And
on a mental level, the epidemic of eating disorders may affect
women of this generation in such a way as to make feminism
seem viscerally unconvincing: Being a woman is evidently nothing to be up in arms about; it makes you hungry, weak, and sick.

Beyond this are other succession problems generated by the
myth. Young women inherited twenty years of the propagandizing
caricature of the Ugly Feminist, so—"I'm feminine, not a feminist," says a college senior in a *Time* magazine report; "I picture a

feminist as someone who is masculine and doesn't shave her
legs." Too many young women do not realize that others pictured
"a feminist" in that way so that they would be sure to respond as
this one does. Others, alarmingly, blame the women's movement
for the beauty backlash against it—"Kathryn," a twenty-five-year-
old quoted by Sylvia Ann Hewlett, describes a party at her law
firm: "I often resent . . . the way women's liberation has increased the expectations of men": Twenty years ago, she complains, a young male lawyer would want to arrive with "a drop-
dead blonde" on his arm, whereas today he and and his colleagues compete to escort the highest achiever—"the only catch
was that these yuppie women had to look every bit as glamorous
as the drop-dead blondes of the past." Finally, the myth seeks to
discourage all young women from identifying with earlier feminists—simply because these are older women. Men grant themselves tradition to hand down through the generations; women are
permitted only fashion which each season renders obsolete. Under that construct, the link between generations of women is
weakened by definition: What came before is rarely held up for
admiration as history or heritage, but derided by fashion's rigid
rule as embarrassingly démodé.

To share a meal with a young woman of the present generation, you have to be prepared to witness signs of grave illness.
You ignore her frantic scanning of the menu, the meticulous way
she scrapes the sauce. If she drinks five glasses of water and sucks
and chews the ice, you mustn't comment. You look away if she
starts to ferret a breadstick into her pocket, and ignore her reck-
less agitation at the appearance of the pastry tray, her long shame-
faced absence after the meal, before the coffee. "Are you okay?"
"I'm *fine*." How dare you ask.

When you share the bill, you haven't shared a meal. The always renewed debate that young people of each generation take
for granted, about how to change the world to suit their vision, is
not going to be renewed for women over a table such as this. The
pastry cart comes first; its gilt handles tower over you, blocking
out the landscape. The world will have to wait. That's how it
works.

There is no villain lurking by the cash register. No visible
enemy has done this to you two; there's only your waiter, and the

block-print tablecloths, the blackboard with the daily menu, the ice bucket full of melting cubes, the discreet hallway that leads to the bathroom with its sliding bolt. Evil, said Hannah Arendt, is banal. But the work is done anyway, and it looks as if it has been done by your own hands. You claim your coats and step outside and part ways, having talked nothing new whatever into life.

Young girls and women are seriously weakened by inheriting the general fallout of two decades of the beauty myth's backlash. But other factors compound these pressures on young women so intensely that the surprise is not how many do have eating diseases, but that any at all do not.

Girls and young women are also starving because the women's movement changed educational institutions and the workplace enough to make them admit women, but not yet enough to change the maleness of power itself. Women in "coeducational" schools and colleges are still isolated from one another, and admitted as men manqué. Women's studies are kept on the margins of the curriculum, and fewer than 5 percent of professors are women, the worldview taught young women is male. The pressure on them is to conform themselves to the masculine atmosphere. Separated from their mothers, young women on campus have few older role models who are not male; how can they learn how to love their bodies? The main images of women given them to admire and emulate are not of impressive, wise older women, but of girls their own age or younger, who are not respected for their minds. Physically, these universities are ordered for men or unwomaned women. They are overhung with oil portraits of men; engraved with the rolling names of men; designed, like the Yale Club in New York, which for twenty years after women were admitted had no women's changing room, for men. They are not lit for women who want to escape rape; at Yale, campus police maps showing the most dangerous street corners for rape were allegedly kept from the student body so as not to alarm parents. The colleges are only marginally concerned with the things that happen to women's bodies that do not happen to the bodies of the men. Women students sense this institutional wish that the problems of their female bodies would just fade away; responding, the bodies themselves fade away.

Added to this isolation and lack of recognition is the unprecedented level of expectation placed on ambitious young women. Older women, in some ways, explored the best of both gender roles: They grew up as women and fought their way into the masculine work force. They learned to affirm the values of women and master the work of men. They are doubly strong. Young women have been doubly weakened: Raised to compete like men in rigid male-model institutions, they must also maintain to the last detail an impeccable femininity. Gender roles, for this generation of women, did not harmonize so much as double: Young women today are expected to act like "real men" and look like "real women." Fathers transferred to daughters the expectations of achievement once reserved for sons; but the burden to be a beauty, inherited from the mothers, was not lightened in response.

Ceremonies of achievement play out this conflict: Meant to initiate young people into a new level of power or expertise, those ceremonies summon an unfeminine emotion—pride. But with each rite of passage through these institutions, payment is exacted from the young woman in the form of "beauty"; placating and flattering to men in power, it is required at these times as proof that she does not mean anything too serious by winning this diploma or this promotion. On one hand, here again the powerful stress the beauty myth so as to neutralize the achievement of the women involved; on the other, women do homage to the myth at such moments in request for its protection, a talisman that will let them get to the next stage unpunished.

In the 1950s, "domesticity" was what mitigated these moments of achievement. As a Listerine ad put it: "What was the diploma compared to those precious sparkling rings Babs and Beth were wearing?" Today "beauty" does the same work: "Only fifteen days until Becky's graduation. I want her to be proud of me too. . . . Alba makes your diet a sweet success." In a Johnnie Walker ad, it takes two high-fashion models to muse that "he thinks it's fine for me to make more than he does." *The New York Times* cites a woman whose boyfriend gave her breast implants for completing her doctorate. A current trend in the United States is for graduating daughters to get breast implant surgery while boys get the traditional grand tour of Europe. The most brilliant female students on campus are often the closest to full starvation.

Women are having breast surgery, liposuction, rhinoplasty, not only as rewards for attaining power—doctorates, inheritances, bat mitzvahs—they are also having these things, and being asked to have them, as antidotes for their having attained this power.

This sacrificial impulse is religious, to propitiate the gods before undertaking the next stage of a journey. And the gods are thirsty; they are asking to be propitiated. "Boys, that's all," said the administrator preparing Rhodes Scholarship interviewees at Yale. "Girls, please stay a few moments for pointers on clothes, posture, and makeup." At the interview luncheon, when boys were asked, "How do you plan to save the world from itself?" a girl was asked, "How do you manage to keep your lovely figure?"

Achievement ceremonies are revealing about the need of the powerful to punish women through beauty, since the tension of having to repress alarm at female achievement is unusually formalized in them. Beauty myth insults tend to be blurted out at them like death jokes at a funeral. Memories of these achievement ceremonies are supposed to last like Polaroid snapshots that gel into permanent colors, souvenirs to keep of a hard race run; but for girls and young women, the myth keeps those colors always liquid so that, with a word, they can be smeared into the uniform shades of mud.

At my college graduation, the commencement speaker, Dick Cavett—who had been a "brother" of the university president in an all-male secret society—was confronted by two thousand young female Yale graduates in mortarboards and academic gowns, and offered them this story: When he was at Yale there were no women. The women went to Vassar. There, they had nude photographs taken in gym class to check their posture. Some of the photos ended up in the pornography black market in New Haven. The punch line: The photos found no buyers.

Whether or not the slur was deliberate, it was still effective: We may have been Elis but we would still not make pornography worth his buying. Today, three thousand men of the class of 1984 are sure they are graduates of that university, remembering commencement as they are meant to: proudly. But many of the two thousand women, when they can think of that day at all, recall the feelings of the powerless: exclusion and shame and impotent, complicit silence. We could not make a scene, as it was our parents' great day for which they had traveled long distances; neither could they, out of the same concern for us.

The sun steamed through the rain, the microphone crackled, the mud churned, we sat still, all wrong, under our hot polyester gowns. The speaker had transposed us for a moment out of the gentle quadrangle, where we had been led to believe we were cherished, and into the tawdry district four blocks away where stolen photographs of our naked bodies would find no buyers. Waiting for the parchment that honored our minds, we were returned with reluctant confusion to our bodies, which we had just been told were worthless. Unable to sit still for the rest of the speeches unless we split our minds, being applauded, from our bodies, being derided, we did so. We wanted the honor, we deserved it. The honor and derision came at the same time from the same podium. We shifted in our seats.

We paid the price asked of us. With moments like that to live through, the unreal-sounding statistics of young women's eating diseases begin to come clear. A split like that makes one nauseous. The pride of four years' hard work and struggle was snatched back from us at the moment we reached for it, and returned to us fouled. There was the taste of someone else's bile in our mouths.

The pressure of beauty pornography and the pressures of achievement combine to strike young women where they are most vulnerable: in their exploration of their sexuality in relation to their sense of their own worth. Beauty pornography makes an eating disease seem inevitable, even desirable, if a young woman is to consider herself sexual and valuable: Robin Lakoff and Raquel Scherr in *Face Value* found in 1984 that "among college women, 'modern' definitions of beauty—health, energy, self-confidence"—prevailed. "The bad news" is that they all had "only one overriding concern: the shape and weight of their bodies. They all wanted to lose 5–25 pounds, even though most [were] not remotely overweight. They went into great detail about every flaw in their anatomies, and told of the great disgust they felt every time they looked in the mirror." The "great disgust" they feel comes from learning the rigid conventions of beauty pornography before they learn their own sexual value; in such an atmosphere, eating diseases make perfect sense.

## The Anorexic/Pornographic Generation

When women of different ages do have the rare opportunity to talk, the gap between older women and those of the anorexic/ pornographic generations causes grave mistranslations. "This is what I say to get their attention," says Betty Friedan of her college audiences.

> "How many of you have ever worn a girdle?" And they laugh. Then I say . . . "It used to be that being a woman in the United States meant that . . . you encased your flesh in rigid plastic casing that made it difficult to breathe and difficult to move, but you weren't supposed to notice that. You didn't ask why you wore the girdle, and you weren't supposed to notice red welts on your belly when you took it off at night." And then I say, "How can I expect you to know what it felt like when you have never worn anything under your blue jeans except panty hose, or little bikinis?" That gets to them. Then I explain how far we've come, where we are now, and why they have to start saying, "I am a feminist."

For many young women in Friedan's audience, the girdle is made of their own flesh. They can't take it off at night. The "little bikinis" have not brought this generation heedless bodily freedom; they have become props that superimpose upon the young women chic pseudosexual scenarios that place new limits on what they can think, how they can move, and what they can eat. The backlash does to young women's minds, so much more free, potentially, than any ever before, what corsets and girdles and gates on universities no longer can. The post-1960 daughter sees more images of impossibly "beautiful" women engaged in "sexual" posturing in one day than her mother saw throughout adolescence: She needs to be shown more if she is to know her place. By saturation in imagery, the potential explosiveness of this generation is safely defused.

Young women born after 1960 have been made ill enough from having seen little representation of sexuality apart from beauty pornography. But they are not as ill as the generation who were children in the 1970s; those even younger women arè sick almost to death. And the daughters of the eighties?

"Preadolescent dieting has increased 'exponentially' in recent years. . . . We know that dieting is rampant in the fourth and fifth grades," reports Vivian Meehan, president of the National Association of Anorexia Nervosa and Associated Disorders. In a survey of 494 middle-class schoolgirls in San Francisco, more than half described themselves as overweight, while only 15 percent were so by medical standards. Thirty-one percent of nine-year-olds thought they were too fat, and 81 percent of the ten-year-olds were dieters. A 1989 article in *The New York Times*, titled "Babes in Makeup Land," describes a new marketing drive of cosmetics for little girls, six-year-olds "painted to the hilt"; one doll, Li'l Miss Makeup, "resembles a girl that's 5 or 6 years old" who, when cold water is painted on, "springs eyebrows, colored eyelids, fingernails, tinted lips and a heart-shaped beauty mark."

These little girls, born around the time of Ronald Reagan's first election, are showing third-generation mutations from the beauty backlash against the women's movement. They are born with a congenital deformity: They lack childhoods. This generation will have even more trouble with life in the body than do daughters of the 1960s and 1970s. Born to compete, they will from their earliest memories associate femaleness with deprivation. Hunger is already being eroticized for today's little girls as an entry into adult sexuality. For a contemporary seven-year-old, to climb onto a scale and to exclaim with horror is as much a ritual of femininity, inextricable from the promise of sexual gratification, as my generation's posing provocatively on high heels in front of mirrors, and of my mother's generation dressing dolls in white satin. If they start dieting at seven and don't have sex until their mid-teens, it will already be too late: They will have spent over half their lives learning masochism in preparation for sexual gratification. They will have had little chance to build up memories of erotic life in the Edenic, undivided, pleasure-seeking, satisfied child's body. They will be learning masochism as they learn sexuality, and will enter a long, insecure adolescence, besieged by further messages of beauty as masochism, unprotected by the integrity of a sexual core innocent of pain.

## Off the Road

The protection of chaperons left behind, the protection of sexual
integrity not yet fully claimed, young women are vulnerable in
brand-new ways. They do have greater leeway to move unaccom-
panied through the world than ever before; but that, ironically,
has created still another new use for eating disorders.

The old claustrophobia has a new irritant, more chafing than
ever. The young girl knows, more than her mother could at her
age, what it is she is missing; she has had a taste. In Christina
Rossetti's poem "Goblin Market," one sister, who did not taste
forbidden fruit, stayed whole. The other took one sip of sweetness and found it addictive. She needed more, she needed to glut
herself, or she would waste away.

The threat of sexual danger makes the girl's body a landscape
on which she must project the outer world that now closes in.
This house arrest of adolescence brings dreams of quest and exploration to a barren awakening. Marrakesh, Malabar, the Spice
Islands, fantasies of discovery collapse, and she learns to put a dot
of highlighter in the center of her upper lip. Her adventures must
be restricted to those in which she can safely be looked at, because the really good adventures will expose her to being looked
at to disastrous effect. Where her male peers go On the Road, she
and the golden shackle of her "beauty" have to turn off it.

As an adolescent, she realizes with mounting horror that they
were not kidding: For her to walk alone will be a fraught activity
forever. Anorexia, bulimia, and exercise fixations work off and
numb the frustration of the claustrophobia that accompanies the
girl's grieving realization that the wide world she had imagined,
and just inherited, is shut down to her by the threat of sexual
violence.

If she were to eat, she would have energy; but adolescence is
arranged for the safe venting of masculine steam. From athletic
events to sexual conquests to a moody walk in the woods, boys
have outlets for that agitation of waiting to fly. But if a girl has her
full measure of wanderlust, libido, and curiosity, she is in a bad
way. With ample stores of sugar to set off the buzz for intellectual
exploration, starch to convert into restlessness in her elongating

legs, fat to fuel her sexual curiosity, and the fearlessness born from a lack of concern over where her next meal will come from— she will get in trouble.

What if she doesn't worry about her body and eats enough for all the growing she has to do? She might rip her stockings and slam-dance on a forged ID to the Pogues, and walk home barefoot, holding her shoes, alone at dawn; she might baby-sit in a battered-women's shelter one night a month; she might skateboard down Lombard Street with its seven hairpin turns, or fall in love with her best friend and do something about it, or lose herself for hours gazing into test tubes with her hair a mess, or climb a promontory with the girls and get drunk at the top, or sit down when the Pledge of Allegiance says stand, or hop a freight train, or take lovers without telling her last name, or run away to sea. She might revel in all the freedoms that seem so trivial to those who could take them for granted; she might dream seriously the dreams that seem so obvious to those who grew up with them really available. Who knows what she would do? Who knows what it would feel like?

But if she *is not careful* she will end up: raped, pregnant, impossible to control, or merely what is now called fat. The teenage girl knows this. Everyone is telling her to be careful. She learns that making her body into her landscape to tame is preferable to any kind of wildness.

Dieting is being careful, and checking into a hunger camp offers the ultimate in care.

# *Violence*

*H*unger makes women's bodies hurt them, and makes women hurt their bodies. Studies of abusers show that violence, once begun, escalates. Cosmetic surgery is the fastest-growing "medical" specialty. More than two million Americans, at least 87 percent of them female, had undergone it by 1988, a figure that had tripled in two years. Throughout the 1980s, as women gained power, unprecedented numbers of them sought out and submitted to the knife. Why surgery? Why now?

From the beginning of their history until just before the 1960s, women's gender caused them pain. Because of puerperal fever and childbed complications, giving birth was cruelly painful until the invention of chloroform in 1860, and mortally dangerous until the advent of antisepsis in the 1880s. Afterward, sex still carried the risk of an illegal abortion, with its dangers of hemorrhage, perforated uterus, and death by blood poisoning. "Labor"

218

for women has meant childbirth, so that work, sex, love, pain, and death, over the centuries, intertwined into a living knot at the center of female consciousness: Love hurt, sex could kill, a woman's painful labor was a labor of love. What would be masochism in a man has meant survival for a woman.

Sex began to lose its sting in 1965, when in the case of *Griswold* v. *Connecticut* the U.S. Supreme Court legalized the sale of contraceptives and the Pill was widely prescribed. It hurt even less from the late 1960s until the late 1980s, when safe abortion was legalized in most Western countries. As women entered the paid work force and lost their dependence on sexual barter for survival, it hurt less still. Changing social mores and the women's movement's championing of female sexuality began to make it imaginable that the pleasure their sex gave women might finally and forever outweigh the pain. The strands of sex and pain in women at last began to separate.

In the strange new absence of female pain, the myth put beauty in its place. For as far back as women could remember, something had hurt about being female. As of a generation ago, that became less and less true. But neither women nor the masculine social order could adapt so abruptly to a present in which femaleness was not characterized and defined by pain. Today, what hurts is beauty.

Many women took on this new version of pain exacted by beauty stoically because freedom from sexual pain left a gap in female identity. Women were expected, and expected themselves, to conform to freedom effortlessly, with superhuman resilience. But freedom is not learned easily overnight. One generation is not long enough to forget five millennia of learning how to bear being hurt. If a woman's sexual sense of self has centered on pain as far back as the record goes, who is she without it? If suffering is beauty and beauty is love, she cannot be sure she will be loved if she does not suffer. It is hard, because of such conditioning, to envisage a female body free of pain and still desirable.

Even aside from the biological pain of women's gender, modern women are just recovering from our long experience of man-made punishment for pleasure. The Greek lawmaker Solon ruled that an unmarried woman caught in a sexual act could be sold into slavery; the emperor Constantine decreed that a virgin who had willingly fornicated must be burned (her penalty was lighter if she had been raped); death was the price a free woman paid for making love with a slave. The laws of Romulus gave a husband the right to kill his adulterous wife. Adulteresses in modern Saudi Arabia are stoned to death. Resistance to the abortifacient pill RU428 derives partly from its relative painlessness. Antiabortion activists often make exceptions for rape and incest, which suggests that it is her desire for sex for which a woman must pay with her pain. And many women, from a memory that extends back through endless mothers, are inclined consciously or not to agree.

Cosmetic surgery processes the bodies of woman-made women, who make up the vast majority of its patient pool, into man-made women. It took over the regions of the female mind left unpoliced when female sexuality stopped hurting, and exploited our willingness to heed an authoritarian voice that announces—as we uneasily try out the alien state of the pain-free women—Not so fast.

## The Walking Wounded

The cosmetic surgery industry is expanding by manipulating ideas of health and sickness. There is a clear historical precedent for what the surgeons are doing. "Healthy" and "diseased," as Susan Sontag points out in *Illness as Metaphor*, are often subjective judgments that society makes for its own purposes. Women have long been defined as sick as a means of subjecting them to social control. What the modern Surgical Age is doing to women is an overt reenactment of what nineteenth-century medicine did to make well women sick and active women passive. The surgical industry has taken over for its own profit motives the ancient medical attitude, which harks back to classical Greece but reached its high point in the Victorian female cult of invalidism, which defines normal, healthy female physiology, drives, and desires as pathological. "In the traditions of Western thought," write Deirdre English and Barbara Ehrenreich in *Complaints and Disorders: The Sexual Politics of Sickness*, "man represents wholeness, strength

and health. Woman is a 'misbegotten man,' weak and in-
complete." Historian Jules Michelet refers to women as "the
walking wounded."

The relation of doctors to women has been less than straight-
forward for most of their history. Healing and tending the sick
were primarily female skills until the Enlightenment; women's
medical effectiveness was one catalyst for the witch burnings that
swept Europe from the fourteenth to the eighteenth centuries.
But the ascent of science and the exclusion of women healers
from the childbed are connected, and the professionalization of
medicine in the nineteenth century deliberately barred women
from their traditional healing role.

The Surgical Age took over from the institutionalization of
female "mental illness," which had in turn overtaken the institutionalization of nineteenth-century hysteria, each phase of medical coercion consistently finding new ways to determine that what
is female is sick. As English and Ehrenreich put it: "Medicine's
prime contribution to sexist ideology has been to describe women
as sick, and as potentially sickening to men." The "vital lie" that
equates femaleness with disease has benefited doctors in each of
these three phases of medical history, guaranteeing them "sick"
and profitable patients wherever middle-class women can be
found. The old edifice of medical coercion of women, temporarily
weakened when women entered medical schools in significant
numbers, has gained reinforcements from the beauty doctors of
the Surgical Age.

The parallels between the two systems are remarkable. Both
arose to answer the need for an ideology that could debilitate and
discredit middle-class women whose education, leisure, and freedom from material constraints might lead them too far into a dangerous emancipation and participation in public life. From 1848
until the enfranchisement of Western women in the first decades
of the twentieth century was a time of feminist agitation of unsur-
passed intensity, and the "Woman Question" was a continuing
social crisis: in backlash, a new ideal of the "separate sphere" of
total domesticity arose. That ideal came, like the beauty myth in
a parallel backlash against women's advancement, with its socially
useful price: the cult of female invalidism, initiated by "a con-
striction in the field of vision which led doctors to focus, with

obsessive concern, on women as organs of reproduction . . . a distortion of perception which, by placing primary emphasis on the sexual organs, enabled men to view women as a creature apart." Showalter also notes that

> during the decades from 1870 to 1910, middle-class women were beginning to organize in behalf of higher education, entrance to the professions, and political rights. Simultaneously, the female nervous disorders of anorexia nervosa, hysteria, and neurasthenia became epidemic; and the Darwinian "nerve specialist" arose to dictate proper feminine behavior outside the asylum as well as in . . . and to oppose women's efforts to change the conditions of their lives.

The Victorian woman became her ovaries, as today's woman has become her "beauty." Her reproductive value, as the "aesthetic" value of her face and body today, "came to be seen as a sacred trust, one that she must constantly guard in the interest of her race."

Where Victorian doctors helped support a culture that needed to view women through ovarian determinism, modern cosmetic surgeons do the same for society by creating a system of beauty determinism. In the last century, notes Showalter, "women were the primary patients in surgical clinics, water-cure establishments, and rest-cure homes; they flocked to the new specialists in the 'female illnesses' of hysteria and neurasthenia, as well as marginal therapies, i.e., 'mesmeric healing,'" just as women are the primary patients of "beauty therapies" in the current backlash. These attitudes, in both ideologies, allow doctors to act as a vanguard in imposing upon women what society needs from them.

## Health

Both the Victorian and the modern medical systems reclassify aspects of healthy femaleness into grotesque abnormality. Victorian medicine "treated pregnancy and menopause as diseases, menstruation as a chronic disorder, childbirth as a surgical event." A

menstruating woman was treated with purgatives, forced medi-
cines, hip baths, and leeches. The regulation of menstruation was
pursued obsessively, just as the regulation of women's fat is today: "The proper establishment of the menstrual function was
viewed as essential to female mental health, not only for the adolescent years but for the woman's entire life-span. Menarche
was"—as the weight gain of puberty is now considered to be—
"the first stage of mortal danger." Maintaining reproduction, like
the maintenance of "beauty," was seen as the all-important
female function threatened by the woman's moral laxness and
mental chaos: Just as they do today, doctors then helped the Victorian woman maintain her "stability in the face of almost overwhelming physical odds," and enforced in her "those qualities of
self-government and industriousness that would help a woman resist the stresses of her body and the weakness of her female
nature."

With the advent of the Victorian women's doctor, the earlier
religious rationale for calling women *morally* sick was changed into
a biomedical one. That in turn has changed into an "aesthetic"
one, bringing us full circle. Our rationale is even more subjective
than the "vital lie" of the Victorians. While their medical termi-
nology had at least to gesture at "objectivity," today's aesthetic
judgments about who is sick and who is well are as impossible to
prove, as easy to manipulate, as a belief about the stain on a
woman's soul. And the modern reclassification makes more
money: A woman who thought she was sick with femaleness
couldn't buy an ultimate cure for her gender. But a woman who
thinks she is sick with female ugliness is now being persuaded
that she can.

The nineteenth-century version of medical coercion looks
quaint to us: How could women have been made to believe that
menstruation, masturbation, pregnancy, and menopause were diseases? But as modern women are being asked to believe that parts
of our normal, healthy bodies are diseased, we have entered a
new phase of medical coercion that is so horrific that no one wants
to look at it at all.

The reclassification of well and beautiful women as sick and
ugly women is taking place without hindrance. Since the nineteenth century, society has tacitly supported efforts of the medical

profession to confine women's lives through versions of this reclassification. Since it is socially necessary work, now as in the last
century, fewer reality checks apply to this than are applied to
medical practices in general; the media is tolerant or supportive;
and the main functionaries, whose work benefits the social order,
are unusually highly compensated.

The purpose of the Victorian cult of female invalidism was
social control. It too was a double symbol, like "beauty": Subjec-
tively, women invalids exerted through it the little power they
had, escaped onerous sexual demands and dangerous childbirth,
and received attention from responsive doctors. But for the establishment, it was a political solution as useful as the Iron Maiden.
As French writer Catherine Clément puts it: "Hysteria [was] tol-
erated because in fact it has no power to effect cultural change; it
is much safer for the patriarchal order to encourage and allow dis-
contented women to express their wrongs through psychosomatic
illness than to have them agitating for economic and legal rights."
Social pressure demanded that leisured, educated, middle-class
women preempt trouble by being sick, and the enforced hypochondria felt to the sufferer like real illness. For similar reasons
today, social pressure requires that women preempt the implications of our recent claim to our bodies by feeling ugly, and that
forcibly lowered self-esteem looks to the sufferer like real "ugliness."

The surgeons are taking the feminist redefinition of health as
beauty and perverting it into a notion of "beauty" as health; and,
thus, of whatever they are selling as health: hunger as health,
pain and bloodshed as health. Anguish and illness have been
"beauty" before: In the nineteenth century, the tubercular
woman—with her glittering eyes, pearly skin, and fevered lips—
was the ideal. *Gender and Stress* describes the media's idealization
of anorexics; the iconography of the Victorians idealized "beautiful" hysterics fainting in front of male doctors, asylum doctors
dwelt lasciviously on the wasted bodies of anorexics in their care,
and later psychiatric handbooks ask doctors to admire the "calm
and beautiful face" of the anesthetized woman who has undergone electroshock therapy. Like current coverage by women's
journalism of the surgical ideal, Victorian journalism aimed at

women waxed lyrical on the sentimental attractiveness of feminine debility, invalidism, and death.

A century ago, normal female activity, especially the kind that
would lead women into power, was classified as ugly and sick. If a
woman read too much, her uterus would "atrophy." If she kept
on reading, her reproductive system would collapse and, according to the medical commentary of the day, "we should have before us a repulsive and useless hybrid." Menopause was depicted
as a terminal blow, "the death of the woman in the woman":
"The end of a woman's reproductive life was as profound a mental upheaval as the beginning," producing, like the modern wan-
ing of "beauty," "a distinct shock to the brain." Then as now,
though with a different rationalization, menopause was represented as causing the feeling that "the world . . . is turned upside
down, that everything is changed, or that some very dreadful but
undefined calamity has happened or is about to happen."

Participation in modernity, education, and employment was
portrayed as making Victorian women ill: "warm apartments, coal-
fires, gas-lights, late hours, rich food," turned them into invalids,
as today, as the skin cream copy puts it, "central heating, air pollution, fluorescent lights, etc." make us "ugly." Victorians protested women's higher education by fervidly imagining the
damage it would do to their reproductive organs; Friedrich Engels
claimed that "protracted work frequently causes deformities of
the pelvis," and it was taken for granted that "the education of
women would sterilize them" and make them sexually unattractive: "When a woman displays scientific interest, then there is
something out of order in her sexuality." The Victorians insisted
that freedom from the "separate sphere" impaired womanhood,
just as we are asked to believe that freedom from the beauty myth
impairs beauty.

Vital lies are resilient. Contraception, for example, is defined
by the medical profession, depending on the social mood, as making women ill or "beautiful": Victorian doctors claimed that any
contraception      caused      "galloping      cancer,      sterility      and
nymphomania in women; . . . the practise was likely to produce
mania leading to suicide." Until the 1920s, it was considered
"distinctly dangerous to health," sterility and "mental degenera-

tion in subsequent offspring" being among its supposed effects. But when society needed sexually available women, although questions about safety and side effects arose at once, women's magazines nonetheless ran enthusiastic stories suggesting that the Pill would keep women young, and make them more "sexy."

In the same way, surgeons—and women's magazines, increasingly dependent on the editorial copy and ad revenue the surgeons provide—are recasting freedom from the beauty myth as disease. Advertisements for holy oils initiated this new definition by imitating medical journalism's photographs of "disease" and "cure." They drew on the worst medical fears of the age, postnuclear cancers and AIDS. "Crow's feet" sounds insignificant compared with the suggestions the ads made of radiation sickness and carcinogenic lesions, cellular chaos and lowered immune systems. Elizabeth Arden's is "the most advanced treatment system of the century," as if aging required chemotherapy. Estée Lauder's "science-proven" Night Repair is applied with a medical syringe and rubber balloon, like a blood transfusion or a liquid drug. Vichy lets your skin "recuperate." Clarins talks of "relapse." Elancyl speaks of fat as a "condition" that "disfigures." Doctors give prescriptions, Clarins a "Beauty Prescription," and Clinique, "Prescriptives." Cancer specialists speak of the "regression" of the illness; so does Clinique: "Stay with your treatment—the temporary 'regression' will stop." Ultima II makes Megadose.

In 1985, Eugenia Chandris in *The Venus Syndrome* called big hips and thighs "a medical problem"; looking at the Paleolithic fertility figures, she committed the solecism of saying that "the problem has troubled women ever since." "The problem," of course, has only troubled women since it has been called a problem—that is, within living memory. Female fat is characterized as if it were not only dead, but carcinogenic: "proliferating cells," breeding more death. The Victorians defined all reproductive activity as illness; today's beauty surgeons define as illness all evidence on the body of its reproductive activity—stretch marks, sagging breasts, breasts that have nursed, and the postpartum weight that accumulates, in every culture, at about ten pounds per pregnancy. Education, of course, never affected a woman's ovaries, just as maternal breasts lose no feeling; nursing *is* erotic.

Nor are they dysfunctional; to the contrary, they have fulfilled a primary function of the breast, lactation. But cosmetic surgeons describe postpartum breasts, as the Victorians described educated ovaries, as "atrophied," a term that healing doctors use to describe the wasted, dysfunctional muscles of paralysis. They reclassify healthy adult female flesh as "cellulite," an invented "condition" that was imported into the United States by *Vogue* only in 1973; they refer to this texture as "disfiguring," "unsightly," "polluted with toxins." Before 1973, it was normal female flesh.

Health makes good propaganda. "'Proof' that women's activities outside the home are detrimental to the health and welfare of themselves, their families and the country as a whole" lent impetus, writes Ann Oakley, to the nineteenth-century cult of domesticity. The ovaries were seen as collective property rather than the woman's own business, as the face and the body outline are seen today. Who can argue with health?

## Institutionalized Reclassification

Respected institutions are participating, as they did in the last century, in this cultural policing of women through reclassification: In 1978, the American Medical Association made the claim that preoccupation with beauty was the same as preoccupation with health. Dr. Arthur K. Balin, president of the American Aging Association, declared to *The New York Times* that "it would benefit physicians to look upon ugliness not as a cosmetic issue but a disease." In professional plastic surgery journals, it is impossible to see where the surgeons differentiate between the cutting open of the cancerous and the healthy breast. Dr. Daniel C. Tostesen of Harvard Medical School, who has accepted $85 million from Shiseido for research, is earning his salary on its behalf: There is, he asserts, a "subtle and continuous gradation" between health and medical interests on the one hand, and "beauty and well-being" on the other. Such dicta affect women more than men, as they are meant to; it is women who are the main surgical patient pool and the buyers of Shiseido products (no mention is made of

the physical appeal, or lack of it, of Drs. Balin and Tostesen).
When the surgeons convene conferences to discuss "the deformities of the aging face," the profile on the announcement is invariably female.

A man is "deformed" if a limb or feature is missing or severely
skewed from the human phenotype. Where women do not fit the
Iron Maiden, we are now being called monstrous, and the Iron
Maiden is exactly that which no woman fits, or fits forever. A
woman is being asked to feel like a monster now though she is
whole and fully physically functional. The surgeons are playing
on the myth's double standard for the function of the body. A
man's thigh is for walking, but a woman's is for walking and looking "beautiful." If women can walk but believe our limbs look
wrong, we feel that their bodies cannot do what they are meant to
do; we feel as genuinely deformed and disabled as the unwilling
Victorian hypochondriac felt ill.

The tragedy of this reclassification is that for most of our history, women have indeed suffered from illness—prolapsed uteri,
early death from ovarian cysts, untreatable venereal diseases and
vaginal infections; poor hygiene, ignorance, shame, and compulsory yearly pregnancy took their toll. Compared with that,
women are now miraculously, unprecedentedly well—but the
myth denies us the experience of our wellness. Only a generation
after the physical dis-ease of femaleness had ended, the new possibility of ease in the female body was ruined for women by the
beauty myth.

Recycled rhetoric about female disease insults women's
healthy bodies: When a modern woman is blessed with a body
that can move, run, dance, play, and bring her to orgasm; with
breasts free of cancer, a healthy uterus, a life twice as long as that
of the average Victorian woman, long enough to let her express
her character on her face; with enough to eat and a metabolism
that protects her by laying down flesh where and when she needs
it; now that hers is the gift of health and well-being beyond that
which any generation of women could have hoped for before—
the Age of Surgery undoes her immense good fortune. It breaks
down into defective components the gift of her sentient, vital
body and the individuality of her face, teaching her to experience
her lifelong blessing as a lifelong curse.

As a result, fully able women may now be less satisfied with their bodies than are disabled people: "Physically handicapped people," reports a recent study quoted in *The New York Times*, "generally express an overall satisfaction about their bodies"—while able-bodied women, we saw, do not. One San Francisco Bay area woman in four would undergo cosmetic surgery given the chance. The word "deformed" is no longer used in polite discourse, except to describe bodies and faces of healthy normal women, where cosmetic surgeons' language constructs out of us the new freak show.

## Is "Health" Healthful?

How healthy is the Surgical Age? Smoking is on the decline in all groups but young women; 39 percent of all women who smoke say they smoke to maintain their weight; one quarter of those will die of disease caused by cigarette smoking—though, to be fair, the dead women's corpses will weigh on average four pounds less than will the bodies of the living nonsmokers. Capri cigarettes are advertised as "the slimmest slim." The late Rose Cipollone, whose husband sued the tobacco industry for her death from lung cancer, started smoking as a teenager because "I thought I was going to be glamorous or beautiful."

Liquid fasts have caused at least sixty deaths in the United States, and their side effects include nausea, hair loss, dizziness, and depression. Compulsive exercise causes sports anemia and stunted growth. Breast implants make cancer detection more difficult. Women delay mammograms for fear of losing a breast and becoming "only half a woman."

The myth is not only making women physically ill, but mentally ill. Attie and Brooks-Gunn in *Gender and Stress* assert that dieting is a chronic cause of stress in women; stress is one of the most serious medical risk factors, lowering the immune system and contributing to high blood pressure, heart disease, and higher mortality rates from cancer. But even worse, the beauty myth in the Surgical Age actually duplicates within women's consciousness the classic symptoms of mental illness.

Schizophrenics are characterized by a disturbed sense of body boundaries. A neurotic's body image is erratic, extremely negative or positive. Narcissists feel that what happens to their bodies does not happen to them. Psychotics have the feeling that parts of their body are falling apart. They display repetitive rubbing, self-mutilation, and fears of sliding into nothingness and disintegration. Surgical expectations and weight fluctuations subject women to weak body boundaries. The stress on appearance gives them erratic, extremely negative or positive views of themselves. A torrent of media images show the female face and body split into pieces, which is how the beauty myth asks a woman to think of her own body parts. A number of beauty practices require of her repetitive rubbing and self-mutilation. When she ages, she is asked to believe that without "beauty" she slides into nothingness and disintegration. Is it possible that by submitting women to the experiences symptomatic of mental illness, we are more likely to become mentally ill? Women are the majority of sufferers from mental illness by a significant majority.

But these facts are not very useful to women, because there is a double standard for "health" in men and women. Women are not getting it wrong when they smoke to lose weight. Our society *does* reward beauty on the outside over health on the inside. Women must not be blamed for choosing short-term beauty "fixes" that harm our long-term health, since our life spans are inverted under the beauty myth, and there is no great social or economic incentive for women to live a long time. A thin young woman with precancerous lungs is more highly rewarded socially than a hearty old crone. Spokespeople sell women the Iron Maiden and name her "Health"; if public discourse were really concerned with women's health, it would turn angrily upon this aspect of the beauty myth.

The prime of life, the decades from forty to sixty—when many men but certainly most women are at the height of their powers—are cast as men's peak and women's decline (an especially sharp irony since those years represent women's sexual peak and men's sexual decline). This double standard is not based on health differences between middle-aged men and women, but on the artificial inequality of the beauty myth. The hypocrisy of the use of "health" as a gloss for the Surgical Age is that the myth's true message is that a woman should live hungry, die young, and leave a pretty corpse.

The Surgical Age's definition of female "health" is not healthy. Are those aspects defined as "diseased" actually sick?

You could see the signs of female aging as diseased, especially if you had a vested interest in making women too see them your way. Or you could see that if a woman is healthy she lives to grow old; as she thrives, she reacts and speaks and shows emotion, and grows into her face. Lines trace her thought and radiate from the corners of her eyes after decades of laughter, closing together like fans as she smiles. You could call the lines a network of "serious lesions," or you could see that in a precise calligraphy, thought has etched marks of concentration between her brows, and drawn across her forehead the horizontal creases of surprise, delight, compassion, and good talk. A lifetime of kissing, of speaking and weeping, shows expressively around a mouth scored like a leaf in motion. The skin loosens on her face and throat, giving her features a setting of sensual dignity; her features grow stronger as she does. She has looked around in her life, and it shows. When gray and white reflect in her hair, you could call it a dirty secret or you could call it silver or moonlight. Her body fills into itself, taking on gravity like a bather breasting water, growing generous with the rest of her. The darkening under her eyes, the weight of her lids, their minute cross-hatching, reveal that what she has been part of has left in her its complexity and richness. She is darker, stronger, looser, tougher, sexier. The maturing of a woman who has continued to grow is a beautiful thing to behold.

Or, if your ad revenue or your seven-figure salary or your privileged sexual status depend on it, it is an operable condition.

If you could make a million dollars a year—the average income of cosmetic surgeons in the United States—by doing so, then female fat can easily enough be called a disease. Or it can be seen for what it is: normal, since even the thinnest healthy women have more fat than men. When you see the way women's curves swell at the hips and again at the thighs, you could claim that that is an abnormal deformity. Or you could tell the truth: 75 percent of women are shaped like that, and soft, rounded hips and thighs and bellies were perceived as desirable and sensual without question until women got the vote. Women's flesh, you could acknowledge, is textured, rippled, dense, and complicated; and the way fat is laid down on female muscle, on the hips and thighs that cradle and deliver children and open for sex, is one of the most provocative qualities of the female body. Or you could turn this too into an operable condition.

Whatever is deeply, essentially female—the life in a woman's expression, the feel of her flesh, the shape of her breasts, the transformations after childbirth of her skin—is being reclassified as ugly, and ugliness as disease. These qualities are about an intensification of female power, which explains why they are being recast as a diminution of power. At least a third of a woman's life is marked with aging; about a third of her body is made of fat. Both symbols are being transformed into operable conditions—*so that* women will only feel healthy if we are two thirds of the women we could be. How can an "ideal" be about women if it is defined as how much of a female sexual characterlsic *does not* exist on the woman's body, and how much of a female life *does not* show on her face?

## Profit

It cannot be about women, for the "ideal" is not about women but about money. The current Surgical Age is, like the Victorian medical system, impelled by easy profits. The cosmetic surgery industry in the United States grosses $300 million every year, and is growing annually by 10 percent. But as women get used to comfort and freedom, it cannot continue to count on profit from women's willingness to suffer for their sex. A mechanism of intimidation must be set in place to maintain that rate of growth, higher than that of any other "medical specialty." Women's pain threshold has to be raised, and a new sense of vulnerability imbedded in us, if the industry is to reap the full profit of their new technology acting on old guilt. The surgeons' market is imaginary, since there is nothing wrong with women's faces or bodies that social change won't cure; so the surgeons depend for their income on warping female self-perception and multiplying female self-hatred.

"The myth of female frailty, and the very real cult of female hypochondria that seemed to support the myth, played directly into the financial interests of the medical profession," according to Ehrenreich and English. In the nineteenth century, competition in the medical profession rose. Doctors were frantic to ensure a reliable patient pool of wealthy women, a "client caste," who could be convinced of the need for regular house calls and lengthy convalescences. Suffragists saw through to the real impetus behind women's invalidism—the doctor's interests and the unnatural conditions that confined women's lives. Mary Livermore, a suffragist, protested "the monstrous assumption that woman is a natural invalid," and denounced "the unclean army of 'gynecologists'" who "seem desirous to convince women that they possess but one set of organs—and that these are always diseased." Dr. Mary Putnam Jacobi traced women's ill health directly to "their new function as lucrative patients." As Ehrenreich and English put it: "As a businessman, the doctor had a direct interest in a social role for women that required them to be sick."

Modern cosmetic surgeons have a direct financial interest in a social role for women that requires them to feel ugly. They do not simply advertise for a share of a market that already exists: Their advertisements create new markets. It is a boom industry because it is influentially placed to create its own demand through the pairing of text with ads in women's magazines.

The industry takes out ads and gets coverage; women get cut open. They pay their money and they take their chances. As surgeons grow richer, they are able to command larger and brighter ad space: The October 1988 issue of *Harper's and Queen* is typical, in pairing a positive article on surgery with the same amount of space, on the same pages, of surgical advertising. In *The New York Times* health supplement of July 1989, advertising for regulated fasts, fat farms, weight-loss camps, surgeons, and eating disorder specialists fills over half the commercial space. By September 1990, the quid pro quo was solid: *Cosmopolitan* provided a slavishly uncritical puff piece in an issue supported by full-page, full-color surgical advertising. The time has arrived when the relationship among cosmetic surgery, ad revenue, risks, and warnings is re-creating cigarette advertising's inhibitions on antismoking journalism before the Surgeon General took his stand. With journalists given little incentive to expose or pursue them (indeed, they are given incentive not to: The premier cosmetic surgeons' organization offers a $500 journalism prize, 2 free plane tickets included), the surgeons' status and influence will continue to rise. Tending cultural, not biological, needs, they may well continue to accumulate power over women's social and economic life or death; if so, soon they should be what many seem to want to be: little gods, whom no one will wish to cross.

If women suddenly stopped feeling ugly, the fastest-growing medical specialty would be the fastest dying. In many states of the United States, where cosmetic surgeons (as opposed to plastic surgeons, who specialize in burns, trauma, and birth defects) can be any nonspecialist M.D., it would be back to mumps and hemorrhoids for the doctors, conditions that advertising cannot exacerbate. They depend for their considerable livelihood on selling women a feeling of terminal ugliness. If you tell someone she has cancer, you cannot create in her the disease and its agony. But tell a woman persuasively enough that she is ugly, you do create the "disease," and its agony is real. If you wrap up your advertisement, alongside an article promoting surgery, in a context that makes women feel ugly, and leads us to believe that other women are competing in this way, then you have paid for promoting a disease that you alone can cure.

This market creation seems not to be subject to the ethics of the genuine medical profession. Healing doctors would be discredited if they promoted behavior that destroyed health in order to profit from the damage: Hospitals are withdrawing investment from tobacco and alcohol companies. The term for this practice, ethical investing, recognizes that some medical profit relationships are unethical. Hospitals can afford such virtue, since their patient pool of the sick and dying is always naturally replenished. But cosmetic surgeons must create a patient pool where none biologically exists. So they take out full-page ads in *The New York Times*—showing a full-length image of a famous model in a swimsuit, accompanied by an offer of easy credit and low monthly terms, as if a woman's breasts were a set of consumer durables— and make their dream of mass disease come true.

## Ethics

Though the Surgical Age has begun, it remains socially, ethically, and politically unexamined. While the last thing women need is anyone telling us what we can or cannot do to our bodies, and while the last thing we need is to be blamed for our choices, the fact that no ethical debate has centered on the supply side of the Surgical Age is telling. This *laissez-faire* attitude is inconsistent for many reasons. Much debate and legislation constrains the purchase of body parts and protects the body from risks posed to it by the free market. Law recognizes that the human body is fundamentally different from an inanimate object when it comes to buying and selling. United States law forbids the commercial barter of the vagina, mouth, or anus in most states. It criminalizes self-maiming and suicide, and rejects contracts based on people assuming personal risks that are unreasonable (in this case, risk of death). Philosopher Immanuel Kant wrote that selling body parts violates the ethical limitations on what may be sold in the marketplace. The World Health Organization condemns the sale of human organs for transplant; British and American law banned it, as did at least twenty other countries. Fetal experimentation is banned in the United States, and in Great Britain Parliament debated the issue bitterly. In the Baby M. case in the United States the court ruled that it is illegal to buy or rent a womb. It is illegal in the United States and Britain to buy a baby. Ethical discussion is raised by the financial pressure on a woman to sell her uterus, or on a man to sell a kidney. Agonizing national debate centers on the life and death of the fetus. Our willingness to wrestle with such issues is taken as a sign of society's moral health.

What the surgeons traffic in is body parts, and the method of the sale is invasive. Experimental fetal tissue is dead; it still raises complex questions. The women subjected to surgical experiments are still alive. Surgeons call tissues on a woman's body dead so that they can profitably kill them. Is a woman entirely alive, or only the parts of her that are young and "beautiful"? Social pressure to let old people die raises questions about eugenics. What about social pressure on a woman to destroy the "deformity" on her healthy body, or to kill off the age in herself? Does that say nothing about society's moral health? How can what is wrong in the body politic be not only right but necessary on the *female* body? Is nothing political going on here?

When it comes to women and the ethical void opened by the Surgical Age, no guidelines apply and no debate follows. The most violent people set limits for themselves to mark that they have not lost their humanity. A soldier balks at killing a baby, the Department of Defense draws the line at poison gas, the Geneva Convention asserts that even in war there remains such a thing as going too far: We agree that civilized people can recognize torture and condemn it. But in this, the beauty myth seems to exist outside civilization: There is as yet no such thing as a limit.

The myth rests on the fallacy that beauty is a form of Darwinism, a natural struggle for scarce resources, and that nature is red in tooth and claw. Even if one is able to accept the fallacy that women's pain for beauty can be justified—as generals justify war—as part of an inevitable evolutionary conflict, one must still recognize that at no point have civilized people said about it, as they do about military excesses, that's enough, we are not animals.

The Hippocratic Oath begins, "First, do no harm." A victim of medical experimentation quoted in Robert Jay Lifton's *The Nazi Doctors* asked the doctors, "Why do you want to operate on me? I am . . . not sick." The actions of cosmetic surgeons directly contradict the medical ethics of healing doctors. Healing doctors follow a strict code, established after the Nuremberg trials, to protect patients from irresponsible experimentation: The code condemns excessive risk in medical experimentation; it absolutely forbids experimentation without a therapeutic purpose; it insists on the patients' free and uncoerced choice to participate; and it compels full disclosure of risks in obtaining patients' "informed consent." Looking at their actions strictly literally, not rhetorically, it's clear that modern cosmetic surgeons are daily violating the medical code of Nuremberg.

Cosmetic surgical techniques appear to be developed in irresponsible medical experiments, using desperate women as laboratory animals: In the first stabs at liposuction in France, powerful hoses tore out of women, along with massive globules of living tissue, entire nerve networks, dendrites and ganglia. Undaunted, the experimenters kept at it. Nine French women died of the *"improved"* technique, *which was called a success* and brought to the United States. Liposuctionists begin their practice in the absence of any hands-on experience during training. "My surgeon has never done that procedure before . . . so he will use me to 'experiment,'" reports a surgery addict. With stomach stapling, "surgeons are continuing to experiment in order to come up with better techniques."

To protect patients from medical experimentation, the Nuremberg Code emphasizes that in order genuinely to consent, patients must know all the risks. Though patients are asked to sign consent forms, it is extremely difficult, if not impossible, to get accurate or objective information about cosmetic surgery. Most coverage stresses women's responsibility to research the practitioners and procedures. But reading only women's magazines, a woman might learn the complications—but not their probability; devoting full-time research to it, she still won't find out the mortality rate. Either no one knows it who should, or no one's telling. A spokeswoman for the American Society of Plastic and Reconstructive Surgeons says, "No one's keeping the figures for a mortality rate. There are no records for an overall death rate." The same is true in Canada. The British Association of Aesthetic Plastic Surgeons also states that statistics are not available. One cosmetic surgery informational source admits to 1 death in 30,000, which must mean that at least 67 American women are dead so far—though these odds are never mentioned in articles in the popular press. Most available sources omit levels of risk and all omit descriptions of levels of pain, as a random survey of popular books on the subject shows: In *About Face*, the authors cover five procedures including liposuction, chemical peel, and chemodermabrasion, but mention neither risks nor pain. *The Beautiful Body Book* covers procedures including breast surgery, dermabrasion, and liposuction without mentioning risks, pain, breast hardening, reoperation rates, or cancer detection difficulties. The author describes breast reduction surgery and "repositioning" surgery (for when, in her words, "the nipple is misplaced"). These procedures permanently kill the erotic response of the nipple. She does mention this side effect only to dismiss it with the astonish-

ing opinion of a "Dr. Brink" who "told me that it is not unusual
for many women with oversized breasts to have little or no feeling
in the nipple area anyway." She goes on to give "facts" that,
typically for such books, are simply wrong: Liposuction, she mis-
states, has resulted in "only four deaths" (*The New York Times*
counted eleven in 1987) and that "to date, no long-term negative
effects have been observed." The Poutney Clinic brochure does
not mention in their list of "risks" pain, loss of nipple sensation in
any of the five breast surgeries they offer, or the risk of death.
The Surgery Advisory Service brochure gives out a flat untruth:
Scar tissue development after breast surgery, it claims, "is rare,"
happening only "very occasionally," though estimates for scarring
actually range from 10 percent of all cases to as many as 70 percent. Cosmetic surgeon Dr. Thomas D. Rees's approach to informed consent is characteristic: to "give [his] patients a paper
designed to provide them with as much practical information as
possible without scaring them half to death about the multitude of
complications" that, despite what he calls their rarity, "could befall them." It is also very difficult to tell which sources are partial:
*The Independent* (London), a respected newspaper, ran a positive
article on surgery, ending in an advertisement for their *Independent
Guide to Cosmetic Surgery* (two pounds), which plays down risk and
advertises all the qualified surgeons in Great Britain. A woman
cannot know what the chances are that a horror story will happen
to her, until it does; her ignorance alone puts the cosmetic surgeons in violation of both the letter and spirit of Nuremberg.

Healing doctors respect the healthy body and invade the diseased only as a last resort; cosmetic surgeons call healthy bodies
sick in order to invade them. The former avoid operating on family members; the latter are the first men to whom technology
grants the ancient male fantasy of mythical Pygmalion, the sculp-
tor who fell in love with his own creation: At least one surgeon
has totally reconstructed his wife. Healing doctors resist being
manipulated by addicts; there is already a class of women who are
addicted to surgery, reports *Newsweek*, "scalpel slaves" who "in-
dulge . . . in plastic surgery the way some of us eat chocolate—
compulsively. Neither cost, pain nor spectacular bruising lessen
[the] desire for a little more whittling." One surgeon gives an
addict a discount for repeat operations. Addicts "go from doctor to

doctor, seeking multiple operations. . . . Their self-scrutiny becomes microscopic. They start complaining about bumps the
average person doesn't see." And the surgeons operate: Dr.
Frank Dunton has cut up one woman at least half a dozen times,
"and expects to keep up the remodelling work. 'I guess it's all
right,' he says, 'as long as her husband doesn't complain.'"

## Safeguards

Medical coercion in service of a vital lie is less regulated than
legitimate medicine. In the nineteenth century, sexual surgery
was risky and unscientific, with few legal checks. Patients were
more likely, until around 1912, to be harmed by medical intervention than helped. Little, according to today's standards, was
known about how the body worked, and strange experiments on
women's reproductive organs were common. The American Medical Association had no legal control over who could call himself a
doctor. Doctors had virtually free rein to peddle opiate-based, addictive snake oils, and miracle cures for vague female maladies.
    The new atrocities are flourishing without intervention from
the institutions that promise to safeguard the welfare of citizens.
In a sexual double standard as to who receives consumer protection, it seems that if what you do is done to women in the name
of beauty, you may do what you like. It is illegal to claim that
something grows hair, or makes you taller, or restores virility, if it
does not. It is difficult to imagine that the baldness remedy
Minoxidil would be on the market if it had killed nine French and
at least eleven American men. In contrast, the long-term effects
of Retin-A are still unknown—Dr. Stuart Yuspa of the National
Cancer Institute refers to its prescription as "a human experiment"—and the Food and Drug Administration has not approved
it; yet dermatologists are prescribing it to women at a revenue of
over $150 million a year.
    The silicone injections of the 1970s, never approved by the
FDA, have hardened "like a sack of rocks," as Dr. Thomas Rees
puts it, in women's breasts. The long-term carcinogenic effect of
silicone is unknown, but surgeons are still injecting it into

women's faces. "Peeling parlors" have appeared where operators
with no medical training at all use acid to cause second-degree
burns on women's faces. It wasn't until 1988 that the FDA
cracked down on quack cures for weight loss aimed at women, a
$25-billion-a-year business. For the forty years before the
crackdown, disreputable physicians prescribed, for "medically approved" weight-loss treatment: amphetamines and related addictive drugs, high doses of digitalis, a highly toxic heart drug,
injections from pregnant women's urine, extended fasting, brain
surgery, jaw wiring, and intestinal bypass. Though all were promoted by doctors, none was backed by long-term animal studies
or clinical trials for safety or effectiveness. Mass-market diet formulas still place dangerous stresses on the body when normal eating is resumed; PPA (phenylpropanolamine), present in diet pills
and herbal weight-loss remedies, causes danger to the heart, but
need not be labeled on the product. Women are still prescribed
addictive cocaine- and amphetamine-derived drugs for weight
loss, but this does not merit the attention of the President's task
force on drugs. This lack of regulation is itself a message to
women, a message that we understand.

In Great Britain, doctors who are not registered by the National Health Service to perform cosmetic surgery invent objec-
tive-sounding organization names—such as the Cosmetic Surgery
Helpline, the Medical Advisory Group, the Surgery Advisory Service—and make use on their literature of the winged staff and
serpents of Asclepius, god of healing and of the medical profession. They mislead women into thinking they are getting impar-
tial information, when what they do is lobby over the phone,
through medically untrained "counselors," for new patients. In
the United States, it was not until 1989, ten years into the Surgical Age, that a congressional hearing was convened by Congressman Ron Wyden (Democrat, Oregon), to investigate what
one witness called "the last refuge of freebooters charging what
the market will bear" and their advertising, which is "often mis-
leading and false . . . preying on the insecurities of American
women." Testimony accused the Federal Trade Commission of a
failure to regulate the "profession," and blamed it for permitting
advertising in the 1970s and then abandoning responsibility for
what the ads had wrought. An M.D/D.P.S. is "board-certified"

by the American Board of Plastic Surgery, and therefore trained; but an American woman who is told that it is her burden to ensure that the surgeon is "board-certified" is unlikely to know that there are over one hundred different "boards" with official-sounding names that go unregulated. Fully 90 percent of cosmetic surgery in the United States is performed in unregulated doctors' offices. Finally, asserted the congressional testimony, "there is no standard method for preoperative screening," so any woman is operable. What did Congress do about the situation once it was staring them in the face? Nothing: The legislation proposed after Congress saw 1,790 pages of shocking testimony is, says Dr. Steve Scott, spokesman for Congressman Wyden's office, more than a year afterward, "on hold." Why? Because it happens to women for beauty, so it is not serious.

## Sexual Surgery

It is particularly not serious if it is sexual. The industry expanded in the 1980s in response to beauty pornography. When AIDS curbed heterosexual promiscuity, men and women had fewer real-life sexual experiences to make them secure in the knowledge that good sex looked all sorts of ways. When there were fewer authentic images of sexuality in people's heads with which they could counteract the influence of commercial images of sexuality, "body sculpting" took on a life of its own, driving the sexes apart into a complementary narcissism no longer even aimed at seduction. Women lifted weights and "got hard"; but it is men who "get hard," and "beauty" is necessary in women to apologize for masculine power: When they were hard all over, they had incisions opened under the folds of their breasts and clear sacs of gel inserted. The muscles were the hypermasculine iron fist; the artificial breasts, the hyperfeminine velvet glove. This ideal was no longer a "naked woman," that vulnerable being. Its breasts made of clear chemicals, it had got rid of as much of the "naked" and the "woman" that could go.

Anywhere from 200,000 to 1 million American women have had their breasts cut open and sacs of chemical gel implanted.

242     THE BEAUTY MYTH

Journalist Jeremy Weir in *Self* magazine puts the number at over a million, and the profits at between $168 million and $374 million. (The operation costs from $1,800 to $4,000.) The breast, he writes, is the part surgeons are cutting into most: 159,300 breast operations in a year, compared with 67,000 face-lifts. The surgery leads to a hardening of scar tissue around the implants in up to seven cases in ten, when the breasts become rock-hard and must be reopened and the implants removed, or the lumps torn apart by the full weight of the surgeon using his bare hands. Saltwater implants deflate and must be extracted; implant manufacturers provide surgeons with routine insurance to cover replacements (surgeons buy the sacs in packs of three pairs of different sizes). Silicone implants leak the substance into the body to unknown effect, medical journals predicting immune-system problems and toxic shock syndrome. Implants make it harder to detect cancer: In a study at the Breast Center in Van Nuys, California, of twenty cancer patients with implants, none of the breast tumors had been detected early, and by the time the disease could be discovered, the cancer had spread to the lymph nodes of thirteen of the women. Dr. Susan Chobanian, a Beverly Hills cosmetic surgeon, says that "very few women withdraw after hearing the risks."

A risk never mentioned in sources available to most women is the death of the nipple: According to Penny Chorlton, "Any surgery on the breast can and probably will adversely affect any erotic stimulation a woman has hitherto enjoyed, and this should be pointed out by the surgeon *in case it is important to the patient* " (italics added). Breast surgery, therefore, in its mangling of erotic feeling, is a form of sexual mutilation.

Imagine this: penis implants, penis augmentation, foreskin enhancement, testicular silicone injections to correct asymmetry, saline injections with a choice of three sizes, surgery to correct the angle of erection, to lift the scrotum and make it pert. Before and after shots of the augmented penis in *Esquire*. Risks: Total numbing of the glans. Diminution of sexual feeling. Permanent obliteration of sexual feeling. Glans rigidity, to the consistency of hard plastic. Testicular swelling and hardening, with probable repeat operations, including scar tissue formation that the surgeon must break apart with manual pressure. Implant collapse. Leakage. Unknown long-term consequences. Weeks of recovery necessary

during which the penis must not be touched. The above procedures are undergone because they make men sexy to women,
or so men are told.

Civilized people will agree that these are mutilations so horrible that a woman should not even be able to think them. I re-
coiled when I wrote them. You, if a woman, probably flinched
when you read them; if you were a man, your revulsion was no
doubt almost physical.

But since women are taught to identify more compassionately
with the body of a man or a child—or a fetus or a primate or a
baby seal—than with our own, we read of similar attacks on our
own sexual organs with numbness. Just as women's sexuality is
turned inside out so that we identify more with male pleasure
than female, the same goes for our identification with pain. One
could protest that breast and penis are not parallel terms, and that
is valid: Breast surgery is not exactly a clitoridectomy. It is only
half a clitoridectomy.

But it is not like real genital mutilation, one could argue, because women choose it. In West Africa, Muslim girls with uncir-
cumcised clitorises can't marry. The tribe's women excise the
clitoris with unsterilized broken bottles or rusty knives, leading
often to hemorrhage and infection, sometimes to death. Women
are the agents there. One could say with as much insight that
those women "do it to themselves."

An estimated twenty-five million women in Africa are sexually
mutilated. The common explanation is that it makes women more
fertile, when the opposite is true. Foot-binding in China also had
a sexual rationale, as Andrea Dworkin has noted: Chinese foot-
binding was believed to alter the vagina, causing "a supernatural
exaltation" during sex, so, as a Chinese diplomat explained, the
system "was not really oppressive," though, Dworkin writes, "the
flesh often became putrescent during the binding and portions
sloughed off from the sole" and "sometimes one or more toes
dropped off." It was the essence of desirability: No Chinese girl
"could bear the ridicule involved in being called a 'large-footed
demon' and the shame of being unable to marry." The rationale
for breast surgery is also sexual desire and desirability.

Like breast surgery, genital mutilation was trivialized: Atroci-
ties that happen to women are "sexual" and not "political," so

the U.S. State Department, the World Health Organization, and UNICEF called them "social and cultural attitudes" and did nothing. At last, though, WHO monitored the practice. Daniel Arap Moi, president of Kenya, banned it in 1982, after he learned that fourteen girls had died.

Western sexual surgery is not new. Normal female sexuality was a disease in the nineteenth century, just as normal breasts are operable today. The role of the nineteenth-century gynecologist was the "detection, judgment and punishment" of sexual disease and "social crime." Pelvic surgery became widespread as a "social reflex," since "orgasm was disease and cure was its destruction."

Victorian clitoridectomy made women behave. "Patients are cured . . . the moral sense of the patient is elevated . . . she becomes tractable, orderly, industrious and cleanly." Modern surgeons claim they make women feel better, and that, no doubt, is true; Victorian middle-class women had so internalized the idea of their sexuality as diseased that the gynecologists were "answering their prayers." Says a face-lift patient of Dr. Thomas Rees's, "The relief was enormous." One of Victorian Dr. Cushing's patients, relieved by the scalpel of the "temptation" to masturbate, wrote, "A window has been opened in heaven [for me]." "It's changed my life," says a rhinoplasty patient of Dr. Thomas Rees's: "As simple as that."

Victorian medical opinion varied on whether female castration worked in returning women to their "normal" role. A Dr. Warner conceded, as do modern surgeons, that the results were probably psychological, not physical. A Dr. Symington-Brown conceded that, but insisted that the operation was still valid because it worked by "shock effect." The Surgical Age likewise reinforces women's submissiveness to the beauty myth with the unspoken background fear: If she is not careful, she will need an operation.

Like the criteria for modern surgery, in which face-lift patients in their twenties are subject to a "preventive" operation that is, in the words of one doctor, "pure marketing hype," the criteria for clitoridectomy were at first narrowly defined but soon became all-encompassing. Dr. Symington-Brown began clitoridectomies in 1859. By the 1860s he was removing labia as well. He became more confident, operating on girls as young as ten, on idiots, epileptics, paralytics, and women with eye problems. As a surgery addict says in *She* magazine, "Once you start, it has a knock-on effect." He operated five times on women who wanted divorces—each time returning wife to husband. "The surgery . . . was a ceremony of stigmatization that frightened most of them into submission. . . .The mutilation, sedation and psychological intimidation . . . seems to have been an efficient, if brutal, form of reprogramming." "Clitoridectomy," writes Showalter, "is the surgical enforcement of an ideology that restricts female sexuality to reproduction," just as breast surgery is of an ideology that restricts female sexuality to "beauty." Victorian women complained of being "tricked and coerced" into treatment, as did the American women who in 1989 described to talk show hostess Oprah Winfrey the genital mutilations inflicted on them without their consent by a surgeon convinced he could improve their orgasms by surgical reconstruction.

It is not coincidental that breast surgery is expanding at a time when female sexuality is such a threat. That was true in Victorian times as well, when doctors treated amenorrhea by placing leeches directly on the vagina or cervix, and cauterized the uterus for discharge with chromic acid. "The operation . . . is not what's important," says a rhinoplasty patient, as Victorian women's "mental agony and physical torture was accounted nothing." Surgeons are becoming media stars. "Glamour and prestige" came to surround the gynecological surgeon, and doctors often advised surgery where less dramatic measures were enough. Ovariotomy "became a fashionable operation in spite of a mortality rate sometimes as high as 40%. *Not only the diseased ovary but the healthy, normal ovary fell prey to the sexual surgeons*" (italics added). One has only to open a cosmetic surgery brochure to see how very normal and healthy are the breasts now "prey to the sexual surgeons."

The modern sexual surgeons display their work with pride; Fay Weldon's *The Life and Loves of a She-Devil* reproduces a current fantasy of the completely reconstructed woman shown off to fellow surgeons at a cocktail party. Victorian doctors boasted of the numbers of ovariotomies they had performed and displayed ovaries arranged on silver platters to admiring audiences at meetings of the American Gynecological Society.

The removal of the ovaries was developed in 1872. The next year, it was recommended for "non-ovarian conditions," espe-

cially masturbation, so that by 1906 about 150,000 American
women were without ovaries. "Non-ovarian conditions" was a social judgment aimed to prevent the "unfit" from breeding and
polluting the body politic. "The 'unfit' included . . . any women
who had been corrupted by masturbation, contraception and abortion . . . from the 1890s until the Second World War, mentally ill
women were 'castrated.'"

The "Orificial Surgery Society" in 1925 offered surgical training in clitoridectomy and infibulation "because of the vast amount
of sickness and suffering which could be saved the gentler sex."
Ten years ago, an Ohio gynecologist offered a $1,500 "Mark Z"
operation to reconstruct the vagina "to make the clitoris more ac-
cessible to direct penile stimulation." A common boast of modern
cosmetic surgeons is that their work saves women from lives of
suffering and misery.

There is a genre of pornography that centers on hurting and
cutting women's breasts. It is frightening that what seems to be
considered erotic about breast surgery is not that it makes women
appear to have bigger or better natural breasts—no one seems
interested in pretending that they look natural; nor that it makes
women more "womanly"; not even that it makes the breasts more
"perfect." What frightens is that the *surgery itself* is being eroticized. A Hungarian magazine features local beauties' breasts
alongside the surgeons who constructed them; *Playboy* has featured the surgery of Mariel Hemingway and Jessica Hahn—not so
much the breasts; the surgery. It is frightening to see that now, in
a woman-fearing era, the thought of scientists cutting open, invading, and artificially reconstructing the breasts of women appears to be emerging as the ultimate erotic triumph.

The artificial reconstruction of the breast may now have become eroticized for women too. It is only after two decades of
beauty pornography curtailing female sexuality that a sexually
dead breast can be seen and felt to be "better" than one that is
sexually alive. The same tacit censorship that edits images of
women's faces and body shapes also edits images of the female
breast, keeping women ignorant about what breasts are actually
like. Culture screens breasts with impeccable thoroughness, almost never representing those that are soft, or asymmetrical, or
mature, or that have gone through the changes of pregnancy.

Looking at breasts in culture, one would have little idea that real breasts come in as many shapes and variations as there are women. Since most women rarely if ever see or touch other women's breasts, they have no idea what they feel like, or of the way they move and shift with the body, or of how they really look during lovemaking. Women of all ages have a fixation—sad in the light of how varied women's breasts really are in texture—on "pertness" and "firmness." Many young women suffer agonies of shame from their conviction that they alone have stretch marks. Since beauty censorship keeps women in profound darkness about other women's real bodies, it is able to make virtually any woman feel that her breasts alone are too soft or low or sagging or small or big or weird or wrong, and to steal from her the full and exquisite eroticism of the nipple.

The trend toward breast surgery is created by a culture that blocks out all breasts that are not the Official Breast, calls the imagery left over from this editing "sex," keeps women ignorant of their own and other women's bodies, and provides a little-monitored service that distributes for several thousand dollars ("Each?" "No, both") the permissible replacement to frantic women.

In a television ad for an American cosmetic surgeon, the actress on screen purrs with the smile of the well-satisfied woman. Nothing on her face looks unusual. It is understood that she is not talking about her face. Women are not cutting their breasts open for individual men, by and large, but so that they can experience their own sexuality. In a diseased environment, they *are* doing this "for themselves." Most are married or in stable relationships. Fully a third are mothers whose breasts have, in the surgeon's words, "atrophied" after pregnancy. Their partners "categorically deny" they encouraged the operations, and protest that they never criticized their lovers' breasts.

This sexual mutilation is not about relations between real men and women. It is about women's sexuality trapped in the beauty backlash, in spite of men who may love them. Soon, not even a loving partner will be able to save many women's sexuality from the knife. Today a woman must ignore her reflection in the eyes of her lover, since he might admire her, and seek it in the gaze of the God of Beauty, in whose perception she is never complete.

What is it about the Official Breast that makes it cancel out all other breasts? Of all shapes and sizes, it best guarantees adolescence. Very young girls, of course, have small breasts, but so do many mature women. Many mature women have large breasts that are not "firm" and "pert." The breast that is high but also large and firm is most likely to belong to a teenager. In a culture which fears the price of women's sexual self-confidence, that breast is the reassuring guarantee of extreme youth—sexual ignorance and infertility.

Freud believed that repression of the libido made civilization; civilization depends at the moment on the repression of female libido: In 1973, *Psychology Today* reports, one fourth of American women surveyed were unhappy with the size or shape of their breasts. By 1986, the number had risen to a third; it was not women's breasts that had changed in the meantime.

*no choice*

This is why many women increasingly can't care that surgery does things to their breasts that might repel a sexual interest that is merely human—rigidification that turns them to the consistency of hard plastic. Women report (at least, articles on surgery report that women report) new sexual fulfillment after the operation, even if their breasts are nerve-dead and rock-hard. How can that be? Many women's sexuality is becoming so externalized by beauty pornography that they may truly be more excited by sexual organs that, though dead or immobile, visually fit into it.

So breast implants, even if they feel bizarre to her lover and cut off sensation in herself, may in fact "free" a woman sexually. They look official. They photograph well. They have become artifact—not-woman—and will never change, the beauty myth's ultimate goal. Plastic body parts won't stop here.

Surgeons are not expected to elicit what will make the woman beautiful in her own eyes, but to guarantee her that they will impose on her body the culture's official fantasy. They seem to have no illusions about their role. An ad in a surgical journal shows a hairy male hand squeezing a glutinous implant. Gel (made, incidentally, by the manufacturers of napalm) bulges out between its fingers. The text asserts that the product "feels natural"—to the squeezing hand.

Medical ethics treats interference in male sexuality as an atrocity. Depo-Provera, a drug that lowers the libido of male criminals, is controversial because it is barbaric to intervene in male sexuality. But female sexuality is still treated by institutions as if it were hypothetical. Not only do factory-produced breasts endanger women's sensual response; many other procedures harm it too. (The Pill, for example, which was supposed to make women "sexier," actually lowers their libido, a side effect of which they are rarely informed.) A risk of eyelid surgery is blindness; a nose job risks damage to the sense of smell; numbness accompanies face-lifts. If the surgical ideal is sensual, there must be other senses than the usual five.

## Numbness

Enough pain makes people numb. Look at a "done-up" woman walking down a wintry street, branches rattling above her. She is wearing a costume, part flamenco dancer, part Carmen, a self-creation that is fragile and arresting. She painted her face for an hour, blending and shading, and now she holds her head as if it were a work of art. Her legs in black silk are numb from the windchill. The deep parting of her dress is open to a blast of wind, which raises tiny hairs on her skin. Her Achilles tendons are ground by the upward pressure of her black-red spike heels, and are relentlessly throbbing. But heads turn, and keep turning: Who's *that*? Each glance is like a shot from a hypodermic. As long as the heads keep turning, she truly is not cold.

A healthy body's reflexes lead it to avoid pain. But beauty thinking is an anesthetic, with the ability to make women more like objects by cauterizing sensation. The beauty index is raising our pain threshold to support surgical technologies. To survive the Surgical Age, we do have to keep ourselves from knowing what we feel. The more we suffer, the more psychological resistance there will be to reopening the mental channels we had to block. In the Milgram Experiments of the 1950s, researchers placed subjects' hands on a lever that they were told would administer electric shocks to people whom they could not see. Then, scientists told them to keep administering increasing levels of shock. The subjects, unwilling to disobey scientific authorities telling them it was right, and cut off from seeing the "victims," raised the electric currents to fatal levels. A woman learns, in the dawn of the Surgical Age, to relate to her body as the experimental subjects related to the shock victims. Separated from it, asked not to see it or feel for it as human, she is being taught by scientific authorities to do her worst.

Electric shock is not just a metaphor. It has been part of the control of women since electricity was in use. Victorian invalids were subjected to galvanic shocks. Electroshock therapy is used typically on women asylum patients, and bears a strong resemblance to the death-and-rebirth ceremonial of cosmetic surgery. Like surgery, it has, claims Elaine Showalter in *The Female Malady*, "the trappings of a powerful religious ritual, conducted by a priestly masculine figure . . . [its magic] comes from its imitation of the death and rebirth ceremony. For the patient it represents a rite of passage in which the doctor kills off the 'bad' crazy self, and resurrects the 'good' self"—in poet Sylvia Plath's vision of electroshock, a good self born again "not of woman." "For this reason, suicidal patients are often comforted by ECT; upon awakening, they feel that in a sense they have died and been born again, with the hated parts of themselves annihilated— literally, electrocuted." Gerald McKnight describes an antiaging "therapy" in which electric shocks are applied to the face. Lancôme makes a "contouring product of extreme precision" that promises to "attack unwanted bulges": It is "the first thermic body contouring shock treatment." Electric shock has encouraged passivity in political dissidents from the Soviet Union to Chile.

Now that women are invited to act as their own electroshock operators, there is no point in detailing case after case that has gone disgustingly wrong, or to say again that the surgery is expensive and very very painful, and that the chances are you will turn your body over to someone who is unregulated, unqualified, and not on your side. Neither is there much point anymore in talking about fatalities.

That apathy is the real issue: The global numbing effect is under way. With every article on surgery that details the horrors of it, as many do, women, ironically, lose a bit more of our ability to feel for our own bodies and identify with our own pain—a survival skill, since with each article, social pressure to undergo those

very horrors will have mounted. Women know about the atroci- ✝
ties; but we cannot feel them anymore.

As the index rises and surgical technologies become more sophisticated, this numbing process will accelerate. Procedures that
still sound barbaric to our ears will soon be absorbed into the en-
croaching numbness. The myth spreads eastward: Procedures that
we have come to tolerate in America still sound nauseating in
Great Britain and revolting in the Netherlands, but next year British women will be able to keep their gorge from rising and Dutch
women will feel merely queasy. Parts of ourselves that we now
admire with pleasure will next year be reclassified as fresh deformities. The pain threshold asked of us will rise and rise. This
projection is just arithmetic: Cosmetic surgery doubled its rate
every five years in the United States, until it tripled in two; it
doubles every decade in Britain. A city of women the size of San
Francisco gets cut open each year in the United States; in Britain,
a village the size of Bath.

The point is that our numbness is catching up to what the
beauty index is asking of us. The reader finishes the article and
looks at the pictures: The woman's face looks as if she has been
beaten across the zygomatic ridge with an iron pipe. Her eyes are
blackened. The skin of the woman's hips is a blanket of bruises.
The woman's breasts are swollen out and yellow like hyperthyroid
jaundiced eyes. The woman's breasts don't move. The blood
crusts under the sutures. The reader, two or three years ago,
thought these images were alarmist. It dawns on her now, they're
promotional. She is no longer expected to react with the revulsion
that she felt at first. Women's magazines set the beauty index.
They've given enormous coverage to surgery, partly because very
little happens in the world of "beauty" that is at all new. These
features have readers believe that we should balk now at nothing,
since it seems that other readers, the competition, are braving it.
The typical article, which details weeks of grisly pain but ends in
happy beauty, provokes in women something like panic buying.

A woman in a shelter for battered women once described her
legs to me as "all one bruise, like they were covered with purplish
tights." In an interview for a book promoting cosmetic surgery,
overheard in a Manhattan coffee shop, a woman who had had
liposuction used a similar image. What needs to be explored are

not the mutilations, but the atmosphere we now inhabit that makes them make no difference.

We have entered a terrifying new age with cosmetic surgery. All limits have broken down. No amount of suffering or threat of disfigurement can serve as a deterrent. What is happening to the female body in relation to cosmetic surgery is like what is happening to the balance of life on the planet. We are at a historic turning point.

The dawn of the Surgical Age in the 1980s did result from some technological advances in the profession. It drew far more energy, though, from the beauty backlash against feminism. The two developments—the means and, more important, *the will* completely to alter women—has brought us to an extraordinary mental upheaval surrounding life in the female form. With the shift in rhetoric that recast pain and mutilation into diminished language, female consciousness has had to reckon with the sort of destruction of the rules that faced human thinking when the atom was split. With the huge expansion of possibility came a huge expansion of danger.

If anything on a woman's body can be changed, something revolutionary—or demonic—has come about in the alternate world of the beauty myth. Does it mean the cruel old economy is blasted apart? That science has indeed opened up a horizon of beauty for all women who can afford it? Does it mean the bitterly rankling caste system, in which some are born "better" than others, is dead, and women are free?

That has been the popular interpretation: The Surgical Age is an unqualified good. It is the American dream come true: One can re-create oneself "better" in a brave new world. It has even, understandably, been interpreted as a feminist liberation: *Ms.* magazine hailed it as "self-transformation"; in *Lear's*, a woman surgeon urges, "Voilà! You are led to freedom." This hopeful female yearning for a magic technology that destroys the beauty myth and its injustice—with a "beauty" that is almost fair because you can earn it with pain and buy it with money—is a poignant, but shortsighted, response.

It is with the same kind of hopefulness that the atom bomb was introduced in the 1950s. The Bomb was presented at the end of total war as a magic equalizer of unequal nations; cosmetic surgery is presented as the miraculous peacekeeper in women's combat under the beauty myth. It took decades for people to recognize the true impact of the nuclear age on human consciousness. Whether or not it would ever be used again, the Bomb changed forever how we thought about the world.

With the Age of Surgery, we are at the very first swell of a wave whose end we cannot see. But the cheerfulness with which we are embracing this technology is as shortsighted as the optimism about the Bomb that flooded the market with Atomic beachwear and cartoon characters. With cosmetic surgery, consciousness inside the female body is undergoing a transformation that may mean we have lost the body's boundaries, so recently defined and defended—and our presurgical orientation inside it—forever.

We are affected by the Bomb whether or not it is detonated. Whether or not a woman ever undergoes cosmetic surgery, her mind is now being shaped by its existence. The *expectation* of surgery will continue to rise. Since the beauty myth works in a mappable balance system, as soon as enough women are altered and critical mass is reached so that too many women look like the "ideal," the "ideal" will always shift. Ever-different cutting and stitching will be required of women if we are to keep our sexuality and our livelihood.

In 1945, we lost the luxury of taking for granted that the world would outlive the individual. Technology made its destruction imaginable. Around 1990, technology introduced the end of the woman-made female body. A woman began to lose the luxury of taking for granted that she had a face and a body that were hers alone in which she could live out her life.

The years between the development of the Bomb and the evolution of Einstein's "new manner of thinking" about war were the most dangerous. Human beings had the means to destroy the world through using new technology in conventional warfare, but had not yet evolved beyond imagining the inevitability of conventional warfare. Today, women have access to the technological capacity to do anything to our bodies in the struggle for "beauty," but we have yet to evolve a mentality beyond the old rules, to let them imagine that this combat among women is not inevitable. Surgeons can now do anything. We have not yet reached the age in which we can defend ourselves with an unwillingness to have "anything" done.

This is a dangerous time.

New possibilities for women quickly become new obligations. It is a short step from "anything can be done for beauty" to "anything *must* be done." What must be worked through before we can start thinking our way to safety is the assertion that women freely choose this pain. We need to ask what "choice" and "pain" mean in relation to women in the Surgical Age.

## Pain

What makes pain exist? Law theorist Suzanne Levitt points out that in the courtroom, in order to prove harm has been done, you have to prove you are worse off than you were before. But, she says, since there is a "background noise" of harm around them, women aren't seen to be hurt when they are hurt. The same concept seems to hold true for recognition of the harm done women for beauty's sake: Since women should be addicted to "beauty," this life-threatening addiction is not real. Since women should suffer to be beautiful—since our suffering *is* beautiful—the pain we feel is "discomfort." Because women's money is not real money but pin money, and because women are fools for "beauty" and a fool and her money are soon parted, fraudulent practices are not fraud and women's play money is fair game. Because women are deformed to begin with, we cannot really suffer deformation. Because we are gullible by nature in search of "beauty," no deception is a scandal.

Pain is real when you can get other people to believe in it. If no one believes it but you, your pain is madness or hysteria or your own unfeminine inadequacy. Women have learned to submit to pain by hearing authority figures—doctors, priests, psychiatrists—tell us that what we feel is not pain.

Women are asked to be stoic in the face of surgical pain as they were asked to be stoic for childbirth. The medieval Church enforced the curse of Eve by refusing to permit any alleviation of the pain of childbirth, according to Andrea Dworkin's analysis of misogyny, *Woman Hating*. "The Catholic objection to abortion," says Dworkin, "centered specifically on the Biblical curse that made childbirth a painful punishment—it did not have to do with the 'right to life' of the unborn fetus." The poet Adrienne Rich reminds women that "patriarchy has told the woman in labor that her suffering was purposive—was *the* purpose of her existence, that the new life she was bringing forth (especially if male) was of value and that her own value depended on bringing it forth." The same is true for the "new life" of surgical "beauty." In maternity wards, asserts the Brighton Women and Science Group in *Alice Through the Microscope*, the mother-to-be "is usually expected to dissociate herself from her body and its behaviour, to remain in control of herself and behave 'well.' The woman who screams in labor, or who cries afterwards, is often made to feel that she *ought not*, that she has lost control, that her own feelings are not natural, or that she should not give in to them." Women who have undergone cosmetic surgery report the same experience.

Most women can think of many occasions on which they were told that what was hurting them was not. I remember a gynecologist with thick and senseless hands, who expanded the speculum angrily and shot a meteor of pain to the base of my spine; the fontanelles in my skull seemed to separate and pain poured in like ice. "Stop making faces," he told me. "This doesn't hurt." Or the electrologist a woman told me about who asked, "Have you ever had electrolysis before?" "Yes," said the woman. "What do you know about it?" "It hurts like hell." "It does not," she contradicted. Or the voices one hears over a rape crisis hot line: "They said they didn't know why I was so upset. There weren't any bruises. It wasn't like he'd hurt me." Or the career woman who described to me her nose surgery: "It was after a bad love affair that I literally cut off my nose to spite my face. They said if I was a good patient there would be no real pain and only a little blood. I couldn't bear it. I said it hurt. They said I was overreacting. There was so much blood my sister fainted when she saw me. They said, 'Now look what you've done.'"

A "scalpel slave" in *She* magazine describes a face peel: "Essentially, it is no different from a second-degree burn. . . . [It] makes you go brown and crispy, then a scab forms and drops off . . . [it] takes several hours because it is so poisonous and you can't risk getting it into the bloodstream." Dr. Thomas Rees minces no words: "Abrasion and peeling traumatizes [*sic*] the skin . . . with either procedure, the skin can be removed too deeply and result in an open wound . . . . deaths [from cardiac arrest] have followed a chemical peel . . . the skin is frozen [for dermabrasion] until it assumes a boardlike quality that facilitates the abrasion from a rotating wire brush impregnated with diamond particles." ("Skin planing," he informs the reader, "originated in World War II, done with sandpaper to remove shrapnel embedded in the skin." Plastic surgery developed after World War I in reaction to wartime mutilations never witnessed before.) A woman who has witnessed skin planing said to an interviewer, "If we found that they were doing that to people in prison, there would be an international outcry and [the country] would be reported to Amnesty International for torture of the most horrific kind." Chemical peeling, that "torture of the most horrific kind," is up, according to Rees, 34 percent.

It is not easy to describe physical pain, and the words we agree on to convey it are rarely adequate. Society has to agree that a certain kind of pain exists in order to ease it. What women experience in the operating theater, under the mask of acid, laid out open to the mouth of the suction machine, passed out cold in wait for the bridge of the nose to be broken, is still private and unsayable.

Their pain is denied through trivialization. "It can be uncomfortable." "There is some discomfort." "A little, little bit of bruising and swelling." One is not yet allowed to compare American and European women's pain for beauty to real pain, to Amnesty International pain. The comparison will be called overstatement. But the comparison must hold, since women are dying of understatement.

Surgery hurts, it hurts. They hold you underwater just long enough to stop you struggling. You breathe with newly cut gills. They haul you out again, logged and twisted, facedown on a bank with no footprints. Your spirit held in suspended animation, they drive a tank carefully over your ignorant body.

Waking up hurts, and coming back to life hurts horribly. A hospital, though it is called "luxurious" or "caring," degrades: Like a prison or a mental institution, wherever the old identity meant trouble, they take away your clothes and give you a numbered bed.

For the time you were under, you lose your life, and you never regain those hours. Visitors come, but you see them through the waters that have closed over your head, another species: the well. Once you have been cut into, no amount of good living can ever erase what you know about how easy, how accommodating death is.

Cosmetic surgery is not "cosmetic," and human flesh is not "plastic." Even the names trivialize what it is. It's not like ironing wrinkles in fabric, or tuning up a car, or altering outmoded clothes, the current metaphors. Trivialization and infantilization pervade the surgeons' language when they speak to women: "a nip," a "tummy tuck." Rees writes, describing a second-degree acid burn over the face: "Remember when you were in school and you skinned your knee and a scab formed?" This baby talk falsifies reality. Surgery changes one forever, the mind as well as the body. If we don't start to speak of it as serious, the millennium of the man-made woman will be upon us, and we will have had no choice.


## Choice

"Beauty's" pain is trivial since it is assumed that women freely choose it. That conviction is what keeps people from seeing that what the Surgical Age is doing to women is human rights abuse. The hunger, the nausea, and surgical invasions of the beauty backlash are political weapons. Through them, a widespread political torture is taking place among us. When a class of people is denied food, or forced to vomit regularly, or repeatedly cut open and stitched together to no medical purpose, we call it torture. Are women less hungry, less bloody, if we act as our own torturers?

Most people will say yes, since women do it to themselves, and it is something that must be done. But it is illogical to conclude that there is a different quality to blood or hunger or second-degree burning because it was "chosen." Nerve endings

cannot tell who has paid for the slicing; a raw dermis is not comforted by the motive behind its burning. People respond il-
logically when confronted with beauty's pain since they believe
that masochists deserve the pain they get because they enjoy it.

But moreover, women learn what we have to do from our environment. Women are sensitive to the signals that institutions
send about what we have to do with our "beauty" to survive, and
the institutions are giving us a very clear message that they en-
dorse any level of violence. If struggle for beauty is women's warfare, the women who draw the line are treated as cowards, as are
male pacifists. "Who's afraid of cosmetic surgery?" taunts a surgeon. Women's choice in the Age of Surgery is not free, so we
have no excuse for refusing to see their pain as real.

Women will have a real choice about cosmetic surgery only
when:

*If we don't do it, we can keep their livelihood.* We saw how
surgical alteration has become a requirement for women's employment and promotion. Surgical brochures emphasize career pressures on women to look "youthful." That requirement is actually
criminal. According to the Occupational Safety and Health Act of
1970, "Employers can no longer . . . purchase the agreement of
workers to subject themselves to unsafe or unhealthful working
conditions." Surgery, Retin-A, and chronic caloric deprivation are
unhealthful and unsafe, but women faced with the professional
beauty qualification lack the choice to resist them and keep their
means of support.

*If we don't do it, we can keep our identities.* "Choice" means
nothing if the choice is to survive or to perish. An animal caught
in a trap doesn't choose to gnaw its leg off. The Iron Maiden is
closing now, with her razor outlines. What has outgrown the edge
is trapped and must be severed. When women talk about surgery,
they speak of "flaws" they "cannot live with," and they are not
being hysterical. Their magazines ask: "Is there life after 40? Is
there life after size 16?" and those questions are no joke. Women
choose surgery when we are convinced we cannot be who we
really are without it. If all women could choose to live with themselves *as* themselves, most probably would. Women's fears of loss
of identity are legitimate. We "choose" a little death over what is

portrayed as an unlivable life; we "choose" to die a bit in order to be born again.

*If we don't do it, we can still keep our places in the community.*   In traditional cultures such as Greece and Turkey, it is considered obscene for older women to wear the bright colors of youth. There are "modern" communities already—Palm Springs, Beverly Hills, Manhattan's Upper East Side—that consider it as shocking for an older woman to leave the skin of her throat uncut.

Men usually think of coercion as a threatened loss of autonomy. For women, coercion often takes a different form: the threat of losing the chance to form bonds with others, be loved, and stay wanted. Men think coercion happens mainly through physical violence, but women see physical suffering as bearable compared with the pain of losing love. The threat of the loss of love can put someone back in line faster than a raised fist. If we think of women as the ones who will jump through hoops of fire to keep love, it is only because the threat of lovelessness has been used so far against women rather than against men as a form of political crowd control.

Women's desperation for beauty is derided as narcissism; but women are desperate to hold on to a sexual center that no one threatens to take away from men, who keep sexual identity in spite of physical imperfections and age. Men do not hear in the same way the message that time is running out, and that they will never again be stroked and admired and gratified. Let a man imagine himself living under that threat before he calls women narcissistic. Fighting for "beauty," many of us understandably believe we are fighting for our lives, for life warmed by sexual love.

With the threat of lost love comes the threat of invisibility. Extreme age shows the essence of the myth's inequality: The world is run by old men; but old women are erased from the culture. A banned or ostracized person becomes a nonperson. Ostracism and banning are effective, and leave no proof of coercion: no bars, no laws, no guns. South African activist Beyers Naude said on British television that "a banning order can easily lead to people breaking down." Few can bear being treated as if they are invisible. Women have face-lifts in a society in which women without them appear to vanish from sight.

Face-lifts cause nerve paralysis, infection, skin ulceration, "skin death," scar overgrowth and postoperative depression. "What a shock! I looked like a truck had hit me! Swollen, bruised, pathetic . . . I looked freakish . . . about this time, I was told, many women begin to cry uncontrollably." "It's quite painful afterward, because your jaw feels dislocated. You can't smile, your face aches . . . I had terrible yellow bruising and trauma." "An angry infection . . . hematoma . . . a half-circle bruise and three distinct lumps, one the size of a giant jawbreaker. . . . Now I enjoy putting on makeup!" Those are quotes in women's magazines from women who have had face-lifts.

I wish I could forget the sight of someone I love lying in St. Vincent's Hospital, bandages on her eyes smeared with a sulfurous matter. An intravenous tube dripped into a delicate vein. Groggy, her head rolled across the pillow like a blinded calf's. She could not see the people who cared for her standing awkwardly around her high-railed bed. Down the magnificent cheekbones, over the celebrated mouth, a line of bright blood descended. She seemed to be lying there because she was sick or hurt, but before she entered the hospital, she hadn't been. She was there because she was less beautiful, some might say, than she used to be.

Women are learning to smile grimly at such tales, because the alternative, we are told, is really intolerable. Old women disappear. Our mothers' mothers disappeared, their social worth diminished when their child rearing days ended.

But whatever the pressures of the present, the surgical future is one without choice.

## Surgical Futures

The Victorians' definition of operable kept expanding. "Moral insanity," like ugliness, was a "definition that could be altered to take in almost any kind of behavior regarded as abnormal or disruptive by community standards," writes Elaine Showalter. "Asylums opened for 'young women of ungovernable temper . . . sullen, wayward, malicious, defying all domestic control; or who want that restraint over their passions without which the female character is lost.'" So does our definition of operable keep expanding, for the same reasons. In the 1970s, intestinal bypass surgery (in which the intestines are sealed off for weight loss) was invented and it multiplied until, by 1983, there were fifty thousand such operations performed a year. Jaw clamps (in which the jaw is wired together for weight loss) were also introduced in the feminist 1970s, and stomach stapling (in which the stomach is sutured together for weight loss) began in 1976. "As time went on," reports *Radiance*, "the criteria for acceptance became looser and looser until now anyone who is even moderately plump can find a cooperative surgeon." Women of 154 pounds have had their intestines stapled together. Though the doctor who developed it restricted the procedure to patients more than 100 pounds overweight, the FDA approved it for "virtually anyone who wants it."

Intestinal stapling causes thirty-seven possible complications, including severe malnutrition, liver damage, liver failure, irregular heartbeat, brain and nerve damage, stomach cancer, immune deficiency, pernicious anemia, liver failure, and death. One patient in ten develops ulcers within six months. Her mortality rate is nine times above that of an identical person who forgoes surgery; 2 to 4 percent die within days, and the eventual death toll may be much higher. Surgeons "aggressively seek out" patients, and "have no trouble getting patients to sign informed consent forms acknowledging the possibility of severe complications and even death."

One is not surprised by now to learn that 80 to 90 percent of stomach and intestinal stapling patients are female.

At last, all women are operable. Liposuction is the fastest-growing of cosmetic surgeries: 130,000 American women underwent the procedure last year, and surgeons sucked 200,000 pounds of body tissue out of them. According to *The New York Times*, as we saw, 11 women have died from the procedure. At least 3 more have died since that article was written.

But I would not have known that from the conversations I had with "counselors" when I posed as a prospective client:

"What are the risks from liposuction?"
"The risks aren't great. There is always a risk from
    infection, that is small and a risk from anesthetic,
    that's small."

"Has anyone ever died?"

"Well, maybe ten years ago, with very obese people."

"Does anyone ever die these days?"

"Oh, *no*."

"What are the risks from liposuction?"

"There are no risks, none at all."

"I read that people have died from it."

"Oh God. Where did you read that?"

*"The New York Times."*

"I know nothing about that. I know nothing about *The New York Times*. I'm sure if that were true it would be making headlines. They make a fuss over the least little thing."

"Are there any risks involved with liposuction?"

"No, no. Generally speaking, no risks involved at all, no, no. No problem at all, no."

"I read that there have been some deaths."

"Mmm. I have heard something about that. But as long as you're in the hands of a skilled practitioner, you should have no problem, no problem."

"What are the risks involved with liposuction?"

"There is very little risk, very little."

"Does anyone ever die from it?"

"I would never think so."

"What are the risks involved with liposuction?"

"They're tiny, very very small. They are very very minimal, whether one million to one or whatever. It's very simple, there's very little to go wrong in terms of permanent side effects—very very little to go wrong."

"Is there any risk of death?"

"None whatsoever, no, no. I haven't heard of any complication like that."

You could call death a permanent side effect. You could definitely call it a complication. Stretching a point, you could say risking your life is the least little thing to fuss about, a very very little risk, tiny, very small, very very minimal. Liposuction deaths aren't real deaths—a comforting thought for the families of the deceased. The surgeons say that "the benefits far outweigh the risks," which is a value judgment about the relative importance of their version of "beauty" to that of a woman's life.

To dwell on the teeny tiny death risk, a surgeon might say, is to overreact: The deaths are a fraction of a percentage of the whole. Surely—for a medically necessary operation. But for the reconstruction of healthy young women? How many will die before it is too many, before we draw around ourselves a line of safety? Fourteen dead women and counting, each of whom had a name, a home, and a future. And each of whom had healthy concentrations of flesh where fat distinguishes female from male sexual development; for which all the rest had to be staked on the wheel, all gambled for double or nothing and, for these fourteen women, all lost. When is it appropriate to notice blood on a doctor's hands? Will we go on to twenty? To thirty? To fifty healthy women dead before we feel resistance, before we question the process that has women gamble their lives for a "beauty" that has nothing to do with us? At this rate, those deaths will be just a matter of time. Liposuction is the fastest-growing procedure in a field that triples every other year. Before this trend escalates until it can never again be considered appropriate, now is the time to stand back and notice fourteen dead bodies, real ones, human ones. Fourteen women dead was enough for Kenya, but not for the United States.

What is liposuction (assuming you live through it)? If you are reading the Poutney Clinic's brochure, it looks like this:

FIGURE IMPROVEMENT BY IMMEDIATE SPOT FAT REDUCTION. . . . One of the most successful techniques is that developed to refine and reshape the figure. With Lipolysis/Suction assisted Lipectomy a tiny incision is made in each area of excess fat. A very slender tube is then inserted and by gentle, skillful movements aided by a powerful and even suction this unwanted (and often unsightly) fat is removed—permanently.

If you are reading an eyewitness account by journalist Jill Neimark, it looks like this:

[A] man force[s] a plastic tube down a naked woman's throat.
He connects the tube to a pump that, for the next two hours,
will breathe for her. Her eyes are taped shut, her arms are
stretched out horizontally and her head lolls a little to the
side. . . . She's in a chemically induced coma known as general anaesthesia . . . what comes next is almost unbelievably
violent. Her surgeon, Dr. Leigh Lachman, begins to thrust
the cannula in and out, as rapid as a piston, breaking through
thick nets of fat, nerves and tissue in her leg. The doctor is
ready to stitch her up. Nearly 2,000 millilitres of tissue and
blood have been sucked out of her, any more would put her
at risk for massive infection and fluid loss leading to shock
and death. . . . He peels the tape back from her lids, and
she stares at him, unseeing. "A lot of people have trouble
coming back. Bringing someone out of anaesthesia is the
most dangerous part of an operation." . . . [which] can lead
to massive infection, excessive damage to capillaries and
fluid depletion resulting in shock and coma.

Liposuction shows the way to the future: It is the first of many
procedures to come for which all women will be eligible by virtue
of being women.


**Eugenics**


Women are surgical candidates because we are considered inferior, an evaluation women share with other excluded groups.
Nonwhite racial features are "deformities" too: The Poutney
Clinic's brochure offers "a Western appearance to the eyes" to
"the Oriental Eyelid," which "lacks a well-defined supratarsal
fold." It admires "the Caucasian or 'Western' nose," ridicules
"Asian Noses," "Afro-Caribbean Noses ('a fat and rounded tip
which needs correction')," and "Oriental Noses ('the tip . . . too
close to the face')." And "the Western nose that requires alteration invariably exhibits some of the characteristics of (nonwhite)
noses . . . although the improvement needed is more subtle."
White women, together with black and Asian women, undergo

surgery not as a consequence of selfish vanity, but in reasonable reaction to physical discrimination.

When we examine the language of the Age of Surgery, a familiar degradation process echoes. In 1938, German relatives of deformed infants requested their mercy killings. It was an atmosphere in which the Third Reich stressed, writes Robert Jay Lifton, "the duty to be healthy," asked its people to "renounce the old individualist principle of 'the right to one's own body,'" and characterized the ill and weak as "useless eaters."

Recall the reclassification process and how it moves, once violence begins, from narrow to wide: The Nazi doctors began by sterilizing people with chronic disabilities, then with minor defects, then "undesirables"; finally, healthy Jewish children were placed in the net because their Jewishness was disease enough. The definition of sick, expendable life soon became "loose, extensive, and increasingly known." The "useless eaters" were simply put on a "fat-free diet" until they starved to death; they had "already been fed insufficiently and the idea of not nourishing them was in the air." Remember the characterization of parts of women as already wounded, numb, deformed, or dead. "These people," the Nazi doctors declared of "undesirables," "are already dead." A language that categorized the "unfit" as already less than alive eased the doctors' conscience: They called them "human ballast," "life unworthy of life," "empty shells of human beings." Remember the use of "health" to rationalize bloodshed; the doctors' worldview was grounded in what Robert Jay Lifton calls "the healing/killing reversal." They stressed the therapeutic function of killing deformed and weak children as a means to heal the body politic, "to ensure that the people realize the full potential of their racial and genetic endowment" and "to reverse racial decay."

Remember the trivializing language of the surgeons; when the German doctors culled children by syringe, it was "not murder, this is a putting-to-sleep." Remember the unqualified surgeons' bureaucratic obfuscations; the Reich Committee for the Scientific Registration of Serious Hereditary and Congenital Diseases, Lifton writes, "conveyed the sense of a formidable medical-scientific registry board, though its leader . . . had his degree in agricultural economics . . . . these 'observation' institutions . . .

provided an aura of medical check against mistakes, when in fact no real examination or observation was made." Medical experimentation was justified on "creatures who, because less than human, can be studied, altered, manipulated, mutilated or killed—in the service . . . ultimately of remaking humankind." Remember numbness; both victims and experimenters existed in a state of "extreme numbing," for in "the Auschwitz atmosphere . . . any kind of experiment was considered possible."

As Lifton writes: "The doctor . . . if not living in a moral situation . . . where limits are very clear . . . is very dangerous."

Progressive dehumanization has a stark, well-documented pattern. To undergo cosmetic surgery, one must feel and society must agree that some parts of the body are not worthy of life, though they are still living. These ideas are seeping into the general atmosphere with a nasty stench of eugenics, for the cosmetic surgeon's world is based on biological supremacy, something Western democracies are not supposed to admire.

## The Iron Maiden Breaks Free

Women are in jeopardy from our current misunderstanding of the Iron Maiden. We still believe that there is some point where surgery is constrained by a natural limit, the outline of the "perfect" human female. That is no longer true. The "ideal" has never been about the bodies of women, and from now on technology can allow the "ideal" to do what it has always sought to do: leave the female body behind altogether to clone its mutations in space. The human female is no longer the point of reference.

The "ideal" has become at last fully inhuman. One model points out in *Cosmopolitan* that "the ideal today is a muscular body with big breasts. Nature doesn't make women like that." And, in fact, women no longer see versions of the Iron Maiden that represent the natural female body. "Today," says Dr. Stephen Herman of Albert Einstein College of Medicine Hospital, "I think, almost every popular model has had some type of breast augmentation operation." "Many models," another women's magazine concedes, "now regard a session with the plastic surgeon as part

of their job requirement." Fifty million Americans watch the Miss
America pageant; in 1989 five contestants, including Miss Florida,
Miss Alaska, and Miss Oregon, were surgically reconstructed by a
single Arkansas plastic surgeon. Women are comparing themselves and young men are comparing young women with a new
breed that is hybrid nonwoman. Women's natural attractions were
never the aim of the beauty myth, and technology has finally cut
the cord. She says, I feel bad about this; he cuts. She says, What
about this here; he cuts.

The specter of the future is not that women will be slaves, but
that we will be robots. First, we will be subservient to ever more
refined technology for self-surveillance, such as the Futurex-5000,
or Holtain's Body Composition Analyzer, a portable fat-analysis
machine with infrared light, and a hand-held computer that applies electrical currents through electrodes placed at wrists and
ankles. Then, to more sophisticated alterations of images of the
"ideal" in the media: "Virtual reality" and "photographic re-
imaging" will make "pefection" increasingly surreal. Then, to
technologies that replace the faulty, mortal female body, piece by
piece, with "perfect" artifice. This is not science fiction: the replacement of women has begun with reproductive technology. In
Great Britain and the United States, research is well under way to
develop an artificial placenta, and, according to science writers,
"we are now moving into an era when we will have the scientific
and technical knowledge to deny women the opportunity to reproduce, or to reproduce only if they use the genetic materials of
others." That is, the technology exists for wealthy white couples
to rent the uteri of poor women of any race to gestate their white
babies. Since childbirth "ruins" the figure, the scenario of rich
women hiring poor ones to do their ungainly reproductive labor is
imminent. And cosmetic surgery has given us little reason to
doubt that when the technology exists for it, poor women will be
pressed to sell actual body material—breasts or skin or hair or
fat—to service the reconstruction of rich women, as people today
sell their organs and blood. If that seems grotesquely futuristic,
cast yourself back just ten years and imagine being told that the
invasive alteration on a mass scale of women's breasts and hips
would come to pass so soon.

Technology will continue radically to destabilize the social

value of the female body. Products are being developed to predetermine sex, with success rates of 70–80 percent; when such
products are available one can expect, based on gender preferences recorded worldwide, that the ratio of women to men will
drop precipitously. In the near future, warns one group of scientists, "women could be bred for particular qualities, like passivity
and beauty." Adjustable breast implants are now a reality, allowing women to be adapted for each partner's preferences. The Japanese have already perfected a lifelike geisha robot with artificial
skin.

But the first signs of the mass production of the female body
are still the exception; the mass production of the female mind is
pervasive. Women are the drugged sex: Between 1957 and 1967,
consumption of psychotropic drugs (sedatives, tranquilizers, anti-
depressants, appetite reducers) increased by 80 percent, and 75
percent of the drug users are female. By 1979, 160 million prescriptions were written for tranquilizers, over 60 million for Valium alone. Sixty to 80 percent of those prescriptions went to
women, and Valium abuse is reported as the most common drug
problem that hospital emergency services deal with. Today, in
Great Britain and the United States, twice as many women as
men take tranquilizers; a scandal in Canada is the overprescribing
of tranquilizers to women. In all three countries, women are the
main subjects of electroshock treatment, psychosurgery, and psychotropic drugs.

This recent history of woman as pharmaceutical subject sets
the stage for "a new era of 'pharmaceutical cosmetics,'" including
Lilly Industries' antidepressant drug Fluoxetine, awaiting approval by the FDA, which will be marketed as a weight-loss pill.
*The Guardian* reports that another, the adrenalinelike ephedrine,
speeds metabolic rate, and a third, DRL26830A, thins subjects
down while inducing "transient tremors." Though of course
"there is concern within the pharmaceuticals industry that they
could create serious ethical problems," industry spokesmen are
already prepared for "setting the stage for more 'cosmetic' rather
than medical use." Women take drugs, one drug agency quoted
in the article reports, "in order to be seen as feminine. The 'feminine' woman . . . is slim, passive, deferential to men and 'does
not exhibit emotions such as anger, frustration or assertiveness.'"

The new wave of cosmetically directed mood enhancers may solve the problem of women once and for all, as we dose ourselves into a state of perpetual cheerfulness, deference, passivity, and chronically sedated slimness.

Whatever the future threatens, we can be fairly sure of this: Women in our "raw" or "natural" state will continue to be shifted from category "woman" to category "ugly," and shamed into an assembly-line physical identity. As each woman responds to the pressure, it will grow so intense that it will become obligatory, until no self-respecting woman will venture outdoors with a surgically unaltered face. The free market will compete to cut up women's bodies more cheaply, if more sloppily, with no-frills surgery in bargain basement clinics. In that atmosphere, it is a matter of time before they reposition the clitoris, sew up the vagina for a snugger fit, loosen the throat muscles, and sever the gag reflex. Los Angeles surgeons have developed and implanted transparent skin, through which the inner organs can be seen. It is, says one witness, "the ultimate voyeurism."

The machine is at the door. Is she the future?

# Beyond the Beauty Myth

*C*an *we* bring about another future, in which it is she who is dead and we who are beautifully alive?

The beauty myth countered women's new freedoms by transposing the social limits to women's lives directly onto our faces and bodies. In response, we must now ask the questions about our place in our bodies that women a generation ago asked about their place in society.

What is a woman? Is she what is made of her? Do a woman's life and experience have value? If so, should she be ashamed for them to show? What *is* so great about looking young?

The idea that a woman's body has boundaries that must not be violated is fairly new. We evidently haven't taken it far enough. Can we extend that idea? Or are women the pliable sex, innately adapted to being shaped, cut, and subjected to physical invasion? Does the female body deserve the same notion of integrity as the male body? Is there a difference between fashions in clothing and fashions in women's bodies? Assuming that someday women can be altered cheaply, painlessly, and with no risk, is

270

that to be what we must want? Must the expressiveness of maturity and old age become extinct? Will we lose nothing if it does?

Does a woman's identity count? Must she be made to want to look like someone else? Is there something implicitly gross about the texture of female flesh? The inadequacy of female flesh stands in for the older inadequacy of the female mind. Women asserted that there was nothing inferior about their minds; are our bodies really inferior?

Is "beauty" really sex? Does a woman's sexuality correspond to what she looks like? Does she have the right to sexual pleasure and self-esteem because she's a person, or must she earn that right through "beauty," as she used to through marriage? What is female sexuality—what does it look like? Does it bear any relation to the way in which commercial images represent it? Is it something women need to buy like a product? What really draws men and women together?

Are women beautiful or aren't we?

Of course we are. But we won't really believe it the way we need to until we start to take the first steps beyond the beauty myth.

Does all this mean we can't wear lipstick without feeling guilty?

On the contrary. It means we have to separate from the myth what it has surrounded and held hostage: female sexuality, bonding among women, visual enjoyment, sensual pleasure in fabrics and shapes and colors—female fun, clean and dirty. We can dissolve the myth and survive it with sex, love, attraction, and style not only intact, but flourishing more vibrantly than before. I am not attacking anything that makes women feel good; only what makes us feel bad in the first place. We all like to be desirable and feel beautiful.

But for about 160 years, middle-class, educated Western women have been controlled by various ideals about female perfection; this old and successful tactic has worked by taking the best of female culture and attaching to it the most repressive demands of male-dominated societies. These forms of ransom were imposed on the female orgasm in the 1920s, on home and children and the family in the 1950s, on the culture of beauty in the

1980s. With this tactic, we waste time in every generation debating the symptoms more passionately than the disease.

We see this pattern of *the self-interested promotion of ideals*—eloquently pointed out in the work of Barbara Ehrenreich and Dierdre English—throughout our recent history. We must bring it up to date with the beauty myth, to get it once and for all. If we don't, as soon as we take apart the beauty myth, a new ideology will arise in its place. The beauty myth is not, ultimately, about appearance or dieting or surgery or cosmetics—any more than the Feminine Mystique was about housework. No one who is responsible for the myths of femininity in every generation really cares about the symptoms at all.

The architects of the Feminine Mystique didn't really believe that a floor in which you could see yourself indicated a cardinal virtue in women; in my own lifetime, when the idea of menstrual psychic irregularity was being clumsily resurrected as a last-ditch way to hold off the claims of the women's movement, no one was really vested in the conviction of menstrual incapacity *in itself*. By the same token, the beauty myth could not care less how much women weigh; it doesn't give a damn about the texture of women's hair or the smoothness of our skin. We intuit that, if we were all to go home tomorrow and say we never meant it really—we'll do without the jobs, the autonomy, the orgasms, the money—the beauty myth would slacken at once and grow more comfortable.

This realization makes the real issues behind the symptoms easier to see and analyze: Just as the beauty myth did not really care what women looked like as long as women felt ugly, we must see that it does not matter in the least what women look like as long as we feel beautiful.

The real issue has nothing to do with whether women wear makeup or don't, gain weight or lose it, have surgery or shun it, dress up or down, make our clothing and faces and bodies into works of art or ignore adornment altogether. *The real problem is our lack of choice.*

Under the Feminine Mystique, virtually all middle-class women were condemned to a compulsive attitude toward domesticity, whatever their individual inclinations; now that this idea is largely dismantled, those women who are personally inclined scrupulous housekeeping pursue it, and those women who couldn't be less interested have a (relatively) greater degree of choice. We got sloppy, and the world didn't end. After we dismantle the beauty myth, a similar situation—so eminently sensible, yet so remote from where we are—will characterize our relationship to beauty culture.

The problem with cosmetics exists only when women feel invisible or inadequate without them. The problem with working out exists only if women hate ourselves when we don't. When a woman is forced to adorn herself to buy a hearing, when she needs her grooming in order to protect her identity, when she goes hungry in order to keep her job, when she must attract a lover so that she can take care of her children, that is exactly what makes "beauty" hurt. Because what hurts women about the beauty myth is not adornment, or expressed sexuality, or time spent grooming, or the desire to attract a lover. Many mammals groom, and every culture uses adornment. "Natural" and "unnatural" are not the terms in question. The actual struggle is between pain and pleasure, freedom and compulsion.

Costumes and disguises will be lighthearted and fun when women are granted rock-solid identities. Clothing that highlights women's sexuality will be casual wear when women's sexuality is under our own control. When female sexuality is fully affirmed as a legitimate passion that arises from within, to be directed without stigma to the chosen object of our desire, the sexually expressive clothes or manner we may assume can no longer be used to shame us, blame us, or target us for beauty myth harassment.

The beauty myth posited to women a false choice: Which will I be, sexual or serious? We must reject that false and forced dilemma. Men's sexuality is taken to be enhanced by their seriousness; to be at the same time a serious person and a sexual being is to be fully human. Let's turn on those who offer this devil's bargain and refuse to believe that in choosing one aspect of the self we must thereby forfeit the other. In a world in which women have real choices, the choices we make about our appearance will be taken at last for what they really are: no big deal.

Women will be able thoughtlessly to adorn ourselves with pretty objects when there is no question that *we* are not objects. Women will be free of the beauty myth when we can choose to use our faces and clothes and bodies as simply one form of self-expression out of a full range of others. We can dress up for our pleasure, but we must speak up for our rights.

Many writers have tried to deal with the problems of fantasy, pleasure, and "glamour" by evicting them from the female Utopia. But "glamour" is merely a demonstration of the human capacity for being enchanted, and is not in itself destructive. We need it, but redefined. We cannot disperse an exploitive religion through asceticism, or bad poetry with none at all. We can combat painful pleasure only with pure pleasure.

But let's not be naive. We are trying to make new meanings for beauty in an environment that doesn't want us to get away with it. To look however we want to look—and to be heard as we deserve to be heard—we will need no less than a feminist third wave.

## Speech

The trouble with any debate about the beauty myth is the sophisticated reflex it uses: It punishes virtually any woman who tries to raise these issues by scrutinizing her appearance. It is striking to notice how thoroughly we comprehend this implied punishment. We know well how it works in a typical beauty myth double bind: No matter what a woman's appearance may be, it will be used to undermine what she is saying and taken to individualize—as her personal problem—observations she makes about aspects of the beauty myth in society.

Unfortunately, since the media routinely give accounts of women's appearance in a way that trivializes or discredits what they say, women reading or watching are routinely dissuaded from identifying with women in the public eye—the ultimate anti-feminist goal of the beauty myth. Whenever we dismiss or do not hear a woman on television or in print because our attention has been drawn to her size or makeup or clothing or hairstyle, the beauty myth is working with optimum efficiency.

For a woman to go public means she must face being subjected to invasive physical scrutiny, which by definition, as we saw, no woman can pass; for a woman to speak about the beauty myth (as about women's issues in general) means that *there is no right way she can look.* There is no unmarked, or neutral, stance allowed women at those times: They are called either too "ugly" or too "pretty" to be believed. This reflex is working well politically: Often today, when women talk about the reasons they do not engage more with women-centered groups and movements, they often focus on differences not in agenda or worldview but in aesthetics and personal style. By keeping the antifeminist origins and reactionary purpose of this direction of attention always in mind, we can thwart the myth. For us to reject the insistence that a woman's appearance *is her speech,* for us to hear one another out beyond the beauty myth, is itself a political step forward.

## Blame

Blame is what fuels the beauty myth; to take it apart, let us refuse forever to blame ourselves and other women for what it, in its great strength, has tried to do. The most important change to aim at is this: When someone tries, in the future, to use the beauty myth against us, we will no longer look in the mirror to see what we have done wrong. Women can organize around discrimination in employment on the basis of appearance only when we examine the usual reactions to such complaints ("Well, why did you wear that tight sweater?" "So, why don't you do something about yourself?") and reject them. We cannot speak up about the myth until we believe in our guts that there is nothing objective about how the myth works—that when women are called too ugly or too pretty to do something we want to do, this has nothing to do with our appearance. Women can summon the courage to talk about the myth in public by keeping in mind that attacks on or flattery of our appearance in public are never at fault. It is all impersonal; it is political.

The reflexive responses that have developed to keep us silent will doubtless increase in intensity: "Easy for you to say." "You're too pretty to be a feminist." "No wonder she's a feminist; look at her." "What does she expect, dressed like that?"

"That's what comes of vanity." "What makes you think they were whistling at you?" "What was she wearing?" "Don't you wish." "Don't flatter yourself." "There's no excuse any more for a woman to look her age." "Sour grapes?" "A bimbo." "Brainless." "She's using it for all she can get." Recognizing these reactions for what they are, it may be easier to brave coercive flattery or insults or both, and make some long-overdue scenes.

This will be hard. Talking about the beauty myth strikes a nerve which, for most of us, is on some level very raw. We will need to have compassion for ourselves and other women for our strong feelings about "beauty," and be very gentle with those feelings. If the beauty myth is religion, it is because women still lack rituals that include us; if it is economy, it is because we're still compensated unfairly; if it is sexuality, it is because female sexuality is still a dark continent; if it is warfare, it is because women are denied ways to see ourselves as heroines, daredevils, stoics, and rebels; if it is women's culture, it is because men's culture still resists us. When we recognize that the myth is powerful because it has claimed so much of the best of female consciousness, we can turn from it to look more clearly at all it has tried to stand in for.

## A Feminist Third Wave

So here we are. What can we do?

We must dismantle the PBQ; support the unionization of women's jobs; make "beauty" harassment, age discrimination, unsafe working conditions such as enforced surgery, and the double standard for appearance, issues for labor negotiation; women in television and other heavily discriminatory professions must organize for wave after wave of lawsuits; we must insist on equal enforcement of dress codes, take a deep breath, and tell our stories.

It is often said that we must make fashion and advertising images include us, but this is a dangerously optimistic misunderstanding of how the market works. Advertising aimed at women works by lowering our self-esteem. If it flatters our self-esteem, it is not effective. Let's abandon this hope of looking to the index fully to include us. It won't, because if it does, it has lost its function. As long as the definition of "beauty" comes from outside women, we will continue to be manipulated by it.

We claimed the freedom to age and remain sexual, but that rigidified into the condition of aging "youthfully." We began to wear comfortable clothing, but the discomfort settled back onto our bodies. The seventies' "natural" beauty became its own icon; the 1980s' "healthy" beauty brought about an epidemic of new diseases and "strength as beauty" enslaved women to our muscles. This process will continue with every effort women make to reform the index until we change our relationship to the index altogether.

The marketplace is not open to consciousness-raising. It is misplaced energy to attack the market's images themselves: Given recent history, they were bound to develop as they did.

While we cannot directly affect the images, we can drain them of their power. We can turn away from them, look directly at one another, and find alternative images of beauty in a female subculture; seek out the plays, music, films that illuminate women in three dimensions; find the biographies of women, the women's history, the heroines that in each generation are submerged from view; fill in the terrible, "beautiful" blanks. We can lift ourselves and other women out of the myth—but only if we are willing to seek out and support and really look at the alternatives.

Since our imaginary landscape fades to gray when we try to think past the myth, women need cultural help to imagine our way free. For most of our history, the representation of women, our sexuality and our true beauty, has not been in our hands. After just twenty years of the great push foward, during which time women sought to define those things for ourselves, the marketplace, more influential than any solitary artist, has seized the definition of our desire. Shall we let women-hating images claim our sexuality for their royalties? We need to insist on making culture out of our desire: making paintings, novels, plays, and films potent and seductive and authentic enough to undermine and overwhelm the Iron Maiden. Let's expand our culture to separate sex from the Iron Maiden.

We'll need to remember, at the same time, how heavily censored our mass culture is by beauty advertisers: As long as prime-time TV and the mainstream press aimed at women are supported by beauty advertisers, the story line of how women are in mass culture will be dictated by the beauty myth. It is understood without directives that stories that center admiringly on an "un-processed" woman will rarely get made. If we could see a sixty-year-old woman who looks her age read the news, a deep fissure would open in the beauty myth. Meanwhile, let's be clear that the myth rules the airwaves *only* because the products of the pro-cess buy the time.

Finally, we can keep our analytical gaze always sharp, being aware of what shapes the Iron Maiden can affect how we see, absorb, and respond to her images. Quickly, with this con-sciousness, they begin to look like what they are—two-dimen-sional. They literally fall flat. It is when they become tedious to us that they will evolve to *adapt* to the sea change in women's moods; an advertiser can't influence a story line if there is no audience. Responding to sheer boredom on women's part, cre-ators of culture will be forced to present three-dimensional images of women in order to involve us again. Women can provoke, through our sudden boredom with the Iron Maiden, a mass culture that does, in fact treat us like people.

In transforming the cultural environment, women who work in the mainstream media are a crucial inside vanguard. I have heard many women in the media express frustration at the limitations surrounding the treatment of beauty myth issues; many report a sense of isolation in relation to pushing those limits. Perhaps de-bate renewed in more political terms about the beauty myth in the media, and the seriousness of its consequences, will forge new alliances in support of those women in print and TV and radio journalism who are eager to battle the beauty myth at ground zero.

Quickly, when we put together a personal counterculture of meaningful images of beauty, the Iron Maiden begins to look like an image of unattractive violence; alternative ways to see start to leap out from the background.

"Rosemary Fell was not exactly beautiful. No, you couldn't have called her beautiful. Pretty? Well, if you took her to pieces. . . . But why be so cruel as to take anyone to pieces?"

(Katherine Mansfield); "To Lily her beauty seemed a senseless thing, since it gained her nothing in the way of passion, release, kinship, or intimacy. . . ." (Jane Smiley); "She was astonishingly beautiful. . . . Beauty had this penalty—it came too readily, came too completely. It stilled life—froze it. One forgot the little agitations; the flush, the pallor, some queer distortion, some light or shadow, which made the face unrecognizable for a moment and yet added a quality one saw forever after. It was simpler to smooth that all out under the cover of beauty. . . ." (Virginia Woolf); "If there is anything behind a face, that face improves with age. Lines show distinction and character: they show that one has lived, that one may know something." (Karen de Crow); "Though she was now over fifty . . . it was easy to credit all one had heard about the passions she had inspired. People who have been much loved retain even in old age a radiating quality difficult to describe but unmistakable. Even a stone that has been blazed on all day will hold heat after nightfall . . . this warm radiance." (Dame Ethyl Smyth).

The beauty cult attests to a spiritual hunger for female ritual and rites of passage. We need to develop and elaborate better women's rituals to fill in the void. Can we evolve more widely among friends, among networks of friends, fruitful new rites and celebrations for the female life cycle? We have baby showers and bridal showers, but what about purification, confirmation, healing, and renewal ceremonies for childbirth, first menstruation, loss of virginity, graduation, first job, marriage, recovery from heartbreak or divorce, the earning of a degree, menopause? Whatever organic form they take, we need new and positive, rather than negative, celebrations to mark the female lifespan.

To protect our sexuality from the beauty myth, we can believe in the importance of cherishing, nurturing, and attending to our sexuality as to an animal or a child. Sexuality is not inert or given but, like a living being, changes with what it feeds upon. We can stay away from gratuitously sexually violent or exploitive images—and, when we do encounter them, ask ourselves to feel them as such. We can seek out those dreams and visions that include a sexuality free of exploitation or violence, and try to stay as conscious of what we take into our imaginations as we now are of what enters our bodies.

An eroticism of equality may be hard to visualize now. Critiques of sexuality tend to stop short with the assumption that sexuality cannot evolve. But for most women, fantasies of objectification or violence are learned superficially through a patina of images. I believe that they can be as easily unlearned by consciously reversing our conditioning—by making the repeated association between pleasure and mutuality. Our ideas of sexual beauty are open to more transformation than we yet realize.

We need, especially for the anorexic/pornographic generations, a radical rapprochement with nakedness. Many women have described the sweeping revelation that follows even one experience of communal all-female nakedness. This is an easy suggestion to mock, but the fastest way to demystify the naked Iron Maiden is to promote retreats, festivals, excursions, that include—whether in swimming or sunning or Turkish baths or random relaxation—communal nakedness. Men's groups, from fraternities to athletic clubs, understand the value, the cohesiveness, and the esteem for one's own gender generated by such moments. A single revelation of the beauty of our infinite variousness is worth more than words; one such experience is strong enough, for a young girl, especially, to give the lie to the Iron Maiden.

When faced with the myth, the questions to ask are not about women's faces and bodies but about the power relations of the situation. Who is this serving? Who says? Who profits? What is the context? When someone discusses a woman's appearance to her face, she can ask herself, Is it that person's business? Are the power relations equal? Would she feel comfortable making the same personal comments in return?

A woman's appearance is more often called to her attention for a political reason than as a constituent of genuine attraction and desire. We can learn to get better at telling the difference—a liberating skill in itself. We need not condemn lust, seduction, or physical attraction—a much more democratic and subjective quality than the market would like us to discover—we need only to reject political manipulation.

The irony is that more beauty promises what only more female solidarity can deliver: The beauty myth can be defeated for good only through an electric resurgence of the woman-centered political activism of the seventies—a feminist third wave— updated to take on the new issues of the nineties. In this decade, for young women in particular, some of the enemies are quieter and cleverer and harder to grasp. To enlist young women, we'll need to define our self-esteem as political: to rank it, along with money, jobs, child care, safety, as a vital resource for women that is *deliberately* kept in inadequate supply.

I don't pretend to have the agenda; I know only that some of the problems have changed. I've become convinced that there are thousands of young women ready and eager to join forces with a peer-driven feminist third wave that would take on, along with the classic feminist agenda, the new problems that have arisen with the shift in *Zeitgeist* and the beauty backlash. The movement would need to deal with the ambiguities of assimilation. Young women express feelings of being scared and isolated "insiders" as opposed to angry and united outsiders, and this distinction makes backlash sense: The best way to stop a revolution is to give people something to lose. It would need to politicize eating disorders, young women's uniquley intense relationship to images, and the effect of those images on their sexuality—ir would need to make the point that you don't have much of a right over your own body if you can't eat. It would need to analyze the antifeminist propaganda young women have inherited, and give them tools, including arguments like this one, with which to see through it. While transmitting the previous heritage of feminism intact, it would need to be, as all feminist waves are, peer-driven: No matter how wise a mother's advice is, we listen to our peers. It would have to make joy, rowdiness, and wanton celebration as much a part of its project as hard work and bitter struggle, and it can begin all this by rejecting the pernicious fib that is crippling young women— the fib called postfeminism, the pious hope that the battles have all been won. This scary word is making young women, who face many of the same old problems, once again blame themselves— since it's all been fixed, right? It strips them of the weapon of theory and makes them feel alone once again. We never speak complacently of the post-Democratic era: Democracy, we know, is a living, vulnerable thing that every generation must renew. The same goes for that aspect of democracy represented by feminism. So let's get on with it.

Women learned to crave "beauty" in its contemporary form because we were learning at the same time that the feminist struggle was going to be much harder than we had realized. The ideology of "beauty" was a shortcut promise to agitating women—a historical placebo—that we could be confident, valued, heard out, respected, and make demands without fear. (In fact, it is doubtful whether "beauty" is the real desire at all; women may want "beauty" so that we can get back inside their bodies, and crave perfection so that we can forget about the whole damn thing. Most women, in their guts, would probably rather be, given the choice, a sexual, courageous self than a beautiful generic Other.)

Beauty advertising copy promises that sort of courage and freedom— "Beachwear for the beautiful and brave"; "A fresh, fearless look," "A funky fearlessness"; "Think radical"; "The Freedom Fighters—for the woman who isn't afraid to speak up or stand out." But this courage and confidence will not be real until we are backed by the material gains that we can achieve only by seeing other women as allies rather than as competitors.

The 1980s tried to buy us off with promises of individual solutions. We have reached the limit of what the individualist, beauty-myth version of female progress can do, and it is not good enough: We will be 2 percent of top management and 5 percent of full professors and 5 percent of senior partners forever if we do not get together for the next great push forward. Higher cheekbones and firmer bustlines clearly won't get us what we need for real confidence and visibility; only a renewed commitment to the basics of female political progress—to child-care programs, effective antidiscrimination laws, parental leave, reproductive choice, fair compensation, and genuine penalties against sexual violence—will do so. We won't have these until we can identify our interests in other women's, and allow our natural solidarity to overcome the organizational obstacles put forward by the competitiveness and rivalry artificially provoked among us by the beauty backlash.

The terrible truth is that though the marketplace promotes the myth, it would be powerless if women didn't enforce it against one another. For any one woman to outgrow the myth, she needs the support of many women. The toughest but most necessary change will come not from men or from the media, but from women, in the way we see and behave toward other women, in the way we see and behave toward other women.

## Generational Collaboration

The links between generations of women need mending if we are to save one another from the beauty myth, and save women's progress from its past historical fate—the periodic reinvention of the wheel. Gill Hudson, editor of *Company*, reveals the extent to which the beauty backlash has propagandized the young: Young women, she says, "absolutely don't want to be known as feminists" because "feminism is not considered sexy." It would be stupid and sad if the women of the near future had to fight the same old battles all over again from the beginning just because of young women's isolation from older women. It would be pathetic if young women had to go back to the beginning because we were taken in by an unoriginal twenty-year campaign to portray the women's movement as "not sexy," a campaign aimed to help young women forget whose battles made sex sexy in the first place.

Since young women will not be encouraged by our institutions to make the connections, we can get past the myth only by actively exploring more useful role models than the glossies give us. We are sorely in need of intergenerational contact: We need to see the faces of the women who made our freedom possible; they need to hear our thanks. Young women are dangerously "unmothered"—unprotected, unguided—institutionally and need role models and mentors. The work and experience of older women gain scope and influence when imparted to students, apprentices, protégés. Yet, both generations will have to resist their externally ingrained impulses against intergenerational collaboration. We are well trained, if young, to shy away from identification with older women; if older, at being a little hard on young women, viewing them with impatience and disdain. The beauty myth is designed artifically to pit the generations of women against one another; our consciously strengthening those links gives back the wholeness of our lifespans that the beauty myth would keep us from discovering.

## Divide and Conquer

The fact is, women are not actually dangerous to one another. Outside the myth, other women look a lot like natural allies. In order for women to learn to fear one another, we had to be convinced that our sisters possess some kind of mysterious, potent secret weapon to be used against us—the imaginary weapon being "beauty."

The core of the myth—and the reason it was so useful as a counter to feminism—is its divisiveness. You can see and hear it everywhere: "Don't hate me because I'm beautiful" (L'Oréal). "I really hate my aerobics instructor—I guess hatred is good motivation." "You'd hate her. She has everything." "Women who get out of bed looking beautiful really annoy me." "Don't you hate women who can eat like that?" "No pores—makes you sick." "Tall, blonde—couldn't you just kill her?" Rivalry, resentment, and hostility provoked by the beauty myth run deep. Sisters commonly remember the grief of one being designated "the pretty one." Mothers often have difficulty with their daughters' blooming. Jealousy among the best of friends is a cruel fact of female love. Even women who are lovers describe beauty competition. It is painful for women to talk about beauty because under the myth, one woman's body is used to hurt another. Our faces and bodies become instruments for punishing other women, often used out of our control and against our will. At present, "beauty" is an economy in which women find the "value" of their faces and bodies impinging, in spite of themselves, on that of other women's. This constant comparison, in which one woman's worth fluctuates through the presence of another, divides and conquers. It forces women to be acutely critical of the "choices" other women make about how they look. But that economy that pits women against one another is not inevitable.

To get past this divisiveness, women will have to break a lot of taboos against talking about it, including the one that prohibits women from narrating the dark side of being treated as a beautiful object. From the dozens of women to whom I have listened, it is clear that the amount of pain a given woman experiences through the beauty myth bears no relationship at all to what she looks like relative to a cultural ideal. (In the words of a top fashion model, "When I was on the cover of the Italian *Vogue,* everyone told me how great I looked. I just thought, 'I can't believe you can't see all those lines.'") Women who impersonate the Iron Maiden may be no less victimized by the myth than the women subjected to their images. The myth asks women to be at once blindly hostile to and blindly envious of "beauty" in other women. Both the hostility and the envy serve the myth and hurt all women.

While the "beautiful" woman is briefly at the apex of the system, this is, of course, far from the divine state of grace that the myth propagates. The pleasure to be had from turning oneself into a living art object, the roaring in the ears and the fine jetspray of regard on the surface of the skin, is some kind of power, when power is in short supply. But it is not much compared to the pleasure of getting back forever inside the body; the pleasure of discovering sexual pride, a delight in a common female sexuality that overwhelms the divisions of "beauty"; the pleasure of shedding self-consciousness and narcissism and guilt like a chainmail gown; the pleasure of the freedom to forget all about it.

Only then will women be able to talk about what "beauty" really involves: the attention of people we do not know, rewards for things we did not earn, sex from men who reach for us as for a brass ring on a carousel, hostility and scepticism from other women, adolescence extended longer than it ought to be, cruel aging, and a long hard struggle for identity. And we will learn that what is good about "beauty"—the promise of confidence, sexuality, and the self-regard of a healthy individuality—are actually qualities that have nothing to do with "beauty" specifically, but are deserved by and, as the myth is dismantled, available to all women. The best that "beauty" offers belongs to us all by right of femaleness. When we separate "beauty" from sexuality, when we celebrate the individuality of our features and characteristics, women will have access to a pleasure in our bodies that unites us rather than divides us. The beauty myth will be history.

But as long as women censor in one another the truths about

our experiences, "beauty" will remain mystified and still most useful to those who wish to control women. The unacceptable reality is that we live under a caste system. It is not innate and permanent; it is not based on sex or God or the Rock of Ages. It can and must be changed. The situation is closing in on us, and there is no long term left to which to postpone the conversation.

When the conversation commences, the artificial barriers of the myth will begin to fall away. We will hear that just because a woman looks "beautiful" doesn't mean she feels it, and she can feel beautiful without looking it at first glance. Thin women may feel fat; young women will grow old. When one woman looks at another, she cannot possibly know the self-image within that woman: Though she appears enviably in control, she may be starving; though she overflows her clothing, she may be enviably satisfied sexually. A woman may be fleshy from high self-esteem or from low; she may cover her face in makeup out of the desire to play around outrageously or the desire to hide. All women have experienced the world treating them better or worse according to where they rate each day: while this experience wreaks havoc with a woman's identity, it does mean that women have access to a far greater range of experience than the snapshots "beauty" takes of us would lead us to believe. We may well discover that the way we now read appearances tells us little, and that we experience, no matter what we look like, the same spectrum of feelings: sometimes lovely, often unlovely, always female, in a commonality that extends across the infinite grids that the beauty myth tries to draw among us.

Women blame men for looking but not listening. But we do it too; perhaps even more so. We have to stop reading each others' appearances as if appearance were language, political allegiance, worthiness, or aggression. The chances are excellent that what a woman means to say *to other women* is far more complex and sympathetic than the garbled message that her appearance permits her.

Let us start with a reinterpretation of "beauty" that is *noncompetitive, nonhierarchical, and nonviolent.* Why must one woman's pleasure and pride have to mean another woman's pain? Men are only in sexual competition when they are competing sexually, but the myth puts women in "sexual" competition in every situation. Competition for a specific sexual partner is rare; since it is not usually a competition "for men," it is not biologically inevitable.

Women compete this way "for other women" partly because we are devotees of the same sect, and partly to fill, if only temporarily, the black hole that the myth created in the first place. Hostile competition can often be proof of what our current sexual arrangements repress: our mutual physical attraction. If women redefine sexuality to affirm our attraction among ourselves, the myth will no longer hurt. Other women's beauty will not be a threat or an insult, but a pleasure and a tribute. Women will be able to costume and adorn ourselves without fear of hurting and betraying other women, or of being accused of false loyalties. We can then dress up in celebration of the shared pleasure of the female body, doing it "for other women" in a positive rather than a negative offering of the self.

And when we let ourselves experience this physical attraction, the marketplace will no longer be able to make a profit out of its representation of men's desires: We, knowing firsthand that attraction to other women comes in many forms, will no longer believe that the qualities that make us desirable are a lucrative mystery.

By changing our prejudgments of one another, we have the means for the beginning of a noncompetitive experience of beauty. The "other woman" is represented through the myth as an unknown danger. "Meet the Other Woman," reads a Wella hair-coloring brochure, referring to the "after" version of the woman targeted. The idea is that "beauty" makes *another* woman—even one's own idealized image—into a being so alien that you need a formal introduction. It is a phrase that suggests threats, mistresses, glamorous destroyers of relationships.

We undo the myth by approaching the unknown Other Woman. Since women's everyday experiences of flirtatious attention derive most often from men reacting to our "beauty," it is no wonder that silent, watching women can be represented to us as antagonists.

We can melt this suspicion and distance: Why should we not be gallant and chivalrous and flirtatious with one another. Let us charm one another with some of that sparkling attention too often held in reserve only for men: compliment one another, show our admiration. We can engage with the Other Woman—catch her eye, give her a lift when she is hitchhiking, open the door when she is struggling. When we approach one another in the street and give, or receive, that wary, defensive shoes-to-haircut glance, what if we meet one another's eyes woman to woman; what if we smile.

This movement toward a noncompetitive idea of beauty is already underway. The myth has always denied women honor. Here and there, women are evolving codes of honor to protect us from it. We withold easy criticism. We shower authentic praise. We bow out of social situations in which our beauty is being used to put other women in the shadows. We refuse to jostle for random male attention. A contestant in the 1989 Miss California Pageant pulls a banner from her swimsuit that reads PAGEANTS HURT ALL WOMEN. A film actress tells me that when she did a nude scene, she refused, as a gesture to women in the audience, to discipline her body first. We are already beginning to find ways in which we won't be rivals and we won't be instruments.

This new perspective changes not how we look but how we see. We begin to see other women's faces and bodies for themselves, the Iron Maiden no longer superimposed. We catch our breath when we see a woman laughing. We cheer inside when we see a woman walk proud. We smile in the mirror, watch the lines form at the corners of our eyes, and, pleased with what we are making, smile again.

Though women can give this new perspective to one another, men's participation in overturning the myth is welcome. Some men, certainly, have used the beauty myth abusively against women, the way some men use their fists; but there is a strong consciousness among both sexes that the real agents enforcing the myth today are not men as individual lovers or husbands, but institutions, that depend on male dominance. Both sexes seem to be finding that the full force of the myth derives little from private sexual relations, and much from the cultural and economic megalith "out there" in the public realm. Increasingly, both sexes know they are being cheated.

But helping women to take the myth apart is in men's own interest on an even deeper level: Their turn is next. Advertisers have recently figured out that undermining sexual self-confidence works whatever the targeted gender. According to *The Guardian*, "Men are now looking at mirrors instead of at girls. . . . Beautiful men can now be seen selling everything." Using images from male homosexual subculture, advertising has begun to portray the male body in a beauty myth of its own. As this imagery focuses more closely on male sexuality, it will undermine the sexual self-esteem of men in general. Since men are more conditioned to be separate from their bodies, and to compete to inhuman excess, the male version could conceivably hurt men even more than the female version hurts women.

Psychiatrists are anticipating a rise in male rates of eating diseases. Now that men are being cast as a frontier market to be opened up by self-hatred, images have begun to tell heterosexual men the same half-truths about what women want and how they see that they have traditionally told heterosexual women about men; if they buy it and become trapped themselves, that will be no victory for women. No one will win.

But it is also in men's interest to undo the myth because the survival of the planet depends on it. The earth can no longer afford a consumer ideology based on the insatiable wastefulness of sexual and material discontent. We need to begin to get lasting satisfaction out of the things we consume. We conceived of the planet as female, an all-giving Mother Nature, just as we conceived of the female body, infinitely alterable by and for man; we serve both ourselves and our hopes for the planet by insisting on a new female reality on which to base a new metaphor for the earth: the female body with its own organic integrity that must be respected.

The environmental crisis demands a new way of thinking that is communitarian, collective and not adversarial, and we need it fast. We can pray and hope that male institutions evolve this sophisticated, unfamiliar way of thinking within a few short years; or we can turn to the female tradition, which has perfected it over five millennia, and adapt it to the public sphere. Since the beauty myth blots out the female tradition, we keep a crucial option for the planet open when we resist it.

And we keep options open for ourselves. We do not need to change our bodies, we need to change the rules. Beyond the myth, women will still be blamed for our appearances by whomever needs to blame us. So let's stop blaming ourselves and stop running and stop apologizing, and let's start to please ourselves once and for all. The "beautiful" woman does not win under the myth; neither does anyone else. The woman who is subjected to the continual adulation of strangers does not win, nor does the woman who denies herself attention. The woman who wears a uniform does not win, nor does the woman with a designer outfit for every day of the year. You do not win by struggling to the top of a caste system, you win by refusing to be trapped within one at all. The woman wins who calls herself beautiful and challenges the world to change to truly see her.

A woman wins by giving herself and other women permission—to eat; to be sexual; to age; to wear overalls, a paste tiara, a Balenciaga gown, a second-hand opera cloak, or combat boots; to cover up or to go practically naked; to do whatever we choose in following—or ignoring—our own aesthetic. A woman wins when she feels that what each woman does with her own body—unforced, uncoerced— is her own business. When many individual women exempt themselves from the economy, it will begin to dissolve. Institutions, some men, and some women, will continue to try to use women's appearance against us. But we won't bite.

Can there be a prowoman definition of beauty? Absolutely. What has been missing is play. The beauty myth is harmful and pompous and grave because so much, too much, depends upon it. The pleasure of playfulness is that it doesn't matter. Once you play for stakes of any amount, the game becomes a war game, or compulsive gambling. In the myth, it has been a game for life, for questionable love, for desperate and dishonest sexuality, and without the choice not to play by alien rules. No choice, no free will; no levity, no real game.

But we can imagine, to save ourselves, a life in the body that is not value-laden; a masquerade, a voluntary theatricality that emerges from abundant self-love. A pro-woman redefinition of beauty reflects our redefinitions of what power is. Who says we need a hierarchy? Where I see beauty may not be where you do. Some people look more desirable to me than they do to you. So what? My perception has no authority over yours. Why should beauty be exclusive? Admiration can include so much. Why is rareness impressive? The high value of rareness is a masculine concept, having more to do with capitalism than with lust. What is the fun in wanting the most what cannot be found? Children, in contrast, are common as dirt, but they are highly valued and regarded as beautiful.

How might women act beyond the myth? Who can say? Maybe we will let our bodies wax and wane, enjoying the variations on a theme, and avoid pain because when something hurts us it begins to look ugly to us. Maybe we will adorn ourselves with real delight, with the sense that we are gilding the lily. Maybe the less pain women inflict on our bodies, the more beautiful our bodies will look to us. Perhaps we will forget to elicit admiration from strangers, and find we don't miss it; perhaps we will await our older faces with anticipation, and be unable to see our bodies as a mass of imperfections, since there is nothing on us that is not precious. Maybe we won't want to be the "after" anymore.

How to begin? Let's be shameless. Be greedy. Pursue pleasure. Avoid pain. Wear and touch and eat and drink what we feel like. Tolerate other women's choices. Seek out the sex we want and fight fiercely against the sex we do not want. Choose our own causes. And once we break through and change the rules so our sense of our own beauty cannot be shaken, sing that beauty and dress it up and flaunt it and revel in it: In a sensual politics, female is beautiful.

A woman-loving definition of beauty supplants desperation with play, narcissism with self-love, dismemberment with wholeness, absence with presence, stillness with animation. It admits radiance: light coming out of the face and the body, rather than a spotlight on the body, dimming the self. It is sexual, various, and surprising. We will be able to see it in others and not be frightened, and able at last to see it in ourselves.

A generation ago, Germaine Greer wondered about women: "What *will* you do?" What women did brought about a quarter century of cataclysmic social revolution. The next phase of our movement forward as individual women, as women together, and as tenants of our bodies and this planet, depends now on what we decide to see when we look in the mirror.

What *will* we see?

# *Acknowledgments*

I owe this book to the support of my family: Leonard and Deborah and Aaron Wolfe, Daniel Goleman, Tara Bennet-Goleman, Anasuya Weil and Tom Weil. I'm expecially grateful to my grandmother, Fay Goleman, on whose unflagging encouragement I depended and whose life—as family services pioneer, professor, wife, mother, and early feminist—gives continual inspiration. I'm grateful to Ruth Sullivan, Esther Boner, Lily Rivlin, Michele Landsberg, Joanne Stewart, Florence Lewis, Patricia Pierce, Alan Shoaf, Polly Shulman, Elizabeth Alexander, Rhonda Garelick, Amruta Slee, and Barbara Browning for their vital contributions to my work. Jane Meara and Jim Landis gave their thoughtful editorial attention very generously. Colin Troup was a ready source of comfort, contentiousness, and amusement. And I am indebted to the theorists of femininity of the second wave, without whose struggles with these issues I could not have begun my own.

# $\mathcal{N}otes$

## The Beauty Myth

*Page*

10 Cosmetic surgery: *Standard and Poor's Industry Surveys* (New York: Standard and Poor's Corp., 1988).

10 Pornography main media category: See "Crackdown on Pornography: A No-Win Battle," *U.S. News and World Report*, June 4, 1984. The Association of Fashion and Image Consultants tripled its membership between 1984 and 1989 alone (Annetta Miller and Dody Tsiantar, *Newsweek*, May 22, 1989). During the five or six years prior to 1986, consumer spending rose from $300 billion to $600 billion.

10 Thirty-three thousand American women, University of Cincinnati College of Medicine, 1984: Wooley, S. C., and O. W. Wooley, "Obesity and Women: A Closer Look at the Facts," *Women's Studies International Quarterly*, vol. 2 (1979), pp. 69–79. Data reprinted in "33,000 Women Tell How They Really Feel About Their Bodies," *Glamour*, February 1984.

10 Recent research shows: See Dr. Thomas Cash, Diane Cash, and Jonathan Butters, "Mirror-Mirror on the Wall: Contrast Effects and Self-Evaluation of Physical Attractiveness," *Personality and Social Psychology Bulletin*, September 1983, vol. 9, no. 3. Dr. Cash's research shows very little connection between "how attractive women are" and "how attractive they feel themselves to be." All the women he treated were, in his terms, "extremely attractive," but his patients compare themselves only to models, not to other women.

11 Very little to me: Lucy Stone, 1855, quoted in Andrea Dworkin, *Pornography: Men Possessing Women* (New York: Putnam, 1981), p. 11.

12 A doll: Germaine Greer, *The Female Eunuch* (London: Paladin Grafton Books, 1970), pp. 55, 60.

12 Myth: See also Roland Barthes's definition: "It [myth] transforms history into nature. . . . Myth has the task of giving an historical intention a natural justification, and making contingency appear eternal." Roland Barthes, "Myth Today," *Mythologies* (New York: Hill and Wang, 1972), p. 129.

Anthropologist Bronislaw Malinowski's definition of "a myth of origin" is relevant to the beauty myth: A myth of origin, writes Ann Oakley, "tends to be worked hardest in times of social strain, when the state of affairs portrayed in the myth are called into question." Ann Oakley, *Housewife: High Value/Low Cost* (London: Penguin Books, 1987), p. 163.

12 Platonic: See Plato's discussion of Beauty in *Symposium*. For varying standards of beauty, see Ted Polhemus, *BodyStyles* (Luton, England: Lennard Publishing, 1988).

12 Sexual selection; Darwin . . . was unconvinced: See Cynthia Eagle Russett, "Hairy Men and Beautiful Women," *Sexual Science: The Victorian Construction of Womanhood* (Cambridge, Mass.: Harvard University Press, 1989), pp. 78–103.

On page 84 Russett quotes Darwin: "Man is more powerful in body and mind than woman, and in the savage state he keeps her in a much more abject state of bondage, than does the male of any other animal; therefore it is not surprising that he should have gained the power of selection. . . . As women have long been selected for beauty, it is not surprising that some of their successive variations should have been transmitted exclusively to the same sex; consequently that they should have transmitted beauty in a somewhat higher degree to their female than to their male offspring, and thus have become more beautiful, according to general opinion, than men." Darwin himself noticed the evolutionary inconsistency of this idea that, as Russett puts it, "a funny thing happened on the way up the ladder: among humans, the female no longer chose but was chosen." This theory "implied an awkward break in evolutionary continuity," she observes: "In Darwin's own terms it marked a rather startling reversal in the trend of evolution."

See also Natalie Angier, "Hard-to-Please Females May Be Neglected Evolutionary Force," *The New York Times*, May 8, 1990, and Natalie Angier, "Mating for Life? It's Not for the Birds or the Bees," *The New York Times*, August 21, 1990.

13 Evolution: See Evelyn Reed, *Woman's Evolution: From Matriarchal Clan to Patriarchal Family* (New York: Pathfinder Press, 1986); and Elaine Morgan, *The Descent of Woman* (New York: Bantam Books, 1979). See especially "the upper primate," p. 91.

13 Goddess: Rosalind Miles, *The Women's History of the World* (London: Paladin Grafton Books, 1988), p. 43. See also Merlin Stone, *When God Was a Woman* (San Diego: Harvest Books, 1976).

13 Wodaabe tribe: Leslie Woodhead, "Desert Dandies," *The Guardian*, July 1988.

In the West African Fulani tribe young women choose their husbands on the basis of their beauty: "The contestants . . . take part in the yaake, a line-up in which they sing and dance, stand on tip-toe and make faces, rolling and crossing their eyes and grimacing to show off their teeth to the judges. They keep this up for hours, aided by the consumption of stimulating drugs beforehand. Throughout all this, old ladies in the crowd hurl criticisms at those who do not live up to the Fulani idea of beauty." [Polhemus, op. cit., p. 21]

See also Carol Beckwith and Marion van Offelen, *Nomads of Niger* (London: William Collins Sons & Co. Ltd., 1984), cited in Carol Beckwith, "Niger's Wodaabe: People of the Taboo," *National Geographic*, vol. 164, no. 4, October 1983, pp. 483–509.

Paleolithic excavations suggest that it has been human males rather than females to whom adornment was assigned in prehistoric societies; in modern tribal communities men generally adorn at least as much as women, and often hold "a virtual monopoly" over adornment. The Sudanese Nuba, the Australian Waligigi, and the Mount Hagen men of New Guinea also spend hours painting themselves and perfecting their hairstyles to attract the women, whose toilette takes only minutes. See Polhemus, op. cit., pp. 54–55.

14 Technologies: See, for example, Beaumont Newhall, *The History of Photography from 1839 to the Present* (London: Secker & Warburg, 1986), p. 31. Photograph *Academie*, c. 1845, photographer unknown.

17 Powerful industries: Diet items are a $74-billion-a-year industry in the United States, totaling one-third the nation's annual food bill. See David Brand, "A Nation of Healthy Worrywarts?," *Time*, July 25, 1988.

17 $33-billion-a-year diet industry: Molly O'Neill, "Congress Looking into the Diet Business," *The New York Times*, March 28, 1990.

17 $300-million-a-year cosmetic surgery industry: *Standard and Poor's Industry Surveys*, op. cit. 1988.

17 $7 billion pornography industry, "Crackdown on Pornography," op. cit.

17 Vital lies: Daniel Goleman, *Vital Lies, Simple Truths: The Psychology of Self-Deception* (New York: Simon and Schuster, 1983), pp. 16–17, quoting Henrik Ibsen's phrase: "The vital lie continues unrevealed, sheltered by the family's silence, alibis, stark denial."

18 A higher calling: John Kenneth Galbraith, quoted in Michael H. Minton with Jean Libman Block, *What Is a Wife Worth?* (New York: McGraw-Hill, 1984), pp. 134–135.

18 Ugly Feminist: Marcia Cohen, *The Sisterhood: The Inside Story of the Women's Movement and the Leaders Who Made It Happen* (New York: Ballantine Books, 1988), pp. 205, 206, 287, 290, 322, 332.

18 Swearing like a trooper: Betty Friedan, *The Feminine Mystique* (London: Penguin Books, 1982), p. 79, quoting Elinor Rice Hays, *Morning Star: A Biography of Lucy Stone* (New York: Harcourt, 1961), p. 83.

19 Unpleasant image: Friedan, op. cit., p. 87.

# Work

*Page*

21 U.S. women in work force: Ruth Sidel, *Women and Children Last: The Plight of Poor Women in Affluent America*, (New York: Penguin Books, 1987), p. 60.

21 British women in paid work: U.K. Equal Opportunities Commission, *Towards Equality: A Casebook of Decisions on Sex Discrimination and Equal Pay, 1976–1981*, pamphlet. See also: U.K. Equal Opportunities Commission, *Sex Discrimination and Employment: Equality at Work: A Guide to the Employment Provisions of the Sex Discrimination Act 1975*, pamphlet, p. 12.

22 Prehistory: Rosalind Miles, *The Women's History of the World* (London: Paladin Grafton Books, 1988), p. 152.

22 Modern tribal societies: Ibid., p. 22.

23 Duchess of Newcastle: The entire quote is: "Women live like *bats* or *owls*, labour like *beasts* and die like *worms*," ibid., p. 192.

23 No work too hard: Ibid., p. 155, quoting Viola Klein, *The Feminine Character: History of an Ideology*, 2d ed. (Urbana: University of Illinois Press, 1971).

23 Fatigue: Ibid., p. 188.

23 Humphrey Institute: Humphrey Institute, University of Minnesota, *Looking to the Future: Equal Partnership Between Women and Men in the 21st Century*, quoted in Debbie Taylor et al., *Women: A World Report* (Oxford: Oxford University Press, 1985), p. 82.

23 Twice as many hours as men: *Report of the World Conference for the United Nations Decade for Women*, Copenhagen, 1980, A/Conf. 94/35.

23 Pakistani women: Taylor et al., op. cit., p. 3.

23 Nonwork: Ann Oakley, *Housewife: High Value/Low Cost* (London: Penguin Books, 1987), p. 53.

23 Rise by 60 percent: Sidel, op. cit., p. 26.

23 France's labor power: Sylvia Ann Hewlett, *A Lesser Life: The Myth of Women's Liberation in America* (New York: Warner Books, 1987).

23 Volunteer work: Yvonne Roberts, "Standing Up to Be Counted," *The Guardian* (London) 1989 interview with Marilyn Waring, author of *If Women Counted: A New Feminist Economics* (San Francisco: Harper & Row, 1988). See also Waring, p. 69.

23 Gross national product: Taylor et al., op. cit., p. 4.

23 Nancy Barrett: "Obstacles to Economic Parity for Women," *The American Economic Review*, vol. 72 (May 1982), pp. 160–165.

24 Thirty-six minutes more: Arlie Hochschild with Anne Machung, *The Second Shift: Working Parents and the Revolution at Home* (New York: Viking Penguin, 1989).

24 Household chores: Michael H. Minton with Jean Libman Block, *What Is a Wife Worth?* (New York: McGraw-Hill), p. 19.

24 75 percent of household work: Hochschild and Machung, op. cit., p. 4. See also Sarah E. Rix, ed., *The American Woman, 1988–89: A Status Report*, Chapter 3: Rebecca M. Blank, "Women's Paid Work, Household Income and Household Well-Being," pp. 123–161 (New York: W. W. Norton & Co., 1988).

24 U.S. married men: Claudia Wallis, "Onward Women!," *Time International*, December 4, 1989.

24 Demand eight hours more: Heidi Hartmann, "The Family as the Locus of Gender, Class and Political Struggle: The Example of Housework," in *Signs: Journal of Women in Culture and Society*, vol. 6 (1981), pp. 366–394.

24 Italy: Hewlett, op. cit.

24 Less leisure: Taylor et al., op. cit., p. 4.

24 Kenya: Ibid.

24 Chase Manhattan Bank: Minton and Block, op. cit., pp. 59–60.

24 U.S. college undergraduates: Wallis, op. cit.

24 Undergraduates in the United Kingdom: U.K. Equal Opportunities Commission, *The Fact About Women Is . . .*, pamphlet, 1986.

25 American women in work force: Sidel, op. cit., p. 60.

25 Marilyn Waring: Quoted in Roberts, op. cit.

25 Patricia Ireland: Quoted in Wallis, op. cit.

26 Women with children in the American work force: Ibid.

26 United Kingdom mothers: U.K. Equal Opportunities Commission, op. cit.

26 Sole economic support: Sidel, op. cit.

26 Marvin Harris: quoted in Minton and Block, op. cit.

28 Title VII: See Rosemarie Tong, *Women, Sex and the Law* (Totowa, N.J.: Rowman and Littlefield, 1984), pp. 65–89.

28 1975 Sex Discrimination Act/Great Britain: See U.K. Equal Opportunities
Commission, *Sex Discrimination and Employment*, especially pp. 12–13:
"Sex discrimination where sex is a 'genuine occupational qualification' for
the job, or for part of the job, because of: (a) Physical form or authen-
ticity—for example, a model or an actor." See also *Sex Discrimination: A
Guide to the Sex Discrimination Act 1975*, U.K. Home Office pamphlet (2775)
Dd8829821 G3371, p. 10.

The Sex Discrimination Act of 1984 in Australia does not cover discrimination on the basis of appearance; as of 1990, the federal attorney general
will extend the jurisdiction of the Human Rights and Equal Opportunity
Commission Act to cover discrimination on the ground of "age, medical
record, criminal record, impairment, marital status, mental, intellectual or
psychiatric disability, nationality, physical disability, sexual preference and
trade union activity," but discrimination on the basis of appearance will not
be addressed. See also Australia, Human Rights and Equal Opportunity
Commission, *The Sex Discrimination Act 1984: A Guide to the Law*, pamphlet,
August 1989.

28 American Dream: Sidel, op. cit., p. 22.

31 Helen Gurley Brown: See *Sex and the Single Girl* (New York: Bernard Geis,
1962).

31 Firing of stewardesses: See Marcia Cohen, op. cit., p. 394. One flight at-
tendant explains that the sexualized cabin atmosphere is expressly designed to diminish male passengers' fear of flying: "They figure mild
sexual arousal will be helpful in getting people's minds off" the danger
(Hochschild, 1983, cited in Albert J. Mills, "Gender, Sexuality and the
Labour Process," in Jeff Hearn et al., *The Sexuality of Organization*
(London: Sage Publications, 1989), p. 94.

32 Or go to prison: *Time*, June 7, 1971, cited in Roberta Pollack Seid, *Never
Too Thin: Why Women Are at War with Their Bodies* (New York: Prentice-
Hall, 1988).

32 Bunny Image: *Weber v. Playboy Club of New York, Playboy Clubs Interna-
tional, Inc., Hugh Hefner*, App. No. 774, Case No. CSF22619-70, Human
Rights Appeal Board, New York, New York, December 17, 1971; see also
*St. Cross v. Playboy Club of New York*, CSF222618-70.

33 "All women are Bunnies": Gloria Steinem, *Outrageous Acts and Everyday
Rebellions* (New York: Holt, Rinehart & Winston, 1983), p. 69.

33 20 percent of management: Hewlett, op. cit.

33 Xerox Corporation: Catherine McDermott won her suit only after an
eleven-year battle in New York courts; Seid, op. cit., p. 22, citing "Dieting: The Losing Game," *Time*, January 20, 1986, p. 54.

33 One sixth of U.S. MBAs: Hewlett, op. cit.

33 Appearance standards: Christine Craft, *Too Old, Too Ugly and Not Deferential
to Men* (New York: Dell, 1988).

34 "Male Anchors: 40 to 50": Ibid., p. 37.

35 "Fortyish women": Ibid., p. 204.

36 IS SHE WORTH IT?: Richard Zoglin, "Star Power," *Time*, August 7, 1989, pp. 46–51. The opening sentence of the article reads: "First there are the blond-haired good looks, striking but somehow wholesome, more high school prom queen than Hollywood glamour puss." Then it continues: "It pains [Sawyer] that her journalistic accomplishments are overshadowed by questions about her looks. . . ." See also the obsession with Jessica Savitch's appearance described in Gwenda Blair, *Almost Golden: Jessica Savitch and the Selling of Television News* (New York: Avon Books, 1988). (The jacket copy reads, "She was the Marilyn Monroe of TV News.")

36 Crippling point of view: Ibid., p. 77.

37 Physical characteristics: *Miller* v. *Bank of America*, 600 F.2d 211 9th Circuit, 1979, cited in Tong, op. cit., pp. 78.

38 *Barnes* v. *Costle*, 561 F.2d 983 (D.C. Circuit 1977), cited in Tong, op. cit., p. 81.

38 Mechelle Vinson: *Meritor Savings Bank, FSB* v. *Vinson*, 106 S. Circuit 2399 (1986).

39 *Hopkins* v. *Price-Waterhouse:* 741 F.2d 1163; S. Ct., 1775. See also Laura Mansuerus, "Unwelcome Partner," *The New York Times*, May 20, 1990.

39 *Nancy Fadhl* v. *Police Department of City and County of San Francisco:* 741 F.2d 1163, cited in Suzanne Levitt, "Rethinking Harm: A Feminist Perspective," unpublished doctoral thesis, Yale University Law School, 1989.

39 *Tamini* v. *Howard Johnson Company, Inc.:* cited in ibid.

39 *Andre* v. *Bendix Corporation:* 841 F.2d 7th Circuit, 1988, cited in ibid.

39 *Buren* v. *City of East Chicago, Indiana:* 799 F.2d 1180 7th Circuit, 1986, cited in ibid.

39 *Diaz* v. *Coleman:* Conversation with counsel Ursula Werner, Yale University Law School, New Haven, Connecticut, April 15, 1989.

39 *M. Schmidt* v. *Austicks Bookshops, Ltd.:* U.K. Industrial Relations Law Reports (IRLR), 1977, pp. 360–361.

40 *Jeremiah* v. *Ministry of Defense:* 1 Queen's Bench (QB) 1979, p. 87; see also *Strathclyde Regional Council* v. *Porcelli*, IRLR, 1986, p. 134.

40 Dan Air: See U.K. Equal Opportunities Commission, "Formal Investigation Report: Dan Air," January 1987. Dan Air lost the case.

40 Costumes: *Maureen Murphy and Eileen Davidson* v. *Stakis Leisure, Ltd.*, The Industrial Tribunals, Scotland 1989.

40 *Sisley* v. *Britannia Security Systems, Ltd.:* Industrial Court Reports, 1983, pp. 628–636.

41 *Snowball* v. *Gardner Merchant, Ltd:* IRLR, 1987, p. 397; see also *Balgobin and Francis* v. *London Borough of Tower Hamlets*, IRLR, 1987, p. 401.

41 *Wileman* v. *Minilec Engineering, Ltd.*: IRLR, 1988, p. 145.

41 200 London models: British Association of Model Agencies.

42 Fifty-four-year-old woman: Hearn et al., op. cit., p. 82.

42 Informal rules: Ibid., p. 149.

42 Contradiction: Ibid., p. 143.

43 Violations: Ibid., p. 148.

43 Sexual harassment: In a survey of nine thousand *Redbook* readers, 88 percent reported sexual harassment in the workplace. Hearn et al., op. cit.,
p. 80.

In the United Kingdom, where there is no specific law against it, 86
percent of managers and 66 percent of employees "had seen" sexual harassment, according to an Alfred Marks Bureau survey; a British Civil Service study found that 70 percent of women employees had been subjected
to it. See British Society of Civil and Public Servants, *Sexual Harassment: A
Trade Union Issue,* pamphlet, p. 14. For more information on sexual harassment, see Constance Backhouse and Leah Cohen, *Sexual Harassment on the
Job* (Englewood Cliffs, N.J.: Prentice-Hall, 1982), and Catharine A. Mac-
Kinnon, *Sexual Harassment of Working Women* (New Haven: Yale University
Press, 1979), especially Chapter 3, "Sexual Harassment: The Experience,"
pp. 25–55. See also p. 17: "How many thousands of employers hire
women for their 'aesthetic' appeal?"

Since 1981, the number of sexual-harassment complaints filed has
nearly doubled, 94 percent of them brought by women, most of them serious charges, i.e., sexual assault, physical contact, or threats of job loss.
Only 31 percent of the decisions favored the plaintiff. See David Terpstra,
University of Idaho, and Douglas Baker, Washington State University,
cited in "Harassment Charges: Who Wins?," *Psychology Today,* May 1989.

43 Provoked the comments: Nancy DiTomaso, "Sexuality in the Workplace:
Discrimination and Harassment," in Hearn et al., op. cit., p. 78. Catharine
A. MacKinnon cites a study by the Working Women United Institute in
which respondents who had been harassed "tend to feel the incident is
their fault, that they must have done something, individually, to elicit or
encourage the behavior, that it is 'my problem.' . . . Almost a quarter of
the women in one study reported feeling 'guilty.'" MacKinnon, *Sexual Harassment of Working Women,* p. 47. Rape defendants' lawyers can legally cite
a woman's "sexually provocative" clothing as evidence in rape cases in
every state except Florida: "Nature of Clothing Isn't Evidence in Rape
Cases, Florida Law Says," *The New York Times,* June 3, 1990.

43 Nonverbal cues ambiguous: Barbara A. Gutek, "Sexuality in the Workplace: Social Research and Organizational Practise," in Hearn et al., op.
cit., p. 61.

44 Molloy: Cited in Deborah L. Sheppard, "Organizations, Power and Sexuality: The Image and Self-Image of Women Managers," in Hearn et al.,
op. cit., p. 150.

44 Success suit: John T. Molloy, "Instant Clothing Power," *The Woman's Dress for Success Book* (New York: Warner Books, 1977), Chapter 1.

44 Equal footing: Ibid.

44 Dress-for-success passé: Molloy remarks that " 'anything goes' articles were written by fashion industry types who were not going to put themselves in a straitjacket by saying that one item worked better than another." Molloy, Ibid., p. 27.

44 Molloy study: Ibid., p. 48.

46 Sizeable minority of men: Gutek, op. cit., pp. 63–64.

46 Use their appearance: "I use my personal appearance to my advantage in getting things accomplished on the job" is a statement that more men agree with than women. According to a recent study by psychologist Andrew DuBrin of the Rochester Institute of Technology, of 300 men and women, 22 percent of men use their appearance to get ahead, as opposed to 14 percent of women; 22 percent of men versus 15 percent of women admit using manipulation, and 40 percent of men versus 29 percent of women use charm. Cited in Marjory Roberts, "Workplace Wiles: Who Uses Beauty and Charm?," *Psychology Today*, May 1989.

According to Barbara A. Gutek: "My surveys found relatively little evidence that women routinely or even occasionally use their sexuality to try to gain some organizational goal. There is even less support for the position that women have succeeded or advanced at work by using their sexuality. . . . In comparison to women, men may not only use sex more often at work, they may be more successful at it!" [Hearn et al., op. cit., pp. 63–64.]

48 Professional elegance: Levitt, op. cit., pp. 31–34.

49 Wherever records have survived: Miles, op. cit., p. 155.

49 1984 U.S. women: Sidel, op. cit., p. 61.

49 Estimates . . . from 54 to. . . : Ibid.

49 In the United Kingdom: Hewlett, op. cit.

49 U.S. pay differential: Hewlett, ibid.

49 Self-worth: Rosabeth Kanter, See *Men and Women of the Corporation* (New York: Basic Books, 1977), cited in Sidel, op. cit., p. 62.

49 Unsure of worth: Ibid., p. 63.

50 20 of 420 occupations: Ibid., p. 61.

50 Arlie Hochschild even found: See Hearn et al., op. cit.; see also Hochschild with Machung, op. cit.

50 Best economic option: Catharine A. MacKinnon, *Feminism Unmodified: Discourses on Life and Law* (Cambridge, Mass.: Harvard University Press, 1987) pp. 24–25, citing Priscilla Alexander, NOW Task Force on Prostitution; the pimp retains much or most of this amount. See also Moira K. Griffin, "Wives, Hookers and the Law," *Student Lawyer*, January 1982, p. 18, cited in MacKinnon, ibid., p. 238.

50 Twice as much: Ibid., p. 238.

50 Miss America's salary: Ellen Goodman, "Miss America Gets Phonier," *The Stockton* (Calif.) *Record*, September 19, 1989.

51 "Severe doubts": Liz Friedrich, "How to Save Yourself from Financial Ruin," *The Observer* (London), August 21, 1988.

51 Shoemaker Mine: Tong, op. cit., p. 84.

51 This sort of imagery anyway: Tong, ibid. See also Zillah R. Eisenstein, *The Female Body and the Law* (Berkeley, Calif.: University of California Press, 1988).

52 Direct comparisons are being made: See *Strathclyde* v. *Porcelli*, op. cit.

52 "Nude female depicted": Ibid.

52 "Gray flannel suit": Maureen Orth, "Looking Good at Any Cost," *New York Woman*, June 1988.

53 Income discrimination. Ibid. Orth cites other examples of these expenses: A-list personal training, $1,240 a month. Retin-A, six visits to dermatologist at $75 each. Electrical "face-building" by Janet Sartin, $2,000 a series, lasts six months. "Female executives now consider the act of maintaining themselves a legitimate business expense," Orth writes. "Maintenance has invaded the tax code." "Models and prostitutes," in MacKinnon, *Feminism Unmodified*, p. 24.

53 Vice-presidents who are women: Wallis, op. cit.

53 Fatigue: Deborah Hutton, "The Fatigue Factor," British *Vogue*, October 1988.

54 A 60 percent shot at being poor: Hewlett, op. cit.

54 American older women: Sidel, op. cit.

54 In Great Britain: Taylor et al., op. cit., p. 14. Benefits for British old women are described in U.K. Equal Opportunities Commission, 1986. *The Fact About Women Is . . .*

54 West German women retiring: Taylor et al. op. cit. p. 34.

54 Private pensions: Sidel, op. cit., p. 161.

54 Year 2000: Taylor et al., op. cit., p. 11, citing UN World Assembly on Aging, Vienna, 1982.

54 Long enough to give them: Hewlett, op. cit.

57 Unions never stopped trying: MacKinnon, *Feminism Unmodified*, p. 227. "Women," MacKinnon also notes, "are randomly rewarded and systematically punished for being women. We are not rewarded systematically and punished at random, as is commonly supposed."

## Culture

*Page*

58 Anonymous women: See Marina Warner, *Monuments and Maidens: The Allegory of the Female Form* (London: Weidenfield and Nicholson, 1985).

58 Men look: John Berger, *Ways of Seeing* (London: Penguin Books, 1988), p. 47.

60 This tradition: Jane Austen, *Emma* (1816) (New York and London: Penguin Classics, 1986), p. 211; George Eliot, *Middlemarch* (1871–72) (New York and London: Penguin Books, 1984); Jane Austen, *Mansfield Park* (1814) (New York and London: Penguin Classics, 1985); John Davie, ed. Jane Austen, *Northanger Abbey, Lady Susan, The Watsons and Sanditon* (Oxford: Oxford University Press, 1985); Charlotte Brontë, *Villette* (1853) (New York and London: Penguin Classics, 1986), p. 214; Louisa May Alcott, *Little Women* (1868–69) (New York: Bantam Books, 1983), p. 237; see also Alison Lurie, *Foreign Affairs* (London: Michael Joseph, 1985); Fay Weldon, *The Life and Loves of a She-Devil* (London: Hodder, 1984); Anita Brookner, *Look at Me* (London: Jonathan Cape, 1984).

61 Blowjobs and sentimentality: "Bookworm," *Private Eye*, January 19, 1989.

62 Out of control: Peter Gay, *The Bourgeois Experience: Victoria to Freud, Volume II: The Tender Passion* (New York: Oxford University Press, 1986), p. 99. Harvard's Radcliffe Annexe and Somerville College and Lady Margaret Hall at Oxford were founded in 1879; Cambridge University opened degrees to women in 1881.

62 To fifty thousand: Janice Winship, *Inside Women's Magazines,* (London: Pandora Press, 1987), p. 7.

62 The press cooperated: John Q. Costello, *Love, Sex, and War: Changing Values, 1939–1945* (London: Collins, 1985).

64 Ideal self: Cynthia White, *Women's Magazines, 1693–1968,* quoted in Ann Oakley, *Housewife: High Value/Low Cost* (London: Penguin Books, 1987), p. 9.

64 Betty Friedan: Friedan, "The Sexual Sell," in *The Feminine Mystique* (London: Penguin Books, 1982), pp. 13–29. All quotes through page 67 are from this source.

65 "toiletries/cosmetics" ad revenue: Magazine Publishers of America, "Magazine Advertising Revenue by Class Totals, January–December 1989," Information Bureau, A.H.B., January 1990.

67 Weren't even spending much money on clothing anymore: Roberta Pollack Seid, *Never Too Thin* (New York: Prentice-Hall, 1989).

67 Style for all: Elizabeth Wilson and Lou Taylor, *Through the Looking Glass: A History of Dress from 1860 to the Present day* (London: BBC Books, 1989), p. 193.

67 Fell sharply: Marjorie Ferguson, *Forever Feminine: Women's Magazines and the Cult of Femininity* (Gower, England: Aldershot, 1983), p. 27.

"What part did women's magazines play in all this [the feminist agenda]?" Ferguson asked. "Most editors busily grappling with the problems of how to target audiences more tightly, or prevent circulation decline, were aware that some changes were taking place outside their offices, but often lacked any systematic information about their nature or extent. . . . Some editors related women going out to work to diminished 'time' and 'need' for women's magazines:

"'Then there is the business of women going out to work. Once you go out to work you have less time; your needs are different, and they might have been answered by either television, newspapers, or by the television programme paper.' (Women's weekly editor)"

Helen Gurley Brown, *Cosmopolitan*'s editor, increased its circulation from 700,000 in 1965 to 2.89 million copies a month in 1981. According to Brown, "*Cosmopolitan* is every girl's sophisticated older sister. . . . *Cosmopolitan* says you can get anything if you really try, if you don't just sit on your backside with your nose pressed to the glass. . . . We carry our profile, one piece on health, one on sex, two on emotions . . . one on man/woman relationships, one on careers, one short story and one part of a major work of fiction, as well as our regular columns." Quoted in Ferguson, p. 37.

67 The Nude Look: Seid, op. cit., p. 217.

67 Diet-related articles rose 70 percent: Ibid., p. 236.

67 To 66 in month of January: Ibid.

68 300 diet books on the shelves: Ibid.

68 Hybrid species, half man and half woman: Gay, op. cit.

68 Senator Lane: Ibid.

68 Degenerate women: Ibid. See also Barbara Ehrenreich and Deirdre English, *Complaints and Disorders: The Sexual Politics of Sickness* (Old Westbury, N.Y.: City University of New York, Feminist Press, 1973).

68 Feminists were denigrated: Gay, op. cit., p. 227.

68 Jealousy will get you nowhere: Marcia Cohen, *The Sisterhood: The Inside Story of the Women's Movement and the Leaders Who Made It Happen* (New York: Fawcett Columbine, 1988), p. 151; quotes from *Commentary* and *The New York Times*, also from Cohen, ibid., p. 261.

68 A bunch of ugly women: Ibid., p. 261.

69 Pete Hamill: Quoted in Cohen, p. 287.

69 Norman Mailer: Quoted in Cohen, p. 290.

69 WOMEN ARE REVOLTING: Ibid., p. 205.

71 Rivers and streams: Ibid., pp. 82–83, 133.

73 Misinformed: April Fallon and Paul Rozin, "Sex Differences in Perceptors of Body Size," *Journal of Abnormal Psychology*, Vol. 92, no. 4 (1983). "Our data suggest women are misinformed and exaggerate the magnitude of thinness men desire."

74 Trust: Cohen, op. cit., p. 91.

74 Pride in their identity: Quoted in J. Winship, op. cit., p. 7.

78 Fragility of the word: Lewis Lapham, *Money and Class in America: Notes on the Civil Religion* (London: Picador, 1989), p. 283.

78 Readers as a market: Lawrence Zuckerman, "Who's Minding the Newsroom?," *Time*, November 28, 1988.

78 Watergate: Thomas Winship, former editor at *The Boston Globe*, quoted in Zuckerman, op. cit.

78 Sell goods: Daniel Lazare, "Vanity Fare," *Columbia Journalism Review* (May/June 1990), pp. 6–8.

78 Atmosphere: Ibid, pp. 6–8. Lazare points out that one American magazine, *Vanity Fair*, gives laudatory coverage of fashion and cosmetics giants; in September 1988 alone, these recipients of editorial promotion took out fifty ad pages at up to $25,000 a page.

79 650 TV messages a week: Mark Muro, "A New Era of Eros in Advertising," *The Boston Globe*, April 16, 1989.

79 Demolish resistance: Ibid.

79 Pornography . . . 7 billion dollars a year: MacKinnon, *Feminism Unmodified*, op. cit., citing Galloway and Thornton, "Crackdown on Pornography—A No-Win Battle," *U.S. News and World Report*, June 4, 1984; see also Catherine Itzin and Corinne Sweet of the Campaign Against Pornography and Censorship in Britain, "What Should We Do About Pornography?," British *Cosmopolitan*, November 1989; J. Cook, "The X-Rated Economy," *Forbes*, September 18, 1978 ($4 billion per year); "The Place of Pornography," *Harper's*, November 1984 ($7 billion per year).
   In the past fifteen years, the industry has increased 1,600 times over and now has more outlets than McDonald's. See Jane Caputi, *The Age of Sex Crime* (Bowling Green, Ohio: Bowling Green State University, Popular Press, 1987).

79 United States alone, a million dollars a day: Consumer Association of Penang, *Abuse of Women in the Media* (Oxford: Oxford University Press, 1985), cited in Debbie Taylor et al., *Women: A World Report*, (Oxford: Oxford University Press, 1985), p. 67.

79 British magazines, Angela Lambert, "Amid the Alien Porn," *The Independent*, July 1, 1989.

79 Swedish pornography: Gunilla Bjarsdal. Stockholm: Legenda Publishing Research, 1989.

79 18 million U.S. men: Taylor et al., op. cit., p. 67.

79 One American man in ten: John Crewdson, *By Silence Betrayed: Sexual Abuse of Children* (New York: Harper & Row, 1988), p. 249.

79 Best read in Canada: Caputi, op. cit., p. 74.

79 Italian pornography: The Institute for Economic and Political Studies, Italy; research by Mondadori Publishing, 1989.

79 Increasingly violent: See Andrea Dworkin, *Pornography: Men Possessing Women* (New York: Putnam, 1981), especially "Objects," pp. 101–128. On Herschel Gordon Lewis, see Caputi, op. cit., p. 91. Also, concerning competition with pornography, see Tony Garnett, director of *Handgun*, Weintraub Enterprises, quoted in "Rape: That's Entertainment?," Jane Mills, producer, *Omnibus*, BBC1, September 15, 1989. According to Garnett, "One of the reasons a film like this is probably financed is because there is a rape scene at the center of it. There was . . . a considerable pressure from the various distributors who controlled it. Most of the people who dealt with it were very disappointed in the film, particularly in the rape because it was not sexually exciting and I was asked if we had any off-cuts that we could re-cut in to make it more sexually exciting because that sells tickets."

80 30 percent U.S. made: "Stars and Stripes Everywhere," *The Observer*, October 8, 1989.

80 71 percent imports: Paul Harrison, *Inside the Third World: The Anatomy of Poverty* (London: Penguin Books, 1980).

80 TV ownership in India: Edward W. Desmond, "Puppies and Consumer Boomers," *Time*, November 14, 1989. (In 1984 Indian advertisers began to sponsor shows.)

80 Worldwide deregulation of airwaves: The Dutch government is concerned about satellite-based pornography and commercial TV from Luxembourg. Some European foreign ministers believe that "by the end of the next decade the US-dominated media empires will have a stranglehold on global broadcasting." [John Palmer, "European Ministers Divided Over US 'Media Imperialism,'" *The Guardian*, Oct. 3, 1989.]

In "Review and Appraisal: Communication and Media," a paper presented to the World Conference to Review and Appraise the Achievements of the United Nations Decade for Women, Nairobi, 1985 (A/CONF.116/5), a worldwide survey found that in the media, there is little representation of women's changing roles. In Mexico, women are "the soul of the home" or the "sex object." In Turkey, the typical woman in the media is "mother, wife, sex symbol"; the Ivory Coast emphasizes her "charm, beauty, frivolity, fragility." Cited in Taylor et al., op. cit., p. 78.

80 $9 billion: "Stars and Stripes Everywhere," op. cit.

80 Glitz blitz: "You Must Be Joking," *The Guardian*, October 10, 1989.

80 Contradictory freedoms: Cynthia Cockburn, "Second Among Equals," *Marxism Today*, July 1989.

80 Glamour: See David Remnick, "From Russia with Lycra," *Gentlemen's Quarterly*, November 1988.

80 *Reform:* David Palliser: *The Guardian*, October 16, 1989.

80 Negoda: "From Russia with Sex," *Newsweek*, April 17, 1989.

80 China: See "The Queen of the Universe," *Newsweek*, June 6, 1988.

80 Tatiana Mamanova: Quoted in Caputi, op. cit., p. 7.

81 Silences: J. Winship, op. cit., p. 40.

81 Looking intelligent: Penny Chorlton, *Cover-up: Taking the Lid Off the Cosmetics Industry* (Wellingborough, U.K.: Grapevine, 1988), p. 47; also Gloria Steinem, "Sex, Lies and Advertising," *Ms.*, September 1990.

81 Ad pressure . . . gray hair: Michael Hoyt, "When the Walls Came Tumbling Down," *Columbia Journalism Review*, March/April 1990, pp. 35–40.

81 Steinem: See Gloria Steinem, *Outrageous Acts and Everyday Rebellions* (New York: Holt, Rinehart and Winston, 1983), p. 4.

82 Her lifetime: Marilyn Webb, "Gloria Leaves Home," *New York Woman*, July 1988.

82 Ten presidents: Lisa Lebowitz, "Younger Every Day," *Harper's Bazaar*, August 1988.

82 More on advertising: Chorlton, op. cit., p. 46.

82 Cosmetic stock: *Standard and Poor's Industry Surveys* (New York: Standard and Poor's Corp., 1988). In the United States, in 1987, the cosmetics, toiletries, and personal care products industry accounted for $18.5 billion, with cosmetics making up 27 percent of that figure; see Robin Marantz Henig, "The War on Wrinkles," *New Woman*, June 1988.

Much of the growth is due to the depressed price of petroleum derivatives, especially ethanol, which is the base of most products. "A major factor underlying the group's performance," according to the 1988 *Standard and Poor's Industry Surveys*, "has been its favorable cost/price ratio."

82 Beauty editors: Chorlton, "Publicity Disguised as Editorial Matter," in *Cover-up*, op. cit., pp. 46–47.

82 Dalma Heyn: Pat Duarte, "Older, but Not Invisible," *Women's Center News* (Women's Center of San Joaquin County, Calif.), vol. 12, no. 12 (August 1988), pp. 1–2.

83 Bob Ciano: Quoted in ibid., p. 2.

84 Advertising revenue: A single issue of *Harper's and Queen*, in October 1988, carried £100,000 worth of ads from cosmetics companies: Gerald McKnight, *The Skin Game: The International Beauty Business Brutally Exposed* (London: Sidgwick and Jackson, 1987), p. 65.

84 Advertising depends on . . . dieting: Magazine Publishers of America, op. cit.

# Religion

88 Pray Your Weight Away!: Roberta Pollack Seid, *Never Too Thin* (New York: Prentice Hall, 1989), p. 107.

90 Tradition: See Carol Gilligan, *In a Different Voice: Psychological Theory and Women's Development* (Cambridge, Mass.: Harvard University Press, 1982).

91 Blessed . . . among women: Roman Catholic missal.

91 Price beyond rubies: Proverbs 3:10–31.

91 Women outnumbered men: Nancy F. Cott, *The Bonds of Womanhood: Woman's Sphere in New England, 1780–1835* (New Haven: Yale University Press, 1977), p. 126.

92 Ministers: See Ann Douglas, *The Feminization of American Culture* (New York: Knopf, 1977).

92 Harriet Martineau: Cott, op. cit., p. 138.

92 Morphology: Ibid., p. 139.

93 Creation story: Genesis, 2:21–23.

93 Be ye . . . perfect: Matthew 5:48.

93 Wilson: Quoted in Gerald McKnight, *The Skin Game: The International Beauty Business Brutally Exposed* (London: Sidgwick & Jackson, 1989), p. 158.

93 Second Class: Oscar Wilde, *Lecture on Art,* cited in Richard Ellman, *Oscar Wilde* (London: H. Hamilton, 1987).

94 Neither male nor female: Galatians 3:28.

94 Men . . . distort theirs positively: Daniel Goleman, "Science Times," *The New York Times*, March 15, 1989, citing April Fallon and Paul Rozin, "Sex Differences in Perceptors of Body Size," *Journal of Abnormal Psychology*, vol. 4 (1983). See also John K. Collins et al., "Body Percept Change in Obese Females After Weight Loss Reduction Therapy," *Journal of Clinical Psychology*, vol. 39 (1983): *All* of sixty-eight eighteen-to-sixty-five-year-old women judged themselves to be fatter than they actually were.

94 Strongly dissatisfied: "Staying Forever Young," *San Francisco Chronicle*, October 12, 1988.

94 Most weight-loss enrollment female: See Eva Szekely, *Never Too Thin* (Toronto: The Women's Press, 1988).

95 Convention: "Views on Beauty: When Artists Meet Surgeons," *The New York Times*, June 20, 1988.

95 Fragen: Ronald Fragen, "The Holy Grail of Good Looks," *The New York Times*, June 29, 1988.

95 Rees: Dr. Thomas D. Rees with Sylvia Simmons, *More Than Just a Pretty Face: How Cosmetic Surgery Can Improve Your Looks and Your Life* (Boston: Little, Brown, 1987), p. 63.

95 Niôsome: Advertisement for Niôsome Système Anti-Age.

96 Kim Chernin: See *The Obsession: Reflections on the Tyranny of Slenderness* (New York: Harper & Row, 1981), p. 39.

97 Menstruation taboos: Rosalind Miles, *The Women's History of the World* (London: Grafton Books, 1988), pp. 108–109.

99 Surveillance: Elaine Showalter, *The Female Malady: Women, Madness and English Culture, 1830–1980* (New York: Pantheon Books, 1985), p. 212.

100 Watch ye therefore: Mark 13:35.

100 Stand naked: Alexandra Cruikshank et al., *Positively Beautiful: Everywoman's Guide to Face, Figure and Fitness* (Sydney and London: Bay Books, 1988), p. 25.

100 Souls: Cott, op. cit., p. 136.

100 Richard Stuart: Seid, op. cit., pp. 169–170.

102 The snares of death: Psalm 116.

106 Men cut off women: Dale Spender, *Man Made Language* (London and New York: Routledge and Kegan Paul, 1985). See also Laura Shapiro, "Guns and Dolls," *Newsweek*, May 28, 1990, and Edward B. Fiske, "Even at a Former Women's College, Men Are Taken More Seriously, A Researcher Finds," *The New York Times*, April 11, 1990.

107 Cult converters and hypnotists: Willa Appel, *Cults in America: Programmed for Paradise* (New York: Holt, Rinehart & Winston, 1983).

108 Stare fixedly: All quotes from cult members are from Appel, ibid.

109 Massive con: McKnight, op. cit., p. 20.

109 Herstein: Ibid., pp. 24–25.

110 Industry insiders: Quoted in ibid., p. 74.

110 Roddick: Quoted in ibid., pp. 55–56.

111 Disney: Quoted in ibid., p. 17.

111 Sugiyama: Quoted in ibid., p. 4.

111 Kligman: Ibid., p. 39.

111 FDA: Ibid., pp. 17–29.

112 To punish anyone: Deborah Blumenthal, "Softer Sell in Ads for Beauty Products," *The New York Times*, April 23, 1988, p. 56.

112 Rejuvenation: British Code of Advertising, Section C.I 5.3.

113 Day care: Felicity Barringer, "Census Report Shows a Rise in Child Care and Its Costs," *The New York Times*, August 16, 1990.

115 Women *are* under attack . . . 44 percent: See Diana E. H. Russell, *Rape: The Victim's Perspective* (New York: Stein & Day, 1975).

115 21 percent . . . abused: Angela Browne, *When Battered Women Kill* (New York: Free Press, 1987), pp. 4–5.

115 One British woman in seven raped: Ruth E. Hall, *Ask Any Woman: A London Inquiry into Rape and Assault* (Bristol, U.K.: Falling Wall Press, 1985).

115 Standard of living declines: Lenore Weitzman, "Social and Economic Consequences of Property, Alimony and Child Support Awards," *University of California Los Angeles Law Review*, vol. 28 (1982), pp. 1118–1251.

115 Child support: See Ruth Sidel, *Women and Children Last: The Plight of Poor Women in Affluent America* (New York: Penguin Books, 1987), p. 104.

115 Median income: Ibid., p. 18.

116 Harassment: See Catharine A. MacKinnon, *Sexual Harassment of Working Women: A Case of Sex Discrimination* (New Haven: Yale University Press, 1979), also Rosemarie Tong, *Women, Sex and the Law* (Totowa, N.J.: Rowman and Littlefield, 1984).

116 Women make . . .: Sidel, op. cit., p. 17.

117 Divorce rate: Debbie Taylor et al., *Women: A World Report* (Oxford: Oxford University Press, 1985), p. 13.

118 Food: Linda Wells, "Food for Thought," *The New York Times Magazine*, July 30, 1989.

120 La Prairie: Anthea Gerrie, "Inject a Little Fun into Your Marriage," "Male and Femail," *Mail on Sunday*, 1988.

120 Fetal tissue: McKnight, op. cit., p. 84.

120 Prices: Quoted in Linda Wells, "Prices: Out of Sight," *The New York Times Magazine*, July 16, 1989.

120 Cost of product: Quoted in McKnight, op. cit., p. 66.

121 Cults: Appel, op. cit., pp. 113–137. See also Chernin, op. cit., pp. 35–36, on cults.

122 Set a watch: Based on Psalm 141:3.

125 Weight Watchers: WW international statistics, Dutch *Viva*, September 1989.

125 Appel, op. cit., p. 1–21.

126 Ibid., p. 31.

126 Ibid., p. 50.

126 Ibid., p. 59.

127 Ibid., p. 61.

127 Ibid., p. 64.

127 Ibid., p. 133.

127 Ibid., 72.

130 Lasch: See Christopher Lasch, *The Culture of Narcissism: American Life in an Age of Diminishing Expectations* (New York: Warner Books, 1979).


## Sex


*Page*

131 Kinsey: Alfred Kinsey et al.: *Sexual Behavior in the Human Female* (Philadelphia: W. B. Saunders Co., 1953); cited in Debbie Taylor et al., *Women: A World Report* (Oxford: Oxford University Press, 1985), p. 62.

131 Destroying it: Rosalind Miles, *The Women's History of the World* (London: Paladin Grafton Books, 1988), p. 115.

132 Sex is learned: See Elaine Morgan, *The Descent of Woman* (New York: Bantam Books, 1972), pp. 76, 77. According to Morgan:
"You might imagine that copulation was such a basic and 'instinctive' process that it would be very little affected by learning and imitation . . . but as far as sex is concerned, you would be wrong, at least about primates. Harlow and Harlow's experiments in the 1950's proved beyond doubt that if a baby monkey is reared in isolation, unable either to experiment with coevals or to observe its elders copulating (which young primates do, with great curiosity and often at hamperingly close quarters, whenever they can), then, when it grows up, it hasn't got the faintest idea how to go about it, and if it is a male, it dies without issue."

136 Jack Sullivan: Quoted in Jane Caputi, *The Age of Sex Crime* (Bowling Green, Ohio: Bowling Green State University Popular Press, 1987), p. 63.

136 Siskel: Quoted ibid., p. 84. Life and art converged in the 1980s: In the novel *Confessions of a Lady Killer*, a sex killer stalks feminists; *Tightrope*, the hero fantasizes strangling a feminist rape-crisis counselor; in December 1989, a man shot fourteen young women in Canada, shouting, "I hate feminists."

137 France: "French Without Fears," *The Observer* (London), September 17, 1989.

137 Screen Actors Guild: "Actresses Make Less Than Men, New Study Says," *San Francisco Chronicle*, August 2, 1990.

138 Next to *Time*: Susan G. Cole, *Pornography and the Sex Crisis* (Toronto: Amanita Enterprises, 1989), p. 37.

138  The authorities in Sweden: Anita Desai, "The Family—Norway," in Taylor et al., op. cit., p. 24.

138  *Spare Rib* censored: Caroline Harris and Jennifer Moore, "Altered Images," *Marxism Today*, November 1988, pp. 24–27.

139  Judy Chicago: Jonetta Rose Barras, "U.D.C.'s $1.6 Million Dinner," *The Washington Times*, July 18, 1990.

139  Canadian women's film was banned: Caputi, op. cit., p. 72.

140  Fantasy lives: Taylor et al., op. cit., p. 66.

141  Less likely to believe a rape victim: Neil M. Malamuth and Edward Donnerstein, eds., *Pornography and Sexual Aggression* (New York: Academic Press, 1984).

141  Desensitizing: Dolph Zillman and Jennings Bryant, "Pornography, Sexual Callousness and the Trivialization of Rape," *Journal of Communication*, vol. 32 (982), pp. 16–18.

141  Trivialize the severity: Donnerstein and Linz: "Pornography: Its Effect on Violence Against Women," in Malamuth and Donnerstein, eds., op. cit., pp. 115–138.

141  Violence alone: Edward Donnerstein and Leonard Berkowitz, "Victim Reactions in Aggressive Erotic Films as a Factor in Violence Against Women," *Personality and Social Psychology Bulletin*, vol. 41, (1981), pp. 710–724.

141  Wendy Stock, "The Effects of Pornography on Women," testimony for the Attorney General's Commission on Pornography, 1985.

141  Carol L. Krafka, "Sexually Explicit, Sexually Violent and Violent Media: Effects of Multiple Naturalistic Exposures and Debriefing on Female Viewers," doctoral thesis, University of Wisconsin, 1985.

143  Consumerism: Barbara Ehrenreich, Elizabeth Hess, and Gloria Jacobs, *Re-Making Love: The Feminization of Sex* (London: Fontana/Collins, 1986), p. 110.

146  Orgasm: For statistics on orgasm, see Shere Hite, *The Hite Report* (London: Pandora Press, 1989), pp. 225–270.

146  Kaplan: Helen Singer Kaplan, *The New Sex Therapy* (New York: Brunner/Mazel, 1974).

147  Seymour Fischer: See *Understanding the Female Orgasm* (New York: Bantam Books, 1973).

147  British women: Wendy Faulkner, "The Obsessive Orgasm: Science, Sex and Female Sexuality," in Lynda Birke et al., *Alice Through the Microscope* (London: Virago Press, 1980), p. 145. See also R. Chester and C. Walker, "Sexual Experience and Attitudes of British Women," in R. Chester and J. Peel, *Changing Patterns of Sexual Behaviour* (London: Academic Press, 1979).

147 Danish women: K. Garde and I. Lunde, "Female Sexual Behaviour: A Study of a Random Sample of Forty-Year-Old Women," *Maturita*, vol. 2 (1980).

147 Sudanese women: A. A. Shandall, "Circumcision and Infibulation of Females," Faculty of Medicine, University of Khartoum; cited in Taylor et al., op. cit., p. 61.

149 Foolishly decides: Alice Walker, "Coming Apart," in *You Can't Keep a Good Woman Down* (San Diego: Harcourt Brace Jovanovich, 1981), pp. 41–53.

149 I fantasize: Nancy Friday, *My Secret Garden: Women's Sexual Fantasies* (London: Quartet Books, 1985), p. 147.

150 Strongly dissatisfied: Dr. Thomas Cash, Diane Cash, and Jonathan Butters, "Mirror-Mirror on the Wall: Contrast Effects and Self-Evaluation of Physical Attractiveness," *Personality and Social Psychology Bulletin*, vol. 9 (3), September 1983.

150 Hutchinson: Jane E. Brody, "Personal Health," *The New York Times*, October 20, 1988.

153 The old man kissed her: Miles, op. cit., pp. 97, 141.

158 Swept away: see Carol Cassell, *Swept Away: Why Women Confuse Love and Sex* (New York: Simon & Schuster, 1984); for a psychoanalytic explanation of the overdetermination of the female body, see Dorothy Dinnerstein, *Sexual Arrangements and the Human Malaise,* (New York: Harper Colophon, 1977).

159 48.7 percent of U.S. abortions: "Paths to an Abortion Clinic: Seven Trails of Conflict and Pain," *The New York Times*, May 8, 1989.

159 1983 random survey: Report of the Los Angeles Commission on Assaults Against Women. See Page Mellish, ed. "Statistics on Violence Against Women," *The Backlash Times*, 1989.

159 By her husband or ex-husband: Diana E. H. Russell, cited in Angela Browne, *When Battered Women Kill* (New York: Free Press, 1987), p. 100. For U.S. marital rape figures of one wife in ten, see David Finkelhor and Kersti Yllo, *License to Rape: Sexual Abuse of Wives* (New York: The Free Press, 1985). Menachem Amir's figures, now thought to be too low, showed rates of rape for black women to be 50 percent; for white women, 12 percent, or one in eight. See Menachem Amir, *Patterns in Forcible Rape* (Chicago: University of Chicago Press, 1971), p. 44. See also Diana E. H. Russell, *Rape in Marriage* (Bloomington: Indiana University Press, 1982), p. 66.

159 Dutch families: see *Geweld tegen vrouwen in heteroseksuele relaties* (Renee Romkers, 1989); *Sexueel misbruik van meisjes door verwanten* (Nel Draijer, 1988).

159 Sweden: Research by Gunilla Bjarsdal. Stockholm: Legenda Publishing Research, 1989. For an international overview of the prevalence of marital rape, see Diana E. H. Russell, "Wife Rape in Other Countries," in *Rape in Marriage*, pp. 333–354.

159 Canada: Caputi, op. cit., p. 54.

159 England: R. Hall, S. James, and J. Kertesz, *The Rapist Who Pays the Rent*
(Bristol, England: Falling Wall Press, 1981). Spousal rape was not a crime
in Canada until 1983, in Scotland until 1982, and is not yet a crime in
England or in many states in the United States.

159 London women: Ruth Hall, *Ask Any Woman: A London Inquiry into Rape and
Sexual Assault* (Bristol, England: Falling Wall Press, 1981).

159 Epidemic: Mellish, op. cit. Also Lenore Walker, "The Battered Woman,"
*The Backlash Times*, 1979, p. 20. Walker estimates that as many as 50 percent of all women will be battered at some point in their lives.

160 Harris poll: See Browne, op. cit.

160 94–95 percent of cases: Ibid., p. 8.

160 Assault each year: Ibid., pp. 4–5.

160 One quarter of violent crime in United States: M. Barret and S. McIntosh,
in Taylor et al., op cit.

160 Researchers in Pittsburgh: Browne, op. cit., pp. 4–5.

160 Canadian married women: Linda McLeod, *The Vicious Circle* (Ottawa: Canadian Advisory Council on the Status of Women, 1980), p. 21. One
woman in Canada raped every 17 minutes: See Julie Brickman, "Incidence
of Rape and Sexual Assault in Urban Canadian Population," *International
Journal of Women's Studies*, vol. 7 (1984), pp. 195–206.

160 NIMH study: Browne, op. cit., p. 9.

160 Incest: Kinsey et al., op. cit., *Sexual Behavior in the Human Female*, cited in
John Crewdson, *By Silence Betrayed: Sexual Abuse of Children in America*
(Boston: Little, Brown, 1988), p. 25.

160 Diana Russell: Reported in ibid., p. 25.

160 Bud Lewis: Ibid., p. 28.

160 Worldwide research . . . year out: Taylor et al., op. cit.

161 Anorexics . . . sexually abused: Deanne Stone, "Challenging Conventional
Thought," an interview with Doctors Susan and Wayne Wooley, *Radiance*,
Summer 1989.

161 Elizabeth Morgan: Quoted in Joyce Egginton, "The Pain of Hiding Hil-
ary," *The Observer*, November 5, 1989.

161 Sexual pleasure . . . not from a good place: Caputi, op. cit., p. 116.

162 Theorists . . . of pornography: See Susan Griffin, *Pornography and Silence*
(London: The Women's Press, 1988); Susan G. Cole, *Pornography and the
Sex Crisis* (Toronto: Amanita, 1989); Andrea Dworkin, *Pornography: Men
Possessing Women* (New York: Putnam, 1981); Gloria Steinem, "Erotica vs.
Pornography," in *Outrageous Acts and Everyday Rebellions* (New York: Holt,
Rinehart and Winston, 1983), pp. 219–232; Susanne Kappeler, *The Por-
nography of Representation* (Minneapolis: University of Minnesota Press,
1986).

163 12 percent of British and American parents: "Striking Attitudes," *The Guardian*, November 15, 1989, citing *The British Social Attitudes Special International Report* by Roger Jowell, Sharon Witherspoon, and Lindsay Brook (London: Social and Community Planning Research, Gower, 1989).

164 MTV: Quoted in Caputi, op. cit., p. 39.

164 Alice Cooper: Adam Sweeting, "Blame It on Alice," *The Guardian*, December 1, 1989.

165 *Ms.* magazine: Robin Warshaw, *I Never Called It Rape: The* Ms. *Report on Recognizing, Fighting and Surviving Date and Acquaintance Rape* (New York: The Ms. Foundation for Education and Communication with Sarah Lazin Books, 1988), p. 83; research by Mary P. Koss, Kent State University, with the Center for Prevention and Control of Rape.

165 Relate directly to acquaintance rape: Ibid., p. 96.

165 "I like to dominate a woman": Survey was conducted by Virginia Greenlinger, Williams College, and Donna Byrne, SUNY-Albany; cited in Warshaw, p. 93.

165 8 percent of college men had raped: Ibid., p. 84. The pornography that respondents read consisted of: *Playboy, Penthouse, Chic, Club, Forum, Gallery, Genesis, Oui* or *Hustler.*

165 58 percent of college males: John Briere and Neil M. Malamuth, "Self-Reported Likelihood of Sexually Aggressive Behavior: Attitudinal versus Sexual Explanations," *Journal of Research in Personality*, Vol. 37 (1983), pp. 315–318.

165 30 percent rated faces showing distress more attractive: Alfred B. Heilbrun, Jr., Emory; Maura P. Loftus, Auburn University; cited in ibid., p. 97. See also: N. Malamuth, J. Heim, and S. Feshbach, "Sexual Responsiveness of College Students to Rape Depictions: Inhibitory and Disinhibitory Effects," *Social Psychology*, vol. 38 (1980), p. 399.

165 Among 3,187 women: Warshaw, op. cit., p. 83.

166 Heart attacks: Ibid., p. 11.

166 Auburn University: Ibid., pp. 13–14. Also at Auburn University, Professor Barry R. Burkhart found that 61 percent of male students said they had sexually touched a woman against her will.

166 Did not call it "rape": Ibid., pp. 3, 51, 64, 66, 117.

166 Violence from dating partner: Browne, op. cit., p. 42.

167 Fourteen- to eighteen-year-olds: See study by Jacqueline Goodchild et al., cited in Warshaw, op. cit., p. 120.

167 A recent survey in Toronto: Caputi, op. cit., p. 119.

169 Preoccupation with face and hair: Daniel Goleman, "Science Times," *The New York Times*, March 15, 1989.

172 William Butler Yeats: "For Ann Gregory," in *The Collected Poems of W. B. Yeats* (London: MacMillan, 1965).

173 Mary Gordon: *Final Payments* (London: Black Swan, 1987).

174 Gertrude Stein: Quoted in Arianna Stassinopoulos, *Picasso: Creator and Destroyer* (New York: Simon & Schuster, 1988).


# Hunger


*Page*

181 Woolf: Virginia Woolf, *A Room of One's Own* (San Diego: Harcourt Brace Jovanovich, 1981); reprint of 1929 edition.

182 Anorexia and Bulimia Association: cited in Joan Jacobs Brumberg, *Fasting Girls: The Emergence of Anorexia Nervosa as a Modern Disease* (Cambridge, Mass: Harvard University Press, 1988), p. 20.

182 AIDS: "AIDS Toll Rises by 50 percent," *Glasgow Herald*, January 7, 1990.

182 5 to 20 percent of women students: Brumberg, op. cit., p. 12.

182 50 percent of college women: *Ms.*, October 1983. A recent University of California at San Francisco survey showed "*all* [italics added] the 18-year-olds said they currently use vomiting, laxatives, fasting, or diet pills to control their weight. [Jane Brody, "Personal Health," *The New York Times*, March 18, 1987.]

182 Bulimic: Cited in Roberta Pollack Seid, *Never Too Thin: Why Women Are at War with Their Bodies* (New York: Prentice Hall, 1989), p. 21.

182 Death rate: L.K.G. Hsu, "Outcome of Anorexia Nervosa: A Review of the Literature," *Archives of General Psychiatry*, vol. 37 (1980), pp. 1041–1042. For a thorough overview of the literature, see L. K. George Hsu, M. D., *Eating Disorders* (New York: The Guildford Press, 1990).

182 Never recover completely: Brumberg, op. cit., p. 24.

183 Medical effects: Brumberg, op. cit., p. 26. According to *The Penguin Encyclopaedia of Nutrition* (New York: Viking, 1985): "The patient's teeth are eroded by acidity of ejected gastric contents. Imbalance of blood chemistry can lead to serious irregularities of the heartbeat, and to kidney failure. Epileptic seizures are not uncommon. Irregular menstrual pattern [leads to infertility]," op. cit.

183 Failure to thrive: Seid, op. cit., p. 26, citing Michael Pugliese et al., "Fear of Obesity: A Cause of Short Stature and Delayed Puberty," *New England Journal of Medicine*, September 1, 1983, pp. 513–518. See also Rose Dosti, "Nutritionists Express Worries About Children Following Adult Diets," *Los Angeles Times*, June 29, 1986.

180 50 percent of British women suffer: Julia Buckroyd, "Why Women Still Can't Cope with Food," British *Cosmopolitan*, September 1989.

183 Spreading to Europe: Hilde Bruch, *The Golden Cage: The Enigma of Anorexia Nervosa* (New York: Random House, 1979), cited in Kim Chernin, *The Obsession: Reflections on the Tyranny of Slenderness* (New York: Harper & Row, 1981), p. 101.

183 Sweden: Cecilia Bergh Rosen, "An Explorative Study of Bulimia and Other Excessive Behaviours," King Gustav V Research Institute, Karolinska Institute, Stockholm, and the Department of Sociology and the School of Social Work, University of Stockholm, Sweden (Stockholm, 1988). "Social seclusion and economic problems were seen as the two most negative effects of bulimia. Although physical consequences were severe, the probands were not deterred by this. . . . In all cases bulimia was said to have caused social withdrawal and isolation" [p. 77].

183 Italian teenagers: Professor N. Frighi, "Le Sepienze," Institute for Mental Health, University of Rome, 1989; study of over 4,435 secondary-school students.

183 Middle-class: Brumberg, *Fasting Girls*, p. 9. Ninety to 95 percent of anorexics are young, white, female, and disproportionately middle- and upper-class. The "contagion" is confined to the United States, Western Europe, Japan, and areas experiencing "rapid Westernization" [Ibid., pp. 12–13]. Recent studies show that the higher the man's income, the lower his wife's weight [Seid, op. cit., p. 16].

184 The look of sickness: Ann Hollander, *Seeing Through Clothes* (New York: Viking Penguin, 1988), p. 151.

184 The average model . . . 23 percent: Reported in Verne Palmer, "Where's the Fat?," *The Outlook*, May 13, 1987, quoting Dr. C. Wayne Callaway, director of the Center for Clinical Nutrition at George Washington University; cited in Seid, op. cit., p. 15.

184 Twiggy: Quoted in Nicholas Drake, ed., *The Sixties: A Decade in Vogue* (New York: Prentice Hall, 1988).

185 Playboy Playmates: See David Garner et al., "Cultural Expectations of Thinness in Women," *Psychological Reports*, vol. 47 (1980), pp. 483–491.

185 25 percent on diets: Seid, op. cit., p. 3.

185 *Glamour* survey: Survey by Drs. Wayne and Susan Wooley, of the University of Cincinnati College of Medicine, 1984: "33,000 Women Tell How They Really Feel About Their Bodies," *Glamour*, February 1984.

187 Obesity . . . heart disease: See "Bills to Improve Health Studies of Women," *San Francisco Chronicle*, August 1, 1990: According to Rep. Barbara Mikulski (Democrat, Maryland), nearly all heart disease research is done on male subjects; the National Institutes of Health spends only 13 percent of its funds on women's health research.

187 J. Polivy and C. P. Herman: "Clinical Depression and Weight Change: A Complex Relation," *Journal of Abnormal Psychology*, vol. 85 (1976), pp. 338–340. Cited in Ilana Attie and J. Brooks-Gunn, "Weight Concerns as Chronic Stressors in Women," in Rosalind C. Barnett, Lois Biener, and Grace K. Baruch, eds., *Gender and Stress* (New York: The Free Press, 1987), p. 237.

188 Other theories: Rudolph M. Bell, *Holy Anorexia* (Chicago and London: The University of Chicago Press, 1985); Kim Chernin, *The Hungry Self: Women, Eating and Identity* (London: Virago Press, 1986); Marilyn Lawrence, *The Anorexic Experience* (London: The Women's Press, 1984); Susie Orbach, *Hunger Strike: The Anorectic's Struggle as a Metaphor for our Age* (London: Faber and Faber, 1986); Eva Szekeley, *Never Too Thin* (Toronto: The Women's Press, 1988); Susie Orbach, *Fat Is a Feminist Issue* (London: Arrow Books, 1989).

190 Rome: Sarah Pomeroy, *Goddesses, Whores, Wives and Slaves: Women in Classical Antiquity* (New York: Shocken Books, 1975), p. 203. Under Trajan, the allowance for boys was sixteen sesterces, twelve for girls; in a second-century foundation, boys were given twenty sesterces to girls' sixteen [Ibid.].

190 Infanticide: M. Piers, *Infanticide* (New York: W, W, Norton, 1978); and Marvin Harris, *Cows, Pigs, Wars and Witches: The Riddles of Culture* (New York: Vintage, 1975).

190 Botswana: See Jalna Hammer and Pat Allen, "Reproductive Engineering: The Final Solution?," in Lynda Birke et al., *Alice Through the Microscope: The Power of Science Over Women's Lives* (London: Virago Press, 1980), p. 224.

190 Less nutritious: See L. Leghorn and M. Roodkowsky, "Who Really Starves?," *Women and World Hunger* (New York, n.a., 1977).

190 Turkey: Debbie Taylor et al., *Women: A World Report* (Oxford: Oxford University Press, 1985), p. 47.

190 Not hungry: While both Kim Chernin and Susie Orbach describe this pattern, they do not conclude that it directly serves to maintain a political objective.

190 Anemic: Taylor et al., op. cit., p. 8, citing E. Royston, "Morbidity of Women: The Prevalence of Nutritional Anemias in Developing Countries," World Health Organization Division of Family Health (Geneva: 1978).

191 In a sample of babies: Susie Orbach, op. cit., pp. 40–41.

192 Healthy twenty-year-old female: Seid, op. cit., p. 175.

192 38 percent body fat: Anne Scott Beller, *Fat and Thin* (New York: Farrar, Straus and Giroux, 1977); for discussion of set-point theory (the weight which the body defends), see Seid, op. cit., p. 182. See also Gina Kolata, "Where Fat Is Problem, Heredity Is the Answer, Studies Find," *The New York Times*, May 24, 1990.

192 Caloric needs: Derek Cooper, "Good Health or Bad Food? 20 Ways to Find Out," *Scotland on Sunday*, December 24, 1989; Sarah Bosely, "The Fat of the Land," *The Guardian*, January 12, 1990.

192 Women who exercise: Seid, op. cit., p. 40.

192 Ovarian cancer: Ibid., p. 29.

192 Inactive ovaries, Saffron Davies, "Fat: A Fertility Issue," "Health Watch," *The Guardian*, June 30, 1988.

192 Frisch: Rose E. Frisch, "Fatness and Fertility," *Scientific American*, March 1988.

192 Low-birthweight babies: *British Medical Journal*, cited in British *Cosmopolitan*, July 1988.

192 But desire: Seid, op. cit., pp. 290–291.

193 Develop breasts: Magnus Pyke, *Man and Food* (London: Weidenfeld and Nicolson, 1970), pp. 140–145.

193 Loyola University: Seid, op. cit., p. 360, quoting Phyllis Mensing, "Eating Disorders Have Severe Effect on Sexual Function," *Evening Outlook*, April 6, 1987.

193 Exercisers lose interest in sex: Seid, op. cit., p. 296, citing Alayne Yatres et al., "Running—An Analogue of Anorexia?," *New England Journal of Medicine*," February 3, 1983, pp. 251–255.

193 Sexless anorexics: Brumberg, op, cit., p. 267.

193 Sexless bulimics: Mette Bergstrom, "Sweets and Sour," *The Guardian*, October 3, 1989.

193 In India: Taylor et al., op. cit., p. 86.

193 Self-inflicted semi-starvation: Seid, op. cit., p. 31.

193 University of Minnesota: See ibid., p. 266; excerpts from Attie and Brooks-Gunn, *Gender and Stress*, op. cit.

194 Social Isolation: See Rosen, op. cit. See also Daniota Czyzewski and Melanie A. Suhz, eds., Hilda Bruch, *Conversations with Anorexics* (New York: Basic Books, 1988). See also Garner et al., op. cit, pp. 483–491.

194 Half-crazed confessions: Seid, op. cit., pp. 266–267.

195 [Dutch] great famine: Pyke, op. cit., pp. 129–130.

195 Lodz ghetto: See Lucian Dobrischitski, ed., *The Chronicles of the Lodz Ghetto* (New Haven: Yale University Press, 1984). See also Jean-Francis Steiner, *Treblinka* (New York: New American Library, 1968).

195 Starvation rations: Paula Dranov, "Where to Go to Lose Weight," *New Woman*, June 1988.

195 Food deprivation: Seid, op. cit., p. 266.

196 Eating diseases caused by dieting: Attie and Brooks-Gunn, op. cit., p. 243:
"According to this perspective, dieting becomes an addiction, maintained by
(1) feelings of euphoria associated with successful weight loss, requiring further caloric restriction to maintain the pleasurable, tension-relieving effects;
(2) physiologic changes by which the body adapts to food deprivation; and
(3) the threat of "withdrawal" symptoms associated with food consumption,
including rapid weight gain, physical discomfort, and dysphoria."

197 Woolf, op. cit., p. 10.

200 Austin Stress Clinic: Raymond C. Hawkins, Susan Turell, Linda H. Jack-
son, Austin Stress Clinic, 1983: "Desirable and Undesirable Masculine and
Feminine Traits in Relation to Students' Dieting Tendencies and Body
Image Dissatisfaction," *Sex Roles*, vol. 9 (1983), p. 705–718.

210 An indifferent eye: The Intercollegiate Eating Disorders Conference, mentioned by Brumberg [op. cit.], did draw many colleges' representatives.
But according to women's centers in several Ivy League universities, eating
diseases are not dealt with beyond self-help groups, and certainly not at an
administrative level. The entire term's budget for the Yale University
Women's Center is $600, up from $400 in 1984. "Diet-conscious female
students report that fasting, weight control and binge eating are a normal
part of life on American college campuses " [Brumberg, op. cit., p. 264,
citing K. A. Halmi, J. R. Falk, and E. Schwartz, "Binge-Eating and
Vomiting: A Survey of a College Population," *Psychological Medicine* 11
(1981), pp. 697–706.]

213 Disgust: Quoted in Robin Tolmach Lakoff and Raquel L. Scherr, *Face
Value: The Politics of Beauty* (London and Boston: Routledge and Kegan
Paul, 1984), pp. 141–142, 168–169.

213 Friedan: Betty Friedan, *Lear's*, "Friedan, Sadat," May/June 1988.

215 Meehan: Quoted in Jean Seligman, "The Littlest Dieters," *Newsweek*, July
27, 1987.

215 Little girls' cosmetics: Linda Wells, "Babes in Makeup Land," *The New
York Times Magazine*, August 13, 1989.

# Violence

*Page*

218 Throughout the 1980s: The figure of more than 2 million Americans was
up from 590,550 in 1986 (a rise of 24 percent from 1984). See *Standard and
Poor's Industry Surveys* (New York: Standard and Poor's Corp., 1988) and
Martin Walker, "Beauty World Goes Peanuts," *The Guardian* (London),
September 20, 1989. But since over 80 percent of eyelifts, facelifts, and
nose operations are on female patients, as are virtually all breast surgery
and liposuction operations, the true female-male ratio must be higher than
87 percent—meaning that cosmetic surgery is only properly understood as
a *processing of femaleness*. See, for figures, Joanna Gibbon, "A Nose by Any
Other Shape," *The Independent* (London), January 19, 1989.

218 Violence, once begun: Angela Browne, *When Battered Women Kill* (New York: Free Press, 1987) p. 106.

220 The Emperor Constantine: Sarah Pomeroy, *Goddesses, Whores, Wives and Slaves: Women in Classical Antiquity* (New York: Shocken Books, 1975), p. 160.

220 Sontag: Susan Sontag, *Illness as Metaphor* (New York: Schocken Books, 1988).

221 Misbegotten man: Barbara Ehrenreich and Deirdre English, *Complaints and Disorders: The Sexual Politics of Sickness* (Old Westbury, N.Y.: The Feminist Press, 1973); "Repulsive and useless hybrid," ibid., p. 28.

221 Michelet: Quoted in Peter Gay, *The Bourgeois Experience, Volume II: The Tender Passion* (New York: Oxford University Press, 1986), p. 82.

221 Separate sphere: See Sarah Stage, *Female Complaints: Lydia Pinkham and the Business of Women's Medicine* (New York: W. W. Norton, 1979), p. 68.

222 1870–1920: Elaine Showalter, *The Female Malady: Women, Madness and English Culture, 1830–1980* (New York: Pantheon Books, 1985), p. 18. See also Mary Livermore's "Recommendatory Letter" and "On Female Invalidism" by Dr. Mary Putnam Jacobi, in Nancy F. Cott, ed., *Root of Bitterness: Documents of the Social History of American Women* (New York: Dutton, 1972), pp. 292, 304.

222 Women were the primary patients: Showalter, op. cit., p. 56.

222 Victorian medicine: Ehrenreich and English, op. cit., p. 60.

224 Catherine Clément: "Enclave Esclave," in Elaine Marks and Isabelle de Courtivron, eds., *New French Feminisms: An Anthology* (New York: Schocken Books, 1981), p. 59.

224 Calm . . . face: Showalter, op. cit.

225 Menopause: John Conolly, "Construction," cited in Showalter, op. cit., p. 59.

225 Modernity: Stage, op. cit., p. 75.

225 Engels: Cited in Ann Oakley, *Housewife: High Value/Low Cost* (London: Penguin Books, 1987), pp. 46–47.

225 Scientific interest: See Peter Gay, *The Bourgeois Experience, Volume II: The Tender Passion* (New York: Oxford University Press, 1986).

226 Questions of safety arose: Vivien Walsh, "Contraception: The Growth of a Technology," The Brighton Women and Science Group, *Alice Through the Microscope: The Power of Science over Women's Lives* (London: Virago Press, 1980), p. 202.

226 Recasting freedom . . . as disease: See Carlotta Karlson Jacobson and Catherine Ettlings, *How to Be Wrinkle Free* (New York: Putnam, 1987): "Wrinkles . . . may not be life threatening in the purest sense, but the stress and anxiety they produce can alter (if not threaten) the quality of life." The authors describe skin "shock treatments meant to 'shock' [skin] back into beautiful shape." According to the authors, Steven Genender injects a toxin into the facial muscle so it will not express emotion; others sever facial muscles, leaving the face impassive.

226 Paleolithic fertility figures: Eugenia Chandris, *The Venus Syndrome* (London: Chatto & Windus, 1985).

227 Balin: "Despite Risks, Plastic Surgery Thrives," *The New York Times*, June 29, 1988.

227 Dr. Tostesen: "Harvard and Japanese Cosmetics Makers Join in Skin Research," *The New York Times*, August 4, 1989. The University of Pennsylvania has also accepted donations from cosmetics manufacturers for a $200,000 chair in "beauty and well-being" research.

229 Disabled people: Daniel Goleman, "Dislike of Own Body Found Common Among Women," *The New York Times*, March 19, 1985.

229 Bay Area: "Staying Forever Young," *San Francisco Chronicle*, October 12, 1988.

229 Rose Cipollone: "Coffin Nails," *The New York Times*, June 15, 1988.

229 Liquid fasts: Carla Rohlfing, "Do the New Liquid Diets Really Work?," *Reader's Digest*, June 1989; see also "The Losing Formula," *Newsweek*, April 30, 1990.

229 Cancer detection more difficult: In a study involving twenty breast-cancer patients with implants, researchers found that none of the tumors had been detected early with X rays, and the cancer had spread to the lymph nodes of thirteen by the time the disease was detected: Michele Goodwin, "Silicone Breast Implants," *The New Haven Advocate*, March 13, 1989. The Public Citizen Health Research Group made the charge to implant manufacturers Dow Corning Corp., citing the manufacturers' own research that 23 percent of female laboratory rats implanted with silicone developed cancer. The Group also points out that implants have been followed only for ten or twelve years, not long enough for the cancers to develop. The literature of the American Society of Plastic and Reconstructive Surgery denies any risk.

229 Mental illness: Stanley Grand, "The Body and Its Boundaries: A Psychoanalytic View of Cognitive Process Disturbances in Schizophrenia," *International Review of Psychoanalysis*, vol. 9 (1982), p. 327.

229 Stress: Daniel Goleman, "Researchers Find That Optimism Helps the Body's Defense System" "Science Times," *The New York Times*, April 20, 1989.

230 Schizophrenia: Daniel Brown, Harvard Medical School, quoted in Daniel Goleman, "Science Times," *The New York Times*, March 15, 1985.

230 Manufacturing mental illness: Eating disorders are mutating into self-mutilation, creating a new wave of young women who cut themselves up. "A growing number of 'self-lacerating' young women . . . One bulimic binged and vomited until she felt so out of control that she 'grabbed a knife and stuck it into [her] stomach.'" [Maggy Ross, "Shocking Habit," *Company*, September 1988]. Three "attractive young women" who feel "physically repulsive" and "evil inside" regularly cut a pattern of up to sixty diagonal slashes on their forearms, feeling numb and detached. "I couldn't stand being so judged," said one [Michele Hanson, "An End to the Hurting," *Elle*, October 1988].

231 A million dollars: Gerald McKnight, *The Skin Game: The International Beauty Business Brutally Exposed* (London: Sidgwick and Jackson, 1989).

232 Surgery profits: *Standard and Poor's Industry Surveys*, 1988.

233 As a businessman: Ehrenreich and English, op. cit., p. 26.

235 Fetal experimentation, human organs: See *The New York Times*, August 1, 1988. See also Wendy Varley, "A Process of Elimination," *The Guardian*, November 28, 1989, and Aileen Ballantyne, "The Embryo and the Law," *The Guardian*, September 8, 1989.

"There are, in a civilized society, some things that money can't buy": Ruling on Baby M. Case. *In re Baby M.*, 537 A2d 1227 (N.J.) 1988; *In re Baby M.*, 225 N.J. Super. 267 (S. Ct., N.J., 1988) 73.

236 Robert Jay Lifton, *The Nazi Doctors: Medical Killing and the Psychology of Genocide* (New York: Basic Books, 1986).

237 Experimentation: "Use me to 'experiment'": Quoted in Maria Kay, "Plastic Makes Perfect," *She*, July 1988.

237 Stomach stapling experiments: Paul Ernsberger, "The Unkindest Cut of All: The Dangers of Weight-Loss Surgery," *Radiance*, Summer 1988.

Dr. Stuart Yuspa of the National Cancer Institute refers to Retin-A/tretonoin prescriptions as "a human experiment." [Jane E. Brody, "Personal Health," *The New York Times*, June 16, 1988.]

237 Nuremberg: The Code of Ethics of Human Experimentation was laid down on August 19, 1947, at the Nuremberg Military Tribunal. [See David A. Frankele, "Human Experimentation: Codes of Ethics," in Amnon Karmi, ed., *Medical Experimentation* (Ramat Gan, Israel: Turtledove Publishing, 1978).] The Berlin Medical School adapted a formulation (by Thomas Percival, 1803), a version of which was later adapted by the American Medical Association, that forbids "risk of any man's life . . . by vain experimentation, or doubtful means" and condemns debasing oneself by employing one's art "for . . . immoral purposes."

In September 1948, the General Assembly of the World Medical Association adopted the Declaration of Geneva: "A doctor shall not in any circumstances do, authorize to be done or condone anything that would weaken the physical or mental resistance of a human being, except for the prevention and treatment of disease."

The Nuremberg Code was "meant to reinstate 'existing general principles of human experimentation accepted by all civilized nations.'" German courts after Nuremburg "have considered every medical operation or other treatment invading the human body technically to be assault and battery, which in general needs to be justified by the patient's informed consent." [A. Karmi, "Legal Problems," in *Medical Experimentation*.]

Without "free choice," the procedure is criminal: "It is generally agreed that scientific experiments cannot be undertaken without the *free consent* of the person subjected to them after having been duly informed." [Gerfried F. Scher, quoted in Karmi, op. cit., p. 100.] Moreover, "the decision to participate in a scientific clinical trial must be perfectly free and uninfluenced by any sort of dependency." [Ibid., p. 101]

Cosmetic surgery violates current codes of medical ethics as well: As the chief U.S. medical adviser at the war trials adapted the code: "The voluntary consent of the human subject is absolutely essential. This means that the person involved should have the legal capacity to give consent, should be so situated as to be able to exercise free power of choice, without the intervention of any element of force, fraud, deceit, duress, overreaching, or other ulterior form of constraint or coercion; and should have sufficient knowledge of the subject matter involved as to enable him to make an understanding and enlightened decision. The duty and responsibility for ascertaining the quality of the consent rests with the experimenter (minors cannot be considered to consent). . . . The degree of risk to be taken should never exceed that determined by the humanitarian importance of the problem to be solved in the experiment." Regarding fraud, deceit, etc.: The State Court of Michigan ruled that the "inherently coercive atmosphere" surrounding one medical experiment made "truly informed consent impossible." Regarding minors' maturity to consent: Cosmetic surgeons have targeted teenage girls as a new market; they operate on them with parental consent in spite of their status as minors.

Regarding nontherapeutic experiments: "The risks to be run must be in *reasonable proportion* to the possible benefits. *If the experiment entails actual risk to the subject's life, his consent is invalid even if he has been informed of this.* . . . The same holds true where there is an actual risk of heavy and lasting damage to the patient's health." [Italics added]

For the patient's own benefit, the experimental nature of new treatments must be disclosed: "His general consent to the treatment without knowing its experimental character is not sufficient." The law governing medical practice in the United States depends on the concepts of Standards of Care to distinguish between those medical and surgical procedures generally accepted by the medical professions and those that are not. According to Martin L. Norton: "We should . . . regard anything done to a patient, which is not for his direct therapeutic benefit or contributory to the diagnosis of his disease, as constituting an experiment." [Ibid., pp. 107–109]

237  1 in 30,000 possibility of death: Joanna Gibbon, *Independent Guide to Cosmetic Surgery* (*The Independent*, 1989), pamphlet, p. 7.

According to the *Guide*, silicone implants for breast augmentation "leach to other parts of the body, and the long-term effects are unknown," and there is a 10 to 40 percent chance that the scar tissue will harden into "a cricket ball," necessitating "a further operation to split the scar capsule." [Ibid., p. 8.] McKnight, op. cit., asserts that the chances are 70 percent that the implants will harden. Dr. Peter Davis at St. Thomas Hospital in England asserts that "Mortality . . . is reported to be up by 10 percent in America." [McKnight, op. cit., pp. 114, 120.] "If [U.S.] doctors were to admit to a 10 percent failure rate, which is normal in our experience out of every thousand facelifts, they'd lose their practice. Take the breast prosthesis we've been inserting for years here—it has a 70 percent complication rate. Yet there are people in America quoting 1 percent. *One of us has to be telling the truth.*"

238 Liposuction deaths: Wenda B. O'Reilly, *The Beautiful Body Book: A Guide to Effortless Weight Loss.* (New York: Bantam, 1989).

238 Liposuction . . . count of eleven: Robin Marantz Henig, "The High Cost of Thinness," *The New York Times Magazine,* February 28, 1988.

238 As many as 90 percent: See McKnight, op. cit. When I asked the spokeswoman for the ASPRS what the likelihood of "capular contraction," in her words, might be, she replied, "It's impossible to say. Some surgeons have ten percent and some have ninety percent." "Aren't there any studies with complication rates?" "No. Every woman's different. It's not fair to a woman to tell her she can't have the operation because there might be these numbers."

238 Addicts: See Maria Kay, "Plastic Makes Perfect," *She,* July 1988: "It's quite painful afterwards, because your jaw feels dislocated . . . you have to go on a liquid diet . . . food particles cause infection if they catch in the stitches, but you can't chew anyway. You can't smile, your face aches. My face swelled up like a hamster's and I had terrible yellow bruising and trauma." Chemical peeling "makes you go brown and crispy, then a scab forms and drops off." See also "Scalpel Slaves Just Can't Quit!," *Newsweek,* January 11, 1988.

239 Double standard: See "Government to Ban Baldness, Sex Drugs," *Danbury* (Conn.) *News Times,* July 8, 1989.

240 Fraud: Paul Ernsberger, "Fraudulent Weight-Loss Programs: How Hazardous?," *Radiance,* Fall 1985, p. 6; "Investigating Claims Made by Diet Programs," *The New York Times,* September 25, 1990.

240 In Britain: The British Medical Association has issued a statement deploring direct access of patients to cosmetic surgery clinics, but the General Medical Council can do nothing about it.

241 90 percent unregulated: Cable News Network, April 19, 1989; also Claude Solnick, "A Nip, a Tuck, and a Lift," *New York Perspectives,* January 11–18, 1991, pp. 12–13.

241 Congressional hearings: See Federal Trade Commission Report, *Unqualified Doctors Performing Cosmetic Surgery: Policies and Enforcement Activities of the Federal Trade Commission,* Parts I, II, and III, Serial no. 101-7.

241 Weir: Jeremy Weir, "Breast Frenzy," *Self,* April 1989.

242 Nipple death: Penny Chorlton, *Cover-up: Taking the Lid Off the Cosmetics Industry* (Wellingborough, U.K.: Grapevine, 1988), p. 244. See also the literature of the American Society of Plastic and Reconstructive Surgeons.

243 Genital mutilation: Gloria Steinem, "The International Crime of Genital Mutilation," in *Outrageous Acts and Everyday Rebellions* (New York: Holt, Rinehart & Winston, 1983), pp. 292–300.

243 Footbinding: Andrea Dworkin, *Woman Hating* (New York: Dutton, 1974), pp. 95–116.

244 Dr. Symington-Brown: Sarah Stage, *Female Complaints: Lydia Pinkham and the Business of Women's Medicine* (New York: W. W. Norton, 1981), p. 77.

245 Weldon: Fay Weldon, *The Life and Loves of a She-Devil* (London: Coronet Books, 1983): "One day, we vaguely know, a knight in shining armour will gallop by, and see through to the beauty of the soul, and gather the damsel up and set a crown on her head, and she will be queen. But there is no beauty in my soul . . . so I must make my own, and since I cannot change the world, I will change myself" (p. 56). Weldon wrote a pro-surgery article for *New Woman*, November 1989.

245 Ovariotomies: Stage, op. cit.; also Ehrenreich and English, op. cit., p. 35.

250 Electroshock: *Newsweek*, July 23, 1956, reports that a behavior-modification program used electric shock when subjects ate their favorite foods; cited in Seid, op. cit., p. 171.

250 Electric shock: Showalter, op. cit., p. 217, citing Sylvia Plath, *The Journals of Sylvia Plath*, Ted Hughes and Frances McCullough, eds. (New York: Dial Press, 1982), p. 318.

254 Harm: Suzanne Levitt, "Rethinking Harm: A Feminist Perspective," Yale Law School, unpublished doctoral thesis, 1989.

255 Right to life: Andrea Dworkin, op. cit., p. 140.

255 Rich: Adrienne Rich, *Of Woman Born: Motherhood as Experience and Institution* (London: Virago Press, 1977).

255 Dissociate: Lynda Birke et al., "Technology in the Lying-In Room," in *Alice Through the Microscope*, op. cit., p. 172.

256 Trivialization: See Lewis M. Feder and Jane Maclean Craig, *About Face* (New York: Warner Books, 1989): "Just as a seamstress can reshape a garment by taking necessary 'nips and tucks,' so the cosmetic surgeon can alter the contours of the facial skin" [p. 161].

258 Health at work: Occupational Safety and Health Act of 1970, United States Code, Title 29, Sections 651–658.

260 Facelifts: "What a shock!," quoted in Jeanne Brown, "How Much Younger My Short Haircut Made Me Look!," *Lear's*, July/August 1988. See also Saville Jackson, "Fat Suction—Trying It for Thighs," *Vogue*, October 1988: "The insides of my thighs are *black*. I am aghast but the surgeon seems quite pleased."

There are several "feminist" readings of cosmetic surgery: Surgeon Michele Copeland, in "Let's Not Discourage the Pursuit of Beauty," *The New York Times*, September 29, 1988, urges women to "burn their bras" with breast surgery. Carolyn J. Cline, M.D., in "The Best Revenge: Who's Afraid of Plastic Surgery?," *Lear's*, July/August 1988, urges women to have facelifts with the exhortation, "Voilà! You've been led to freedom."

260 Moral insanity: The term is attributed to asylum innovator John Conolly, cited in Showalter, op. cit., p. 48. See also Phyllis Chesler, Ph.D., *Women and Madness* (Garden City, N.Y.: Doubleday, 1972).

261 Stomach stapling: See Paul Ernsberger, "The Unkindest Cut of All," op. cit.

261 200,000 pounds of fat: Harper's Index, *Harper's*, January 1989.

263 Neimark: Jill Neimark, "Slaves of the Scalpel," *Mademoiselle*, November 1988, pp. 194–195.

265 Lifton: Robert Jay Lifton, *The Nazi Doctors: Medical Killing and the Psychology of Genocide* (New York: Basic Books, 1986), p. 31.

266 Any kind of experiment: Ibid., p. 294.

266 "The doctor . . .": Relevant to the discussion, the reader is reminded of the Oath of Hippocrates. It reads:

I swear by Apollo Physician, by Asclepius, by Health, by Panacea, and by all the gods and goddesses, making them my witnesses, that I will carry out, according to my ability and judgment, this oath and this indenture. . . . I will use treatment to help the sick according to my ability and judgment, but never with a view to injury or wrongdoing. . . . I will keep pure and holy both in my life and my art. In whatsoever house I enter, I will enter to help the sick, and I will abstain from all intentional wrongdoing and harm. . . . now if I carry out this oath, and break it not, may I gain forever reputation among all men for my life and for my art; but if I transgress it and forswear myself, may the opposite befall me.

265 "These people are already dead": Attributed to Nazi doctor Karl Bunding, quoted in ibid., p. 47.

265 The Reich Committee: Ibid., p. 70.

265 Liberating therapy for the race: Ibid., p. 26.

265 Trivialization: Ibid., p. 57.

265 Expansion of categories: Ibid., p. 56. "Excessive zeal" was widespread, excused as a product of "the idealism of the time."

265 Life unworthy of life: Ibid., p. 302.

266 The doctor . . . very dangerous: Ibid., p. 430.

266 *Cosmopolitan:* Catherine Houck, "The Rise and Fall and Rise of the Bosom," *Cosmopolitan*, June 1989.

266 Every popular model: Dr. Steven Herman, quoted in *Glamour*, September 1987.

267 Miss America: Ellen Goodman, "Misled America: The Pageant Gets Phonier," *Stockton* (Calif.) *Record*, September 19, 1989.

267 Artificial placenta: Jalna Hammer and Pat Allen, "Reproductive Engineering: The Final Solution?," in *Alice Through the Microscope*, op. cit., p. 221. Also being researched are an artificial skin, and a pill that manipulates the pituitary gland to promote height.

267 Grossman: Edward Grossman, quoted in Hammer and Allen, op. cit., p. 210, lists the "benefits" that will accrue from an artificial placenta. Grossman reports that the Chinese and Russians are both interested in the artificial placenta.

267 Moving into an era: Hammer and Allen, op. cit., p. 211.

267 Gestate their white babies: Lecture, Catharine A. MacKinnon, Yale University Law School, April 1989. In 1990, a custody suit was brought for an infant carried to term in a genetically unrelated "rented" uterus.

268 To predetermine sex: Hammer and Allen, op. cit., p. 215.

268 Passivity and beauty: Ibid., p. 213.

268 Psychotropic drugs: Oakley, op. cit., p. 232.

268 Valium: Ruth Sidel, *Women and Children Last: The Plight of Poor Women in Affluent America* (New York: Penguin Books, 1987), p. 144.

268 Tranquilizers: Debbie Taylor et al., *Women: A World Report* (Oxford: Oxford University Press, 1985) p. 46.

268 Amphetamines first appeared in 1938, their dangers unknown. By 1952, 60,000 pounds of them were produced in the United States annually, with doctors prescribing them regularly for weight loss: Roberta Pollack Seid, *Never Too Thin: Why Women Are at War with Their Bodies* (New York: Prentice Hall, 1989) p. 106.

268 Sedated slimness: John Allman, "The Incredible Shrinking Pill," *The Guardian*, September 22, 1989.

# Bibliography

## The Beauty Myth

de Beauvoir, Simone. *The Second Sex.* New York: Penguin, 1986. (1949)

Greer, Germaine. *The Female Eunuch.* London: Paladin Grafton Books, 1985.

Reed, Evelyn. *Sexism and Science.* New York: Pathfinder Press, 1978.

———. *Woman's Evolution: From Matriarchal Clan to Patriarchal Family.* New York: Pathfinder Press, 1975.

Russett, Cynthia Eagle. *Sexual Science: The Victorian Construction of Womanhood.* Cambridge, Mass.: Harvard University Press, 1989.

Stone, Merlin. *When God Was a Woman.* San Diego: Harvest, 1976.

Walker, Barbara G. *The Crone: Woman of Age, Wisdom, and Power.* New York: Harper & Row, 1988.

## Work

Anderson, Bonnie S., and Judith P. Zinsser. *A History of Their Own: Women in Europe from Prehistory to the Present.* Vols. I and II. New York: Harper & Row, 1988.

Cava, Anita. "Taking Judicial Notice of Sexual Stereotyping (*Price Waterhouse* v.

*Hopkins*, 109 S. Ct. 1775)," in *Arkansas Law Review*. Vol. 43 (1990), pp. 27–56.

Cohen, Marcia. *The Sisterhood: The Inside Story of the Women's Movement and the Leaders Who Made It Happen*. New York: Fawcett Columbine, 1988.

Craft, Christine. *Too Old, Too Ugly, and Not Deferential to Men*. New York: Dell, 1988.

Eisenstein, Hester. *Contemporary Feminist Thought*. London: Unwin Paperbacks, 1985.

Eisenstein, Zillah R. *The Female Body and the Law*. Berkeley: University of California Press, 1988.

Hearn, Jeff; Deborah L. Sheppard; Peta Tancred-Sheriff; and Gibson Burrell, eds. *The Sexuality of Organization*. London: Sage Publications, 1989.

Hewlett, Sylvia Ann. *A Lesser Life*. New York: Warner Books, 1986.

Hochschild, Arlie, with Anne Machung. *The Second Shift: Working Parents and the Revolution at Home*. New York: Viking, 1989.

Kanowitz, Leo. *Women and the Law: The Unfinished Revolution*. Albuquerque: University of New Mexico Press, 1975.

Lefkowitz, Rochelle, and Ann Withorn, eds. *For Crying Out Loud: Women and Poverty in the United States*. New York: Pilgrim Press, 1986.

MacKinnon, Catharine A. *Feminism Unmodified: Discourses on Life and Law*. Cambridge, Mass.: Harvard University Press, 1987.

————. *Sexual Harassment of Working Women*. New Haven: Yale University Press, 1979.

————. *Toward a Feminist Theory of the State*. Cambridge, Mass.: Harvard University Press, 1989.

Miles, Rosalind. *The Women's History of the World*. London: Paladin, 1989.

Millett, Kate. *Sexual Politics*. London: Virago, 1985.

Minton, Michael, with Jean Libman Block. *What Is a Wife Worth?* New York: McGraw-Hill, 1983.

Molloy, John T. *The Woman's Dress for Success Book*. New York: Warner Books, 1977.

Oakley, Ann. *Housewife; High Value/Low Cost*. London: Penguin, 1987.

Richards, Janet Radcliffe. "The Unadorned Feminist" in *The Sceptical Feminist: A Philosophical Enquiry*. Harmondsworth, England: Penguin, 1980.

Radford, Mary F. "Beyond *Price Waterhouse* v. *Hopkins* (109 S. Ct. 1775): A New Approach to Mixed Motive Discrimination" in *North Carolina Law Review*. Vol. 68 (March 1990), pp. 495–539.

————. "Sex Stereotyping and the Promotion of Women to Positions of Power," in *The Hastings Law Journal*. Vol. 41 (March 1990), pp. 471–535.

Rix, Sarah E., ed. *The American Woman, 1988–89: A Status Report*. New York: W. W. Norton, 1988.

Rowbotham, Sheila. *Woman's Consciousness, Man's World*. Harmondsworth, England: Penguin, 1983.

Sidel, Ruth. *Women and Children Last: The Plight of Poor Women in Affluent America*. New York: Penguin, 1986.

Swan, Peter N. "Subjective Hiring and Promotion Decisions in the Wake of Ft.

Worth (*Watson* v. *Fort Worth Bank & Trust,* 108 S. Ct. 2777), Antonio (*Wards Cove Packing Co., Inc.* v. *Antonio,* 109 S. Ct. 2115) and Price Waterhouse (*Price Waterhouse* v. *Hopkins,* 109 S. Ct. 1775)," in *The Journal of College and University Law.* Vol. 16 (Spring 1990), pp. 553–72.

Taylor, Debbie et. al. *Women: A World Report.* Oxford: Oxford University Press, 1985.

Tong, Rosemary. *Women, Sex, and the Law.* Totowa, N.J.: Rowman & Allanheld, 1984.

Steinem, Gloria. *Outrageous Acts and Everyday Rebellions.* New York: Holt, Rinehart and Winston, 1983.

Waring, Marilyn. *If Women Counted: A New Feminist Economics.* New York: Harper & Row, 1988.

## Religion

Appel, Willa. *Cults in America: Programmed for Paradise.* New York: Henry Holt, 1983.

Cott, Nancy F. *The Bonds of Womanhood: "Woman's Sphere" in New England, 1780–1835.* New Haven: Yale University Press, 1977.

———. *Root of Bitterness: Documents of the Social History of American Women.* New York: Dutton, 1972.

Galanter, Marc, ed. *Cults and Religious Movements: A Report of the American Psychiatric Association.* Washington, D.C.: The American Psychiatric Association, 1989.

Halperin, David A., ed. *Psychodynamic Perspectives on Religion, Sect and Cult.* Boston: J. Wright, PSG, Inc., 1983.

Hassan, Steven. *Combating Cult Mind Control.* New York: Harper & Row, 1988.

Lasch, Christopher. *The Culture of Narcissism: American Life in an Age of Diminishing Expectations.* New York: W. W. Norton, 1979.

McKnight, Gerald. *The Skin Game: The International Beauty Business Brutally Exposed.* London: Sidgwick & Jackson, 1989.

## Culture

Berger, John. *Ways of Seeing.* London: Penguin Books, 1988.

Brookner, Anita. *Look at Me.* London: Triad Grafton, 1982.

Chorlton, Penny. *Cover-up: Taking the Lid Off the Cosmetics Industry.* Wellingborough, England: Grapevine, 1988.

Ferguson, Marjorie. *Forever Feminine: Women's Magazines and the Cult of Femininity.* Brookfield, England: Gower, 1985.

Friedan, Betty. *The Feminine Mystique.* London: Penguin Books, 1982.

——. *The Second Stage*. New York: Summit Books, 1981.

Gamman, Lorraine, and Margaret Marshment, eds. *The Female Gaze: Women as Viewers of Popular Culture*. London: The Women's Press, 1988.

Gay, Peter. *The Bourgeois Experience: Victoria to Freud. Volume I: Education of the Senses*. Oxford: Oxford University Press, 1984.

——. *The Bourgeois Experience: Victoria to Freud. Volume II: The Tender Passion*. Oxford: Oxford University Press, 1986.

Kent, S., and J. Morreau, eds. *Women's Images of Men*. New York: Writers and Readers Publishing, 1985.

Lapham, Lewis H. *Money and Class in America: Notes on the Civil Religion*. London: Picador, 1989.

Oakley, Ann. *The Sociology of Housework*. Oxford: Basil Blackwell, 1985.

Reich, Wilhelm. *The Mass Psychology of Fascism*. New York: Penguin Books, 1978.

Root, Jane. *Pictures of Women: Sexuality*. London: Pandora Press, 1984.

Wilson, Elizabeth, and Lou Taylor. *Through the Looking Glass: A History of Dress from 1860 to the Present Day*. London: BBC Books, 1989.

Winship, Janice. *Inside Women's Magazines*. London: Pandora Press, 1987

## Sex

Brownmiller, Susan. *Against Our Will: Men, Women and Rape*. New York: Simon & Schuster, 1975.

Carter, Angela. *The Sadean Woman: An Exercise in Cultural History*. London: Virago Press, 1987.

Caputi, Jane. *The Age of Sex Crime*. London: The Women's Press, Ltd., 1987.

Cassell, Carol. *Swept Away: Why Women Fear Their Own Sexuality*. New York: Simon & Schuster, 1984.

Chodorow, Nancy J. *Feminism and Psychoanalytic Theory*. New Haven: Yale University Press, 1989.

Cole, Susan G. *Pornography and the Sex Crisis*. Toronto: Amanita, 1989.

Coward, Rosalind. *Female Desire: Women's Sexuality Today*. London: Paladin, 1984.

Crewdson, John. *By Silence Betrayed: The Sexual Abuse of Children in America*. New York: Harper & Row, 1988.

Danica, Elly. *Don't: A Woman's Word*. London: The Women's Press, 1988.

Dinnerstein, Dorothy. *Sexual Arrangements and the Human Malaise*. New York: Harper Colophon, 1976.

Dworkin, Andrea. *Pornography: Men Possessing Women*. London: The Women's Press, 1984.

Ehrenreich, Barbara, and Deirdre English. *For Her Own Good: 150 Years of the Experts' Advice to Women*. New York: Anchor/Doubleday, 1979.

————, Elizabeth Hess, and Gloria Jacobs. *Re-Making Love: The Feminization of Sex*. New York: Anchor/Doubleday 1986.

Estrich, Susan. *Real Rape*. Cambridge, Mass.: Harvard University Press, 1987.

Finkelhor, David. *Sexually Victimized Children*. New York: The Free Press, 1979.

————, and Kersti Yllo. *License to Rape: Sexual Abuse of Wives*. New York: The Free Press, 1985.

Firestone, Shulamith. *The Dialectic of Sex*. New York: Bantam, 1971.

Friday, Nancy. *My Secret Garden: Women's Sexual Fantasies*. New York: Pocket Books, 1974.

Foucault, Michel. *The History of Sexuality. Vol. 1: An Introduction*. New York: Vintage, 1980.

Griffin, Susan. *Pornography and Silence*. New York: Harper & Row, 1984.

Hite, Shere. *The Hite Report on Female Sexuality*. London: Pandora Press, 1989.

Katz, Judy H. *No Fairy Godmothers, No Magic Wands: The Healing Process After Rape*. Saratoga, Calif.: R&E Publishers, 1984.

Kinsey, A. C.; W. B. Pomeroy; C. E. Martin; and P. H. Gebhard, eds. *Sexual Behavior in the Human Female*. Philadelphia: W. B. Saunders Co., 1948.

Minot, Susan. *Lust and Other Stories*. Boston: Houghton Mifflin, 1989.

Mitchell, Juliet, and Jacqueline Rose, eds.; Jacques Lacan and The Ecole Freudienne. *Feminine Sexuality*. London: MacMillan, 1982.

————. *Psychoanalysis and Feminism: Freud, Reich, Lang and Women*. New York: Vintage Books, 1974.

Russell, Diana E. H. *The Politics of Rape: The Victim's Perspective*. New York: Stein & Day, 1984.

————. *Rape in Marriage*. Bloomington, Ind.: Indiana University Press, 1990.

————. "The Incidence and Prevalence of Intrafamilial and Extrafamilial Sexual Abuse of Female Children," in *International Journal of Child Abuse and Neglect*, 7 (1983), pp. 133–139.

Snitow, Ann; Christine Stansell; and Sharon Thompson; eds. *The Powers of Desire*. New York: Monthly Review Press, 1983.

Suleiman, Susan Rubin. *The Female Body in Western Culture*. Cambridge, Mass.: Harvard University Press, 1986.

Vance, Carol S., ed. *Pleasure and Danger: Exploring Female Sexuality*. Boston: Routledge and Kegan Paul, 1984.

Warshaw, Robin. *I Never Called It Rape*. New York: Harper & Row, 1988.

Woolf, Virginia. *Three Guineas*. New York: Penguin Books, 1982.

Walker, Alice. *You Can't Keep a Good Woman Down*. San Diego: Harvest, 1988.

# Hunger

Atwood, Margaret. *The Edible Woman*. London: Virago Press, 1989.

Barnett, Rosalind C.; Lois Biener; and Grace K. Baruch, eds. *Gender and Stress*. New York: The Free Press, 1987.

Bell, Rudolph. *Holy Anorexia*. Chicago: The University of Chicago Press, 1985.
Bruch, Hilde; Danita Czyzewski; and Melanie A. Suhr, eds. *Conversations with Anorexics*. New York: Basic Books, 1988.
———. *Eating Disorders: Obesity, Anorexia Nervosa and the Person Within*. London: Routledge and Kegan Paul, 1974.
———. *The Golden Cage: The Enigma of Anorexia Nervosa*. London: Open Books, 1978.
Brumberg, Joan Jacobs. *Fasting Girls: The Emergence of Anorexia Nervosa as a Modern Disease*. Cambridge, Mass.: Harvard University Press, 1988.
Chernin, Kim. *The Hungry Self: Women, Eating and Identity*. London: Virago Press, 1986.
———. *The Obsession: Reflections on the Tyranny of Slenderness*. New York: Perennial Library, 1981.
Hollander, Ann. *Seeing Through Clothes*. New York: Penguin, 1988.
Hsu, L. K. George. *Eating Disorders*. New York: The Guilford Press, 1990.
Jacobus, Mary; Evelyn Fox Keller; and Sally Shuttleworth; eds. *Body/Politics: Women and the Discourses of Science*. New York: Routledge, 1990. See especially, Susan Bordo, "Reading the Slender Body," pp. 83–112.
Lawrence, Marilyn. *The Anorexic Experience*. London: The Women's Press, 1988.
———, ed. *Fed Up and Hungry*. London: The Women's Press, 1987.
Orbach, Susie. *Fat Is a Feminist Issue*. London: Hamlyn, 1979.
———. *Hunger Strike: The Anorectic's Struggle as a Metaphor for our Age*. London: Faber and Faber, 1986 (especially pp. 74–95).
Pomeroy, Sarah B. *Goddesses, Whores, Wives and Slaves: Women in Classical Antiquity*. New York: Schocken Books, 1975.
Pyke, Magnus. *Man and Food*. London: Weidenfeld & Nicolson, 1970.
Seid, Roberta Pollack. *Never Too Thin: Why Women Are at War with Their Bodies*. New York: Prentice-Hall, 1989.
Szekeley, Eva. *Never Too Thin*. Toronto: The Women's Press, 1988.
Tolmach Lakoff, Robin, and Raquel L. Scherr. *Face Value: The Politics of Beauty*. Boston: Routledge and Kegan Paul, 1984.
Woolf, Virginia. *A Room of One's Own*. San Diego: Harvest/HBJ, 1989.

## Violence

Brighton Women and Science Group. *Alice Through the Microscope: The Power of Science Over Women's Lives*. London: Virago Press, 1980.
Chesler, Phyllis. *Women and Madness*. Garden City. N.Y.: Doubleday & Co., 1972.
Dworkin, Andrea. *Letters from a War Zone: Writing 1976–1987*. London: Secker & Warburg, 1988.
———. *Woman Hating*. New York: E. P. Dutton, 1974.

Kappeler, Susanne. *The Pornography of Representation*. Minneapolis: University of Minnesota Press, 1986.

Karmi, Amnon, ed. *Medical Experimentation*. Ramat Gan, Israel: Turtledove Publishing, 1978.

Koonz, Claudia. *Mothers in the Fatherland: Women, the Family and Nazi Politics*. London: Methuen, 1987.

Lifton, Robert Jay. *The Nazi Doctors: Medical Killing and the Psychology of Genocide*. New York: Basic Books, 1986.

Rich, Adrienne. *Of Woman Born: Motherhood as Experience and Institution*. New York: Virago Press, 1986.

Showalter, Elaine. *The Female Malady: Women, Madness and English Culture, 1830–1980*. New York: Penguin, 1987.

Silverman, William A. *Human Experimentation: A Guided Step into the Unknown*. Oxford: Oxford University Press, 1985.

Solomon, Michael R., ed. *The Psychology of Fashion*. Lexington, Mass.: Lexington Books, 1985.

Sontag, Susan. *A Susan Sontag Reader*. New York: Vintage Books, 1983.

Stage, Sarah. *Female Complaints: Lydia Pinkham and the Business of Women's Medicine*. New York: W. W. Norton, 1981.

Weldon, Fay. *The Life and Loves of a She-Devil*. London: Coronet Books, 1983.

## General

Banner, Lois W. *American Beauty*. New York: Knopf, 1983.

Brownmiller, Susan. *Femininity*. New York: Simon & Schuster, 1984.

Freedman, Rita Jackaway. *Beauty Bound*. Lexington, Mass.: Lexington Books, 1986.

Hatfield, Elaine, and Susan Sprecher. *Mirror, Mirror: The Importance of Looks in Everyday Life*. Albany: State University of New York Press, 1986.

Kinzer, Nora Scott. *Put Down and Ripped Off: The American Woman and the Beauty Cult*. New York: Crowell, 1977.

# Index